MY PAST AND THOUGHTS

MY PAST AND THOUGHTS
The Memoirs of Alexander Herzen

VOLUME II

*Translated from the Russian
by Constance Garnett*

faber and faber

This edition first published in 2008
by Faber and Faber Ltd
3 Queen Square, London WC1N 3AU

Printed by Books on Demand GmbH, Norderstedt

All rights reserved
Translation © Constance Garnett, 1924

The right of Constance Garnett to be identified as translator of this work
has been asserted in accordance with Section 77 of the
Copyright, Designs and Patents Act 1988

This book is sold subject to the condition that it shall not, by way of
trade or otherwise, be lent, resold, hired out or otherwise circulated
without the publisher's prior consent in any form of binding or cover other than
that in which it is published and without a similar condition including this
condition being imposed on the subsequent purchaser

A CIP record for this book is available from the British Library

ISBN 978–0–571–24542–0

Our authorised representative in the EU for product safety is
Easy Access System Europe, Mustamäe tee 50, 10621 Tallinn, Estonia
gpsr.requests@easproject.com

CONTENTS

PART III

VLADIMIR ON THE KLYAZMA
(1838—1839)

CHAPTER XIX:—The Two Princesses *page* 1

CHAPTER XX:—The Forlorn Child *page* 11

CHAPTER XXI:—Separation *page* 29

CHAPTER XXII:—In Moscow while I was away

page 50

CHAPTER XXIII:—The Third of March and the Ninth of May 1838 *page* 63

CHAPTER XXIV:—The Thirteenth of June 1839

page 87

PART IV

MOSCOW, PETERSBURG, AND NOVGOROD
(1840—1847)

CHAPTER XXV:—Dissonance —A New Circle— Desperate Hegelianism—V. Byelinsky, M. Bakunin, and others—A Quarrel with Byelinsky and Reconciliation— Argument with a Lady at Novgorod—Stankevitch's Circle
page 104

CHAPTER XXVI:—Warnings—The Promotion Office —A Minister's Secretariat—The Third Section—The Story of a Sentry—General Dubbelt—Count Benckendorf—Olga Alexandrovna Zherebtsov—My Second Exile *page* 151

CHAPTER XXVII :—The Provincial Government—I am under my own Supervision—The Duhobors and Paul—The Paternal Rule of the Landowners—Count Araktcheyev and the Military Settlements—A Ferocious Investigation—Retirement *page* 188

CHAPTER XXVIII :—Grübelei—Moscow after Exile—Pokrovskoe—The Death of Matvey—Father Ioann

page 207

CHAPTER XXIX :—Our Friends— The Moscow Circle—Table Talk—The Westerners (Botkin, Ryedkin, Kryukov, and Yevgeny Korsh)—On the Grave of a Friend *page* 227

CHAPTER XXX :—Our 'Opponents'—The Slavophils and Panslavism — Homyakov — The Kireyevskys—K. S. Aksakov—P. Y. Tchaadayev *page* 254

CHAPTER XXXI :—My Father's Death—My Heritage—The Partition—Two Nephews *page* 304

CHAPTER XXXII :— The Last Visit to Sokolovo—The Theoretical Rupture—A Strained Position—Dahin! Dahin! *page* 340

CHAPTER XXXIII :—A Police-Officer in the Part of a Valet—The Police-Master Kokoshkin—'Disorder in Order'—Dubbelt Once More—The Passport *page* 353

APPENDIX (TO CHAPTER 29):—N. H. Ketscher—Basil and Armance *page* 365

PART III
VLADIMIR ON THE KLYAZMA
(1838—1839)

Do not expect from me long accounts of my inner life of that period. . . . Terrible events, troubles of all sorts, are more easily put upon paper than quite bright and cloudless memories. . . . Can happiness be described?

Fill in for yourselves what is lacking, divine it with the heart— while I will tell of the external side, of the setting, only rarely, rarely touching by hint or by word, on its holy secrets.

Chapter 19

THE TWO PRINCESSES

WHEN I was five or six years old and was very naughty, Vera Artamonovna used to say: 'Very well, very well, you wait a bit, I'll tell the princess as soon as she comes.' I was at once subdued by this threat and begged her not to complain.

Princess Marya Alexeyevna Hovansky, my father's sister, was a stern, forbidding old woman, stout and dignified, with a birth-mark on her cheek and false curls under her cap; she used to screw up her eyes as she spoke, and to the end of her days, that is to the age of eighty, rouged and powdered a little. Whenever I fell into her hands she worried me; there was no end to her lecturing and grumbling; she would scold me for anything, for a crumpled collar, or a stain on my jacket, would declare I had not gone up to kiss her hand properly, and make me go through the ceremony again. When she had finished lecturing me, she would sometimes say to my father, as with her finger-tips she took a pinch out of a tiny gold snuff-box: 'My dear, you should send your spoilt child to me to be corrected; he would be as soft as silk when he had been a month in my hands.' I knew that they would not give me up to her, but I shivered with horror at those words.

My terror of her passed off with the years, but I never liked the old princess's house; I could not breathe freely in it, I was not myself there, but like a trapped hare looked uneasily from one side to the other to make my escape.

The old princess's household was not in the least like my father's or the Senator's. It was an old-fashioned, orthodox Russian household in which they kept the fasts, went to early matins, put a cross on the doors on the Eve of Epiphany, made marvellous pancakes on Shrove Tuesday, ate pork with horse-radish, dined exactly at two o'clock and supped at nine. The European influences which had infected her brothers and turned them somewhat out of their native rut had not touched the old princess's existence; on the contrary, she disapproved of the way in which 'Vanyusha and Lyovushka,' as she called my father and uncle, had been corrupted by 'that France.'

Princess Marya Alexeyevna lived in the lodge of the house occupied by her aunt, Princess Anna Borissovna Meshtchersky, a maiden lady of eighty.

This Princess Meshtchersky was the living and almost solitary link connecting all the seven ascending and descending branches of the family. At the chief holidays all the relations gathered about her. She reconciled those who were at variance and brought together those who had drifted apart. She was respected by all, and she deserved it. At her death family ties were loosened and lost their rallying-point, and the relations forgot each other.

She had finished the education of my father and his brothers; after the death of their parents she looked after their property until they came of age. She put them into the Guards, and she made marriages for their sisters, I do not know how far she was satisfied with the results of her bringing up, which with the help of a French engineer, a kinsman of Voltaire, had turned them into landowners and *esprits forts*, but she knew how to retain their esteem, and her nephews, though not greatly disposed to feelings of obedience and reverence, respected their old aunt and often obeyed her to the end of her life.

Princess Anna Borissovna's house, by some miracle preserved at the time of the fire of 1812, had not been repaired nor redecorated for fifty years: the hangings that covered the walls were faded and blackened; the lustres on the chandeliers, discoloured by heat and turned into smoky topazes by time, shook and tinkled, shining dingily when any one walked across the room. The heavy, solid mahogany furniture, ornamented with carvings that had lost all their gilt, stood gloomily along the walls; chests of drawers with Chinese incrustations, tables with little copper trellis-work, rococo porcelain dolls—all recalled a different age and different manners.

Grey-headed flunkeys sat in the vestibule, occupied with quiet dignity in various trifling tasks, or sometimes reading half aloud a prayer-book or a psalter, the pages of which were darker than its cover. Boys stood at the doors, but they were more like old dwarfs than children— they never laughed nor raised their voices.

A deathly silence reigned in the inner apartments; only, from time to time, there was the mournful cry of a cockatoo, its luckless faltering effort to repeat a human word, the bony tap of its beak against its perch, covered with tin, and the disgusting whimper of a little old monkey, shrunken and consumptive, that lived in the big drawing-room, on a little shelf of the tiled stove. The monkey, dressed like a *débardeur*, in full, red trousers, gave to the whole room a peculiar and extremely unpleasant smell. In another big drawing-room hung a number of family portraits of all sizes, shapes, periods, ages, and costumes. These portraits had a peculiar interest for me, especially from the contrast between the originals and their semblances. The young man of twenty with a powdered head, dressed in a light-green embroidered, full-skirted coat, smiling courteously from the canvas, was my father. The little girl with dishevelled curls and a bouquet of roses, her face adorned with a patch, mercilessly tight-laced into the shape of a wine-glass, and thrust into an enormous crinoline, was the formidable old Princess Marya Alexeyevna.

The stillness and the stiffness grew more marked as one approached the princess's room. Old maidservants in white caps with wide frills moved to and fro with little teapots, so softly that their footsteps were inaudible; from time to time a grey-headed manservant in a long coat of stout dark-blue cloth appeared at the doors, but his footsteps too were as inaudible, and when he gave some message to the elder maidservant, his lips moved without making a sound.

The little, withered, wrinkled, but by no means ugly, old lady, Princess Anna Borissovna, was usually sitting or reclining on the big clumsy sofa, propped up with cushions. One could scarcely distinguish her; everything was white, her dressing-jacket, her cap, the cushions, the covers on the sofa. Her waxen white face of lace-like fragility together with her faint voice and white dress gave her an air of something that had passed away and was scarcely breathing.

The big English clock on the table with its loud-measured spondee—tick-tack, tick-tack—seemed marking off the last quarters of an hour of her life.

Between twelve and one, Princess Marya Alexeyevna would enter and settle herself with dignity in a big easy-chair. She was dull in her empty apartments. She was a widow, and I still remember her husband, a little grey-headed old gentleman who drank liqueurs and homemade beverages on the sly; he never played an important part in the house, and was accustomed to obey his wife implicitly—though he sometimes rebelled against her in words, especially after his secret potations. The princess would be surprised at the great effect produced on her spouse by the minute glass of vodka which he drank officially before dinner, and she would leave him in peace to play the whole morning with his blackbirds, nightingales, and canaries, which trilled shrilly against each other; he trained some of them with a little organ, others by whistling to them himself; he used to drive off very early to the bird-market to exchange, sell, and buy birds; he took an artistic delight in succeeding, as he supposed, in cheating a dealer. . . . And so he spent his profitable existence, until one morning, after whistling to his canaries, he fell forward on his face and two hours afterwards died.

His widow was left alone. She had had two daughters, both of whom married not for love but simply to escape from the maternal yoke. Both died in their first childbirth. The princess was really an unlucky woman, but her troubles rather warped her character than softened it. Her misfortunes made her not milder, not kinder, but harder and more forbidding.

Now she had no one left but her brothers and her old maiden aunt. She had scarcely parted from the latter all her life, and after her husband's death she took complete control of the old lady's household, and ruled her with a rod of iron under the pretext of looking after her and caring for her wants.

Old women of all sorts, either living with Princess Anna Borissovna or staying temporarily in her house, were always ranged along the walls or sitting in the various corners. Half saints and half vagrants, rather depraved and very devout, sickly and extremely unclean, these old women trailed from one old-fashioned house to another: in one they were fed, in another presented with an old shawl; from one place they were sent grain and fuel, from another linen and cabbage; and so they somehow made both ends meet. Everywhere they were regarded as a nuisance, everywhere they were passed over, everywhere put in the lowest seat, and everywhere received through dullness and emptiness and, most of all, through love of gossip. In the presence of other company these mournful figures were usually silent, looking with envious hatred at each other. . . . They sighed, shook their heads, made the sign of the cross, and muttered to themselves the number of their stitches, prayers, and perhaps even words of abuse. On the other hand, *tête à tête* with their benefactresses, they made up for their silence by the most treacherous gossip about all the other benefactresses who received them, fed them, and made them presents.

They were continually begging from Princess Anna Borissovna, and in return for her presents, often made without the knowledge of Princess Marya Alexeyevna, who did not like indulging them, brought her holy bread, hard as a stone, and useless woollen and knitted articles of their own make, which the old lady afterwards sold for their benefit, regardless of the unwillingness of the purchasers.

Besides birthdays, namedays, and other holidays, the most solemn gathering of kinsmen and friends in Princess Anna Borissovna's house took place on New Year's Eve. On that day she 'elevated' the Iversky Madonna. The holy ikon was carried through all the apartments by monks and priests, chanting. Princess Anna Borissovna, the first to kiss the cross, walked under it, and after her all the visitors, men and maid servants, old people and children. Then they all congratulated her on the New Year, and made her all sorts of trifling presents such as are given to children. She would play with them for a few days, then give them away.

My father used to drag me off every year to this heathen ceremony; everything was repeated in exactly the same order, except that some old men and women were every year missing, and their names were intentionally avoided, until the old lady herself would say: 'Our Ilya Vassilyevitch is no longer here, the Kingdom of Heaven be his! . . . Whom will the Lord summon this year?' and she would shake her head dubiously.

And the ticking of the English clock would go on marking off the days, the hours, the minutes, and at last it reached the fatal second. The old lady felt unwell on getting up one day; she walked about the rooms and was no better; her nose began bleeding, and very violently; she felt faint and exhausted, and lay down fully dressed on her sofa, fell quietly asleep . . . and never woke again. She was over ninety.

She left her house and the greater part of her property to her niece, the widowed princess, but did not hand on to her the inner significance of her life. Princess Marya Alexeyevna could not maintain the—in its own way—artistic role of head of the family, of the patriarchal link connecting many threads. With the death of Princess Anna Borissovna an aspect of gloom came over everything, as in mountainous places at sunset, long dark shadows lay upon all. Princess Marya Alexeyevna shut up her aunt's house and remained living in the lodge; the big house was surrounded by weeds, the walls and frames grew blacker and blacker; the porch, in which ungainly yellow dogs were for ever asleep, fell out of the perpendicular.

Friends and relations came less frequently, her house was deserted, she was distressed at it, but did not know how to improve things.

The only survivor of the whole family, she began to

be apprehensive for her own useless life, and mercilessly repulsed everything that could disturb her physical or moral equilibrium and cause her uneasiness or annoyance. Afraid of the past and of memories, she removed every object that had belonged to her daughters, even their portraits. It was the same with her aunt's belongings— the cockatoo and the monkey were exiled to the servants' hall, and then turned out of the house. The monkey lived out its days in the coachman's quarters at the Senator's, choking with the smell of rank tobacco and amusing the stable-boys.

The egoism of self-preservation has a fearfully hardening effect on the heart of the old. When her last surviving daughter's condition was quite hopeless, the mother was persuaded to leave her and return home, *and she went*. At home she at once ordered spirits of various sorts and cabbage leaves for putting on her head to be got ready, that she might have everything necessary at hand when *the terrible news* should come. She did not take leave of her dead husband nor of her daughter, she did not see them after their death and was not at their funerals. When later on the Senator, her favourite brother, died, she guessed what had happened from a few words dropped by her nephew, and *begged him* not to tell her the melancholy news nor any details of the end. With these precautions against one's own heart, and such an accommodating heart, one may well live to eighty or ninety in perfect health and with undisturbed digestion.

However, in justification of Princess Marya Alexeyevna, I must say that this monstrous avoidance of everything melancholy was more in fashion with the spoilt aristocrats of last century than it is now. The celebrated Kaunitz[1] in his old age sternly forbade any one's death,

---

[1] Kaunitz (1711-1794) was for over forty years the leading statesman of Austria under Maria Theresa and Joseph 11., and one of the most prominent figures in European politics. —(*Translator's Note.*)

or the smallpox, of which he was very much afraid, to be mentioned before him. When the Emperor Joseph II. died, his secretary, not knowing how to announce the fact to Kaunitz, decided to say, 'the Emperor now reigning, Leopold.' Kaunitz understood and, turning pale, sank into an armchair, asking no questions. His gardener avoided the word 'grafting' (in Russian the same word as 'inoculation') for fear of reminding him of smallpox.

He heard of the death of his own son by chance from the Spanish ambassador. And people laugh at ostriches who hide their heads under their wings to escape danger!

To preserve her peace untroubled, the old princess established a special sort of police, and entrusted the supervision of her safety to skilled hands.

Besides the old women dependents inherited from Princess Anna Borissovna, she had a permanent lady companion living with her. This post of honour was filled by the healthy, rosy-cheeked widow of a Zvenigorod government clerk, very proud of 'being a lady' and of her dead husband's rank of assessor; a quarrelsome and irrepressible woman who could never forgive Napoleon the premature death of her Zvenigorod cow, who perished in the war of 1812. I remember how seriously troubled she was on the death of Alexander I. upon the question of the width of the crape weepers that would be appropriate to her rank.

This woman played a very insignificant part in the household while Princess Anna Borissovna was alive, but afterwards she managed so adroitly to humour the widowed princess's caprices and apprehensive anxiety about herself, that she obtained the same control over her as the princess herself had had over her aunt.

Draped in her official weepers, this Marya Stepanovna bounced about the house like a ball from morning to night; she shouted and made an uproar, gave the servants no peace, made complaints against them, investigated the misdeeds of the maids, slapped the boys and pulled them by the ears, raced off into the kitchen, raced off into the stable, brushed away the flies, rubbed the princess's feet, and made her take her medicine. The members of the household no longer had access to their mistress; the woman was a regular Araktcheyev, a Biron, in fact, a Prime Minister. The widowed princess, a haughty and, in the old-fashioned style, well-bred woman, was often, especially at first, annoyed by the Zvenigorod widow, by her shrill voice and market-woman's manners, but she gradually put more and more confidence in her, and saw with delight that Marya Stepanovna considerably decreased the household expenses, which had not been over-high before. For whom the princess was saving her money it is hard to say; she had no near relatives except her brothers, who were twice as wealthy as she was.

For all that, the princess was really dull after the death of her husband and daughters, and was glad when an old Frenchwoman who had been her daughters 'governess, came to spend a fortnight with her, or when her niece from Kortcheva paid her a visit. But these were only passing and exceptional distractions, and the tedious society of her 'lady companion' did not fill the intervals satisfactorily.

An occupation, a plaything, and an entertainment had been provided for her in a very natural way not long before her aunt's death.

Chapter 20

THE FORLORN CHILD

IN the middle of 1825 'the Chemist,' who found his father's affairs in great confusion, sent his brothers and sisters from Petersburg to the Shatskoye estate; he assigned them the house there and their keep, proposing to arrange for their education and their future later on. My aunt, Princess Marya Alexeyevna, drove over to have a look at them. A child of eight caught her attention by her mournfully pensive face; my aunt put her in the carriage, took her home and kept her.

The mother was delighted, and went off with the other children to Tambov.

The Chemist gave his consent—it did not matter to him.

'Remember all your life,' Marya Stepanovna kept saying to the little girl when they had reached home, 'remember that the Princess is your *benefactress* and pray that her days may be long. What would you be without her?'

And so into this lifeless house, gloomily oppressed by two irrepressible old women, one full of whims and caprices, the other her indefatigable spy, devoid of all trace of delicacy or tact, a child was brought, torn from everything familiar to her, strange to everything surrounding her, and adopted out of boredom as people take a puppy, or as my aunt's husband used to keep canaries.

The little girl with a pale face and blue shadows under her eyes was sitting at the window in a long woollen dress of deep mourning when my father brought me a few days later to visit my aunt the princess. She was sitting in silence, scared and bewildered, gazing out of the window, afraid to look at anything else.

My aunt called her up and introduced her to my

father. Always frigid and ungracious, he patted her carelessly on the shoulder, observed that his late brother had not known what he was about, abused 'the Chemist,' and began talking of something else.

The little girl had tears in her eyes; she sat down again by the window and again fell to looking out.

A hard life was beginning for her. Not one warm word, not one tender glance, not one caress; beside her, around her, strangers, wrinkled faces, yellow cheeks, decrepit creatures whose life was smouldering out. Princess Marya Alexeyevna was always stern, exacting, and impatient, and she kept the forlorn child at such a distance that it could never enter her head to take refuge with her, to find warmth or comfort in being near her, or to shed tears. Visitors took no notice of her. Marya Stepanovna put up with her as one of the princess's whims, as something superfluous which she must not harm; she even made a show of protecting the child and making a fuss over her before the princess, especially if visitors were present.

The child did not grow used to her surroundings, and a year later was as little at home as on the day of her arrival, and was even more depressed. Even Princess Marya Alexeyevna was surprised at her 'seriousness,' and sometimes, seeing her sitting dejectedly for hours together at her little embroidery frame, would say to her: 'How is it you don't play and run about?' The little girl would smile, flush, and thank her, but stay where she was.

And the old lady left her in peace, in reality caring nothing about the child's sadness and doing nothing to relieve it. Holidays came, other children were given playthings, other children talked of treats, of new clothes. . . . No presents were given to the little orphan. The princess considered that she had done enough for her in giving her shelter; she had shoes, what did she want with dolls? And in fact she did not need them—she did not know how to play; besides, she had no one to play with.

Only one creature realised the forlorn child's position; an old nurse had been put in charge of her, and she alone loved the child simply and naïvely. Often in the evening when she undressed her she would ask: 'But why is it you are so sad, my little lady?' The child would throw herself on her neck and weep bitterly, and the old woman would shed tears and shake her head as she went away with the candlestick in her hand.

So the years passed. She did not complain, she did not murmur; only, at twelve she longed for death.

'It always seemed to me,' she wrote, 'that I had come by mistake into this life, and that soon I should go home again—but where was my home? . . . When we drove out of Petersburg I saw a great mound of snow over my father's grave; when my mother left me in Moscow she vanished on the wide unending road. . . . I wept bitterly and prayed God to take me quickly home. . . . My childhood was most mournful and bitter; how many tears I shed unseen, how many times before I understood what prayer meant I would get up secretly at night (not even daring to say my prayers except at the fixed time) and pray to God that some one might love me and pet me. I had no amusement nor plaything which could interest or comfort me, for, if anything were given me, it was invariably accompanied by the words: "You don't deserve it." Every rag I received from them I paid for with my tears: afterwards I got over that; I was overcome by a craving for knowledge, and envied other children for nothing more than for their lessons. Many praised me, thought I had abilities, and said compassionately: "If only that child had a chance." "She would astonish the world," I added inwardly, and my cheeks glowed; I hurried away with visions of my pictures, my pupils, and meanwhile they would not give me a piece of paper nor a pencil. . . . The longing to get into another world grew stronger and stronger, and with it my scorn for my dark prison-house and its cruel sentinels; I was continually repeating the lines from "The Monk":

> "A mystery this; already I know
> All the sorrow of life, in the spring of my days."

'Do you remember, we were once staying with you long ago in the other house and you asked me if I had read Kozlov and repeated just that passage from him? A shudder ran over me, I smiled, hardly able to keep from crying.'

There was always a strain of deep melancholy in her heart; it was never quite absent, and only at times hushed at some radiant moment.

Two months before her death, going back once more to her childhood, she wrote: 'Around me all was old, bad, cold, dead, false; my education began with upbraidings and insults, and the result of this was estrangement from all, distrust of their kindness, aversion for their sympathy, and absorption in my own inner life. . . .'

But to be able to be absorbed in one's own inner life one must have not only a terribly deep nature into which one can retreat at will, but a terrific strength of independence and self-sufficiency. Very few can live their own life in hostile and vulgar surroundings from the oppression of which there is no escape. Sometimes the spirit is broken by it, sometimes the health gives way.

Loneliness and harsh treatment at the tenderest age left a dark trace on her soul, a wound which never fully healed.

'I do not remember,' she writes in 1837, 'any time when I could utter the word "mother" freely and spontaneously, any person on whose bosom I could lay my head in security, forgetting everything. I have been a stranger to all since I was eight years old; I love my mother . . . but we do not know each other.'

Looking at the pale face of the twelve-year-old girl, at her big eyes with rings round them, at her tired listlessness and everlasting depression, many thought she was one of the predestined victims of consumption, those victims marked out by the finger of death from childhood with a special imprint of beauty and premature thoughtfulness. 'Perhaps,' she says, 'I should not have survived this struggle if I had not been saved by our meeting.'

And I was so slow to understand her and read her heart!

Till 1834 I failed to appreciate the richly gifted nature that was unfolding beside me, although nine years had passed since the old princess had presented her to my father in her long woollen dress. It is easy to explain. She was shy, I was absorbed in my many interests; I was sorry for the child who sat so solitary and depressed in the window, but we did not see each other very often. It was only rarely and always unwillingly that I went to Princess Marya Alexeyevna's; still more rarely did she bring her to see us. Besides, my aunt's visits almost always left unpleasant impressions. She usually quarrelled with my father over trifles and, though they had not seen each other for two months, they said nasty things to each other, hiding them in affectionate phrases, just as nasty medicines are covered with a coat of sugar. 'My dear boy,' the princess would say; 'My dear girl,' my father would answer, and the quarrel would go on as before. We were always glad when the princess departed. Moreover, it must not be forgotten that at that time I was completely absorbed by my political dreams and my studies, and lived in the university and my comrades.

But what had she to live in, besides her melancholy, during those long dark nine years, surrounded by silly fanatics, haughty relations, tedious monks, and fat priests 'wives, hypocritically patronised by the 'lady companion,' not allowed to go farther from the house than the gloomy courtyard overgrown with weeds and the little garden at the back?

From the foregoing lines it may be seen that the princess was not particularly lavish in her expenditure on the education of her adopted child. Her moral training she undertook herself; it consisted in external observances and in the development of a complete system of hypocrisy. The child had from early morning to be laced in, stiffly erect, with her hair properly dressed: this might be admissible so far as it was not injurious to health; but the princess put her soul in stays as well as her waist, suppressing every open spontaneous feeling; she insisted on a smile and an air of gaiety when the child was sad, on amiable phrases when she wanted to cry, on an appearance of interest in everything indiscriminately—in fact, on continual duplicity.

At first the poor girl was taught nothing on the pretext that learning early was useless; later on, that is *three or four years later*, wearied by the observations made by the Senator and even by outsiders, the princess made up her mind to arrange for her to be taught, keeping the strictest economy in view. For this purpose she took advantage of an old governess who considered herself under obligations to the princess and sometimes stood in need of her assistance. In this way the French language was brought down to the lowest price; on the other hand, it was taught à *bâtons rompus*.

But the Russian language, too, was equally cheapened; to teach it and all other subjects, the princess engaged the son of a priest's widow, to whom she had been a benefactress—of course, at no special expense to herself; through her good offices with the Metropolitan the widow's two sons had been made priests in the cathedral. The tutor was their elder brother, the deacon of a poor parish, burdened with a large family. He was in the lowest depths of poverty, was glad of any payment, and dared not haggle over terms with his brothers' benefactress.

Nothing could have been more pitiful, more insufficient than such an education, and yet all went well, it all brought forth marvellous fruits, so little is needed for development if only there is something to develop.

The poor deacon, a tall, thin, bald man, was one of those enthusiasts whom neither years nor misfortunes can cure of their dreams; on the contrary, their troubles tend to keep them in a state of mystic contemplation. His faith, which approached fanaticism, was sincere and not without a shade of poetry. Between these two, the father of a hungry family and the forlorn child fed on the bread of charity, a good understanding sprang up at once.

The deacon was received in the princess's household as a poor man, defenceless, and at the same time mild-tempered, usually is received, with barely a nod, or barely a condescending word. Even the 'lady companion' thought it necessary to show her disdain; while he scarcely noticed either them or their manners, taught his subjects with love, was touched by his pupil's readiness of understanding, and could move her to tears. This the old princess could not understand; she scolded the child for being a cry-baby and was greatly displeased, declaring that the deacon was upsetting her nerves. 'This is really too much,' she said, 'it's unchildlike!'

Meanwhile the old man's words were opening before the young creature another world, attractive in a very different way from that in which religion itself was turned into an affair of diet, reduced to keeping the fasts, and going to church at night, in which everything was limited, artificial, and conventional, and cramped the soul with its narrowness. The deacon put the Gospel into his pupil's hands—and it was long before she let it go again. The Gospel was the first book she read, and she read it over and over again, with her one friend Sasha, her old nurse's niece, now a young maid of the princess's.

Later on I knew Sasha very well. Where and how she had managed to develop her intelligence I never could understand, as she spent her childhood between the coachman's quarters and the kitchen, and never left the maids 'room, but she was extraordinarily developed. She was one of those innocent victims who perish unnoticed in the servants' quarters, and more often than we suppose, crushed by the conditions of serfdom. They perish not only without compensation, without commiseration, without an hour of brightness, without a joyful memory, but without knowing, without themselves suspecting, what is perishing in them and how much is dying with them. Their mistress says with vexation: 'The wretched girl was just beginning to be trained to her work when she took to her bed and died.' . . . The seventy-year-old housekeeper grumbles: 'What are servants coming to nowadays? They are worse than any young lady,' and goes to the funeral dinner. The mother weeps and weeps and begins to drink—and that is the end.

And we pass hurriedly by, not seeing the terrible dramas enacted at our feet, thinking we have more important things to fill our time, and feeling that we have done our part with a few roubles and a kindly word. And then all at once astounded, we hear the heart-rending moan with which the crushed spirit reveals itself for all time, and, as though awakening from sleep, we ask ourselves whence came that spirit, that strength.

Princess Marya Alexeyevna killed her maid, unintentionally and unconsciously, of course; she worried her to death over trifles, broke her heart, oppressed her whole life, wore her out with humiliations, with harshness and insensibility. For several years she forbade her marriage, and only allowed it when she could see consumption in her suffering face.

Poor Sasha, poor victim of the loathsome, accursed Russian life defiled by serfdom, by death you escaped to freedom! And yet you were incomparably happier than others in the gloomy bondage of the princess's house: you met a friend, and the affection of her whom you loved so immeasurably was with you to the grave. You cost her many tears; not long before her own death she still thought of you, and blessed your memory as the one bright image of her childhood!

The two young girls (Sasha was a little the elder) used to get up early in the mornings when all the household was still asleep, read the Gospel and pray, going out into the courtyard under the open sky. They prayed for the princess and her lady-companion, besought God to soften their hearts; they invented ordeals for themselves, ate no meat for weeks together, dreamed of a nunnery and of the life beyond the grave.

Such mysticism is in keeping with adolescence, with the age in which everything is still a secret, still a religious mystery, when the awakening thought is not yet shining clearly through the mists of early morning, and the mist is not yet dissipated by experience nor passion.

At quiet and gentle moments, I loved in after years to hear of these childish prayers, with which one full life began and one unhappy existence ended. The image of the forlorn child outraged by coarse patronage, and of the slave girl outraged by her hopeless bondage, praying for their oppressors in the neglected courtyard, filled the heart with tenderness, and breathed a rare peace upon the spirit.

The pure and gracious being, whom no one of those near her in the princess's senseless household appreciated, won, besides the devotion of the deacon and Sasha, a warm response and homage from all the servants. These simple people saw in her more than a kind and gracious young lady, they divined in her something higher for which they felt reverence, they had faith in her. The girls of the princess's household, when they were going to their wedding, would beg her to pin some ribbon with her own hands. One young maidservant—I remember her name was Yelena—was suddenly taken very ill; it turned out to be acute pleurisy, there was no hope of saving her, the priest was sent for. The frightened girl kept asking her mother if she were dying; the mother, sobbing, told her that God would soon summon her. Then the sick girl besought her mother with bitter tears to fetch her young lady that she might come herself to bless her with the holy ikon for the other world. When she came the sick girl took her hand, laid it on her forehead, and repeated: 'Pray for me, pray for me!' The young girl, herself in tears, began praying in a low voice, and the sick girl died as she prayed. All in the room knelt round, crossing themselves; Natalie closed the dead girl's eyes, kissed the cold forehead, and went away.[1]

Only cold and narrow natures know nothing of this romantic period; they are as much to be pitied as those frail and feeble beings in whom mysticism outlives youth and remains for ever. In our age this does not happen

[1] Among my papers are several letters of Sasha's written between 1835 and 1836. Sasha was left behind in Moscow while her friend was in the country with the princess. I cannot read this simple and passionate whisper of the heart without deep feeling. 'Can it be true,' she writes, 'that you are coming? Ah, if you really did come, I don't know what would happen to me. You would not believe how often I am thinking of you, almost all my desires, all my thoughts, all, all, all are with you. . . . Ah, Natalya Alexandrovna, how splendid you are, how sweet, how noble!—but I cannot express it. Truly, these are not studied words, they are straight from the heart. . . .'

In another letter she thanks Natalie for writing so often. 'It is really too good, but there, that's you, you,' and she ends the letter with the words: 'They keep interrupting me, I embrace you, my angel, with true immeasurable love. Give me your blessing!'

with realistic natures; but how could the secular influences of the nineteenth century penetrate into the princess's house, every crevice was so well padded?

A crack was found, nevertheless.

My Kortcheva cousin used sometimes to come on a visit to the princess. She was fond of the 'little cousin,' as one is fond of children, especially if they are unhappy, but she did not understand her. With amazement, almost with horror, she discovered later on her exceptional nature, and, impulsive in everything, at once determined to make up for her neglect. She begged from me Hugo, Balzac, or anything new I might have. 'The little cousin,' she said to me, 'is a genius, we ought to do what we can for her!'

The 'big cousin'—and I cannot help smiling at this name for her, for she was a tiny creature—at once communicated to her protégée every stray thought in her own mind, Schiller's ideas and the ideas of Rousseau, revolutionary ideas picked up from me and the dreams of a lovesick girl picked up from herself. Then she secretly lent her French novels, verses, poems; they were for the most part books that had appeared since 1830. With all their defects, they stimulated thought, and stirred and fired youthful hearts. In the novels and stories, the poems and songs of that period, whether the author intended it or not, there was always a strong vein of social feeling: everywhere social sores were revealed and the moan of the hungry, innocent slaves of labour could be heard; even by that date their murmur and complaint was no longer feared as a crime.

I need hardly say that my cousin lent the books without any discrimination, without any explanations, and I imagine that there was no harm in that; there are natures which never need help, support, guidance from others, who always walk most safely where there is no fence.

Another person who carried on the secular influence

of my Kortcheva cousin was soon added to the list. The princess at last made up her mind to take a governess, and to avoid expense engaged a young Russian girl who had only just left boarding-school.

Russian governesses do not cost much, at any rate they did not in the 'thirties, yet for all their defects they were better than the majority of French girls from Switzerland, of retired courtesans and actresses who catch at teaching in despair as their last resource for earning their bread, a resource needing neither talent nor youth, nothing in fact but the ability to pronounce 'Hrrrra' and the manners *d'une dame de comptoir*, which is often taken in the provinces for 'good' manners. Russian governesses come from boarding-schools, or educational establishments, and so have had some sort of regular education, and are free from the petty-bourgeois tone which the foreign women bring in with them.

The French governesses of to-day must be distinguished from those who used to come to Russia before 1812. In those days France was less bourgeois and the women who came to Russia belonged to quite a different social stratum. To some extent they were the daughters of *émigrés* and of ruined noblemen, or widows of officers, often their deserted wives. Napoleon used to marry off his warriors in the way that our landowners used to marry their serfs, without much regard for love or inclination. He wanted, by these marriages, to unite his new military aristocracy with the old nobility; he wanted to knock his Skalozubs[1] into shape by means of their wives. Accustomed to blind obedience, they married without protest, but soon abandoned their wives, finding them too stiff for the festivities of the

[1] Skalozub, a character in Griboyedov's celebrated play, 'Woe from Wit' (or perhaps better, 'Sorrow comes from having Sense'), is the typical coarse, ignorant, blustering military bully.—(*Translator's Note.*)

barracks and the bivouac. The poor women made their way to England, to Austria, to Russia. The old Frenchwoman who used to stay with the princess belonged to this class of old-fashioned governess. She spoke with a smile in choice language and never made use of a single strong expression. She was entirely made up of good manners and never forgot herself for a minute. I am convinced that even at night in her bed she was more preoccupied with the proper way of sleeping than with sleeping.

The young governess was an intelligent, bright, energetic girl with a good share of boarding-school enthusiasm and an innate feeling for what is fine. Active and ardent, she brought more life and movement into the existence of her pupil and friend.

There had been a tone of mourning, of melancholy in the sad and depressing friendship with the consumptive Sasha. Her company, together with the deacon's teachings and the absence of every kind of diversion, was drawing the young girl away from the world, from men. This third person, young, full of life and gaiety, and at the same time sympathetic with everything dreamy and romantic, came in the nick of time: she drew her back to earth, to the basis of truth and reality.

At first the pupil to some extent adopted her Amelia's external manners; a smile was more often to be seen on her face, and her conversation grew livelier; but within a year the natures of the two girls defined their mutual attitude. The careless, charming Amelia gave way before the stronger nature and was completely dominated by her pupil, saw with her eyes, thought her thoughts, lived in her smile and in her affection.

Before I had finished my studies at the university, I took to going more frequently to the princess's house. The young girl seemed pleased when I came, and sometimes her cheeks glowed and her talk grew more animated, but she quickly withdrew into her usual dreamy stillness, recalling the cold beauty of sculpture or Schiller's 'Mädchen aus der Fremde' who checked all approach.

It was not unsociability nor coldness, but an active inner life; not understood by others, she did not as yet even understand herself, and had rather a dim presentiment than a knowledge of what was in herself. In her lovely features there was still something incomplete, not fully expressed, they lacked a spark, a touch of the sculptor's chisel which would decide whether she was destined to pine and fade away in a barren desert, knowing neither herself nor life, or to reflect the glow of passion, to be enfolded by it, and to live, perhaps to suffer—certainly, indeed, to suffer, but to live abundantly.

I first saw the token of life coming out on her half-childish face on the eve of our long separation.

Well I remember her eyes with quite a different light in them, and all her features with their significance transformed, as though penetrated by a new thought, a new fire . . . as though the secret had been guessed and the inner mist dissipated. This was when I was in prison. A dozen times we said good-bye, and still we could not bear to part. At last my mother, who had come with Natalie[1] to the Krutitsky Barracks, resolutely got up to

[1] I know very well how affected the French translation of names sounds, but a name is a traditional thing and how is one to change it? Besides, all unslavonic names are with us, as it were, shortened and less musical; we, educated to some extent, 'not in the law of our fathers,' in our youth 'romanticised' names, while the powers in authority 'Slavonised' them. As a man is promoted and attains to influence at court, the letters in his name are changed—thus, for instance, Count Strogonov remained to the end of his days Sergeyey Grigoryevitch, but Prince Golitsyn was always called Sergiey Mihalovitch. The last example of such a transformation we saw in General Rostovtsov, celebrated in connection with the Fourteenth of December; throughout the reign of Nicholas he was Yakov, as was Yakov Dolgoruky, but with the accession of Alexander II. he became Iakov, the same as the brother of our Lord!

go. The young girl shuddered, turned pale, squeezed my hand with unnatural force, and repeated, turning away to hide her tears, 'Alexandr, don't forget your sister.'

The gendarme saw them out and set to walking to and fro. I flung myself on my bed and long gazed at the door behind which that bright apparition had vanished. 'No, your brother will not forget you,' I thought.

Next day I was taken to Perm, but before I speak of our separation I will tell of something else that prevented me, before my prison days, from understanding Natalie better and growing more intimate with her. I was in love!

Yes, I was in love, and the memory of that pure youthful love is as dear to me as the memory of a spring day spent by the sea among flowers and singing. It was a dream, full of much that was lovely, that vanished as dreams usually do vanish!

I have mentioned already that there were very few women in our circle, especially of the sort with whom I could have been on intimate terms: my affection for my Kortcheva cousin, at first ardent, gradually became quieter in tone. After her marriage we saw each other less often, and then she went away. A vague yearning for a warmer, tenderer feeling than the affection of my men friends hovered about my heart. Everything was ready, all that was lacking was 'she.' In one of the families of our acquaintance there was a young girl with whom I quickly made friends. It was a strange chance that brought us together. She was betrothed, when all at once some dissension arose, her fiancé abandoned her and went off to the other end of Russia. She was in despair, overcome with distress and mortification. With deep and sincere sympathy I saw how she was being consumed by grief. Without daring to hint at the cause, I tried to comfort her and distract her mind, brought her novels, read them aloud to her, told her long stories, and sometimes neglected to prepare for my lectures at the university in order to stay longer with the distressed girl.

Gradually her tears fell less frequently, from time to time a smile glimmered through them; her despair passed into a languid melancholy; soon she began to feel alarmed for her past, she struggled with herself and defended it against the present, from a *point d'honneur* of the heart, as a soldier defends the flag, though he knows that the battle is lost. I saw these last clouds faintly lingering on the horizon and, myself carried away, with a beating heart, softly, softly drew the flag out of her hands, and by the time she had given it up I was in love. We believed in our love. She wrote verses to me, I wrote whole essays to her in prose, and then we dreamed together of the future, of exile, of prisons. She was ready for anything. The external side of life never took a very dear shape in our imaginations; dedicated to the conflict with a monstrous power, we felt success almost incredible. 'Be my Gaetana,' I said to her after reading Saintine's[1] 'The Mutilated Poet,' and I used to fancy how she would follow me to the Siberian mines.

'The Mutilated Poet' was the poet who wrote a lampoon upon Sixtus v. and gave himself up when the Pope promised not to inflict the death penalty. Sixtus v. ordered his tongue and hands to be cut off. The figure of the luckless victim, choked by the mass of ideas which swarmed in his brain and found no outlet, could not but attract us in those days. The martyr's sad and exhausted eyes found peace when they rested with gratitude and some remnant of happiness on the girl who had loved him in old days and did not abandon him in misfortune. Her name was Gaetana.

This first experience of love was soon over, but it was

[1] Xavier Saintine (1798-1865), a French writer of whose many plays and stories only Picciola, *or the Prisoner's Flower* is still well known,—(*Translator's Note.*)

perfectly sincere. Perhaps, indeed, it was right for this love to pass, or it would have lost its finest, most fragrant quality, its innocent freshness, its nineteen-year-old charm. Lilies of the valley do not flower in winter.

And can it be, my Gaetana, that you do not recall our meeting with the same serene smile, can it be that there is any bitterness mixed with your memory of me after twenty-two years? That would be very grievous to me. And where are you, and how have you spent your life?

I have lived my life and now am going slowly downhill, broken, and morally 'mutilated.' I seek no Gaetana, I go over the memories of the past and meet your image joyfully. . . . Do you remember the window in the corner facing the little side street into which I had to turn, and how you always came to it to watch me pass, and how disappointed I was if you did not come to it, or moved away before I had time to turn?

But I do not want to meet you in reality; in my imagination you have remained with your youthful face, your *blond cendré* curls: remain as you were. And you, too, if you think of me, will remember a slender lad with sparkling eyes and fiery words, and may you think of him like that and never know that the eyes have lost their lustre, that I have grown heavy, that my brow is furrowed, that long ago my face lost the radiant, eager look of old days which Ogaryov used to call 'the look of hope.' And, indeed, hope too is gone.

We ought to be to each other as we were then . . . neither Achilles nor Diana grow old. . . . I do not want to meet you as Larin met Princess Alina:[1]

> 'Do you remember Grandison?
> Cousin, how is Grandison?—
> Oh, Grandison! In Moscow living,
> On Christmas Eve he left his card,
> A son of his was married lately.'

---

[1] *From Pushkin's Yevgeny Onyegin.—(Translator's Note.)*

The last glow of dying love lighted up for a moment the prison vault, warmed the heart with its old dreams, and then each took our separate paths. She went away to the Ukraine while I was going into exile. Since then I have had no tidings of her.

Chapter 21

SEPARATION

*'Ah, people, wicked people,
You separated their . . .'*

SO my first letter to Natalie ended, and it is noteworthy that, frightened by the word 'hearts,' I did not write it. And I signed the letter 'your brother.'

How dear 'my sister' was then to me and how continually in my thoughts is clear from the fact that I wrote to her from Nizhni, and from Perm on the very day after my arrival there. The word 'sister' expressed all that was recognised in our affection; I liked it immensely and I like it now, used not as the limit of the feelings but, on the contrary, as the mingling of them all; in it are united affection, love, the tie of kinship, a common devotion, the surroundings of childhood, and habitual association. I had called no one by that name before, and it was so precious to me that even in later years I often used it to Natalie.

Before I fully understood our relations, and perhaps just because I did not understand them fully, a temptation awaited me which has not left so bright a memory as my episode with Gaetana; a temptation that humiliated me and cost me much regret and inner distress.

Having very little experience of life, and being flung into a world completely strange to me, after nine months of prison, I lived at first carelessly without taking stock of what I saw; the new country, the new surroundings made me rather dizzy. My social position was transformed. In Perm and in Vyatka I was regarded very differently from in Moscow; there I had been a young man living in my father's house, here in this stagnant waste I was independent, and was accepted as a government official, although I was not exactly one. It was not hard for me to perceive that without much effort I might play the part of a man of the world in the drawing-rooms beyond the Volga and the Kama, and be a lion in Vyatka society.

In Perm, before I had time to look about me, the landlady to whom I had gone to take lodgings asked me whether I wanted a kitchen garden and whether I was keeping a cow ! It was a question by which I could, with horror, judge the depth of my descent from the academic heights of student life. But at Vyatka I made acquaintance with all the world, especially with the younger people of the merchant class, which is much better educated in these remote provinces than in those nearer the centre, though they are no less given to drink and debauchery. Distracted from my usual pursuits by office work, I led a restlessly idle life; owing to my peculiar impressionability, or perhaps mobility, of character and absence of experience, adventures of all sorts might well be expected.

From a coquettish passion *de l'approbativité* I tried to please right and left indiscriminately, forced my sympathies, made friends over a dozen words, became far more intimate than I need, recognised my mistake a month or two later, said nothing from delicacy, and dragged a weary chain of false relations until it was broken by an absurd quarrel in which I was blamed for capricious impatience, ingratitude, and inconstancy.

At first I did not live alone in Vyatka. A strange and comic figure, which from time to time appears at all the turning points of my life, at all its important events, the person who drowns to make me acquainted with Ogaryov, and waves a handkerchief from Russia when I cross the frontier at Taurogen—K. I. Sonnenberg—was living with me in Vyatka; I forgot to mention this when I described my exile.

This was how it happened: at the moment when I was being sent to Perm, Sonnenberg was preparing to go to the Fair at Irbit. My father, who always liked to complicate everything simple, suggested to Sonnenberg that he should go to Perm and there *furnish my house*, in return undertaking to pay his travelling expenses.

At Perm Sonnenberg zealously set to work, that is, to the purchase of unnecessary articles, all sorts of crockery, saucepans, bowls, glass, and provisions. He went himself to Obva to procure a Vyatka horse *ex ipso fonte*. When everything was complete I was transferred to Vyatka. We sold, half-price, the goods he had purchased and left Perm. Sonnenberg, conscientiously carrying out my father's wishes, thought it his duty to go to Vyatka too to furnish my house. My father was so well pleased with his devotion and self-sacrifice that he offered him a salary of a hundred roubles a month so long as he would stay with me. This was more profitable and more secure than Irbit—and he was in no hurry to leave me.

In Vyatka he bought not one but three horses, one of which belonged to himself, though it too was bought at my father's expense. These horses raised us considerably in the esteem of Vyatka society. Karl Ivanovitch, as I have mentioned already, was, in spite of his fifty years and the rather glaring defects of his features, a great flirt, and entertained the agreeable conviction that every girl and woman who came near him risked the fate of the moth flying round a lighted candle. Karl Ivanovitch had no intention of wasting the effect produced by the horses, but tried to turn them to advantage on the erotic side. Moreover, all our circumstances were favourable to his designs; we had a verandah looking out into a courtyard beyond which there was a garden. From ten o'clock in the morning Sonnenberg, arrayed in

Kazan morocco leather boots, a gold embroidered *tibiteyka*, and a Caucasian *beshmyet*, with an immense amber mouthpiece between his lips, would sit on watch, pretending to be reading. The *tibiteyka* and the amber mouthpiece were all aimed at three young ladies who lived in the next house. The young ladies for their part were interested in the new arrivals and gazed with curiosity at the oriental-looking doll smoking on the verandah. Karl Ivanovitch knew when and how they secretly lifted their blind, thought that things were going swimmingly—and tenderly blew a light coil of smoke in the direction of the objects of his devotion.

Soon the garden gave us the opportunity of making our neighbours' acquaintance. Our landlord had three houses, and the garden was shared in common by them. In one of the houses we were living, together with the landlord and his stepmother, a fat, flabby widow who looked after him so masterfully and with such jealousy that it was only on the sly that he ventured to speak to the ladies of the garden. In the second house lived the young ladies and their parents, and the third house stood empty. Within a week Karl Ivanovitch was quite at home with the ladies of our garden. He would spend several hours a day swinging the young girls in the swing and running to fetch their capes and sunshades, in fact he was *aux petits soins*. The young ladies were more free in their behaviour with him than with anybody else, because he was more beyond suspicion than Caesar's wife: a mere glance at him was enough to check the faintest breath of scandal.

In the evening I too used to walk into the garden, from that herd instinct which makes people do what others are doing, apart from any inclination. To the garden came, besides the lodgers, their acquaintances; the chief subject of talk and interest was flirtation and watching one another. Karl Ivanovitch devoted himself to sentimental espionage with the vigilance of a Vidok,[1] and always knew who walked oftenest with whom, and who looked significantly at whom. I was a terrible bone of contention for all the secret police of our garden; the ladies and the men wondered at my reserve, and for all their efforts could not discover on whom I was dancing attendance, and who particularly attracted me; and indeed it was not easy to do so, for I was not dancing attendance on any one and I did not find any of the young ladies particularly attractive. In the end they were vexed and offended by this, they began to consider me proud and sarcastic, and the young ladies' friendliness grew perceptibly cooler—though every one of them tried her most killing glances upon me when we were alone.

While things were like this, one morning Karl Ivanovitch informed me that the landlady's cook had opened the shutters of the third house and was cleaning the windows. The house had been taken by a family who had arrived in the town.

The garden was entirely absorbed in details concerning the new arrivals. The unknown lady, who was either tired from the journey or had not yet had time to unpack, as though to spite us, refused to show herself outside. Every one tried to see her at a window or in the porch, some succeeded, while others watched for days together in vain; those who saw her reported her pale and languid, interesting, in short, and good-looking. The young ladies said that she looked melancholy and ill. A young clerk in the governor's office, a sprightly and quite intelligent fellow, was the only one who knew the

[1] The reference is probably to Bulgarin, a journalist in close relations with Benckendorf (Chief of the Secret Police). This Bulgarin made many petty personal attacks on Pushkin, who in a well-known poem addresses him by the name Vidok-Figlyarin.—(*Translator's Note,*)

strangers. He had once served in the same provincial town with them, and every one besieged him with questions.

The sprightly clerk, pleased at knowing what other people did not know, held forth endlessly upon the charms of their new neighbour. He praised her to the skies, declared that you could see she was a lady from Petersburg or Moscow. 'She is intelligent,' he repeated, 'charming, cultured, but she won't look at fellows like us. Ah, upon my soul,' he added, suddenly turning to me, 'there's a happy thought; you must keep up the honour of Vyatka society and get up a flirtation with her. . . . Why, you are from Moscow, you know, and in exile; no doubt you write verses. She's a heaven-sent find for you.'

'What nonsense you do talk,' I said, laughing, but I flushed crimson: I longed to see her.

A few days later I met her in the garden and found that she really was a very charming blonde. The gentleman who had talked about her introduced me. I was agitated and was as little able to hide it as my companion his smile.

The shyness due to vanity passed and I got to know her; she was very unhappy and, deceiving herself by assumed composure, was pining away and languishing in a sort of indolence of the heart.

Madame R—— was one of those secretly passionate natures only to be met among women of a fair complexion. The ardour of their hearts is masked by the mildness and gentleness of their features; they turn pale with emotion, and their eyes do not flash but rather grow dim when feeling brims over. Her languid eyes looked exhausted with a vague craving, her yearning bosom heaved irregularly. There was something restless and electric in her whole being. Often when walking in the garden she would suddenly turn pale and, inwardly troubled or agitated, would answer absent-mindedly and hurry into the house. It was just at those moments that I liked to look at her.

I soon saw what was passing within her. She did not love her husband and could not love him; she was twenty-five, he was over fifty, yet that disparity she might have got over, but the difference of education, of interests, of temperament, was too great.

Her husband scarcely ever came out of his room; he was a dry, harsh, old man, an official with pretensions to being a landowner, irritable like all invalids and like most people who have lost their fortune. She was sixteen when she was married to him and then he had some property, but afterwards he had lost everything at cards and was forced to go into the service for a living. Two years before he was transferred to Vyatka he began to fall into ill-health, a sore on his leg developed into disease of the bone. The old man became surly and ill-humoured, was afraid of his illness, and looked with helpless suspicion and uneasiness at his wife. She waited upon him with mournful self-sacrifice, but she did this only as her duty. Her children could not give all that her yearning heart craved.

One evening, speaking of one thing and another, I said that I should very much like to send my cousin my portrait, but that I could not find a man in Vyatka who could hold a pencil.

'Let me try,' said the lady. 'I used to draw rather successful portraits in pencil.'

'I shall be delighted. When?'

'To-morrow before dinner, if you like.'

'Of course. I will come to-morrow at one o'clock.'

All this was in her husband's presence; he said not a word.

Next morning I got a note from Madame R——. It was the first I had ever received from her. She very courteously and circumspectly informed me that her husband was not pleased at her having offered to draw my portrait, begged me not to judge harshly of the whims of an invalid, said that he must not be worried, and, in conclusion, offered to make the sketch some other day, saying nothing about it to her husband, that he might not be annoyed by it.

I warmly, perhaps excessively warmly, thanked her. I did not accept her offer to draw the portrait in secret, but nevertheless these two notes made us much more intimate. Her attitude to her husband, upon which I could never have touched, was openly expressed; a secret understanding, a league against him, was unconsciously formed between us.

In the evening I went to see them—not a word was said about the portrait. If her husband had been cleverer he must have guessed what had happened; but he was not clever. I thanked her with my eyes, she answered with a smile.

Soon they moved into another part of the town. The first time I went to see them I found her alone in a barely furnished drawing-room; she was sitting at the piano, her eyes were tear-stained. I begged her to go on; but the music halted, she played false notes, her hands trembled, the colour left her face. 'How stifling it is!' she said, getting up quickly from the piano.

In silence I took her hand, a weak, feverish hand; her head, like a flower grown too heavy, as though passively obeying some external force, sank on my breast, she pressed her forehead against me and instantly fled.

Next day I received a rather frightened note from her, trying to throw a sort of mist over what had passed; she wrote of the terribly nervous condition in which she had been when I came in, of scarcely remembering what had happened. She apologised for her behaviour—but the thin veil of her words could not conceal the passion that glowed through them.

I went to see them; that day her husband was a little better, though he had not risen from his bed since they had been in their new quarters. I was worked up by excitement, played the fool, fired off witty jokes, talked all sorts of nonsense, made the invalid almost die with laughter, and of course all that was to cover her embarrassment and my own. Moreover, I felt that the laughter was intoxicating her and drawing her on.

.   .   .   .   .   .

This orgy of love lasted for a month; then my heart was as it were tired, exhausted; I began to have moments of depression, I studiously concealed them, tried not to believe in them, wondered what was passing within me —while still love was cooling.

I began to feel constrained by the presence of the old man. It was awkward and hateful for me in his company. Not that I felt myself in the wrong as regards the man who had the civil and ecclesiastical rights of property in a woman who could not love him and whom he was incapable of loving, but my double part struck me as humiliating; hypocrisy and duplicity are the vices most foreign to my nature. While growing passion was in the ascendant I thought of nothing, but as soon as it was somewhat cooler I began to have doubts.

One morning Matvey came into my bedroom with the news that old R—— 'had passed away.' I was overcome by a strange feeling at this news, I turned on the other side and was in no hurry to dress. I did not want to see the dead man. Vitberg came in, quite ready to go out. 'What!' he said, 'you 're still in bed! Haven't you heard what's happened? I expect poor Madame R—— is all alone, let us go and see, make haste and dress.' I dressed—and we went.

We found Madame R—— in a swoon or in a sort of nervous lethargy. There was no pretence about it: her husband's death had recalled her helpless position;

she was left alone with her children in a strange town, without money, without friends or relations. Besides, she had on previous occasions fallen into this cataleptic condition, which was brought on by some violent shock and lasted several hours. Pale as death, with her face cold and her eyes closed, she lay, from time to time giving a gasp, and breathless in the intervals.

Not one woman came to help her, to show her sympathy, to look after the children or the house. Vitberg remained with her, the prophetic clerk and I undertook to see after things.

The old man, looking black and sunken, lay in his uniform on the drawing-room table, frowning as though he were angry with me. We laid him in the coffin, and two days later lowered him into the grave. After the funeral we went back to the dead man's house; the children in their black frocks with crape weepers huddled in the corner, more amazed and frightened than grieved: they whispered together and walked on tiptoe. Madame R—— sat with her head leaning on her hands, as though pondering, and did not say a single word.

In that drawing-room, on that sofa I had waited for her, listened to the sick man moaning and the drunken servant swearing. Now everything was so black. . . . In the midst of funereal surroundings and the smell of incense, I was haunted by vague and gloomy recollections of words and minutes of which I still could not think without tenderness.

Her grief gradually subsided and she looked more resolutely at her position; then, little by little, other thoughts began to light up her careworn and despondent face. Her eyes rested upon me with a sort of agitated inquiry, as though she were waiting for something . . . a question . . . an answer. . . .

I said nothing—and she, frightened, alarmed, began to feel doubts.

Then I saw that her husband had in reality been an excuse for me in my own eyes—love had burnt itself out in me. It was not that I had no feeling for her, far from it, but the feeling was not what she wanted. I was now occupied by a different order of ideas, and that outburst of passion seemed to have possessed me simply to make another feeling clear to myself. Only one thing I can say in my defence—I was perfectly sincere in my infatuation.

While I had lost my head and did not know what to do, while with cowardly weakness I was waiting for the chances of time and circumstance, time and circumstance complicated my position still further.

Tyufyaev, seeing the helpless position of a young and beautiful widow left without any support in a remote town in which she was a stranger, like the true 'father of the province,' showed her the tenderest solicitude. At first we all thought that he felt real sympathy for her. But soon Madame R—— observed with horror that his attentions were by no means so simple. Two or three dissolute governors before him had kept Vyatka ladies as mistresses, and Tyufyaev, following their example, lost no time but at once began making declarations of love to her. Madame R—— of course responded with cold disdain and mockery to his elderly blandishments. Tyufyaev would not recognise himself rebuffed, but persisted in his insolent attentions. Seeing, however, that he was making little progress, he gave her to understand that her children's future lay in his hands, that without his assistance she could not place them in schools at government expense, and that he on his side would not exert himself in her favour if she did not adopt a less chilly attitude to him. The insulted woman sprang up like a wild beast wounded. 'Kindly leave my house and don't dare to set foot in it again,' she said, pointing to the door.

'Ough, what a temper you have got!' said Tyufyaev, trying to turn things off with a jest.

'Pyotr, Pyotr,' she shouted in the entry, and the terrified Tyufyaev, fearing a public scandal, abashed and humiliated, fled to his carriage, gasping with fury.

In the evening Madame R—— told Vitberg and me all that had happened. Vitberg at once realised that the Lovelace put to flight and insulted would not leave the poor woman in peace; Tyufyaev's character was pretty well known to us all. Vitberg resolved at all costs to save her.

Persecutions soon followed. The petition with regard to the children was presented in such a way that refusal was inevitable. The landlord and the shopkeepers demanded payment with remarkable insistence. God knows what might not be expected; the man who had done Petrovsky to death in a madhouse was not to be trifled With.

Though burdened with an immense family and weighed down by poverty, Vitberg did not hesitate for one minute, but invited Madame R—— to move with her children into his house two or three days after his wife's arrival in Vyatka. In his house Madame R—— was safe, so great was the moral power of this exile. His inflexible will, his noble appearance, his fearless words, his scornful smile were dreaded even by the Vyatka Shemyaka.[1]

I lived in a wing apart in the same house and dined at Vitberg's table, and so here we were under the same roof, just when we ought to have been seas apart.

In this close proximity she soon saw that there was no bringing back the past.

Why had she met me, at that time so unstable? She might have been happy, she deserved to be happy. The

[1] Shemyaka was a prince of ancient Russia, whose injustice is still remembered in the proverbial expression, a 'Shemyaka's judgment.'—(Translator's *Note*.)

sorrowful past was over, a new life of love and harmony was so possible for her! Poor woman! Was it my fault that this storm-cloud of love which had swooped down upon me so irresistibly, so ardently, intoxicated me, drew me on, and then melted away?

I lived in a state of anxious perturbation. Perplexed, foreseeing trouble, and dissatisfied with myself, again I turned to dissipation and sought distraction in noise, was vexed at finding it and vexed at not finding it, and awaited a few lines from Natalie as for a breath of pure air in the midst of sultry heat. The gentle image of the child on the verge of womanhood rose brighter and brighter above all this ferment of passion. My outburst of passion for Madame R—— made my own heart clear to me and revealed its secret.

More and more absorbed by my feeling for my faraway cousin, I had not clearly analysed the sentiment that bound me to her. I was used to the feeling and did not watch closely to see whether it had changed or not.

My letters became more and more troubled; on the one hand I felt deeply not only the wrong I had done Madame R——, but the fresh wrong I did her in the lying of which I was guilty by my silence. It seemed to me that I had fallen, that I was unworthy of any other love . . . while my love was growing and growing.

The name of *sister* began to fret me, affection now was not enough for me, that gentle feeling seemed cold. Her love was apparent in every line of her letters, but that did not satisfy me. I wanted not only love but the very word itself, and I wrote: 'I am going to put a strange question to you. Do you believe that the feeling you have for me is only affection? Do you believe that the feeling I have for you is only affection? I don't believe it.'

'You seem somewhat troubled,' she answered. 'I knew your letter frightened you much more than it frightened me. Set your mind at rest, dear, it has changed absolutely nothing in me, it could not make me love you more, or less.'

But the word had been uttered: 'The mist has vanished,' she writes,' all is clear and bright again.'

With unclouded joy she gave herself up to the feeling that had been given its name; her letters are one youthful song of love rising from a childish whisper to lyrical heights.

'Perhaps at this moment,' she writes, 'you are sitting in your study, not writing, not reading, but pensively smoking a cigar, and your eyes are fixed on the vague distance and you have no answer for the greeting of any one who comes in. Where are your thoughts? What are you seeing? Do not answer, let them come to me. . . .'

'Let us be childish, let us fix an hour for both of us to be in the open air, an hour in which we can both be sure that nothing separates us but distance. At eight o'clock in the evening you, too, are surely free? Or else I go out as just now upon the steps—and come back at once thinking that you are indoors.'

'Looking at your letters, at your portrait, thinking of my letters, of my bracelet, I wished I could skip a century and see what will be their fate. The things which have been for us holy relics, which have healed us, body and soul, with which we have talked and which have to some extent replaced us to each other in absence; all these weapons with which we have defended ourselves from others, from the blows of fete, from ourselves, what will they be when we are gone, will their virtue, their soul remain in them, will they awaken, will they warm some other heart, will they tell the story of us, of our sufferings, of our love, will they win one tear? How sad I feel when I imagine that your portrait will one day hang unknown in some one's study, or a child perhaps will break the glass and efface the features.'

My letters were not like this[1]; in the midst of full, enthusiastic love there is a note of bitter vexation with myself and repentance; the dumb reproaches of Madame R—— were gnawing at my heart and troubling the clear radiance of my feeling; I seemed to myself a liar, and yet I had not been lying.

How could I acknowledge the position? How was I to tell Madame R—— in January that I had made a mistake in August when I spoke of my love? How could she believe in the truth of my story—a new love would have been easier to understand, treachery would have been simpler. How the far-away image of the absent could enter into conflict with the present, how another love could have crossed that mountain barrier and become stronger and more recognised—that I did not understand myself, but I felt that it was all true.

Moreover, Madame R—— herself with the elusive agility of a lizard slipped away from any serious explanation; she had an inkling of danger, was lost in conjecture, and at the same time was avoiding the truth. It was as though she had a foreboding that my words would reveal terrible facts, after knowing which all would be over, and she cut short all talk at the point where it was becoming dangerous.

[1] The difference between the style of Natalie's letters and mine is very great, especially in the early part of our correspondence; afterwards it was less unequal and in the end becomes similar. In my letters, together with genuine feeling there are affected expressions, far-fetched high-flown phrases, the influence of the school of Hugo and the new French novelists is apparent. There is nothing of the sort in her letters, her language is simple, poetic, and sincere, the only influence that can be discerned in it is the influence of the Gospel. At that time I was still trying to write in the grand style and wrote badly, because it was not my own language. A life in spheres cut off from practical experience, and top much reading prevents a young man for years from speaking and writing naturally and simply. Intellectual maturity only begins when the style is established and has taken its final form.

At first she was looking about her; for a few days she thought she had found her rival in a charming, lively young German girl whom I liked as a child, with whom I was at ease just because it had never entered her head to flirt with me, nor mine to flirt with her. A week later she perceived that Paulina was not at all dangerous. But I cannot go further without saying a word about the latter.

In the government dispensary at Vyatka there was a German chemist, and there was nothing strange about that, but what is strange is that his assistant was Russian and was called Bolman. With this latter I became acquainted; he was married to the daughter of a Vyatka government clerk, a lady who had the longest, thickest, and most beautiful hair I have ever seen. The dispenser himself, Ferdinand Rulkovius, was at first absent, and Bolman and I used to drink together various 'fizzing drinks' and artistic cordials compounded from the pharmacy. The dispenser was away in Reval, there he made the acquaintance of a young girl and offered her his hand; the girl, who hardly knew him, married him rashly, as a girl generally does, and a German girl in particular; she had no notion even into what wilds he was taking her. But when after the wedding she had to set off, she was overcome with terror and despair. To comfort his bride, the dispenser invited a young girl of seventeen, a distant relation of his wife, to go with them to Vyatka. She, even more rashly, with no idea of what was meant by Vyatka, consented. Neither of the German girls spoke a word of Russian, and in Vyatka there were not four men who spoke German. Even the teacher of that language in the high school did not know it, a fact which surprised me so much that I actually ventured to ask him how he managed to teach it.

'With the grammar,' he answered, 'and with dialogues.'

He further explained that he was really a teacher of mathematics, but that, as there was no post vacant, he was meanwhile teaching German, and that he received, however, only half the salary.[1] The Germans were dying of ennui, and seeing a man who, if he could not speak German well, could at least do so intelligently, were highly delighted, regaled me with coffee and some sort of '*Kalteschale*,' told me all their secrets, their hopes and their wishes, and within two days called me their friend and still more hospitably treated me to sweet cakes and pastries flavoured with spices. Both were fairly well educated, that is, knew Schiller by heart, played the piano, and sang German songs. There the likeness between them ended. The dispenser's wife was a tall, fair, lymphatic woman, very good-looking but sleepy and listless; she was extremely good-natured and, indeed, with her physique it would have been hard to be anything else. Being convinced once for all that her husband was her husband, she loved him quietly and steadily, looked after the kitchen and the linen, read novels in her leisure moments, and in due time successfully bore the chemist a daughter with white eyebrows and eyelashes and a scrofulous constitution.

Her friend, a short, dark brunette, vigorously healthy, with big black eyes and an independent air, was a beauty of the sturdy peasant type; a great deal of energy was apparent in her words and movements, and when at times

[1] On the other hand, the enlightened government appointed as French master in the same Vyatka high school the celebrated Orientalist Vernikovsky, who was a colleague of Kovalevsky's and Mickiewicz's, and was exiled in connection with the Philarets' case.[*]

---

[*] The Philarets or 'lovers of virtue' were a students' society of the Vilna University in the first quarter of the nineteenth century. Their object was to promote learning, to help the poor, and to preach ideals of goodness and justice. Tovjanski and Mickiewicz were members of it.—(*Translator's Note*.)

the dispenser, a dull, close-fisted fellow, made somewhat discourteous observations to his wife, while she listened with a smile on her lips and a tear on her eyelash, Paulina would flush crimson and give the offending husband such a look that he would instantly subside, pretend to be very busy, and go off to his laboratory to pound and mix all sorts of nasty things for the preservation of the health of the Vyatka officials.

I liked the simple-hearted girl who knew how to stand up for herself, and I do not know how it happened, but it was to her I first talked of my love and translated some of Natalie's letters. Only one who has lived for long years with people who are completely alien know how precious are these confidences of the heart. I rarely talk of my feelings, but there are moments, even now, when the longing to express myself becomes insufferable, and at that time I was four-and-twenty, and I had only just realised my love. I could bear separation, I could have borne silence too, but, meeting with another child on the threshold of womanhood, in whom everything was so unaffectedly simple, I could not refrain from giving away my secret. And how grateful she was for my confidence, and how much good she did me!

Vitberg's always serious conversation sometimes wearied me; fretted by my difficult relations with Madame R——, I could not be at my ease with her. Often in the evening I used to go off to Paulina, read foolish stories aloud to her, listen to her ringing laugh and to her singing, especially for my benefit, 'Das Mädchen aus der Fremde'—by which she and I understood another 'maiden from a strange land,' and the clouds were dissipated, there was an unfeigned gaiety, an untroubled serenity in my heart, and I would go home in peace when the dispenser, after stirring his last mixture and preparing his last ointment, began boring me with absurd political inquiries—not, however, before I had drunk a 'draught' of his mixing and eaten the herring salad mixed by the little white hands *der Frau Apothekerin*.

.   .   .   .   .   .

Madame R—— was wretched, while with pitiful weakness I waited for time to bring some chance solution and prolonged the half-deception. A thousand times I longed to go to Madame R——, to throw myself at her feet, to tell her everything, to face her wrath, her contempt . . . but it was not indignation that I feared—I should have been glad of it—I feared her tears. One must have endured many evil experiences to be able to bear a woman's tears, to be able to feel doubts while they trickle still warm over the flushed cheek. Besides, her tears would have been sincere.

A good deal of time passed like this. Rumours began to reach me that my exile might soon come to an end. The day no longer seemed so remote on which I should fling myself into a chaise and dash off to Moscow, familiar faces hovered before my imagination and among them, foremost of them, the cherished features; but scarcely did I abandon myself to these dreams when the pale, mournful figure of Madame R—— would rise up on the other side with tear-stained eyes, full of pain and reproach, and my joy was troubled: I felt sorry, terribly sorry for her.

I could no longer remain in a false position, and plucking up all my courage I made up my mind to get out of it. I wrote her a full confession. Warmly, openly, I told her the whole truth. Next day she said she was ill and did not leave her room. All the sufferings of a criminal, the fears that he will be unmasked, I passed through on that day. She had another attack of her nervous stupor —I dared not visit her.

I wanted my repentance to be complete. I shut myself up with Vitberg in his study and told him the whole story. At first he was astonished, then he listened to me not as a judge but as a friend, did not worry me with questions, did not preach to me with stale morality, but devoted himself to helping me find means for softening the blow—he alone could do that. His affection was very warm for those of whom he was fond. I had been afraid of his rigorous morals, but his affection for me and for Madame R—— completely outweighed that. Yes, in his hands I could leave the unhappy woman to whose hard lot I had given the finishing blow, in him she found strong moral support and authority. She respected him like a father.

In the morning Matvey gave me a note. I had scarcely slept all night. With a trembling hand I broke the seal. She wrote gently, in a noble and deeply mournful spirit; the flowers of my eloquence had not concealed the snake beneath them, in her words of resignation could be heard the stifled moan of a wounded heart, the cry of pain, repressed by a supreme effort. She blessed me on my way to my new life, wished me happiness, called Natalie a sister, and held out a pleading hand to us for forgetfulness of the past and friendship for the future —as though she had been to blame!

Sobbing, I read her letter over and over again. *Qua I cuor tradisti!*

Later on I met her. She gave me her hand affectionately, but we felt awkward; each of us had left something unsaid, each of us tried to avoid touching on something.

A year ago I heard of her death.

When I left Vyatka I was for a long time worried by the thought of Madame R——. As I regained my composure I set to work to write a story of which she was the heroine. I described a young nobleman of the period of Catherine who has abandoned the woman who loves him and married another. She pines away and dies. The news of her death is a heavy blow to him, he becomes gloomy and pensive, and at last goes out of his mind.

His wife, an ideal of gentleness and self-sacrifice, after trying everything, leads him in one of his quieter moments to the Dyevitchy Convent and kneels down with him at the unhappy woman's grave, begging her forgiveness and her intervention. From the windows of the convent the words of a prayer reach them, soft feminine voices sing of forgiveness—and the young man recovers. The story was a failure. At the time when I wrote it Madame R—— had no thought of coming to Moscow, and the only man who guessed that there was anything between us was the 'ubiquitous German,' K. I. Sonnenberg. After my mother's death in 1851, we had no news from him. In 1860 a tourist, describing his acquaintance with Karl Ivanovitch, now a man of eighty, showed me a letter from him. In a postscript the old man told him of the death of Madame R—— and said that my brother had had her buried in the Novo Dyevitchy Convent!

I need hardly say that neither of them knew anything about my story.

Chapter 22
IN MOSCOW WHILE I WAS AWAY

MY peaceful life in Vladimir was soon troubled by news from Moscow which reached me now from all sides and deeply distressed me. To make this intelligible I must go back to 1834.

The day after I was arrested in 1834 was the nameday of my aunt, the princess, and so when Natalie had parted from me in the graveyard she had said: 'Until to-morrow'; she was expecting me, several members of the family had arrived, when suddenly my cousin made his appearance and told them the full details of my arrest. This news, utterly unexpected, gave her a shock; she got up to go into the other room, and after taking two steps fell unconscious on the floor. The princess saw it all and understood it all; she determined to oppose this love from the beginning by every means in her power.

What for?

I do not know : she had of late, that is after I had finished my studies, been very well disposed to me; but my arrest and rumours of our free-thinking attitude, of our giving up the Orthodox Church and entering the Saint Simon 'sect,' infuriated her; from that time forward she never spoke of me except as 'that unhappy son of brother Ivan's.' The Senator had to use all his authority to induce her to allow Natalie to go to the Krutitsky Barracks to say good-bye to me.

Fortunately I was exiled and the princess had plenty of time before her.

'And where is this Perm or Vyatka? He'll be sure to break his neck there, or have it broken for him; and in any case he'll forget her there.'

But as though to spite the princess, I had an excellent memory. Natalie's correspondence with me, for a long time concealed from the old lady, was at last discovered, and she sternly forbade the maids and menservants to receive letters for the young girl, or to take letters to the post.

'So I daresay some fine morning that unhappy son of my brother's will open the door and walk in; it's no use wasting time thinking about it, and putting things off— we'll make a match for her and save her from the political criminal who has no religion or principles.'

The princess, sighing, would talk of the poor, forlorn girl, saying that she had scarcely anything, that it would not do for her to pick and choose, that she would like to see her settled in her own lifetime. She had, as a fact, with the help of her dependents, settled, after a fashion, the fate of one distant cousin who had no dowry by marrying her off to an attorney of some sort. A nice, good-natured, and well-educated girl, she married to satisfy her mother; two years later she died, but the attorney was still living, and from gratitude was still looking after her Excellency's affairs. In this case, however, the bride was not portionless, the princess was prepared to treat her like her own daughter, to give her a dowry of a hundred thousand roubles and to leave her something in her will besides. On such terms suitors are always to be found, not only in Moscow but everywhere else, especially when there is the title of princess as well as a 'lady companion' and numerous 'old women' in attendance.

The whispering, the negotiations, rumours, and maid-servants brought Princess Marya Alexeyevna's intention to the ears of the unhappy victim of so much solicitude. She told the 'lady companion' that she would not accept any offer of marriage. Then followed an insulting and ruthless persecution without one trace of delicacy, a petty persecution pursuing her every minute and catching her at every step, at every word.

'Imagine bad weather, terrible cold, wind, rain, an overcast, as it were, expressionless sky, a very horrid little room which looks as though a corpse had just been carried out of it, and these *children*, who have no aim, no pleasure even, making a noise, shouting, spoiling and defiling everything near them; and it would be bad enough if one had simply to look at them, but when one is forced to be in their company . . .' she writes in one letter from the country where the princess had gone for the summer; and she goes on: 'there are three old women sitting here with us, and they are all three describing how their late husbands were paralysed and how they used to look after them; and it is chilly enough without that.'

Now systematic persecution was added to these surroundings, and it was practised not only by the princess but also by the wretched old women, who were perpetually worrying Natalie, persuading her to be married and abusing me; as a rule, she said nothing in her letters of the continual annoyances she had to endure, but sometimes bitterness, humiliation and boredom were too much for her. 'I don't know,' she writes, 'whether they can invent anything more to oppress me. Can they possibly have wit enough for that? Do you know that I am actually forbidden to go into another room, even to move to another seat in the same room? It is a long while since I have played the piano; lights were brought and I went into the drawing-room, thinking they might be merciful, but no, they brought me back and set me knitting; perhaps, at least I might sit at another table— I can't endure being beside them—might I do even that I No, I must sit just here beside the priest's wife, listen, look, and talk, while they speak of nothing but Filaret or criticise you. For a moment I felt vexed, I flushed crimson, then all at once my heart was weighed down by a feeling of bitter sadness, not because I had to be their slave, ho . . . I felt horribly sorry for them.'

Matchmaking negotiations were formally beginning.

'A lady has been here who is fond of me, and whom I am not for that reason fond of. . . . She is doing her very utmost to settle things for me, and she made me so angry that I sang after her—

> "I had rather be dressed in my winding-sheet
> Than the wedding veil without my sweet."'

A few days later, 26th October 1837, she writes: 'What I have been through to-day, my dear, you can't imagine. They dressed me up and dragged me off to Madame S——, who has been extremely gracious to me ever since I was a child; Colonel Z—— goes there every Tuesday to play cards. Imagine my position: on the one side the old ladies at the card-table, on the other all sorts of disgusting figures, and he . . . The conversation, the company—everything was so alien to me, so strange and horrid, so lifeless and vulgar, I was more like a statue than a living creature. Everything that was going on seemed like an oppressive nightmare. I kept asking like a child to go home, they would not heed me. The attention of the host and of *the visitor* overwhelmed me; he got as far as writing half my monogram in chalk. Oh dear, I am not strong enough and I can look for support to no one of those who might be a help; I am all alone on the edge of a precipice, and a whole crowd of them are doing everything they can to push me over; sometimes I am weary, my strength fails me and you are not near and I cannot see you in the distance; but the mere thought of you—and my soul is stirred and ready to do battle again in the armour of love.'

Meanwhile every one liked the Colonel: the Senator was friendly to him, and my father gave it as his opinion that 'a better match could not be expected and should not be desired.' 'Even his Excellency D. P. (Golohvastov) is pleased with him,' wrote Natalie. The princess said nothing directly to Natalie, but restricted her freedom even more severely and hurried things on. Natalie tried to play the part of a complete imbecile in his presence, hoping to repel him, but not at all; he went on coming more and more frequently.

'Yesterday,' she writes, 'Amelia was here and this is what she said: "If I heard that you were dead I should cross myself with joy and thank God." She is right in a great deal but not altogether; her soul living only in sorrow could fully grasp the sufferings of my spirit, but the bliss with which love fills it she could scarcely understand.'

But the princess was not losing heart. 'Wishing to have a clear conscience, the princess invited a priest who is a friend of Z—— and asked him whether it would not be a sin to marry me against my will. The priest said it would be actually a godly work to make so good a provision for an orphan. I am sending for my own priest,' Natalie adds,' and shall tell him the whole story.'

'*October* 30*th*.—My clothes are here, my attire for to-morrow, and the ikon, the rings; all sorts of arrangements and preparations have been made, and not a word to me. The Nasakins and others have been invited. They are preparing a surprise for me and I am preparing a surprise for them.

'*Evening.* —Now a family council is going on. Lyov Alexeyevitch (the Senator) is here. You urge me to be strong—there is no need, my dear. I am equal to extricating myself from the awful, loathsome scenes into which they are dragging me on the chain. Your image is bright above me, there is no need to fear for me, and my very distress and sadness are so sacred and have taken so firm a hold on my soul that tearing them away would hurt even more, the wounds would re-open.'

However, though they did their best to mask and cover

up the position, the Colonel could not avoid seeing the positive aversion of his proposed bride; he began to be less frequent in his visits, declared himself ill, and even hinted at some addition to the dowry; this greatly incensed the princess, but she got over even that humiliation and was ready to give her an estate near Moscow as well. This concession he had apparently not anticipated, for after it he disappeared altogether.

Two months passed quietly. All at once the news came that I had been transferred to Vladimir. Then the princess made her last desperate effort to marry off her protegee. One of her acquaintances had a son, an officer, who had just returned from the Caucasus; he was young, cultivated, and a very decent fellow. The princess condescended so far as herself to suggest to his sister that she should 'sound' her brother and see whether he cared for the match. He yielded to his sister's representations. The young girl did not care to play the same disgusting and tedious part a second time, so, seeing that the position was taking a serious turn, she wrote to the young man a letter, told him directly, openly, and simply that she loved another man, trusted herself to his honour and begged him not to add to her sufferings.

The officer with great delicacy drew back. The princess was amazed and affronted and made up her mind to find out what had happened. The officer's sister, to whom Natalie had spoken herself, and who had promised her brother to say nothing to the princess, told the whole story to the 'lady companion'; the latter of course at once reported it to her mistress.

The princess almost choked with indignation. Not knowing what to do, she ordered the young girl to go upstairs to her room and not to show herself; not content with that, she ordered her door to be locked and put two maids on guard; then she wrote notes to her two brothers and one of her nephews and asked them to come and give her advice, saying that 'she was so distressed and upset that she could not think what to do in the misfortune that had befallen her.' My father refused, saying that he had plenty of worries of his own, that there was no need to attach such importance to what had happened, and that he was a poor judge in affairs of the heart. The Senator and D. P. Golohvastov appeared next evening in answer to her summons. They talked for a long time without reaching any conclusion and at last asked to see the prisoner. The young girl came in, but she was no longer the shy, silent, forlorn girl they had known. Unflinching firmness and stubborn determination were apparent in the calm and proud expression of her face; this was not a child but a woman who had come to defend her love—my love.

The sight of the prisoner on her trial confounded her judges. They were awkward; at last Dmitry Pavlovitch, *l'orateur de la famille*, expatiated at length on the cause of their coming together, the distress of the princess, her heartfelt desire to settle her protégée's future, and the strange opposition on the part of her for whose benefit it was all being done. The Senator with a nod and a movement of his finger expressed his assent to his nephew's words. The princess said nothing but sat with her head turned away, sniffing salts.

The prisoner on her trial heard all they had to say and asked with straightforward simplicity what they required of her.

'We have no thought of requiring anything from you,' observed the nephew. 'We are here at Aunt's desire to give you sincere advice. A match excellent in all respects is offered to you.'

'I cannot accept it.'

'What is your reason for that?'

'You know it.'

The orator of the family coloured a little, took a pinch

of snuff, and screwing up his eyes went on: 'There is a great deal to which objection might be urged. I would call your attention to the very small ground for your hopes. It is so long since you have seen our unfortunate Alexandr; he is so young and impetuous—are you certain of him?'

'Yes, and whatever his intentions may be, I cannot change mine.'

The nephew had exhausted his eloquence; he got up saying: 'God grant that you may not regret it! I feel very anxious about your future.' The Senator scowled; the luckless girl now appealed to him. 'You have always shown me sympathy,' she said to him. 'I implore you, save me, do what you like but take me out of this life. I have done no harm to any one, I ask for nothing, I am not trying to do anything, I am only refusing to deceive a man and ruin myself by marrying him. What I have to endure on account of it you cannot imagine; it pains me to have to say this in the presence of the princess, but to put up with the slights, the insulting words, the hints of her friends is top much for me. I cannot, I ought not to allow it, for insulting me is insulting . . .' Her nerves gave way, the tears gushed from her eyes; the Senator leapt up and walked about the room in agitation.

Meanwhile the 'lady companion,' boiling over with fury, could not restrain herself and said, addressing the princess: 'So that's our nice, modest girl, there 's gratitude for you.'

'Of whom is she speaking?' shouted the Senator. 'How is it, sister, you allow that woman, devil knows what she is, to speak like that of your brother's daughter in your presence? And if it comes to that, why is this drab here at all? Did you invite her to the family council too? Is she a relation or what?'

'My dear,' answered the panic-stricken princess,' you know what she is to me and how she looks after me.'

'Yes, yes, that's all very nice, let her give you your medicine and what you like; that's not what I am talking about. I ask you, *sœur*, why is she here when family affairs are being discussed, and how dare she put her word in? One might suppose it was all her doing, and then you complain—Hey, my carriage!'

The 'lady companion' flushed, and ran out of the room in tears.

'Why do you spoil her like this?' the Senator went on, carried away; 'she fancies she is sitting in the tavern at Zvenigorod; how is it you aren't disgusted by it?'

'Leave off, my dear, please,' the poor princess groaned, 'my nerves are so upset—oh! You can go upstairs and stay there,' she added, addressing her niece.

'It's time to be done with all this Bastille business. It's all nonsense and leads to nothing,' observed the Senator and took his hat.

Before driving away, he went upstairs; Natalie, overcome by all that had passed, was sitting in an armchair with her face hidden, weeping bitterly. The old man patted her on the shoulder and said:

'Calm yourself, calm yourself, it will all come right. You must just try not to make sister angry with you; she is an invalid, you must humour her; after all, she only wishes for your good, you know; but, there, you shan't be married against your will, I'll answer for that.'

'Better a nunnery, a boarding-school, to go to Tambov to my brother, or to Petersburg, than to endure this life any longer,' she answered.

'Come, come! try and soothe my sister, and as for that fool of a woman I'll teach her not to be rude.'

The Senator, as he crossed the drawing-room, met the 'lady companion': 'I'll ask you not to forget yourself,' he shouted at her, holding up a menacing finger; she went sobbing into the bedroom where the princess lay on the bed while four maids rubbed her hands and feet, moistened her temples with vinegar, and poured Hoffman's drops on lumps of sugar.

So ended the family council.

It is clear that the girl's position was hardly likely to be improved by what had happened; the 'lady companion' was more on her guard, but, cherishing now a personal hatred for Natalie, and desirous of avenging the affront to herself, she poisoned her existence by petty indirect means. I need hardly say that the princess acquiesced in this ignoble persecution of a defenceless girl.

This had to be ended. I made up my mind to come forward, and wrote a long, calm, and sincere letter to my father. I told him of my love and, foreseeing his reply, added that I did not want to hurry him, that I should give him time to see whether it was a passing feeling or not, and that all that I begged of him was that the Senator and he would enter into the poor girl's position and would remember that they had the same rights over her as the princess herself.

My father answered that he could not endure meddling in other people's affairs, that what the princess did in her own house was not his business; he advised me to abandon foolish ideas 'induced by the idleness and ennui of exile,' and added that I had much better prepare myself for travel in foreign lands. We had often talked in past years of a tour abroad, he knew how passionately I wished for it, but found endless difficulties and always ended by saying: 'You must first dose my eyes, then you'll be free to go to the ends of the earth.' In exile I had lost all hope of going abroad, I knew how hard it would be to get permission, and, besides, it would have seemed a lack of delicacy to insist on a voluntary separation after the involuntary one. I remembered the tears quivering on his old eyelids when I was setting off to Perm . . . and now here was my father taking the initiative and suggesting I should go!

I had been open, I had written sparing the old man, asking so little—and he had answered with irony and strategy.

'He doesn't want to do anything for me,' I said to myself, 'like Guizot he advocates *la non-intervention*. Very well then, I'll act myself, and now good-bye to concessions.' I had not once before thought about the ordering of the future; I believed, I knew that it was mine, that it was ours, and I left the details to chance; the consciousness of love was enough for us, our desires did not go beyond a momentary interview. My father's letter forced me to take the future into my own hands. It was useless to wait—*cosa fata capo ha!* My father was not very sentimental, while as for the princess—

> 'Let her weep,
> Her tears mean nought!'

Just at that time my brother and Ketscher came to stay in Vladimir. Ketscher and I spent whole nights together, talking, recalling the past, laughing through our tears, and laughing till we cried. He was the first of our set whom I had seen since we left Moscow. From him I heard the chronicles of our circle, what changes had taken place in it, and what questions were absorbing it, what fresh people had arrived, where those who had left Moscow were, and so on. When we had discussed everything I told him of my plans. After considering how I ought to act, Ketscher concluded with a proposition the absurdity of which I only appreciated afterwards. Desirous of trying every peaceful method, he offered to go to my father and to talk to him seriously. I agreed.

Ketscher, of course, was better fitted for any good deed, and, in fact, for any evil deed, than for diplomatic negotiations, particularly with my father. He had in a marked degree all the characteristics that were calculated to ruin any chance of success. His very appearance was enough to make any conservative depressed and alarmed. A tall figure, with hair strangely dishevelled and arranged on no fixed principle, with a harsh countenance reminiscent of a number of the members of the Convention of 1793, and especially of Marat, with the same big mouth, the same hard, disdainful lines about the lips, and the same expression of mournful and exasperated gloom; to this must be added spectacles, a wide-brimmed hat, extreme irritability, a loud voice, lack of all habit of self-control, and the power of arching his eyebrows higher and higher as he grew more indignant. Ketscher was like Laravigny in George Sand's excellent novel, *Horace*, with an admixture of something of the Pathfinder and Robinson Crusoe, as well as an element purely Muscovite. His open, generous temperament had set him from childhood in direct conflict with the world surrounding him; he did not conceal his antagonism and was accustomed to it. A few years older than we, he was continually scolding us and was dissatisfied with every one. He used to quarrel and bring accusations against us and make up for it all by the simple good-nature of a child. His words were rough, but his feelings were tender and we forgave him much.

Imagine him, this last of the Mohicans with the face of a Marat, this 'friend of the people,' setting off to advise my father! Many times afterwards I made Ketscher describe their interview; my imagination was unequal to picturing all the oddity of this diplomatic intervention. It took place so unexpectedly that for a moment my old father lost his bearings and began explaining the weighty reasons which led him to oppose my marriage; then, recovering himself, he changed his tone and asked Ketscher on what grounds he had come to discuss a matter which was none of his business. The conversation took a more bitter tone. The diplomatist, seeing that his position was not improving, tried to frighten the old man about my health, but it was too late, and the interview ended, as might have been expected, in a series of malignant sarcasms from my father and rude rejoinders from Ketscher.

He wrote to me: 'Expect nothing from the old man.' That was all I wanted. But what was I to do? How was I to begin? While I was thinking over a dozen different plans a day and unable to decide between them, my brother was preparing to return to Moscow.

That was on the first of March 1838.

Chapter 23[1]
The Third of March and the Ninth of May 1838

IN the morning I wrote letters; when I had finished we sat down to dinner. I could not eat, we said nothing, I felt unbearably oppressed—it was between four and five, at seven the horses were to come round.

---

[1] A fragment of this chapter was published in the *Polar Star*, vol.i. page 79, together with the following note:
Who is entitled to write his reminiscences?
Every one.
Because no one is obliged to read them.
In order to write one's reminiscences it is not at all necessary to be a great man, nor a notorious criminal, nor a celebrated artist, nor a statesman—it is quite enough to be simply a human being, to have something to tell, and not merely to desire to tell it but at least some little ability to do so.

Every life is interesting; if not the personality, then the environment, the country are interesting, life itself is interesting. Man likes to enter into another existence, he likes to touch the subtlest fibres of another's heart, and to listen to its beating . . . he compares, he checks it by his own, he seeks in himself confirmation, justification, sympathy. . . .

But may not memoirs be tedious, may not the life described be colourless and commonplace?

Then we shall not read it—there is no worse punishment for a book than that.

Moreover, that is no drawback to the writing of memoirs. Benvenuto Cellini's *Diary* is not interesting because he was an excellent worker in gold but because it is in itself as interesting as any novel.

The fact is that the very word 'entitled' to this or that form of composition does not belong to our epoch, but dates from an era of intellectual immaturity, from an era of poet-laureates, doctors' caps, peddling savants, certificated philosophers, diplomaed metaphysicians and other Pharisees of the Christian world. Then the act of writing was regarded as something sacred, a man writing for the public used a high-flown unnatural choice language, he 'expounded' or 'sang.'

We simply talk; for us writing is the same sort of secular pursuit, the same sort of work or amusement as any other. In this connection it is difficult to dispute 'the right to work.' Whether the

At the same time next day he would be in Moscow while I—and every minute my pulse beat faster.

'I say,' I said at last to my brother, looking at my plate, 'will you take me with you to Moscow?'

He put down his fork and looked at me uncertain whether he had heard me aright.

'Take me through the town gate as your servant, I want nothing more, do you agree?'

'Yes if you like, only, you know, afterwards you'll . . .'

It was too late, his 'if you like' was already in my blood, in my brain. The idea that had only flashed upon me a minute before had now taken deep root.

'What is there to discuss, anything may happen—and so you'll take me?'

---

work will win recognition and approval is quite a different matter.

A year ago I published in Russia part of my memoirs under the title of *Prison and Exile*. I published it in London at the beginning of the war. I did not reckon upon readers nor upon any attention outside Russia. The success of that book exceeded all expectations: the *Revue des* Deux Mondes, the most chaste and rigid of journals, published half the book in a French translation; the clever and learned *Athenaeum* printed extracts in English; the whole book has appeared in German and is being published in England.

That is why I have ventured to print extracts from other parts.

In another place I speak of the immense importance my memoirs have for me personally, and the object with which I began writing them. I confine myself now to the general remark that the publication of contemporary memoirs is particularly useful for us Russians. Thanks to the censorship, we are not accustomed to anything being made public, and the slightest publicity frightens, checks, and surprises us. In England any man who appears on any public stage, whether as a huckster of letters or a guardian of the press, is liable to the same hisses and applause as the actor in the lowest theatre in Islington or Paddington. Neither the Queen nor her husband are excluded. It is a mighty curb!

Let our Imperial Actors of the secret and open police, who have been so well protected from publicity by the censorship and paternal punishments, know that sooner or later their deeds will come into the light of day.

'Of course—I don't mind—only . . .'

I jumped up from the table.

'Are you going?' asked Matvey, anxious to put in a word.

'I am,' I answered in such a tone that he said no more. 'I'll be back the day after to-morrow, if any one comes tell them I have a headache and am asleep, in the evening light the candles, and now get me my linen and my bag.'

The bells were tinkling in the yard.

'Are you ready?'

'Yes, and so good luck to us.'

By dinner-time next day the bells ceased tinkling, we were at Ketscher's door. I bade them call him out. A week before, when he had left me in Vladimir, there had been no idea of my coming, and hence he was so surprised on seeing me that at first he did not say a word and then went off into a peal of laughter: but soon looked anxious and led me indoors. When we were in his room he first carefully locked the door and then asked me: 'What has happened?'

'Nothing.'

'Then why are you here?'

'I couldn't stay in Vladimir, I want to see Natalie—that's all, and you must arrange it, and this very minute, because I must be back at home by to-morrow.'

Ketscher looked into my face and raised his eyebrows.

'What folly, the devil knows what to call it, to come like this with no need and nothing prepared! Have you written, have you fixed a time?'

'I have written nothing.'

'Upon my word, my boy, but what are we to do with you? It's beyond anything, it's raving madness!'

'That's just the point, that you must think what to do without losing a minute.'

'You're a fool,' said Ketscher with conviction, raising

his eyebrows higher than ever. 'I should be glad, very glad indeed, if it were a failure, it would be a lesson to you.'

'And rather a long lesson if I am caught. Listen: as soon as it is dark we'll go to the princess's house, you shall call some one out into the road, one of the servants, I'll tell you which—and then we'll see what to do. What do you say to that?'

'Well, there's no help for it, we'll go, we'll go; but I should like you not to succeed in seeing her! Why on earth didn't you write yesterday?'—and Ketscher, pulling his broad-brimmed hat over his brows with an air of dignity, threw on a black cloak lined with red.

'Oh, you hateful grumbler!' I said to him as we went out, and Ketscher, laughing heartily, repeated: 'But really it's enough to make a hen laugh, to come like this without sending a word; it's beyond anything.'

I could not stay at Ketscher's—he lived terribly far away, and his mother had visitors that day. He took me to an officer of hussars whom he knew to be an honourable man, and who, having never been mixed up with political affairs, was not under police supervision. The officer, a man with long moustaches, was sitting at dinner when we went in; Ketscher told him what we had come about. The officer in reply poured me out a glass of red wine and thanked us for the confidence we put in him; then he took me into his bedroom, which was adorned with saddles and saddle-cloths so that one might have supposed that he slept on horseback.

'Here is a room for you,' he said; 'no one will disturb you here.' Then he called his orderly, a hussar, and told him not to let any one go into that room on any pretext. I found myself again under the guardianship of a soldier, with this difference, that at the Krutitsky Barracks the gendarme had been keeping me from all the world, while here the hussar was keeping all the world from me.

AT THE PRINCESS'S HOUSE

When it was quite dark, Ketscher and I set off. My heart beat violently when I saw again the familiar streets and houses which I had not seen for nearly four years. . . . Kuznetsky Bridge, Tversky Boulevard . . . and here was Ogaryov's house; they had clapped an immense heraldic crest on it and it looked different. In the lower storey, where we spent such happy youthful days, a tailor was living. . . . Here was Povarsky Street—I held my breath: in the corner window of the little room there was a candle burning, that was her room, she was writing to me, she was thinking of me, the candle twinkled so gaily, it seemed twinkling *to me*.

While we were considering how best to call some one out into the street, one of the princess's young footmen ran out towards us.

'Arkady,' I said as he reached us. He did not recognise me. 'How is this,' I said, 'don't you know your own people?'

'Oh, is it you?' he cried.

I put my finger on my lips and said: 'If you would like to do me a friendly service, deliver this little note at once, as quickly as you can, through Sasha or Kostinka, do you understand? We will wait for the answer round the corner, and don't breathe a word to any one of having seen me in Moscow.'

'Don't be uneasy, we'll do it all instantly,' answered Arkady, and he skipped back into the house.

We walked up and down the side-street for about half an hour before a little, thin, old woman came out, flustered and looking about her; this was that same brisk servant girl who in 1812 had begged the French soldiers for '*manger*' for me; we had called her Kostinka ever since I was a child. The old woman took my face in both hands and showered kisses upon it

'So you've flown to see us,' she said. 'Ah, you headstrong boy, when will you learn sense, you foolish darling?—and you've given our young lady such a fright that she almost fainted.'

'And have you a note for me?'

'Yes, yes, he is impatient,' and she gave me a scrap of paper.

A few words had been scribbled in pencil with a trembling hand: 'My God, can it be true—you, here! To-morrow between five and six in the morning I will expect you. I can't believe it, I can't believe it! surely it must be a dream!'

The hussar again put me into his orderly's keeping. At half-past five next morning I stood leaning against a lamp-post, waiting for Ketscher, who had gone in at the side-gate of the princess's house. I will not attempt to describe what was passing in me while I waited at the lamp-post; such moments remain one's own secret because there are no words for them.

Ketscher beckoned to me. I went in at the little gate, a boy who had grown up since I left showed me in with a friendly smile, and here I was in the hall which at one time I used to enter yawning, though now I was ready to fall on my knees and kiss every plank on the floor. Arkady led me into the drawing-room and went out. I sank exhausted on the sofa, my heart throbbed so violently that it hurt me, and besides I was frightened. I linger over my story for the sake of spending longer over these memories, though I see that my words give a poor idea of them.

She came in all in white, dazzlingly lovely; three years of separation and the struggles she had been through had given the finishing touches to her features and her expression.

'This is you,' she said in her soft, gentle voice.

We sat down on the sofa and remained silent.

The expression of joy in her eyes almost approached suffering. I suppose when the feeling of happiness reaches its highest point it is mingled with an expression of pain, for she said to me: 'How exhausted you look!'

I held her hand, she leaned her head on the other, and there was no need for us to talk . . . a few brief phrases, two or three reminiscences, words from our letters, some idle remarks about Arkady, about the hussar, about Kostinka, that was all.

Then the old woman came in, saying that it was time for me to go, and I got up without protesting, and she did not try to keep me . . . our hearts were so full, all thoughts of more or less, of shorter or longer, all vanished before the fullness of the present. . . .

When we had passed the town gate, Ketscher asked: 'Well, have you settled anything?'

'Nothing.'

'But you talked to her?'

'Not a word about that.'

'Does she consent?'

'I didn't ask, of course she consents.'

'Well, upon my soul, you behave like a child, or a lunatic,' observed Ketscher, raising his eyebrows and shrugging his shoulders with indignation.

'I'll write to her and then to you, and now, good-bye. Now drive ahead full speed!'

It was thawing, the spongy snow was black in places, the endless white plain lay on both sides, little villages flashed by with their smoke, then the moon rose and shed a different light on everything; I was alone with the driver and kept looking out, yet all the while was there with her, and the road and the moon and the fields were somehow mixed up with the princess's drawing-room. And, strange to say, I remembered every word uttered by the nurse, by Arkady, even by the maid who had led me out to the gate, but what I had said to her and what she had said to me I could not remember!

Two months were spent in making arrangements. I had to borrow money, and to get her baptismal certificate; it appeared that the princess had taken it. One of my friends—swearing, bribing, treating policemen and clerks—succeeded by all sorts of false statements in getting another from the Consistory.

When everything was ready, we, that is Matvey and I, set off.

At dawn on the eighth of May we were at the last posting-station before Moscow. The drivers had gone to get horses. The air was heavy, there were drops of rain, and it seemed as though a storm were coming on; I remained in the covered chaise and hurried on the driver. Some one spoke near me in a strange, high, sing-song voice. I turned round and saw a pale, thin girl of about sixteen, in rags and with her hair hanging about her; she was begging. I gave her some small silver coin, she laughed seeing it, but instead of going away clambered on to the box of the chaise, turned towards me and began muttering half-coherent sentences, looking straight into my face; her eyes were clouded and pitiful, wisps of hair fell over her face. Her sickly face, her unintelligible mutterings, together with the light of early morning, aroused a sort of nervous uneasiness in me.

'She's crazy, you know, that is, she is simple,' observed the driver. 'And where are you poking yourself? I 'll give you a lash with the whip and then you 'll know! Upon my soul, I will, you shameless hussy!'

'Why are you scolding, what have I done to you—here your master's given me a silver bit, and what harm have I done you?'

'Well, he's given it to you, and so be off to your devils in the forest.'

'Take me with you,' added the girl, looking piteously at me, 'do, really, take me. . . .'

'To put you in a show in Moscow as a freak, some

sea monster, 'observed the driver.' Come, get down, we 're just off.'

The girl made no attempt to move, but kept looking pitifully at me. I begged the driver not to hurt her, he lifted her gently under his arm and set her on the ground. She burst out crying and I was ready to cry with her.

Why had this creature crossed my path just on that day, just as I was driving into Moscow? I thought of Kozlov's 'Mad Girl,' and she, too, had been met near Moscow.

We drove off, the air was full of electricity, unpleasantly heavy and warm. A dark blue storm-cloud with grey streamers reaching to the earth was slowly trailing over the fields, and all at once a zig-zag of lightning ran slanting through it, there was a clap of thunder and the rain came down in torrents. We were nearly seven miles from the Rogozhsky Gate and after reaching Moscow had an hour's drive to the Dyevitchy field. We reached A——'s, where Ketscher was to wait for me, literally without a dry thread on us.

Ketscher was not there. He was at the bedside of a dying woman, E. D. Levashev. This woman was one of those marvellous products of Russian life which reconcile one to it, one of those types whose whole existence is an heroic feat, unseen by any but a small circle of friends. How many tears she had wiped away, how much comfort she had brought to more than one broken heart, of how many young lives she had been the support, and how much she had suffered herself! 'She spent herself in love,' Tchaadayev, one of her closest friends, who dedicated his celebrated letter about Russia to her, said to me.

Ketscher could not leave her; he wrote that he would come about nine o'clock. I was alarmed by this news. A man absorbed by a great passion is a dreadful egoist; in Ketscher's absence I could see nothing but an obstacle in my path. . . . When it struck nine, when the bells began ringing for evening service and then another, quarter of an hour passed, I was overcome by feverish anxiety and cowardly despair. . . . Half-past nine—no, he would not come, the sick woman was probably worse, what was I to do? I could not remain in Moscow, one incautious word from the maid or the old nurse in the princess's house would give everything away. To go back was possible, but I felt I had not the strength to go back.

At a quarter to ten Ketscher appeared in a straw hat with the drowsy face of a man who has not slept all night. I rushed up to him and as I embraced him showered reproaches upon him. Ketscher, frowning, looked at me and asked: 'Why, isn't half an hour enough to get from A——' s to Povarsky Street? I might have been gossiping with you here for an hour, and I daresay it would have been very nice, but I could not bring myself to leave a dying friend sooner than I need for the sake of that. She sends you her greetings,' he added, 'she blessed me with her dying hand, hoping for the success of our enterprise, and gave me a warm shawl in case of need.' The dying woman's greetings were particularly precious to me. The warm shawl was very useful in the night, and I had no time to thank her nor to press her hand . . . soon afterwards she died.

Ketscher and A—— set off. Ketscher was to drive out of the town with Natalie, while A—— was to come back and tell me whether everything had gone off successfully and what I was to do. I was left waiting with his charming and delightful wife; she had herself only lately been married, and, being an ardent, passionate nature, she took the warmest interest in our enterprise. She tried with feigned gaiety to assure me that everything was going splendidly, though she was herself so fretted by anxiety that her face was continually changing. We sat together in the window and conversation did not flow easily; we were like children shut up in an empty room as a punishment. Two hours passed in this way.

There is nothing in the world more shattering, more unendurable than inactivity and suspense at such moments. Friends make a great mistake in taking the whole burden off the shoulders of the principal *patient*. They ought to invent duties for him if there are none, to overwhelm him with physical exertions, to distract his mind with work and arrangements.

At last A—— came in, we rushed to meet him.

'Everything is going gloriously, I saw them gallop off,' he shouted to us from the yard.' You go at once out at the Rogozhsky Gate, there by the little bridge you will see the horses not far from Perov's restaurant. Good luck to you! And change your cab half-way, so that your second cabman may not know where you have come from.'

I flew like an arrow from the bow. . . . And here was the little bridge not far from Perov's; there was no one there, and on the other side of the bridge, too, there was no one. I drove as far as the Izmailovsky Menagerie, there was no one. I dismissed the cabman and went forward on foot. Walking backwards and forwards, at last I saw on another road a carriage of some sort. A handsome young coachman was standing by it. 'Has a tall gentleman in a straw hat driven by here,' I asked him, 'and not alone, with a young lady?'

'I have seen no one,' the coachman answered reluctantly.

'With whom did you come here?'
'With gentlefolks.'
'What is their name?'
'What is that to you?'
'What a fellow you are really, if it was nothing to do with me, I should not be asking you.'

The coachman gave me a searching look and smiled—apparently my appearance disposed him more favourably to me.

'If you have business with them then you ought to know their names yourself.'

'You are a regular flint; well, I want a gentleman named Ketscher.'

The coachman smiled again, and pointing towards the graveyard said: 'There, do you see something black in the distance? That's himself, and the young lady is with him; she did not bring her hat, so Mr. Ketscher gave her his, luckily it was a straw one.'

Again this time we met in a graveyard!

With a faint cry she flung herself on my neck.

'And it's for ever!' she cried.

'For ever,' I repeated. Ketscher was touched, tears gleamed in his eyes, he took our hands and in a trembling voice said, 'Friends, be happy!' We embraced him. This was our real wedding!

For over an hour we waited in the private dining-room of Perov's restaurant, and still the carriage and Matvey did not come! Ketscher frowned. The possibility of trouble never entered our heads, we were so happy there, the three of us, and as much at home as though we had always been together. There was a wood in front of the windows, from the storey below came strains of music and a gypsy chorus; the weather was lovely after the storm.

I was not, like Ketscher, afraid of the police being put on our track by the princess; I knew that she stood too much on her dignity to let a policeman be mixed up in our family affairs. Besides, she never took any step without consulting the Senator, nor the Senator without consulting my father; my father would never consent to the police stopping me in Moscow or near Moscow, which would mean my being sent to Bobruisk or to Siberia for disobedience to the will of the Most High. The only possible danger was from the secret police, but it had all been done so quickly that it was hard for them to know it. Besides, if they had got an inkling of anything, it would never occur to any one that a man who had secretly returned from exile and was eloping with his bride would be quietly sitting in Perov's restaurant where people were coming in and out from morning to night.

At last Matvey appeared with the carriage.

'One more glass,' commanded Ketscher.

And we set off.

And then we were alone, that is, the two of us, flying along the Vladimir road.

At Bunkovo while they were changing horses we went into the inn. The old hostess came to ask us whether we would like anything; and, looking at us good-naturedly, said: 'How young and pretty your good lady is, and the two of you, God bless you, make a pretty pair.' We blushed up to our ears and did not dare to look at each other, but asked for tea to cover our confusion. Between five and six next day we reached Vladimir. There was no time to be lost; leaving Natalie with the family of an old official, I rushed off to find whether everything was ready. But who was there to get things ready in Vladimir?

There are good-natured people everywhere. A Siberian regiment of Uhlans was stationed at Vladimir at the time; I was only very slightly acquainted with the officers, but, meeting one of them rather often in the public library, I took to bowing to him; he was very polite and charming. A month later he admitted that he knew me and my story in 1834 and told me that he was himself a student of the Moscow University. When I was leaving Vladimir and looking about for some one in whose hands to leave various arrangements, I thought of this officer, and told him openly what I wanted.

Genuinely touched by my confidence, he pressed my hand, promised to do everything, and kept his word.

He was awaiting me in full dress uniform, with white facings, with his casque uncovered, with a cartridge-case across his shoulder, and all sorts of cords and trimmings. He told me that the bishop had given the priest permission to marry us, but had bidden him first show the baptismal certificate. I gave the officer the baptismal certificate, while I went off to another young man who had also been a Moscow student. He was serving his two provincial years in accordance with the new regulation, in the governor's office, and was almost dying of boredom.

'Would you like to act as best man?'

'Whose best man?'

'Mine.'

'Yours?'

'Yes, yes, mine.'

'Delighted. When?'

'At once.'

He thought that I was joking, but when I briefly told him how it was, he skipped with delight. To be best man at a clandestine wedding, to have to make arrangements, possibly to get into trouble, and all that in a little town absolutely without any diversions! He promised at once to get a carriage and four horses and ran to his chest of drawers to see whether he had a clean white waistcoat.

As I drove away from him, I met my Uhlan with a priest sitting on his knee. Imagine a smart, gaily attired officer in a little droshky with a stout priest, adorned with a huge, flowing beard, and arrayed in a silk cassock, which kept catching in all the Uhlan's useless accoutrements. This sight might have attracted attention not only in the street that led from the Golden Gate of Vladimir, but in the Paris boulevards, or even in Regent Street. But the Uhlan did not think of that, and, indeed, I only

PREPARATIONS FOR WEDDING

thought of it afterwards. The priest had been going from house to house holding services, as it was St. Nicholas' Day, and my cavalry officer had captured him by force and requisitioned him. We drove off to the bishop's.

To explain the position I must describe how the bishop came to be involved in it. The day before I went away the priest who had agreed to marry us suddenly announced that he would not do so without the bishop's sanction, that he had heard something and was afraid to do it. In spite of all my eloquence, as well as the Uhlan's, the priest was obstinate and stuck to his point. The Uhlan suggested the priest of his regiment. The latter, a priest with a cropped head and shaven skin, wearing a long, full-skirted coat and trousers tucked into his high boots, and placidly smoking a soldier's pipe, though affected by certain details of our proposition, yet refused to perform the ceremony, declaring, in a mixture of Polish and White Russian, that he was strictly forbidden to marry 'civilians.'

'And we are still more strictly forbidden to be witnesses and best men at such marriages without permission,' observed the officer.

'That's a different matter, as God's above us, it's a different matter.'

'God helps those who help themselves,' I said to the Uhlan. 'I'll go straight to the bishop. And by the way, why don't you ask permission?'

'That won't do. The Colonel would tell his wife and she'd gossip about it all over the place. Besides, he'd very likely refuse it.'

Bishop Parfeny of Vladimir was a clever, austere, rough old man; managing and self-willed, he might equally well have been a governor or a general, and, indeed, I think he would have been more in his right place as a general than as a monk; but it had turned out otherwise, and he ruled his diocese as he would have ruled a division in the Caucasus. I noticed in him far more of the qualities of an administrator than of one dead to the things of this life. He was, however, rather harsh than ill-natured; like all business-like men, he grasped questions quickly and clearly and was furious when people talked nonsense to him or did not understand him. It is far easier to come to an understanding with men of that sort than with soft but weak or irresolute persons. In accordance with the custom of all provincial towns, on arriving in Vladimir I went once after mass to call on the bishop. He received me graciously, gave me his blessing, and regaled me with sturgeon; then invited me to come some evening and talk to him, saying that his eyes were failing and he could not read in the evening. I went two or three times; he talked about literature, knew all the new Russian books and read the magazines, and so we got on splendidly together. Nevertheless, it was with some alarm that I knocked at his episcopal door.

It was a hot day. His Reverence the bishop received me in the garden. He was sitting under a big, shady lime tree, and had taken off his monk's cap and let his grey locks flow in freedom. A bald, impressive-looking head-priest was standing before him, bareheaded, and right in the sun, reading some document aloud; his face was crimson and big drops of perspiration stood out on his forehead, he screwed up his eyes at the dazzling whiteness of the paper with the sunlight upon it, yet he did not dare to move nor did the bishop tell him to step out of the sun.

'Sit down,' he said after blessing me, 'we are just finishing, these are our little Consistory affairs. Read,' he added to the head-priest, and the latter, after mopping his face with a dark blue handkerchief and coughing aside, set to reading again.

'What news have you to tell me?' Parfeny asked me, handing the pen to the head-priest, who seized this excellent opportunity to kiss his hand.

I told him of the priest's refusal.

'Have you the necessary papers?' I showed him the governor's permission.

'Is that all?'

'Yes.'

Parfeny smiled: 'And on the lady's side?'

'There is a baptismal certificate; it will be brought on the day of the wedding.'

'When is the wedding?'

'In two days.'

'Have you found a house?'

'Not yet.'

'There you see,' Parfeny said to me, putting his finger on his lips and pulling his mouth towards his cheek, one of his favourite tricks; 'you're an intelligent and well-read man, but you won't catch an old sparrow by putting salt on its tail. There is something shady about it, so, since you have come to me, you had much better tell me all about it truthfully. Then I'll tell you straightforwardly what can be done and what can't, and in any case my advice will do you no harm.'

My case seemed to me so clear and so just that I told him the whole story, without, of course, going into unnecessary details. The old man listened attentively and often looked into my face. It appeared he was an old acquaintance of the princess's, and therefore could to some extent judge for himself of the truth of my account.

'I understand, I understand,' he said when I had finished. 'Well, let me write a letter to the princess on my own account.'

'I assure you that no effort at peace will lead to anything, her ill-humour and exasperation have gone too far. I have told your Reverence all about it, as you desired, now

I will add that if you refuse to help me I shall be forced to do secretly, stealthily, by bribes, what I am doing now quietly, but straightforwardly and openly. I can assure you of one thing, neither prison nor a fresh term of exile will stop me.

'You see,' said Parfeny, getting up and stretching, 'what a headstrong fellow you are. Perm has not been enough for you, you are not broken in yet. Am I saying that I forbid it? Get married if you like, there is nothing unlawful about it; but it would have been better peacefully with the consent of the family. Send me your priest, I'll persuade him somehow; only remember one thing, without the proper certificate on the bride's side don't you attempt it. So it's a case of "Neither prison nor exile"—upon my word, what are people coming to! Well, the Lord be with you! Good luck to you, only you'll get me into trouble with the princess.'

And so in addition to the Uhlan officer his Reverence Parfeny, bishop of Vladimir and Suzdal, came into our conspiracy.

When as a preliminary measure I had asked the governor's permission, I had not spoken of my marriage as though it were clandestine; silence about that was the surest means of avoiding talk about it, and nothing could be more natural than the arrival of my future bride in Vladimir, since I had not the right to leave it. It was also natural that under the circumstances we should wish the wedding to be as quiet as possible.

When we arrived with the priest at the bishop's on the ninth of May, his servitor told us that he had gone to his country house and would not be back until night. It was already between seven and eight in the evening, weddings cannot be celebrated after ten, and the next day was Saturday. What was to be done? The priest was scared. We went in to see the head-monk, the bishops chaplain; he was drinking tea with rum in it and was in the most affable frame of mind. I told him our difficulty, he poured me out a cup of tea and insisted on my adding rum to it; then he took out immense silver spectacles, read the baptismal certificate, turned it over, looked at the other side where there was nothing written, folded it up, and giving it back to the priest said: 'It's all perfectly regular.'

The priest still hesitated. I told the chaplain that if I were not married to-day it would be terribly upsetting for me.

'Why put it off?' he said. 'I will tell his Reverence; marry them, Father Ioann, marry them—in the name of the Father, the Son, and the Holy Ghost, Amen.'

There was nothing for the priest to say, he drove off to write out our names while I galloped off for Natalie.

When we were driving out at the Golden Gate alone together, the sun, which had till then been hidden by the clouds, shed a dazzling light upon us with its last bright, red glow, and so triumphantly and joyously that we both said in one breath: 'That's to see us off!' I remember her smile at the words and the pressure of her hand.

The littte church of the sledge-drivers 'quarter was empty, there were neither choristers nor lighted candelabra. Five or six common soldiers of the Uhlan regiment came in as they were passing, and went out again. The old deacon chanted in a soft, faint voice, Matvey looked at us with tears of joy, our young best men' stood behind us with the heavy crowns with which all the drivers of Vladimir were crowned. The deacon with a shaky hand passed us the silver bowl of union . . . it grew dark in the church, only a few candles glowed here and there; all this was, or seemed to us, extremely picturesque just from its simplicity. The bishop drove by, and seeing the church doors open stopped and sent to inquire what was happening. The priest, turning a little pale, went out himself to him, and returning a minute later with a cheerful face, said to us: 'His Reverence sends you his episcopal blessing and bade me tell you he is praying for you.'

By the time we were driving home the news of our clandestine marriage was all over the town; ladies were waiting on the balconies and the windows were open. I let down the carriage windows and was a little vexed that the darkness prevented me from showing my 'fair bride.'

At home we drank two bottles of wine with Matvey and the 'best men,' the latter stayed twenty minutes with us, and then we were left alone, and again, as at Perov's, that seemed so natural that we were not in the least surprised at it, though for months afterwards we could not get over the wonder of it.

We had three rooms, we sat at a little table in the drawing-room, and forgetting the fatigue of the last few days we talked half the night.

To have a crowd of outsiders at the wedding festivities has always seemed to me something coarse, unseemly, almost cynical; why this premature lifting of the veil from love, this initiation of indifferent casual spectators into the privacy of the family? How all these hackneyed greetings, commonplace vulgarities, stupid allusions, must wound the poor girl who is thrust into the public eye in the part of bride . . . not one delicate feeling is spared, the luxury of the bridal chamber, the charm of the night attire displayed, not only for the visitors but for every idle gazer. And afterwards the first days of the new life that is beginning, in which every minute is precious, which ought to be spent far away in solitude, are, as though in mockery, passed in endless dinners and exhausting balls, amidst a crowd.

Next morning we found two rose-bushes and an immense nosegay awaiting us in the dining-room. Dear, kind Yulia Fyodorovna (the governor's wife), who took a warm interest in our romance, had sent them. I embraced and kissed her footman and then we went off to see her. As the bride's trousseau consisted of two dresses, the one in which she had travelled and the other one in which she had been married, she put on the wedding dress.

From Yulia Fyodorovna's we drove to the bishop's; the old man himself led us into the garden, with his own hands cut us a nosegay of flowers, told Natalie how I had tried to frighten him with the prospect of my own ruin, and in conclusion advised her to study housekeeping. 'Do you know how to salt cucumbers?' he asked Natalie.

'I do,' she answered, laughing.

'Oh, I don't feel sure of it. And you know, it is essential!'

In the evening I wrote a letter to my father. I begged him not to be angry at the accomplished fact, and, 'since God had united us,' to forgive me and add his blessing. My father as a rule wrote me a few lines once a week; he did not write one day earlier or later in reply, and even began his letter exactly as usual: 'I received your letter of the ioth of May, at half-past five the day before yesterday, and from it learned, not without regret, that God had united you with Natasha. I do not repine against the will of God in anything, but submit blindly to the trials which He lays upon me. But since the money is mine and you have not thought it necessary to regard my wishes, I must inform you that I shall not add one kopeck to your present allowance of one thousand silver roubles a year.'

How spontaneously we laughed at this distinction between the spiritual and temporal power.

And yet how we needed something more! The money I had borrowed was all spent. We had nothing, absolutely nothing, no clothes, no linen, no crockery.

We sat shut up in a little flat because we had nothing to go out in. Matvey with a view to economy made a desperate effort to transform himself into a cook, but except beefsteaks and collops he could cook nothing, and so for the most part confined himself to ready-cooked provisions, ham, salt fish, milk, eggs, cheese, and extremely hard cakes flavoured with mint and not in their first youth. Dinner was an endless source of amusement to us; sometimes we had milk first by way of soup, and sometimes last by way of dessert. Over this Spartan fare we used to recall, smiling, the long process of the sacred ritual of dinner at the princess's and at my father's, where half a dozen flunkeys ran about the room with bowls and dishes, cloaking under the magnificent *mise en* scène the really very unattractive fare.

So we struggled along in poverty for a year. 'The Chemist' sent us ten thousand paper roubles; more than six thousand of this went to pay our debts, and what remained was a great help. At last even my father was tired of attacking us like a fortress by hunger, and without adding to my allowance he began sending us presents of money, though I never dropped a hint about money after his famous *distinguo*!

I began looking for another lodging. A big, deserted manor-house with a garden was to let. It belonged to the widow of a prince who had ruined himself at cards, and it was being let very cheaply because it was far away and inconvenient, and, above all, because the princess bargained to keep part of it, in no way separated from the rest, for her son, a spoilt fellow of thirty, and for the servants. No one would agree to this partial possession; I at once accepted it, for I was fascinated by the loftiness of the rooms, the size of the windows, and the big, shady garden. But this very loftiness and spaciousness made a very amusing contrast with our complete lack of movable belongings and articles of the first necessity. The princess's housekeeper, a good-natured old woman, who was greatly attracted by Matvey, provided us at her own risk, first with a table-cloth, then with cups, then with sheets, then with knives and forks.

What bright and untroubled days we spent in the little three-roomed flat at the Golden Gate and in the princess's immense house! . . . There was a big, scarcely furnished drawing-room, in it we were sometimes taken by such childishness that we raced about it, jumped over the chairs, lighted candles in all the candelabra ensconced on the wall, and after illuminating the room *a giorno*, recited poetry. Matvey and our maid, a young Greek girl, took part in everything and 'played the fool' as much as we did. Discipline was 'not maintained' in our household.

And for all this childishness our life was full of a deep earnestness. Cast away in the quiet, peaceful little town, we were completely devoted to each other. From time to time came news of some one of our friends, a few words of warm sympathy, and then again we were alone, absolutely alone. But in this solitude our hearts were not closed by our happiness; on the contrary, they were more open to every interest than ever before; we led a full and many-sided life, we thought and read, gave ourselves up to every pursuit and again concentrated on our love; we compared our thoughts and dreams, and saw with amazement how endless was our sympathy, how in all the subtlest turns and twists of feeling and thought, taste and antipathy, all was kinship and harmony. The only difference was that Natalie brought into our union a gentle, mild, gracious element, the characteristics of a young girl with all the poesy of a loving woman, while I brought lively activity, my *semper in* motu, infinite love, and, moreover, a medley of earnest ideas, laughter, 'dangerous' thoughts and Utopian projects.

My desires had reached a standstill, I was satisfied, I

lived in the present, I expected nothing from the morrow, I carelessly trusted that it would take nothing from me. Personal life could give nothing more, it had reached the limit; any change could but diminish it, on one side or another.

In the spring Ogaryov came from his exile for a few days. He was then in the very height of his powers; he was soon to pass through painful experiences; at moments he seemed to feel that trouble was near, but he could still turn round and look upon the lifted hand of destiny as a dream. I myself thought then that the storm-clouds would be dissipated; carelessness is characteristic of everything young and not devoid of strength, and in it is expressed a trust in life and oneself. The feeling of complete mastery over one's fate lulls us asleep . . . while dark clouds and black-hearted people draw us without a word to the edge of the precipice.

And well it is that man either does not suspect, or can shut his eyes and forget. Where there is apprehension there can never be complete happiness; complete happiness is serene as the sea in the calm of summer. Apprehension gives its peculiar, feverish, morbid thrill which fascinates like the thrill of suspense at cards, but how far away it is from the feeling of harmonious infinite peace. And so, whether it be a dream or not, I deeply prize that trust in life, before life itself has refuted it and has awakened one. . . . The Chinese die for the coarse illusion of it given by opium.

So I ended this chapter in 1853 and so I end it now.

Chapter 24

The Thirteenth of June 1839

ONE long, winter evening towards the end of 1838 we were sitting, as always, alone, reading and then not reading, talking and then being silent, and in silence continuing the talk. There was a hard frost outside, and even in the room it was not at all warm. Natasha did not feel well and was lying on the sofa, covered with a cloak. I was sitting on the floor near her; my reading did not get on, she was inattentive, thinking of something else and absorbed, and her face kept changing.

'Alexandr,' she said, 'I have a secret, come nearer and I will tell you in your ear, but guess it yourself.'

I did guess, but insisted on her telling me. I longed to hear this news from her: she told me, we looked at each other in excitement and with tears in our eyes.

How rich is the human heart in the capacity for happiness, for joy, if only people know how to give themselves up to it without being distracted by trifles. As a rule the present is spoilt by external worries, empty cares, irritable fussiness, all the rubbish which is brought upon us in the midday of life by the vanity of vanities, and the stupid ordering of our everyday life. We waste our best minutes, we let them slip through our fingers as though we had an endless store of them. We are usually thinking of to-morrow, of next year, when we ought with both hands to be clasping the brimming cup which life itself, unbidden, with her customary lavishness, holds out to us, and to drink and drink of it until the cup passes into other hands. Nature does not care to waste time offering it and pressing us.

One would have thought nothing could have been added to our happiness, and yet the news of the coming child opened new vistas of feeling, new raptures, hopes and apprehensions of which we had before known nothing.

Love, a little scared and agitated, grows more tender, is more anxious in its solicitude, from the egoism of two it becomes not a mere egoism of three but the sacrifice of two for a third; family life begins with the child. A new element is entering into life, a mysterious person is knocking at its portals, a guest who is yet is not, but whose coming is essential, who is eagerly awaited. What will he be? No one knows, but whatever he may be like, he is a happy stranger, with what love he is met on the threshold of life!

And then there is the agonising anxiety: would he be born alive or not? There are so many unhappy possibilities. The doctor smiles at the questions: 'He knows nothing or will not say,' one thinks; everything is still hidden from outsiders; there is no one to ask, besides one is shy.

And then the child gives signs of life. I know no loftier and more religious feeling than that which fills the heart at feeling the first movements of the future being, struggling and stretching its immature muscles, that first touch with which the father blesses the newcomer and yields a place for him in his life.

'My wife,' a French bourgeois said to me once, 'my wife'—and seeing that there were neither ladies nor children present, added in an undertone— 'is pregnant.'

Indeed, the muddle of all our moral conceptions is such that pregnancy is looked upon as something improper. Though childbirth should claim unconditional respect for the mother, whoever she may be, the facts are kept secret not from a feeling of respect or spiritual delicacy, but from a regard for propriety. All that is the depravity of idealism, the corruption of monasticism, the accursed immolation of the flesh; it all comes from that unhappy dualism which draws us like Magdeburg hemispheres in opposite directions. Jeanne Deroin,[1] in spite of her socialism, hints in her Almana*ch des F*emmes that in time children will be born differently. How differently?— As the angels are born.—Well, that makes it clear.

Honour and glory to our teacher, the old realist Goethe. He had the courage to set the woman with child beside the innocent maidens of romanticism, and did not fear to mould in his mighty verse the changing forms of the future mother, comparing them with the supple limbs of the future woman.

Truly the woman who bears with the memory of past transports the whole cross of love, all its burden, sacrificing beauty and time, suffering, feeding from her own bosom, is one of the most beautiful and touching figures.

In the Roman elegies, in the Weaver, in Gretchen and her despairing prayer, Goethe has expressed all the solemn beauty with which nature surrounds the ripening fruit and all the thorns with which society crowns that vessel of the future life.

Poor mothers, who hide as though it were shame the traces of love, how brutally and mercilessly the world persecutes them, and persecutes them at the very time when the woman needs peace and kindness, savagely poisoning for her those priceless moments in which life droops fainting under the weight of happiness.

Gradually the secret is with horror discovered: the luckless mother at first tries to persuade herself that it is fancy, but soon doubt is impossible; with despair and tears she follows every movement of her babe, she would like to check the secret workings of its life, to turn it back, she hopes for some misfortune as a mercy, as pardon— while inexorable nature goes its way; she is young and healthy!

---

[1] Jeanne Deroin was a disciple of Saint Simon who published an *Almanach des* Femmes in 1851.—(*Translator's Note.*)

To force a mother to desire the death of her own child, and sometimes even more, to drive her to be its murderess and then to punish her, or to cover her with shame if the mother's heart is too strong for her—how intelligently and morally is society organised!

And who has weighed, who has considered what passes in her heart while the mother crosses the terrible path from love to fear, from fear to despair, to crime, to madness, for infanticide is physiological abnormality. She too has had, of course, moments of forgetfulness, in which she has passionately loved her coming little one, only the more because his existence was a secret between them; there have been times when she has dreamed of his little feet, of his milky smile, has kissed him in his sleep, has found in him a likeness to one who has been so dear to her. . . .

'But do they feel it? Of course there are unhappy victims . . . but . . . the others, but the average?'

It would be hard, one fancies, to sink lower than those bats that flit about at night in the fog and slush of the London streets, those victims of ignorance, poverty, and want, with whom society guards its respectable women from the excesses of their admirers' sensuality . . . in them, of course, it would be hardest of all to assume traces of maternal feeling, would it not?

Allow me to tell you of a little incident that occurred to me. Three years ago I met a young and beautiful girl. She belonged to the higher ranks of prostitution, that is, did not democratically walk the streets, but lived in bourgeois style, kept by a merchant. It was at a public ball; the friend who was with me knew her and invited her to drink a bottle of wine with us in the gallery, she, of course, accepted the invitation. She was a merry, careless creature, and probably like Laura in Pushkin's *Don Juan* was never worried by the fact that far away in Paris it was cold while she heard the watchman in Madrid cry 'The sun is shining.' . . . After swallowing the last glass she rushed back to the ponderous whirl of the English dances and I lost sight of her.

This winter, one wet evening I crossed the street to stand under the Arcade in Pall Mall to escape the streaming rain; a poorly dressed woman, shivering with cold, was standing under the lamp-post in the archway, probably on the watch for her prey. Her features struck me as familiar, she glanced at me, turned away and tried to shrink out of sight, but I had time to recognise her. 'What has happened to you?' I asked her with sympathy. Her sunken cheeks were suffused with bright crimson, whether from shame or consumption I do not know, but it did not seem like rouge; those two years and a half had made her look ten years older.

'I was ill for a long time and was very unfortunate,' with a look of great distress she glanced towards her shabby clothes.

'But where is your friend?'

'He was killed in the Crimea.'

'Why, but he was a merchant, wasn't he?'

She was confused, and instead of answering, said: 'I am very ill even now, and besides I have no work at all. Why, have I changed so much?' she asked, looking at me suddenly in embarrassment.

'Very much: in those days you were like a little girl, and now I shouldn't mind betting that you have children of your own.'

She flushed crimson, and with a sort of terror asked: 'How did you know that?'

'Well, you see, I do know. Now tell me, what really has been happening to you?'

'Nothing, only you are right, I have got a little boy . . . if only you knew,' and at those words her face brightened, 'what a splendid, handsome little fellow he is, even the neighbours all admire him. But that man married a rich girl and went away to the Continent. The baby was born afterwards. He is to blame for my position. At first I had money and used to buy him everything in the biggest shops, but now things have got worse and worse and I have taken everything to "my uncle." I have been advised to put baby out in the country, it certainly would be better for him, but I can't; I look at him, I just look at him and feel, no, we had better die together; I tried to find a situation, but they won't take me with the baby. I went back to mother's, she was all right, she 's got a kind heart, she forgave me, she is fond of the boy and makes a lot of him; but for five months now she has been bedridden—what with the doctor to pay and the medicine and then, as you know yourself, coal and bread and everything so dear this year, there was nothing but starvation before us there. So I——,' she paused, 'of course, it would be better to throw myself in the Thames than . . . but there 's baby and I 'm sorry for him, whom should I leave him to, and you know he 's such a darling!'

I gave her something and in addition took out a shilling and said: 'And spend that on something for your baby.' She took the coin joyfully, held it in her hand, and all at once, giving it back to me, added with a mournful smile: 'Since you are so kind, buy him something yourself in some shop here, a toy or something, for no one has ever given him a present, poor little darling, since he was born.'

I looked with emotion at this *lost* woman and pressed her hand affectionately.

The zealous champions of ladies with camellias and pearls would do better to leave velvet furniture and rococo boudoirs alone and look at the wretched, starved, and shivering prostitution close at hand, the fatal prostitution which forces its victims down the road to ruin and gives no chance for rallying nor repentance. Scavengers more often find precious stones in the gutter than amongst the tinsel of tawdry finery.

That reminded me of that clever translator of *Faust*, poor Gérard de Nerval, who shot himself last year. He had not been home for five or six days. It was discovered at last that he was spending his time in the lowest dens near the town gates, as Paul Niquet used to do, that there he had made friends with thieves, with low creatures of all sorts, was treating them to drink, playing cards with them, and sometimes sleeping under their protection. His old friends tried to persuade him to come away and to put him to shame, Nerval, defending himself good-naturedly, once said to them: 'Let me tell you, my friends, you are fearfully conventional. I assure you that the society of these people is no worse than that of any others I have been among.' He had been suspected of madness; after that saying I imagine the suspicion passed into conviction!

The fatal day was approaching and everything became more and more dreadful. I looked at the doctor and the mysterious face of the midwife with slavish reverence. Neither Natasha nor I nor our young maid knew anything about it; luckily, at my father's request, an elderly lady, an intelligent, practical, and capable woman called Praskovya Andreyevna, came from Moscow to stay with us. Seeing our helplessness she took the reins of management entirely into her own hands and I obeyed her like a nigger.

One night I felt a hand touch me, I opened my eyes. Praskovya Andreyevna was standing before me in a nightcap and dressing-gown with a candle in her hand; she told me to send for the doctor and the midwife. I was petrified as though the news were something quite unexpected. I felt as though I should have liked to take a dose of opium, turn over on the other side and sleep through the danger . . . but there was no help for it. I dressed with trembling hands and rushed to wake Matvey.

A dozen times I ran out from the bedroom into the hall to listen for a carriage in the distance. Everything was still but for the faint, faint rustle of the breeze of morning in the warm June air of the garden; the birds were beginning to sing, the crimson dawn threw a light flush over the leaves, and again I hurried back to the bedroom, pestered kind Praskovya Andreyevna with stupid questions, squeezed Natasha's hands convulsively, did not know what to do, trembled and was in a fever . . . but at last the chaise rattled on the bridge—thank God, it was in time!

At eleven o'clock in the morning I started as from a violent electric shock when the loud scream of a new-born baby reached my ear. 'A boy,' Praskovya Andreyevna called to me as she went towards the cradle; I would have taken the baby from the pillow, but I could not, my hands trembled so violently. The thought of danger (which often indeed is only beginning at this stage) that had weighed upon me vanished at once, a wild joy took possession of my heart as though all the bells were pealing for a festival of festivals! Natasha smiled at me, smiled at the baby, wept and laughed, and only her broken breathing, her weary eyes, and deathly pallor reminded me of the struggle, the agony that she had just passed through.

Then I left the room, I could bear no more. I went into my study and flung myself on the sofa, at the end of my strength, and lay for half an hour without definite thought, without definite feeling, in a sort of anguish of bliss.

That face of exhausted ecstasy, that joy flitting on the brink of death upon the mother's countenance, I recognised again in Vandyke's Madonna in the Corsini Gallery at Rome. The baby has just been born, they are holding it up to the mother; exhausted, with not a drop of blood in her face, faint and weary, she smiles, while her tired eyes rest on the baby with a look of infinite love.

It must be admitted that the Virgin Mother is quite

THE VIRGIN MOTHER

out of keeping with the celibate religion of Christianity. With her, life, love, gentleness cannot but break into the everlasting funeral, the dread day of judgment, and the other horrors of Church theology.

That is why Protestantism has rejected the Virgin Mother *only* from its barn-like chapels, from its factories of God's word. She really does interfere with Christian propriety, she cannot escape from her earthly nature, she warms the cold church, and in spite of everything remains a woman, a mother. She makes up for the supernatural conception by the natural birth, and snatches a blessing on her labour from the lips of monastic worshippers who curse everything bodily.

Michael Angelo and Raphael grasped that in their painting.

In 'The Day of Judgment' in the Sistine Chapel, in that massacre of St. Bartholomew in the other world, we see the Son of God going to preside over the executions; He has already lifted His hand . . . He will give the signal, and tortures? agonies will follow, the last trump will sound, the universal *auto-da-fé* will begin crackling; but—the Mother, trembling and suffering for all, presses up to Him in horror, and is imploring Him on behalf of the sinners; looking at her He will perhaps be softened and forget His cruel' Woman, what hast thou to do with me?' and will not give the signal.

The Sistine Madonna is Mignon after the child's birth, she is frightened at her incredible fate, helpless. . . .

'Was hat man dir, du armes Kind, gethan?'

Her inner peace is shattered, she has been told that her son is the Son of God, that she is the Mother of God; she looks with a sort of nervous ecstasy, with mesmeric clairvoyance she seems to be saying: 'Take Him, He is not mine.' But at the same time she presses Him to herself as though, if she could, she would fly with Him far away and would simply fondle and feed at her bosom not the Saviour of the world but her own babe. And all this is because she is a human mother and has no kinship with Isis and Rhea and all the other gods of the female sex.

That is why it has been so easy for her to conquer the cold Aphrodite, that Ninon L'Enclos of Olympus, whose children no one troubles about. Mary with her babe in her arms, with her eyes always gently looking down upon Him, surrounded by the halo of womanliness and the holiness of motherhood, is nearer to our hearts than the golden-haired Aphrodite.

To my thinking Pius ix. and his Conclave were very consistent in proclaiming the unnatural or, in their language, immaculate conception of the Virgin. Mary, born naturally like you and me, would naturally stand up for men and sympathise with us: in her the living reconciliation of flesh and spirit would steal into religion. If even she was not humanly born, there is nothing in common between her and us, she will not feel for us, and the flesh is once more damned—and the Church more essential than ever for salvation.

It is a pity that the Pope is a thousand years too late. That, it seems, is Pius ix.'s fate. *Troppo tardi, Santo Padre, siete sempre e sempre—troppo tardi!*

When I wrote this part of my Memoirs I had not our old letters. I got them in 1856. After reading them over I had to correct two or three passages, not more. My memory had not betrayed me. I should have liked to add a few of Natalie's letters, and at the same time I am restrained by a sort of dread and cannot decide the question whether I ought to lay bare our life any further, and whether those lines so dear to me might not meet with a cold smile.

Among Natalie's papers I found my own notes to her,

written partly before prison and partly from the Krutitsky Barracks. . . . Some of them I append to this part. Perhaps they will not seem superfluous to those who are fond of tracing the sources of men's destinies, perhaps such will read them with that nervous interest with which we look through the microscope at the development of the living organism.

I [1]

August 15th, 1832.

DEAR NATALYA ALEXANDROVNA,—To-day is your birthday; I should very much have liked to wish you many happy returns in person, but there really is no possibility. I am sorry I have not been to see you for so long, but circumstances have quite prevented me from disposing of my time as I should have liked. I hope that you will forgive me, and wish you the full development of all your talents and all the treasures of happiness which fate bestows on the pure in heart.—Your devoted   A. H.

II

July 5th or 6th, 1833.

You are wrong, Natalya Alexandrovna. You are quite wrong in thinking that I should confine myself to one letter—here is another for you. It is extremely pleasant to write to persons with whom one is in sympathy, there are so few of them, so few that one wouldn't use a quire of paper on them in a year.

I am a graduate, that is true, but they did not give me the gold medal. I have a silver medal—*one of three*!

A. H.

P. S.—To-day there was the prize-giving, but I didn't go for I don't care to be second.

---

[1] These little notes were kept by Natalie, and on many of them she wrote a few words in pencil. I could not preserve any of the letters she wrote to me in prison. I was obliged to destroy them all at once.

III

(At the beginning of 1834.)

Natalie! we are expecting you impatiently. M—— hopes that in spite of E——I——'s threats yesterday Amelia Mihailovna will be sure to come too, and so, till we meet,—Wholly yours,   A. H.

IV

KRUTITSKY BARRACKS,
December 10th, 1834.

I have just written a letter to the colonel in which I have asked for a permit for you, there is no answer yet. It will be harder for you to arrange it, but I rely on Mother. You were in luck in regard to me, you were the last of my friends whom I saw before my arrest [we parted confidently hoping to see each other soon at nine o'clock, but at two I was already in the police-station], and you will be the first to see me again. Knowing you, I know that that will give you pleasure, let me assure you that it will me too. To me you are a sister.

There is not much for me to say about myself. I have settled down and grown used to being a prisoner. The most dreadful thing for me is the separation from Ogaryov, he is essential to me. I have not seen him once—that is, not properly—though on one occasion I was sitting alone in a little lobby (at the committee), my examination was over; from my window the lighted porch could be seen; a chaise was brought round, I rushed instinctively to the window, opened the little pane and saw an adjutant get in together with Ogaryov. The chaise drove off and he had no chance to see me. Can we be fated to perish by a mute, inglorious death, of which no one will hear? Why then has nature given us spirits craving for activity, for glory? Can that be a mockery? But no, faith, strong and living, glows here in my heart, there is a providence watching over us! I am reading with delight *The Lives of the Saints*; there you have examples of self-sacrifice, there you have men!

I have just received the answer, it is not cheering—they refuse the permit.

Good-bye, remember and love your brother.

V

December 31st, 1834.

I will never take upon myself the responsibility which you lay upon me, never! you have a great deal that is *your own*, why then do you give yourself up to my will like this? I want you to make *of yourself whatever you can make of yourself*; for my part I undertake to assist that development, to remove obstacles.

As for your position, it is not so bad for your development as you imagine. You have a great advantage over many; as soon as you began to understand yourself, you found yourself alone, alone in the whole world. Others have known a father's love and a mother's tenderness—you have not had them. No one has cared to look after you, you have been left to yourself. What can be better for development? Thank your fates that no one did look after you, they would have instilled something alien to you, they would have warped your childish soul—now it is too late.

VI

Krutitsky Barracks,
February 1835.

I am told you have an idea of going into a nunnery; don't expect me to smile at the idea, I understand it, but it needs to be very, very thoroughly weighed. Can it be that the thought of love has never stirred your bosom? A nunnery means despair, there are no nunneries now for prayer. Can you doubt that you will one day meet a man who will love you, whom you will love? How joyfully I shall press his hand and yours. He will be happy. If that *he* does not appear—then go into a nunnery, that is a million times better than a vulgar marriage.

I understand *le ton d'exaltation* of your letters—*you are in love!* If you write to me that you are seriously in love I'll say nothing—a brother's authority stops at that. But I must have you say those words. Do you know what ordinary men are? They may of course make some people happy—but can they make you happy, Natasha? You think too little of yourself! Better into a nunnery than into the common herd. Remember one thing, that I say this because I am your brother, *because I am proud of you and for you*.

I have received another letter from Ogaryov; here is an extract from it: 'L'autre jour done je repassais dans ma mémoire toute ma vie. Un bonheur qui ne m'a jamais trahi, c'est ton amitié. De toutes mes passions, une seule qui est restée intacte c'est mon amitié pour toi, car mon amitié est une passion.'

In conclusion, one word more. What is so strange about it if he does love you? What would he be if he did not love you, seeing a shade of attention on your side? But I beseech you don't tell him of your love—not for a long time.

Farewell.—Your brother, ALEXANDR.

VII

What marvels happen in the world, Natalie! Before I got your last letter I had answered all your questions. I have heard that you are ill and melancholy. Take care of yourself, drink resolutely the—not so much bitter as —loathsome cup which your *benefactors* fill for you.

And after that on another sheet of paper follows:—

Natasha, my dear, my sister, for God's sake don't lose heart, despise these abominable egoists, you make too much allowance for them, despise them all—they are wretches! It was an awful moment for me when I read your letter to Amelia. My God, what a position I am in! What can I do for you? I swear that no brother loves his sister more than I do you, but what can I do?

I received your letter and am pleased with you. Forget him, if that is how it is; it was an experiment, and if it had really been love it would not have been expressed like that.

VIII

Krutitsky Barracks,
April 2nd.

My heart is torn to shreds, I have not been so crushed, so shattered, all the while I have been in prison as now. It is not exile that is the cause of it. What do I care whether it is Perm or Moscow, Moscow is no better than Perm. Let me tell you all about it.

On the 31st of March we were summoned to hear our sentence. It was a glorious, magnificent day. Twenty fellows were gathered together, who were to be immediately scattered, some to the cells of the fortresses, others to distant towns, while all of them had spent nine months in captivity. They all sat, a noisy, merry company, in the big hall. When I went in, Sokolovsky, with a beard and a moustache, threw himself on my neck, and S—— was there too. Ogaryov was brought in a good while after me, and all rushed to greet him; we embraced with tears and a smile. Everything rose up in my heart, I lived, I was a youth, I pressed every one's hand, in fact it was one of the happiest moments of my life. I had not a gloomy thought. At last the sentence[1] was read out.

All was well, but yesterday—damnation take it!—has shattered me in every nerve. Obolensky is being confined in the same place with me. When the sentence had been read us, I asked leave of Tsinsky for us to see each other and was given permission. On returning I went to see him, and meanwhile they had forgotten to tell the colonel about the permission. Next day that black. guard of an officer S—reported the matter to the colonel, and in that way I got three of the very best officers into trouble who had shown me no end of kindness; they were all reprimanded and all punished, and now have to be on duty for three weeks (and it is Easter!) without being relieved. Vassilyev the gendarme has been flogged, and all through me. I bit my fingers, cried, raged, and the first thought that came into my head was revenge. I told things about the officer which may ruin him (he used to go off somewhere with a prisoner), and then remembered that he is a poor man and the father of seven children; but ought one to spare the sneak? Did he spare others?

IX

April 10th, 1835. Nine o'clock.

A few hours before departure I am still writing, and writing to you—my last word as I go away shall be for you. Bitter is the feeling of separation, and involuntary separation, but such is the fate to which I have given myself up, it draws me on and I submit. When shall we see each other? Where? All that is dark, but bright is the thought of your affection, the exile will never forget his charming sister.

[1] I omit it.

Perhaps . . . but I cannot finish, for they have come for me—and so farewell for long, but, on my word, not for ever, I cannot think that.

All this is written in the presence of the gendarmes.

Traces of tears can be seen on this note and the word *perhaps* has been twice underlined by her. Natalie carried this note about with her for several months.

PART IV

MOSCOW, PETERSBURG, AND NOVGOROD

(1840–1847)

Chapter 25

Dissonance—A New Circle—Desperate Hegelianism—V. Byelinsky, M. Bakunin, and others—A Quarrel with Byelinsky and Reconciliation—Argument with a Lady at Novgorod—Stankevitch's Circle.

AT the beginning of 1840 we left Vladimir and the poor, narrow Klyazma. With anxiety and an aching heart I left the little town where we were married. I foresaw that the same simple, deep, spiritual life would not come again, and that we should have to take in our sails.

Our long, solitary walks out of the town, where, lost among the meadows, we felt so keenly the spring in nature and the spring in our hearts, would never come again. . . .

The winter evenings when, sitting side by side, we closed the book and listened to the crunch of sledge-runners and the jingle of bells that reminded us of the 3rd of March 1838 and our journey of the 9th of May would never come again. . . .

They will never come again!

In how many keys and for how many ages men have known and repeated that 'the May of life blossoms once and never again,' and yet the June of mature age with its hard work, with its stony roads, catches a man unawares. Youth, all unheeding, floats along in a sort of algebra of ideas, feelings, and yearnings, is little interested in the concrete, little touched by it, and then comes love, the unknown quantity found; all is concentrated on one person, through whom everything passes, in whom the universal becomes precious, in whom the artistic becomes beautiful; then, too, the young are untouched by the external, they are devoted to each other, let the grass grow as it will!

And it does grow, together with the nettles and the thistles, and sooner or later they begin to sting or prick.

We knew that we could not take Vladimir with us, but still we thought that our May was not yet over. I even fancied that in going back to Moscow I was going back to my student days. All the surroundings helped to maintain the illusion. The same house, the same furniture—here was the room where Ogaryov and I, shut in together, used to conspire two paces away from the Senator and my father, and here was my father himself, grown older and more bent, but just as ready to scold me for coming home late. 'Who is lecturing to-morrow? Where is the class? I am going from the university to Ogaryov's. . . .' It was 1833 over again!

Ogaryov was actually there.

He had received permission to go to Moscow a few months before me. Again his house became a centre where friends, old and new, met. And although the old unity was no more, every one was in sympathy with him.

Ogaryov, as I have had occasion to observe already, was endowed with a peculiar magnetism, a feminine quality of attraction. For no apparent reason others are drawn to such people and cling to them; they warm, unite, and soothe them, they are like an open table at which every one sits down, renews his strength, rests, grows calmer and more stout-hearted, and goes away a friend.

His acquaintances swallowed up a great deal of his time; he suffered at times from this, but still kept his doors open, and met every one with his gentle smile. Many people thought it a great weakness. Yes, time was lost and wasted, but the love, not only of intimate friends, but of outsiders, of the weak, was won; that is worth as much as reading and other pursuits.

I never can make out how people like Ogaryov can be accused of idleness. The standards of the factory and the workhouse do not apply in their case. I remember that in our student days Vadim and I were once sitting over a glass of wine when he suddenly became more and more gloomy, and all at once with tears in his eyes repeated the words of Don Carlos (who quoted them from Julius Caesar): 'Twenty-three and nothing done for eternity!' This so mortified him that with all his might he brought his open hand down upon the green wine-glass and cut it badly. All that is so, but neither Caesar nor Don Carlos and Posa, nor Vadim and I explained why we must do something for eternity. There is work and it has to be done, and is it to be done for the sake of the work, or for the sake of being remembered by mankind?

All that is somewhat obscure: and what is work?

Work, business.[1] . . . Officials recognise as such only civil and legal affairs, the merchant regards nothing but commerce as work, military men call it their work to strut about like cranes armed from head to toe in times of peace. To my thinking, to serve as the link, as the centre of a whole circle of people, is a very great work, especially in a society both disunited and fettered. No one has reproached me for idleness, and many people have liked some of the things I have done; but they do not know how much of all that I have done has been the reflection of our talks, our arguments, the nights we spent idly strolling about the streets and fields, or still more idly sitting over a glass of wine.

[1] English in the original.—(*Translator's Note*.)

But soon a chilly air reminding us that spring was over penetrated even into these surroundings. When the joy of meeting had subsided and festivities were over, when we had said most of what we had to say, and had to go on our way again, we perceived that the careless, happy life which we sought from memories was no longer to be found in our circle, and especially not in Ogaryov's house. Friends were noisy, arguments were lively, sometimes wine flowed, but it was not light-hearted, not as light-hearted as in old days. Every one had a hidden thought, something unspoken; there was a feeling of strain: Ogaryov looked melancholy and Ketscher raised his eyebrows fiercely. An intrusive note made a jangling discord in our harmony; all the warmth, all the friendliness of Ogaryov could not drown it.

What I had dreaded a year before had come to pass, and it was even worse than I had thought.

Ogaryov had lost his father in 1838, and had married not long before his father's death. The news of his marriage frightened me, it had all happened so quickly and unexpectedly. The rumours that had reached me about his wife were not altogether favourable to her, yet he wrote with enthusiasm and was happy; I put more faith in him, but still I was uneasy.

At the beginning of 1839 they had come for a few days to Vladimir. It was our first meeting since the auditor Oransky read us our sentence. We were in no mood to be critical. I only remember that for the first few minutes her voice struck me unpleasantly; but that momentary impression passed in the radiance of our joy. Yes, those were the days of fullness and bliss, when a man all unsuspecting reaches the highest limit, the utmost boundary of personal happiness. There was not a shade of gloomy memory, not the faintest dark foreboding, it was all youth, friendship, love, exuberant strength, energy, health, and an endless road before us. Even the mood of mysticism which had not yet passed quite away gave a festive solemnity to our meeting, like chiming bells, choristers, and burning incense.

There was a small iron crucifix on a table in my room. 'On your knees!' said Ogaryov, 'and let us give thanks that we are all four here together.' We knelt down beside him and embraced, wiping away our tears.

But one of the four scarcely needed to wipe them away. Ogaryov's wife looked at the proceedings with some astonishment. I thought at the time that this was *retenue*, but she told me herself afterwards that this scene had struck her as affected and childish. Of course it might strike one so looking on at it as an outsider, but why was she looking on at it as an outsider? Why was she so sober at that moment of intoxication, so middle-aged in the midst of our youthfulness?

Ogaryov went back to his estate, while she went to Petersburg to try and obtain permission for him to return to Moscow.

A month later she passed through Vladimir again, alone. Petersburg and two or three aristocratic drawing-rooms had turned her head. She longed for external splendour, she was allured by wealth. Will she get over it, I wondered. Such opposite tastes may lead to many troubles. But wealth was something new to her and so were drawing-rooms and Petersburg, perhaps it was a momentary infatuation; she was intelligent and she loved Ogaryov—and I hoped.

In Moscow they were more apprehensive that she would not get over it so easily. An artistic and literary circle rather flattered her vanity, but her chief efforts were not turned in that direction. She would have consented to have a place for artists and savants in her aristocratic drawing-room; she forcibly drew Ogaryov into frivolous society in which he was bored to death. His more intimate friends began to notice it, and Ketscher, who had long been scowling over it, angrily proclaimed his *veto*. Hot-tempered, vain, and unused to control herself, she wounded a vanity as sensitive as her own. Her angular, rather frigid manners and sarcasms, uttered in the voice which at our first meeting had so strangely jarred on me, provoked a violent opposition. After carrying on a feud for two months with Ketscher who, though he was right fundamentally, was continually in the wrong formally, and arousing the hostility of several persons who were, perhaps owing to their material position, too ready to take offence, she found herself brought face to face with me.

She was afraid of me. In me she wanted to test herself and to discover once for all which was to take the upper hand, friendship or love, as though one or the other must take the upper hand. There was more in this than the desire to gain the day in a capricious quarrel, there was a consciousness that I opposed her views more strongly than any of them; there was envious jealousy and feminine love of power in it too. With Ketscher she disputed till she shed tears, and every day she quarrelled with him as angry children quarrel, but without exasperation; she could not look at me without turning pale and trembling with hatred. She reproached me for revolting pride, and for destroying her happiness through conceited claims to Ogaryov's exclusive friendship. I felt this was unjust and became cruel and merciless in my turn. She herself confessed to me five years later that she had had thoughts of poisoning me—so violent was her hatred. She broke off all acquaintance with Natalie because of her love for me and the affection all our friends had for her.

Ogaryov suffered. No one spared him, neither she nor I nor the others. We chose his heart (as he himself expressed it in a letter) 'for our field of battle,' and did not consider that whichever gained the day he suffered equally. He swore to reconcile us, he tried to soften the awkwardness of the position and we were reconciled; but wounded vanity cried aloud and smarting resentment flared into warfare at a word. Ogaryov saw with horror that everything he prized was falling to pieces, that his holy things were not sacred to the woman he loved, that she was a stranger—but he could not cease to love her. We were his own people—but he saw with grief that even we did not spare him one drop of the cup of bitterness fate forced upon him. He could not roughly sunder the ties of *Naturgewalt* that bound him to her, nor the strong ties of sympathy that bound him to us; in any case his heart could not but bleed, and, conscious of that, he tried to keep both her and us—gripped convulsively her hands and ours—while we savagely strained apart, tearing him to pieces like executioners!

Man is cruel and only prolonged suffering softens him; the child is cruel in its ignorance, the young man is cruel in the pride of his purity, the priest is cruel in the pride of his holiness, and the doctrinaire in the pride of his learning—we are all merciless, and most of all merciless when we are in the right. The heart is usually melted and grows soft after severe wounds, after the wings have been burnt, after acknowledged downfalls, after the panic which makes a man cold all over when alone, without witnesses, he begins to suspect what a weak and worthless creature he is. His heart grows softer; as he wipes away the sweat of shame and horror, afraid of an eye-witness, he seeks excuses for *himself* and finds them for *others*. The part of judge, of executioner, from that moment excites his loathing.

I was far from that stage in those days!

The feud was carried on intermittently. The exasperated woman, pursued by our intolerance, got further and further entangled, could not go forward, struggled, fell—and did not change. Feeling that she could not be victorious, she burned with vexation and *dépit*, with jealousy in which there was no love. Her confused ideas, taken disconnectedly from George Sand's novels and from our conversations, and never clearly thought out, carried her from one absurdity to another—to eccentricities, which she took for originality and independence, to that form of feminine emancipation in virtue of which women arbitrarily deny all that they dislike in the existing and accepted order, while they obstinately cling to all the rest.

The gulf was becoming impassable, but for a long time yet Ogaryov spared her, for a long time he still tried and hoped to save her. And whenever for a minute some tender feeling was awakened or poetic chord was touched in her, he was ready to forget the past for ever and begin a new life of harmony, peace, and love; but she could not restrain herself, she lost her balance and every time sank lower. Thread by thread their tie was painfully broken, till the last thread snapped without a sound— and they parted for ever.

In all this one question presents itself that is not quite easily answered. How was it that the strong, sympathetic influence that Ogaryov exercised on all around him, which drew outsiders into higher spheres, into general interests, glided over that woman's heart without leaving any fruitful trace upon it? And yet he loved her passionately and put more soul and effort into saving her than into all the rest; and she herself loved him at first, of that there is no doubt.

I have thought a great deal about this. At first, of course, I put the blame on one side only, but afterwards I began to understand that this strange, monstrous fact has an explanation and that there is really no contradiction in it. To have an influence on a sympathetic circle is far easier than to have an influence on one woman. To preach from the pulpit, to sway men's minds from the platform, to teach from the lecturer's desk, is far easier than to educate one child. In the lecture-room, in the church, in the club, similarity of interests and aspirations takes the foremost place; men meet there for the sake of them, and all that is needed is to develop them farther. Ogaryov's circle consisted of his old comrades of the university, young artists, literary or scientific men; they were united by a common religion, a common language, and still more by a common hatred. Those for whom this religion was not really a living question gradually dropped off, while others came to fill their places, and the circle itself, as well as its thinking, was the stronger for the free play of selection and the community of conviction that bound them together.

Intimacy with a woman is a purely personal matter, based on some secret physiological affinity, unaccountable, resting on passion. We are first intimate, afterwards we become acquainted. Among people whose life is not marked out for them, not dominated by one idea, equilibrium is easily established; everything with them happens casually, he yields half and she half, and if they do not, it does not much matter. On the other hand, a man devoted to his idea discovers with horror that it is strange to the creature he has brought so close to him. He sets to work in haste to awaken her, but as a rule only frightens or muddles her. Torn away from the traditions from which she has not freed herself, and flung across a sort of abyss with nothing to fill it, she believes that she is emancipated—conceitedly, arrogantly rejects the old at random, accepts the new indiscriminately. There is disorder and chaos in her head and in her heart . . . the reins are flung down, egoism is unbridled . . . while we imagine that we have accomplished something and preach to her as in the lecture-room.

The gift for education, the gift of patient love, of complete, of persevering devotion is more rarely met with than any other. No mother's passionate love nor dialectical skill can replace it.

Is not this the reason why people torment children and sometimes grown-up people too—that it is so hard to educate them and so easy to flog them? When we punish, are we not revenging ourselves for our own incapacity?

Ogaryov saw that even then; that was why all (and I among them) reproached him for being too gentle.

The circle of young people that gathered round Ogaryov was not our old circle. Only two of his old friends, besides us, were in it. Tone, interests, pursuits, all were changed. Stankevitch's friends took the lead in it; Bakunin and Byelinsky stood at their head, each with a volume of Hegel's philosophy in his hand, and each filled with the youthful intolerance inseparable from deep and passionate convictions.

German philosophy had been grafted on the Moscow University by M. G. Pavlov. The Chair of Philosophy had been abolished since 1826. Pavlov gave us an introduction to philosophy by way of physics and agricultural science. It would have been hard to learn physics at his lectures, impossible to learn agricultural science; but they were extremely profitable. Pavlov stood at the door of the section of Physics and Mathematics and stopped the student with the question: 'You want to acquire knowledge of nature? but what is nature? what is knowledge?'

This was extremely valuable: our young students enter the university entirely without philosophical preparation; only the divinity students had any conception of philosophy, and that an utterly distorted one.

By way of answer to these questions, Pavlov expounded the doctrines of Schelling and of Oken with a conciseness and a clarity such as no teacher of natural philosophy had shown before. If he did not attain complete lucidity in anything it was not his fault, but was due to the cloudiness of Schelling's philosophy. Pavlov may more justly be blamed for stopping short at this Mahabharata of philosophy instead of passing on to the austere initiation into Hegelian logic. But even he went no farther than the introduction and general outline, or at any rate he led others no farther. Such a halt at the beginning, such incompleteness, houses without roofs, foundations without houses, and splendid vestibules leading to a humble dwelling, are quite in the spirit of the Russian people. Are we not perhaps satisfied with vestibules because our history is still knocking at the gate?

What Pavlov did not do was done by one of his pupils —Stankevitch.

Stankevitch, also one of the *idle* people who accomplish *nothing*, was the first disciple of Hegel in the Moscow circle. He had made a profound study of German philosophy, which appealed to his aesthetic sense: endowed with exceptional abilities, he drew a large circle of friends into his favourite pursuit. This circle was extremely remarkable, from it came a regular legion of savants, writers and professors, amongst whom were Byelinsky, Bakunin and Granovsky.

Before our exile there had been no great sympathy between our circle and Stankevitch's. They disliked our almost exclusively political tendency, while we disliked their almost exclusively theoretical interests. They considered us *Frondeurs* and French, we thought them sentimentalists and German. The first man who was acknowledged both by us and by them, who held out the hand of friendship to both and by his warm love for both and his conciliating character removed the last traces of mutual misunderstanding, was Granovsky; but when I arrived in Moscow he was still in Berlin, while poor Stankevitch at the age of twenty-seven was dying on the shore of the Lago di Como.

Sickly in constitution and gentle in character, a poet

DESPERATE HEGELIANISM 115

and a dreamer, Stankevitch was naturally bound to prefer contemplation and abstract thought to living and purely practical questions; his artistic idealism suited him, it was 'the crown of victory' on his pale, youthful brow that bore the imprint of death. The others had too much physical vigour and too little poetical feeling to remain long absorbed in speculative thought without passing on into life. Exclusive preoccupation with theory is utterly opposed to the Russian temperament, and we shall soon see how the Russian spirit transformed Hegel's philosophy and how the vitality of our nature asserted itself in spite of all the tonsures of the philosophic monks. But at the beginning of 1840 the young people surrounding Ogaryov had as yet no thought of rebelling against the letter on behalf of the spirit, against the abstract on behalf of life.

My new acquaintances received me as people do receive exiles and old champions, people who come out of prison or return out of captivity or banishment, that is, with respectful indulgence, with a readiness to receive us into their alliance, though at the same time refusing to yield a single point and hinting at the fact that they are 'to-day' and we are already 'yesterday,' and exacting the unconditional acceptance of Hegel's phenomenology and logic, and their interpretation of it, too.

They discussed these subjects incessantly, there was not a paragraph in the three parts of the *Logic*, in the two of the *Aesthetic*, the *Encyclopaedia*, and so on, which had not been the subject of furious battles for several nights together. People who loved each other were parted for weeks at a time because they disagreed about the definition of 'all-embracing spirit,' or had taken as a personal insult an opinion on 'the absolute personality and its existence in itself.' Every insignificant treatise published in Berlin or other provincial or district towns of German philosophy was ordered and read into tatters, so that the leaves fell out in a few days, if only there were a mention of Hegel in it. Just as Francœur in Paris wept with delight when he heard that in Russia he was taken for a great mathematician and that all the youthful generation made use of the same letters as he did when they solved equations of various degrees, tears of delight might have been shed by all those forgotten Werders, Marheinekes, Michelets, Ottos, Vatkes, Schallers, Rosenkrantzes, and even Arnold Ruge,[1] whom Heine so wonderfully well dubbed 'the gate-keeper of the Hegelian philosophy,' if they had known what pitched battles they were exciting in Moscow, how they were being read, and how they were being bought.

Pavlov's great value lay in the extraordinary clarity of his exposition, a clarity in which none of the depth of German thought was lost; the young philosophers, on the contrary, adopted a conventional language; they did not translate philosophical terms into Russian, but transferred them whole, even, to make things easier, leaving all the Latin words *in crudo*, giving them orthodox terminations and the endings of the Russian declensions.

I have the right to say this because, carried away by the current of the time, I wrote myself exactly in the same way, and was actually surprised when Perevoshtchekov, the well-known astronomer, described my language as the 'twittering of birds.' No one in those days would have hesitated to write a phrase like this: 'The concretion of abstract ideas in the sphere of plastics presents that phase of the self-seeking spirit in which, defining

[1] Arnold Ruge (1802-1880) began his political career with six years' imprisonment in connection with the Burschenschaft movement, founded the *Deutsche Jahrbücher*, the journal of the Young Hegelian School, and some ten years later *Die Reform*, a more definitely political paper. From 1849 he lived in England, advocated a universal democratic state, and wrote many books, of which his autobiography is now of most interest.—(*Translator's Note*.)

itself for itself, it passes from the potentiality of natural immanence into the harmonious sphere of pictorial consciousness in beauty.' It is remarkable that here Russian words, as in the celebrated dinner of the generals of which Yermolov spoke, sound even more foreign than Latin ones.

German learning—and it is its chief defect—has become accustomed to an artificial, heavy, scholastic language, just because it has lived in academies, that is, in the monasteries of idealism. It is the language of the priests of learning, a language for the faithful, and no one of the uninitiated understood it. A key was needed for it, as for a cryptograph letter. The key is now no mystery; when they understood it, people were surprised that very sensible and very simple things were said in this strange jargon. Feuerbach was the first to begin using a more human language.

The mechanical copying of the German learned jargon was the more unpardonable as the leading characteristic of our language is the extreme ease with which everything is expressed in it—abstract ideas, the lyrical sensations of the heart, 'life's mouse-like flitting,' the cry of indignation, sparkling mischief, and overwhelming passion.

Another mistake, far graver, went hand in hand with this distortion of language. Our young philosophers distorted not merely their phrases but their understanding; their attitude to life, to reality, became scholastic, bookish; it was that learned conception of simple things at which Goethe mocks with such genius in the conversation of Mephistopheles with the student. Everything in reality direct, every simple feeling, was lifted into abstract categories and came back from them without a drop of living blood, a pale, algebraic shadow. In all this there was a naïveté of a sort, because it was all perfectly sincere. The man who went for a walk in Sokolniky went in order to give himself up to the pantheistic feeling of his unity with the cosmos; and if on the way he happened upon a drunken soldier or a peasant woman who got into conversation with him, the philosopher did not simply talk to them, but defined the essential substance of the people in its immediate and phenomenal manifestation. The very tear glistening on the eyelash was strictly referred to its proper classification, to *Gemüth* or 'to the tragic in the heart.'

It was the same thing in art. A knowledge of Goethe, especially of the second part of *Faust* (either because it was inferior to the first or because it was more difficult), was as obligatory as the wearing of clothes. The philosophy of music took a foremost position. Of course, no one ever spoke of Rossini; to Mozart they were indulgent, though they did think him childish and poor. On the other hand, they made philosophical investigations into every chord of Beethoven and greatly respected Schubert, not so much, I think, for his superb melodies as for the fact that he chose philosophical themes for them, such as 'the divine omnipotence' and 'Atlas.' French literature, everything French in fact, and, incidentally, everything political also, shared the interdict laid on Italian music.

From the above, it is easy to see on what field we were bound to meet and do battle. So long as we were arguing on the theme that Goethe was objective but that his objectivity was subjective, while Schiller as a poet was subjective but that his subjectivity was objective, and *vice versa*, everything went peaceably. Questions that aroused more passion were not slow to make their appearance.

While Hegel was Professor in Berlin, partly from old age, but far more from satisfaction with his position and the respect he enjoyed, he purposely screwed his philosophy up above the earthly level and kept himself in an environment from which all contemporary interests and passions became somewhat indistinct, like buildings and villages seen from a balloon; he did not like to be entangled in these accursed practical questions with which it is difficult to deal and which must receive a positive answer. How revolting this artificial and disingenious dualism was in a doctrine which set out from the elimination of dualism can readily be understood. The real Hegel was the modest Professor at Jena, the friend of Hoelderlin, who hid his *Phenomenology* under his coat when Napoleon entered the town; then his philosophy did not lead to Indian quietism nor to the justification of the existing forms of society, nor to Prussian Christianity; then he had not read his lectures on the Philosophy of Religion, but had written things of genius such as the article on the executioner and the death penalty, printed in Rosenkrantz's biography.

Hegel confined himself to the sphere of abstractions in order to avoid the necessity of touching upon empirical deductions and practical applications; the one domain which he, very adroitly, selected for the practical application of his theories was the calm, untroubled ocean of aesthetics. He rarely ventured into the light of day, and but for a minute, wrapped up like an invalid, and even then left behind in the dialectic maze just those questions most interesting to the modern man. The extremely feeble intellects (Gantz is the only exception) who surrounded him accepted the letter for the thing itself and were pleased by the empty play of dialectics. Probably the old man felt at times sore and ashamed at the sight of the limited outlook of his excessively complacent pupils. If the dialectic method is not the development of the reality itself, the lifting of it, so to speak, into thought, it becomes a purely external means of driving all sorts of things through a series of categories, an exercise in logical gymnastics, as it was with the Greek Sophists and the mediaeval scholastics after Abelard.

The philosophical phrase which did the greatest harm, and in virtue of which the German conservatives strove to reconcile philosophy with the political régime of Germany—'all that is real is rational'—was the principle of sufficient reason and of the correspondence of logic and fact expressed in other words. Hegel's phrase, wrongly understood, became what the words of the Christian Girondist Paul were at one time: 'There is no power but from God.' But if all powers are from God, and if the existing social order is justified by reason, the struggle against it, since it exists, is also justified. These two sentences accepted in their formal meaning are pure tautology; but whether tautology or not, Hegel's phrase led straight to the recognition of the existing authorities, led to a man's sitting with folded hands, and that was just what the Berlin Buddhists wanted. Though such a view is diametrically opposed to the Russian spirit, our Moscow Hegelians were genuinely misled and accepted it.

Byelinsky, the most active, impulsive, and dialectically passionate, fighting nature, was at that time preaching an Indian stillness of contemplation and theoretical study instead of conflict. He believed in that theory and did not flinch before any of its consequences, nor was he held back by considerations of moral propriety nor the opinion of others, which has such terrors for the weak and those who lack independence. He was free from timidity for he was strong and sincere; his conscience was clear.

'Do you know that from your standpoint,' I said to him, thinking to impress him with my revolutionary ultimatum, 'you can prove that the monstrous tyranny under which we live is rational and ought to exist?'

'There is no doubt about it,' answered Byelinsky, and proceeded to recite to us Pushkin's 'Anniversary of Borodino.'

That was more than I could stand and a desperate battle raged between us. Our feud reacted upon the others, the circle fell apart into two groups. Bakunin tried to reconcile, to explain, to persuade, but there was no real peace. Byelinsky, irritated and dissatisfied, went off to Petersburg, and from there fired off his last furious shot at us in an article which he called 'The Anniversary of Borodino.'

Then I broke off all relations with him. Though Bakunin argued hotly, he began to reconsider things, his revolutionary tact drove him in another direction. Byelinsky reproached him for weakness, for concessions, and went to such exaggerated extremes that he scared his own friends and followers. The chorus was on Byelinsky's side, and looked down upon us, haughtily shrugged their shoulders and considered us behind the times.

In the midst of this feud I saw the necessity *ex ipso fonte bibere* and began studying Hegel in earnest. I even think that a man who has not *lived through* Hegel's phenomenology and Proudhon's contradictions of political economy, who has not passed through that furnace and been tempered by it, is not complete, not modern.

When I had grown used to Hegel's language and mastered his method, I began to perceive that Hegel was much nearer to our standpoint than to the standpoint of his followers; he was so in his early works, he was so everywhere where his genius had got out of hand and had dashed forward forgetting the gates of Brandenburg. The philosophy of Hegel is the algebra of revolution, it emancipates a man in an extraordinary way and leaves not a stone standing of the Christian world, of the world of outlived tradition. But, perhaps with intention, it is badly formulated. Just as in mathematics—only there with more justification—men do not go back to the definition of space, movement, force, but continue the dialectical development of their laws and qualities, so in the formal understanding of philosophy, after once becoming accustomed to the first principles, men go on merely drawing deductions. Any one new to the subject who has not stupefied himself by the method being turned into a habit is pulled up just by these traditions, by these dogmas which have been accepted as thoughts. To people who have long been studying the subject and are consequently not free from preconceptions, it seems astonishing that others should not understand things that are 'perfectly clear.' How can any one fail to understand such a simple idea as, for instance, 'that the soul is immortal and that what perishes is only the personality,' a thought so successfully developed by the Michelet of Berlin; or the still more simple truth that the absolute spirit is a personality, conscious of itself through the world, and at the same time having its own self-consciousness?

All these things seemed so easy to our friends, they smiled so condescendingly at 'French' objections, that I was for some time crushed by them and worked and worked to reach an exact understanding of their philosophic jargon.

Fortunately scholasticism is as little natural to me as mysticism, and I stretched its bow until the string snapped and the scales dropped from my eyes. Strange to say, it was an argument with a lady that brought me to it.

I had the year before at Novgorod become acquainted with a general. I made his acquaintance just because no one could have been less like a general.

There was a painful feeling in his house, there were tears in the air, it was obvious that death had passed through it. His hair was prematurely grey and his kindly, mournful smile was, even more than his wrinkles, expressive of suffering. He was about fifty. The traces of a fate that had cut off living branches was still more clearly imprinted on the pale, thin face of his wife. It was too quiet in their house. The general studied mechanics, while his wife spent her mornings giving

French lessons to some poor children; when they had gone she took up a book, and the only things that suggested a different, bright, fragrant life were the flowers, of which there were many, and the playthings in a cupboard—but no one ever played with them.

They had had three children: two years before I knew them an exceptionally gifted boy of nine had died; a few months later another child died of scarlet fever; the mother hastened into the country to save the last child by change of air and came back a few days later with a little coffin in the carriage with her.

Their life had lost its meaning, it was ended, and continued without object, without need. Their existence was maintained by the compassion of each for the other; the one comfort left them was the deep conviction that each was essential to enable the other to bear the cross. I have seen few more harmonious marriages, though, indeed, it was hardly a marriage, for it was not love that bound them together but a deep comradeship in misfortune; their fate held them tight and kept them together with the little cold hands of those three, and the hopeless emptiness around them and before them.

The bereaved mother was completely given up to mysticism; she found relief from her misery in the world of mysterious reconciliations, she was deceived by the flattery that religion pays the human heart. For her, mysticism was no light thing, it was no mere dream, it meant having her children again, and she was defending them when she defended her religion. But, as she had an extremely active intelligence, she challenged discussion and knew her strength. I have met, both before and since, many mystics of various kinds, from Vitberg and the followers of Tovjanski,[1] who acknowledged Napoleon

---

[1] Tovjanski was a Pole, and at one time a member of the Society of Philarets. He held that there were many Messiahs, of whom Napoleon was one and himself another.—(*Translator's Note*.)

as the military incarnation of God and took off their caps when they passed the Vendôme Column, to the now-forgotten 'Ma-Pa,'[1] who told me himself of his interview with God which took place on the high-road between Montmorency and Paris. They were all hysterical people who worked on the nerves, impressed the fancy, or the heart, mixed up philosophical conceptions with an arbitrary symbolism, and did not care to come out into the open field of logic.

But it was upon that field L——D—— took a firm and fearless stand. Where and how she had succeeded in obtaining such artistic skill in argument I do not know. Altogether women's development is a mystery; there is nothing: just dress and dances, mischievous back-biting and novel reading, making eyes and shedding tears—and all at once titanic will, mature thought, colossal intelligence make their appearance. The young girl carried away by her passions vanishes, and before you stands Théroigne de Méricourt,[2] the beauty of the tribune, swaying multitudes of the people, or a Princess Dashkov, sword in hand, on horseback, at eighteen, in the midst of a turbulent crowd of soldiers.

In L——D—— everything was complete, she had no doubts, no wavering, no theoretical weakness; even the Jesuits or the Calvinists can hardly have been so harmoniously consistent in their doctrine as she.

Deprived of her little ones, she had come, instead of hating death, to hating life. That is just what is needed

---

[1] His real name was Gaunot, and he was an adventurer well known in Paris between 1830 and 1850. He went in for being a god and called his religion *evadisme* (from Eve and Adam), and himself Mapah from *mater* and *pater*. He suggested to Dumas that the latter should become his chief disciple.

[2] Théroigne de Méricourt, called 'l' Amazone de la liberté,' assisted at the taking of the Bastille and became a popular heroine. Later on she was publicly whipped by a crowd of women, and lost her reason in consequence of this outrage.—(*Translator's Notes.*)

for Christianity, that complete apotheosis of death: the contempt for earth, the contempt of the body has no other meaning. Hence the attack upon everything living and realistic, enjoyment, health, gaiety, the free joy of existence. And L——D—— had reached the point of disliking both Goethe and Pushkin.

Her attacks on my philosophy were original. She used ironically to declare that all our dialectical subtleties and elaborate constructions were just the beating of the drum, the noise with which cowards try to drown the terrors of their conscience.

'You will never,' she used to say, 'get to a personal god, nor to the immortality of the soul, by any philosophy, and none of you have the courage to be atheists and reject the life beyond the grave. You are too human not to be horrified by those conclusions, so you invent your logical miracles to throw dust in the eyes and to arrive at what is given by religion in a simple and childlike way.'

I objected, I argued, but I was inwardly conscious that I had no complete proofs and that she had a firmer footing on her ground than I on mine.

To complete my discomfiture, the inspector of the Medical Board must needs turn up to support me; he was a good-natured man, but one of the most ridiculous Germans I have ever met. A devoted worshipper of Oken and Carus,[1] he argued by means of quotations, had a ready-made answer for everything, never had doubts about anything, and imagined that he was completely in accord with me.

The doctor lost his temper, grew furious the more readily as he could not hold his own by other means, looked upon L——D——'s views as feminine caprice, took refuge in Schelling's lectures on the academic

[1] Carus, K.G.(1789-1869), a distinguished German physiologist, author of numerous works on anatomy, physiology, and allied subjects.—(*Translator's Note*.)

doctrine, and read extracts from Burdach's *Physiology* to prove that there is an eternal and spiritual element in man, and that some personal *Geist* is hidden in nature.

L——D——, who had long ago passed through these 'back premises' of pantheism, confuted him, and, smiling, glanced from him to me. She was, of course, more in the right than he, and I was vexed and conscientiously racking my brains, while the good doctor was laughing triumphantly. These arguments interested me so much that I set to work upon Hegel with new zest. The worry of my uncertainty did not last long, the truth flashed before my eyes and began to grow clearer and clearer; I inclined to my opponent's side, but not in the way she wished.

'You are perfectly right,' I said to her, 'and I am ashamed of having argued against you; of course there is no personal spirit, nor immortality of the soul, and that is why it has been so hard to prove that there is. See how simple and natural it all becomes without those gratuitous assumptions.'

She was troubled by my words but quickly recovered herself and said: 'I am sorry for you, but perhaps it is for the best, you will not long remain in that position, it is too empty and depressing, while,' she added, smiling, 'our doctor is incurable, he has no fears, he is in such a fog that he does not see one step before him.'

Her face was paler than usual, however.

Two or three months later, Ogaryov passed through Novgorod. He brought me Feuerbach's *Wesen des Christenthums*; after reading the first pages I leapt up with joy. Away with the trappings of masquerade, no more muddle and equivocations! We are free men and not the slaves of Xanthos, there is no need for us to wrap the truth in myth.

In the heat of my philosophic ardour I began my series

of articles on 'Dilettantism in Science,' in which, among other things,, I paid the doctor out.

Now let us go back to Byelinsky.

A few months after his departure to Petersburg in 1840 we too arrived there. I did not go to see him. Ogaryov took my quarrel with Byelinsky very much to heart; he knew that Byelinsky's absurd theory was a passing malady, and, indeed, I knew it too. But Ogaryov was kinder. At last by his letters he brought about a meeting. Our interview was at first cold, unpleasant, and strained, but neither Byelinsky nor I was very diplomatic and in the course of trivial conversation I mentioned the article on 'The Anniversary of Borodino.' Byelinsky jumped up from his seat and, flushing crimson, said with great simplicity, 'Well, thank God, we've come to it at last. I am so stupid I did not know how to begin. . . . You've won the day; three or four months in Petersburg have done more to convince me than all the arguments. Let us forget that nonsense. It is enough to say that the other day I was dining at a friend's and there was an officer of the Engineers there; my friend asked him if he would like to make my acquaintance. "Is that the author of the article on 'The Anniversary of Borodino'?" the officer asked him in his ear. "Yes." "No, thank you very much," he answered dryly. I heard it all and could not restrain myself. I pressed the officer's hand warmly and said to him: "You 're an honourable man, I respect you. . . ." What more would you have?'

From that moment up to Byelinsky's death we went hand in hand. Byelinsky, as was to be expected, fell upon his former theory with all the stinging vehemence of his language and all his furious energy. The position of many of his friends was not very much to be envied. *Plus royalistes que le roi*, with the courage of misfortune they tried to defend their theories, while not averse to an honourable truce. All those who had enough sense and vitality went over to Byelinsky's side; only the obstinate formalists and pedants were left far behind. Some of them reached such a point of German suicide through dead and scholastic learning that they lost all living interest and were themselves lost, leaving no trace. Others became orthodox Slavophils. Strange as the combination of Hegel and Stefan Yavorsky[1] may appear, it is more possible than might be supposed; the Byzantine theology is just such a superficial casuistry and play with logical formulas as Hegel's dialectics, formally understood. Some of the articles in the *Moskvityanin* are a magnificent instance of the extremes to which, with talent, the unnatural union of philosophy and religion can be brought.

Byelinsky by no means abandoned Hegel's philosophy when he renounced his one-sided interpretation of it. Quite the contrary, it is from this point that his living, apt, original combination of philosophical with revolutionary ideas begins. I regard Byelinsky as one of the most remarkable figures of the period of Nicholas. After the liberalism which had somehow survived 1825 in Polevoy, after the gloomy article of Tchaadayev, Byelinsky appears on the scene with his caustic scepticism, won by suffering, and his passionate interest in every question. In a series of critical articles he touches in season and out of season upon everything, everywhere true to his hatred of authority and often rising to poetic inspiration. The book he reviewed usually served him as a starting-point, but he abandoned it half-way and threw himself into some question. The line 'That's what kindred are' in *Onyegin* is enough for him to summon family life before the judgment seat and to pick family relations to pieces down to the last shred. Who does not

[1] Stefan Yavorsky was a famous monk and theologian of the eighteenth century.—(*Translator's Note.*)

remember his articles on 'The Tarantass,'[1] on 'Turgenev's Parasha,'[2] on 'Derzhavin,' on 'Motchalov,'[3] and 'Hamlet'? What fidelity there is to his principles, what fearless consistency, what adroitness in navigating between the sandbanks of the censorship, what boldness in his attacks on the aristocracy of literature, on the writers of the first three grades, on the high officials of literature who are always ready to defeat an opponent if not by fair means by foul, if not by criticism then by information to the police. Byelinsky scourged them mercilessly, goading the petty vanity of the frigid mediocre writers of eclogues, lovers of culture, benevolence, and sentimentality; he turned into derision their precious ideas, the poetical dreams fostered by their elderly brains, their naïveté, hidden under an Anna ribbon.

How they hated him for it!

The Slavophils on their side began their official existence with the war upon Byelinsky; he drove them by his taunts to the *murmolka* and the *zipun*[4]; one need only recall that Byelinsky had formerly written in *Notes of the Fatherland*, while Kireyevsky called his excellent journal *The European*; no better proof than these titles could be found to show that at first the difference was only between shades of opinion and not between parties.

Byelinsky's articles were awaited with feverish expectation in Petersburg and Moscow from the 25th of every month. Half a dozen times the students would call in at the coffee-houses to ask whether the *Notes of the Fatherland* had been received; the heavy volume was snatched from hand to hand. 'Is there an article of

[1] 'The Tarantass,' a story by Count Sologub, author of various comedies and novels satirising the official class.

[2] Parasha, an early poem of Turgenev's.

[3] Motchalov, the great Russian actor, was particularly famous for his playing of Hamlet.

[4] *Murmolka*, a peasant cap, and *zipun* a long homespun peasant coat.—(*Translator's Notes*.)

Byelinsky's?' 'Yes,' and it was devoured with feverish interest, with laughter, with argument . . . and three or four cherished convictions and reputations were no more.

Sokobelev, the governor of the Peter-Paul fortress, might well say in jest to Byelinsky when he met him on the Nevsky Prospect: 'When are you coming to us? I have a nice warm little cell all ready that I am keeping for you.'

I have spoken in another book of Byelinsky's development and of his literary activity, here I will only say a few words about himself.

Byelinsky was very shy and quite lost his head in an unfamiliar or very numerous company; he knew this and did the most absurd things in trying to conceal it. Ketscher persuaded him to go to visit a lady; as they approached her house Byelinsky became more and more depressed, kept asking whether they could not go another day, and talked of having a headache. Ketscher, who knew him, would accept no excuse. When they arrived Byelinsky set off running as soon as they got out of the sledge, but Ketscher caught him by the overcoat and led him to be introduced to the lady.

He sometimes put in an appearance at Prince Odoevsky's literary diplomatic evenings. At these there were crowds of people who had nothing in common except a certain apprehension of and aversion for each other: clerks from the Embassies and Saharov[1] the archaeologist, painters and A. Meiendorf,[2] several councillors of the cultured sort, Ioakinth Bitchurin[3] from Pekin,

[1] Saharov, Ivan Petrovitch (1807-1863), a well-known archaeologist and ethnographist, was a doctor of medicine and lecturer on palaeology. His discoveries are now regarded somewhat sceptically, but he did much for Russian antiquarian study.

[2] Meiendorf, Alexander Kazimirovitch (1788-1865), a writer on historical and geographical subjects.

[3] Ioakinth Bitchurin (1777-1853), a monk and at one time an

people who were half gendarmes and half literary men, others who were wholly gendarmes and not at all literary men. A——K—— was so much in evidence there that generals took him for an authority. The hostess looked with inner grief upon her husband's vulgar tastes, and gave way to them much as Louis-Philippe at the beginning of his reign indulged the tastes of his electors by inviting to the balls at the Tuileries whole *rez-de-chaussées* of brace-makers, grocers, shopkeepers, shoemakers, and other worthy citizens.

Byelinsky was utterly lost at these evenings, between some Saxon ambassador who did not understand a word of Russian and some officer of the secret police who understood even words that were not uttered. He was usually ailing for two or three days afterwards and cursed the man who had persuaded him to go.

One Saturday, as it was New Year's Eve, Odoevsky took it into his head to mix punch *en petit comité* when the principal guests had dispersed. Byelinsky would certainly have gone away, but he was prevented by a barricade of furniture; he was somehow stuck in a corner and a little table was set before him with wine and glasses on it; Zhukovsky in the white trousers of his uniform, with gold braid on them, was sitting sideways opposite him. Byelinsky bore it in patience a long time, but, seeing no chance of his lot improving, he began moving the table a little; the table yielded at first, then lurched over and fell with a bang on the floor, while the bottle of Bordeaux very deliberately began to empty itself over Zhukovsky. He jumped up while the red wine began to trickle down his trousers; there was a great fuss and to-do, one servant rushed up with a napkin to rub the wine into the other parts of the trousers, and another picked up the broken wine-

archimandrite, head of the Orthodox Mission to Pekin, and later on a translator from the Chinese in the Ministry of Foreign Affairs, was an authority on Chinese language and history.—(*Translator's Notes.*)

glasses . . . while this bustle was going on Byelinsky disappeared and, though it was not long before his end, ran home on foot.

Dear Byelinsky! how angry and upset he was by such incidents long afterwards, with what horror he used to recall them, walking up and down the room and shaking his head without the trace of a smile.

But in that shy man, that frail body, there dwelt a mighty spirit, the spirit of a gladiator! Yes, he was a powerful fighter! he could not preach or lecture, what he needed was disputation. If he met with no objection, if he was not stirred to irritation, he did not speak well, but when he felt stung, when his cherished convictions were touched upon, when the muscles of his cheeks began to quiver and his voice broke, then he was worth seeing; he pounced upon his opponent like a panther, he tore him to pieces, made him ridiculous, made him a piteous object, and incidentally developed his own thought, with extraordinary force, with extraordinary poetry. The discussion would often end in blood which flowed from the sick man's throat; pale, gasping, with his eyes fixed on the man with whom he was speaking, he would lift his handkerchief to his mouth with shaking hand and stop, deeply mortified, crushed by his physical weakness. How I loved and how I pitied him at those moments!

Worried by the financial sharks of literature, morally fettered by the censorship, surrounded in Petersburg by people little sympathetic to him, and consumed by a disease to which the Baltic climate was fatal, he became more and more irritable. He shunned outsiders, was savagely shy, and sometimes spent weeks together in gloomy inactivity. Then the publishers sent note after note demanding copy, and the enslaved writer, grinding his teeth, took up his pen and wrote the venomous articles quivering with indignation, the indictments which so impressed their readers.

Often, utterly exhausted, he would come to us to rest, and lie on the floor with our two-year-old child; he would play with him for hours together. While we were only the three of us things went swimmingly, but if there came a ring at the bell, a spasmodic grimace passed over his face and he would look about him uneasily, trying to find his hat; though with Slav weakness he often remained. Then a word, an observation uttered not to his liking would lead to the most original scenes and disputes. . . .

Once he went in Passion Week to dine with a literary man and Lenten dishes were served. 'Is it long,' he asked, 'since you became so devout?' 'We eat Lenten fare,' answered the literary gentleman, 'simply for the sake of the servants.' 'For the sake of the servants,' said Byelinsky, and he turned pale. 'For the sake of the servants,' he repeated, and flung down his dinner napkin. 'Where are your servants? I'll tell them that they are deceived, any open vice is more humane than this contempt for the weak and uneducated, this hypocrisy in support of ignorance. And do you imagine that you are free people? You are in the same boat with all the tsars and priests and slaveowners. Goodbye, I don't eat Lenten fare for the edification of others, I have no servants!'

Among the Russians who might be classified as inveterate Germans, there was one graduate of our university who had lately arrived from Berlin; he was a good-natured man in blue spectacles, stiff and decorous; he had come to a standstill for ever after upsetting and enfeebling his brains with philosophy and philology. A doctrinaire and to some extent a pedant, he was fond of holding forth in edifying style. On one occasion at a literary evening in the house of the novelist who kept the fasts for the sake of his servants, this gentleman was preaching some sort *honnête et modéré* twaddle.

Byelinsky was lying on a couch in the corner and as I passed him he took me by the lapel of my coat and said: 'Do you hear the rubbish that monster is talking? My tongue has been itching to answer him, but my chest hurts and there are a lot of people. Be a father to me, make a fool of him somehow, squash him, crush him with mockery, you can do it better—come, comfort me.'

I laughed and told Byelinsky that he was setting me on like a bulldog at a rat. I scarcely knew the man and had hardly heard what he said.

Towards the end of the evening, the gentleman in blue spectacles, after abusing Koltsov for having abandoned the national costume, suddenly began talking of Tchaadayev's famous letter and concluded his commonplace remarks, uttered in that didactic tone which of itself provokes derision, with the following words: 'Be that as it may, I consider his action contemptible and revolting: I have no respect for such a man.'

There was in the room only one man closely associated with Tchaadayev, and that was I. I shall have a great deal to say about Tchaadayev later on, I always liked and respected him and was liked by him; I thought it was unseemly to let this absurd remark pass. I asked him dryly whether he supposed that Tchaadayev had written his letter disingenuously or from interested motives.

'Not at all,' answered the gentleman.

An unpleasant conversation followed; I mentioned that the epithets 'revolting and contemptible' were themselves revolting and contemptible when applied to a man who had boldly expressed his opinion and had suffered for it. He talked to me of the people making up one whole, of the unity of the fatherland, of the crime of disturbing that unity, of sacred things that must not be touched.

All at once Byelinsky cut short my words, he leapt up from his sofa, came up to me as white as a sheet and, slapping me on the shoulder, said: 'Here you have them, they have spoken out—the inquisitors, the censors—keeping thought in leading-strings . . .' and so he went on and on. With savage inspiration he spoke, interspersing grave words with deadly sarcasms: 'We are strangely sensitive: men are flogged and we don't resent it, sent to Siberia and we don't resent it, but here Tchaadayev, you see, has picked holes in the national honour, he mustn't dare to speak; to talk is impudence, a flunkey must never speak! Why is it that in more civilised countries where one would expect national susceptibilities to be more developed than in Kostroma and Kaluga words are not resented?'

'In civilised countries,' replied the gentleman in blue spectacles with inimitable self-complacency,' 'there are prisons in which they confine the senseless creatures who insult what the whole people respect . . . and a good thing too.'

Byelinsky seemed to tower above us, he was terrible, great at that moment. Folding his arms over his sick chest, and looking straight at his opponent, he answered in a hollow voice: 'And in still more civilised countries there is a guillotine for those who think that a good thing.'

Saying this, he sank exhausted in an easy-chair and ceased speaking. At the word guillotine our host turned pale, the guests were uneasy and a pause followed. The blue-spectacled gentleman was annihilated, but it is just at such moments that human vanity gets out of hand. Turgenev advises that, when one has gone such lengths in argument that one begins to feel frightened, one should move one's tongue ten times round the inside of one's mouth before uttering a word.

Our opponent, unaware of this homely advice, continued uttering feeble trivialities, addressing himself rather to the rest of the company than to Byelinsky. 'In spite of your intolerance,' he said at last, 'I am certain that you would agree with me . . .'

'No,' answered Byelinsky, 'whatever you might say I shouldn't agree with anything!'

Every one laughed and went in to supper. The gentleman in blue spectacles picked up his hat and went away.

Suffering and privation soon completely undermined Byelinsky's sickly constitution. His face, particularly the muscles about his lips, and the gloomily fixed look in his eyes testified equally to the intense workings of his spirit and the rapid dissolution of his body.

I saw him for the last time in Paris in the autumn of 1847; he was in a very bad way, afraid of speaking aloud, and only at moments his old energy revived and its ebbing fires glowed brightly. It was at such a moment that he wrote his letter[1] to Gogol.

The news of the revolution of February found him still alive; he died taking its glow for the flush of the rising dawn.

So this chapter ended in 1854; since that time much has changed. I have been brought much closer to that period, nearer to the more remote past, through persons who are here, through the arrival of Ogaryov and two books, Annenkov's *Biography of Stankevitch* and the two first parts of Byelinsky's complete works. From the windows suddenly thrown open the fresh air of the fields, the young breath of spring has been wafted into the hospital wards. . . .

Stankevitch's correspondence was unnoticed when it came out. It appeared at the wrong moment. At the end of 1857 Russia had not yet come to herself after the

[1] The reference is to the open letter in which Byelinsky expressed his passionate indignation at the *Correspondence with Friends*, published by Gogol.—(*Translator's Note*.)

funeral of Nicholas, she was expectant and hopeful; that is the worst mood for receiving reminiscences . . . but the book is not lost. It will remain one of the rare monuments from which any man who can read can find what was buried without a word in the wretched graveyard of those days. The dead years, from 1825 to 1855, will soon be utterly lost; the human tracks, swept away by the police, will have vanished, and future generations will come to a standstill in bewilderment before the smooth level waste, seeking the lost channels of thought which were really never interrupted. The current was apparently checked, Nicholas tied up the main artery— but the blood flowed along side-channels. And it is just these capillaries which have left their trace in the works of Byelinsky and the correspondence of Stankevitch.

Thirty years ago, the Russia of the future existed exclusively among a few boys, hardly more than children, so insignificant and unnoticed that there was room for them under the heels of the great boots of the autocracy —and in them was the heritage of the 14th of December, the heritage of a purely national Russia, as well as of the learning of all humanity. This new life struggled on like the grass that tries to grow at the mouth of the still smouldering crater.

In the very jaws of the monster these children stand out unlike other children; they grow, develop, and begin to live a different life. Weak, insignificant, unsupported, on the contrary persecuted by all, they might easily have perished, leaving no trace, but they survive, or, if they die on their way, all does not die with them. They are the rudimentary germs, the embryos of history, barely perceptible, barely existing, like embryos in general.

Little by little, groups of them are formed. What is more nearly akin to them gathers round their centres; then the groups repel one another. This splitting up gives them width and many-sidedness in their development; after developing to the end, that is to the extreme, the branches unite again by whatever names they may be called—Stankevitch's circle, the Slavophils, or our little circle.

The leading characteristic of them all is a profound feeling of aversion for official Russia, for their environment, and at the same time the impulse to get out of it— and in some a vehement desire to get rid of it.

The objection that these circles, unnoticed both from above and from below, form an exceptional, a casual, a disconnected phenomenon, that the education of the young people was for the most part exotic, alien, and that they rather express the translation of French and German ideas into Russian than anything of their own, seems to us quite groundless.

Possibly at the end of last and the beginning of this century there was in the aristocracy a sprinkling of Russian foreigners who had sundered all ties with the national life; but they had neither living interests, nor circles based on convictions, nor a literature of their own. They died out without leaving fruit. Victims of the divorce from the people brought about by Peter the Great, they remained eccentric and whimsical, they were men not merely superfluous but undeserving of pity. The war of 1812 put an end to them—the old generation lived on, but none of the younger developed in that direction. To include among them men of the stamp of Tchaadayev would be the greatest mistake.

Protest, denunciation, hatred for one's country if you will has a completely different significance from indifferent aloofness. Byron, lashing at English life, fleeing from England as from the plague, remained a typical Englishman. Heine, trying through exasperation at the loathsome political state of Germany to turn French, remained a genuine German. The highest protest against Judaism—Christianity—is filled with the spirit of Judaism. The separation of the states of North America from England could lead to war and hatred, but it could not make the Americans un-English.

As a rule, it is with great difficulty that men abandon their physiological memories and the mould in which they are cast by heredity; to do so a man must either be peculiarly passionless and lacking in individual characteristics or must be absorbed in abstract pursuits. The impersonality of mathematics, the unhuman objectivity of nature do not call forth those sides of the soul and do not awaken them; but as soon as we touch upon questions of life, of art, of morals, in which a man is not only an observer and investigator, but at the same time himself an interested party, then we find a physiological limit — which it is very hard to cross with old blood and brains unless one could erase from them all traces of the songs of the cradle, of the fields and the hills of home, of the customs and whole setting of the past.

The poet or the artist in his truest work is always national. Whatever he does, whatever aim and thought he may have in his work, he consciously or unconsciously expresses some elements of the national character and expresses them more deeply and more clearly than the very history of the people. Even when renouncing everything national, the artist does not lose the chief characteristics from which it can be recognised to what people he belongs. Both in the Greek 'Iphigenia' and in the Oriental 'Divan' Goethe was a German. Poets really are, as the Romans called them, prophets; only they do not foretell what is not and will be by chance, but put into words what is unrecognised, what exists in the dim consciousness of the masses, what is already slumbering in them.

Everything that has existed from time immemorial in the soul of the Anglo-Saxon peoples is drawn together as in a ring by one personality; and every fibre, every hint, every attempt, fermenting from generation to generation, unconscious of itself, has taken form and language.

Probably no one supposes that the England of the Elizabethan times—the majority of the people anyway—had a clear understanding of Shakespeare; they have no distinct understanding of him even now—but then they have no distinct understanding of themselves either. But I do not doubt that when an Englishman goes to the theatre he understands Shakespeare instinctively, through sympathy. At the moment when he is listening to the play, something becomes clearer and more familiar to him. One would have thought that a people so capable of rapid comprehension as the French might have understood Shakespeare too. The character of Hamlet, for instance, is so universally human, especially in the stage of doubts and hesitation, in the consciousness of some black deeds being perpetrated about him, some betrayal of what is great for the sake of something that is mean and trivial, that it is hard to imagine that any people could fail to understand him, but in spite of every trial and effort, Hamlet remains alien to the Frenchman.

If the aristocrats of the past century, who systematically despised everything Russian, remained in reality incredibly more Russian than the house-serfs remained peasants, it is even more impossible that the younger generation could have lost their Russian character because they studied science and philosophy and French and German books. A section of the Slavs at Moscow reached the point of ultra-Slavism with Hegel in their hands.

The very circles of which I am speaking came into existence in natural response to a deep inner need of the Russian life of that period.

We have spoken many times of the stagnation that followed the catastrophe of 1825. The moral level of society sank, development was interrupted, everything progressive and energetic was struck out of life. Those who remained—frightened, weak, distracted—were petty and insignificant; the worthless creatures of the generation of Alexander occupied the foremost place; little by little they changed into cringing officials, lost the savage poetry of revelry and of the audacity of the privileged class together with every shadow of independent dignity; they served persistently, they served until they reached high positions, but they never became great personages. Their day was over.

Under this great world of society, the great world of the people maintained an indifferent silence; nothing was changed for them—their plight was bad, but no worse than before, the new blows fell not on their scourged backs. Their time had not yet come. Between this roof and this foundation children were the first to raise their heads, perhaps because they did not suspect how dangerous it was; but, be that as it may, with these children Russia, stunned and stupefied, began to come to life again.

What impressed them was the complete contradiction of the words they were taught with the facts of life around them. Their teachers, their books, their university spoke one language and that language was intelligible to heart and mind. Their father and mother, their relations, and all their surroundings spoke another with which neither mind nor heart was in agreement—but with which the dominant authorities and financial interests were in accord. This contradiction between education and ordinary life nowhere reached such proportions as among the nobility of Russia. The shaggy German student with his round cap covering a seventh part of his head, with his world-shaking sallies, is far nearer to the German *Spitzburger* than is supposed, while the French *collégien*, thin with vanity and emulation, is already *en herbe l'homme raisonnable qui exploite sa position*.

The number of educated people amongst us has always

been extremely small; but those who were educated have always received an education, not perhaps very thorough, but fairly general and humane: it made men of all with whom it succeeded. But a man was just what was not wanted either for the hierarchical pyramid or for the successful maintenance of the landowning régime. The young man had either to dehumanise himself—and the greater number did so—or to stop short and ask himself: 'But is it absolutely essential to go into the service? Is it really a good thing to be a landowner?' After that for some, the weaker and more impatient, there followed the idle existence of a cornet on the retired list, the sloth of the country, the dressing-gown, eccentricities, cards, wine; for others a time of trial and inner travail. They could not live in complete moral disharmony, nor could they be satisfied with a negative attitude of withdrawal; awakened thought demanded an outlet. The various solutions of these questions, all equally harassing for the young generation, determined their distribution into various circles.

Thus, for instance, our little circle was formed in the university and found Sungurov's circle there already. His, like ours, was concerned rather with politics than with learning. Stankevitch's circle, which came into existence at the same time, was equally near both and equally remote from both. He went by another path, his interests were purely theoretical.

Between 1830 and 1840 our convictions were too youthful, too ardent and passionate, not to be exclusive. We could feel a cold respect for Stankevitch's circle, but we could not be intimate with its members. They traced philosophical systems, were absorbed in self-analysis, and found peace in a luxurious pantheism from which Christianity was not excluded. We were dreaming how to get up a new league in Russia on the pattern of the Decembrists and looked upon knowledge itself as merely a means. The government did its best to strengthen us in our revolutionary tendencies.

In 1834 all Sungurov's circle was sent into exile and—vanished.

In 1835 we were exiled. Five years later we came back, hardened by our experience. The dreams of youth had become the irrevocable determination of maturity. This was the most brilliant period of Stankevitch's circle. Stankevitch himself I did not find in Moscow—he was in Germany; but it was just at that moment that Byelinsky's articles were beginning to attract the attention of every one.

On our return we measured our strength with them. The battle was an unequal one; basis, weapons, and language—all were different. After fruitless skirmishes we saw that it was our turn now to undertake serious study and we too set to work upon Hegel and the German philosophy. When we had sufficiently assimilated that, it became evident that there was no ground for dispute between us and Stankevitch's circle.

The latter was inevitably bound to break up. It had done its work—and had done it most brilliantly; its influence on the whole of literature and academic teaching was immense—one need but recall the names of Byelinsky and Granovsky; Koltsov was formed in it, Botkin, Katkov, and others belonged to it. But it could not remain an exclusive circle without passing into German formalism—men who are alive and Russian are not capable of that.

Besides Stankevitch's circle, there was another circle, formed during our exile and in the same relation with them as we; its members were afterwards called Slavophils. The Slavophils approached from the opposite side the vital questions which occupied us, and were far more absorbed in living work and real conflict than Stankevitch's circle.

It was natural that Stankevitch's society should split up between them and us. The Aksakovs and Samarin joined the Slavophils, that is, Homyakov and the Kireyevskys. Byelinsky and Bakunin joined us. The closest friend of Stankevitch, the most nearly akin to him in his whole nature, Granovsky, was one of us from the day he came back from Germany.

If Stankevitch had lived, his circle would still have broken up. He would himself have gone over to Homyakov or to us.

By 1842 the sifting in accordance with natural affinity had long been complete, and our camp stood in battle array face to face with the Slavophils. Of that conflict we will speak in another place.

In conclusion I will add a few words concerning the elements of which Stankevitch's circle was composed; that will throw a light on the strange underground currents which were silently undermining the strong crust of the Russo-German régime.

Stankevitch was the son of a wealthy landowner of the province of Voronezh, and was at first brought up in all the ease and freedom of a landowner's life in the country; then he was sent to the Ostrogozhsk school (and that was something quite original). For fine natures a wealthy and even aristocratic education is very good. Comfort gives unfettered freedom and space for growth and development of every sort, it saves the young mind from premature anxiety and apprehension of the future, and provides complete freedom to pursue the subjects to which it is drawn.

Stankevitch's development was broad and harmonious; his artistic, musical, and at the same time reflective and contemplative nature showed itself from the very beginning of his university career. Stankevitch's special faculty, not only for deeply and warmly understanding, but also for reconciling, or as the Germans say 'removing' contradictions, was due to his artistic temperament. The craving for harmony, proportion, and enjoyment makes such people indulgent as to the means; to avoid seeing the well they cover it over with canvas. The canvas will not stand a push, but the yawning gulf does not vex the eye. In this way the Germans reached pantheistic quietism and slumbered tranquilly upon it; but such a gifted Russian as Stankevitch could not remain 'tranquil' for long.

This is evident from the first question which involuntarily troubled Stankevitch immediately after he left the university.

His university studies were finished, he was left to himself, he was no longer led by others, *but he did not know what he was to do*. There was nothing to go on with, there was no one and nothing around that appealed to a living man. A youth, taking stock of his surroundings and having had time to look about him after school, found himself in the Russia of those days in the position of a traveller awakening in the steppe; one might go where one would—there were traces, there were bones of those who had perished, there were wild beasts and the empty desert on all sides with its dull menace of danger, in which it is easy to perish and impossible to struggle. The one thing which could be pursued was study.

And so Stankevitch persevered in the pursuit of learning. He imagined that it was his vocation to be an historian, and began studying Herodotus; it could be foreseen that nothing could come of that pursuit.

He would have liked to be in Petersburg in which there was such a rush of activity of a sort and to which he was attracted by the theatre and by nearness to Europe; he would have liked to be an honorary superintendent of the school at Ostrogozhsk. He determined to be of use in that 'modest career'—that was even less successful than Herodotus. He was in reality drawn to Moscow, to Germany, to his own university circle, to his own interests. He could not exist without intimate friends (another proof that there were at hand no interests very near to his heart). The craving for sympathy was so strong in Stankevitch that he sometimes invented intellectual sympathy and talents and saw and admired in people qualities which were completely non-existent in them.[1]

But—and in this lay his personal power—he did not often need to have recourse to such fictions, at every step he met wonderful people, he had the faculty of meeting them, and every one to whom he opened his heart remained his passionate friend for life; and to every such friend Stankevitch's influence was either an immense benefit or an alleviation of his burden.

In Voronezh Stankevitch used sometimes to go to the one local library for books. There he met a poor young man of humble station, modest and melancholy. It turned out that he was the son of a cattle-dealer who had business with Stankevitch's father over sales. Stankevitch befriended the young man; the cattle-dealer's son was a great reader and fond of talking of books. Stankevitch got to know him well. Shyly and timidly the youth confessed that he had himself tried his hand at writing verses and, blushing, ventured to show them. Stankevitch was amazed at the immense talent not conscious nor confident of itself. From that minute he did not let him go until all Russia was reading Koltsov's songs with enthusiasm. It is quite likely that the poor cattle-dealer, oppressed by his relations, unwarmed by sympathy or recognition, might have wasted his songs on the empty steppe beyond the Volga over which he drove his herds,

[1] Klyutchnikov vividly expressed this in the following image: 'Stankevitch is a silver rouble that envies the size of a copper piece.'—Annenkov, *Biography of Stankevitch*, p. 133.

and Russia would never have heard those exquisite, truly national songs, if Stankevitch had not crossed his path.

When Bakunin finished his studies at the school of artillery, he received a commission as an officer in the Guards. It is said that his father was angry with him and himself asked that he should be transferred into the regular army. Cast away in some God-forsaken village of White Russia with his battery, he grew morose and unsociable, left off performing his duties, and would lie for whole days together on his bed wrapped in a sheepskin. The commander of his battery was sorry for him; he had, however, no alternative but to remind him that he must either do his duties or go on the retired list. Bakunin had no suspicion that he had a right to take the latter course and at once asked to be relieved of his commission. On receiving his discharge he came to Moscow, and from that date (about 1836) life began in earnest for him. He had studied nothing before, had read nothing, and scarcely knew German. With great dialectical abilities, with a gift for obstinate, persistent thinking, he had strayed without map or compass in a world of fantastic projects and efforts at self-education. Stankevitch perceived his talents and set him down to philosophy. Bakunin learnt German on Kant and Fichte and then set to work upon Hegel, whose method and logic he mastered to perfection, and to whom did he not preach it afterwards? To us and to Byelinsky, to ladies and to Proudhon.

But Byelinsky drew as much from the same source; Stankevitch's views on art, on poetry and its relation to life, grew in Byelinsky's articles into that powerful modern criticism, into that new outlook upon the world and upon life which impressed all thinking Russia and made all the pedants and doctrinaires draw back from Byelinsky with horror. It was Stankevitch's lot to initiate Byelinsky into the mysteries; but the passionate, merciless, fiercely intolerant talent that carried Byelinsky beyond all bounds wounded the aesthetically harmonious temperament of Stankevitch.

And at the same time it was Stankevitch who encouraged the gentle, loving, dreamy, and at that time melancholy Granovsky. Stankevitch was a support and an elder brother to him. His letters to Granovsky are full of charm and beauty—and how Granovsky loved him!

'I have not yet recovered from the first shock,' wrote Granovsky soon after Stankevitch's death, 'real grief has not touched me yet; I am afraid of it in the future. Now I am still unable to believe that my loss is possible —only at times there is a stab at my heart. He has taken with him something essential to my life. To no one in the world was I so much indebted. His influence over us was always unbounded and always fruitful of good.'

And how many could say that! Perhaps have said it!

In Stankevitch's circle only he and Botkin[1] were well-to-do and completely free from financial anxieties. The others made up a very mixed proletariat. Bakunin's relations gave him nothing; Byelinsky, the son of a petty official of Tchembary, expelled from Moscow University for 'lack of ability,' lived on the scanty pay he got for his articles. Krassov,[2] on taking his degree, went to a situation at a landowner's in some province, but life with this patriarchal slaveowner so terrified him that he came back on foot to Moscow with a wallet on his back, in the winter, together with some peasants in charge of a train of wagons. Probably a father or mother of each one

[1] Botkin, Vassily Petrovitch (1810-1865), the self-taught son of a merchant, was a fine critic and authority on art and literature. His criticism was greatly valued by his friends, and his writings (chiefly articles in magazines) give no idea of his real importance in the history of Russian culture. His brother was the great physician.

[2] Krassov, Vassily Ivanovitch (1810-1855), a poet, at one time professor or literature in Kiev. His brother Ivan was a teacher of history in the Petersburg secondary schools.—(*Translator's Notes*.)

of them when giving them their blessing had said—and who dare reproach them for it—'Come, mind you work hard at your studies; and when you have taken your degree you must make your own way, there is nobody to leave you anything, we've nothing to give you either; you must make a career for yourself and think about us too.' On the other hand, Stankevitch had probably been told that he could take a prominent position in society, that he was called by wealth and birth to play a great part—while in Botkin's household every one, from his old father down to the clerks, urged upon him by word and example the necessity of making money, of piling up more and more.

What was it touched these men? what inspiration re-created them? They had no thought, no care for their social position, for their personal advantage, for their security; their whole life, all their efforts were bent on the public good regardless of all personal interests; some forgot their wealth, others their poverty, and went forward, without looking back, to the solution of theoretical questions. The interests of truth, the interests of learning, the interests of art, *humanitas*, swallowed up everything.

And note that the renunciation of this world was not confined to the time at the university and two or three years of youth. The best men of Stankevitch's circle are dead; the others have remained what they were to this day. Byelinsky, worn out by work and suffering, fell a fighter and a beggar. Granovsky, delivering his message of learning and humanity, died as he mounted his platform. Botkin did not, in fact, become a merchant . . . not one of them 'distinguished themselves' in the government service.

It was just the same in the two other circles, the Slavophils and ours. Where, in what corner of the Western world of to-day, do you find such groups of devotees of thought, of zealots of learning, of fanatics of conviction—whose hair turns grey but whose enthusiasms are for ever young?

Where? Point to them. I boldly throw down the challenge—and I only except for the moment one country, Italy—and measure the paces for the conflict, *i.e.*, I will not let my opponent escape from statistics into history.

We know how great was the interest in theory and the passion for truth and religion in the days of such martyrs for science and reason as Bruno, Galileo, and the rest; we know, too, what the France of the Encyclopaedists was in the second half of the eighteenth century; but later? Later *sta viator!*

In the Europe of to-day there is no youth and there are no young men. The most brilliant representative of the France of the last years of the Restoration and of the July dynasty, Victor Hugo, has protested against my saying this. He speaks especially of the young France of the 'twenties, and I am ready to admit that I have been too sweeping[1]—but beyond that I will not yield one step even to him. I have their own admissions. Take *Les Mémoires d'un Enfant du Siècle*, and the poems of Alfred de Musset, recall the France depicted in George Sand's letters, in the contemporary drama and novels, and in the cases in the law courts.

But what does all that prove? A very great deal; and in the first place that the Chinese shoes of German manufacture in which Russia has hobbled for a hundred and fifty years, though they have caused many painful corns, have evidently not crippled her bones, since whenever she has had a chance of stretching her limbs, such fresh young energies have been apparent. That does not guarantee the future, but it does make it extremely *possible*.

---

[1] Victor Hugo, after reading *My Past and Thoughts*, in the French translation, wrote me a letter in defence of the youth of France at the period of the Restoration.

Chapter 26

WARNINGS—THE PROMOTION OFFICE—A MINISTER'S SECRETARIAT—THE THIRD SECTION—THE STORY OF A SENTRY—GENERAL DUBBELT—COUNT BENCKENDORF—OLGA ALEXANDROVNA ZHEREBTSOV—MY SECOND EXILE

THOUGH we were so comfortable in Moscow, we had to move to Petersburg. My father insisted upon it. Count Strogonov, Minister of Home Affairs, commanded me to enter his secretariat, and we set off there at the end of the summer of 1840.

I had, however, been in Petersburg for two or three weeks in December 1839.

It had happened in this way. When I was relieved from police supervision and received the right to visit the 'residence and the capital,' as K. Aksakov called Petersburg and Moscow respectively, my father definitely preferred the 'residence' on the Neva to the ancient capital. Count Strogonov, the director of the university, wrote to his brother and I had to present myself to him. But that was not all. I had been recommended by the governor of Vladimir for the grade of collegiate assessor; my father wanted me to receive this grade as soon as possible. In the Promotion Office the provinces take their turn; this turn comes with the pace of a tortoise, unless special wires are pulled. They almost always are; their cost is excessive because a whole province may be taken outside its regular turn, but a single name must not. Therefore all have to be paid for, 'or else some would be getting an advantage for nothing.' Usually the officials to be promoted get up a subscription and send a delegate to represent them; but on this occasion my father took all the expense upon himself, and in that way several of the titular councillors of Vladimir were indebted to him for becoming assessors eight months before the proper time.

When he sent me off to Petersburg to attend to this business, my father repeated once more, as he said good-bye to me, 'For God's sake, be careful; be on your guard with every one, from the conductor of the *diligence* to the acquaintances to whom I am giving you letters. Do not trust any one. Petersburg nowadays is not what it was in our time. There is sure to be a spy or two in every company. *Tiens-toi pour averti.*' With this commentary on Petersburg life I got into a diligence of the earliest pattern, *i.e.* having all the defects gradually eliminated from later ones, and drove off.

When I reached Petersburg at nine o'clock in the evening, I took a sledge and drove to St. Isaac's Square. I wanted that to be the place with which I was to begin my acquaintance with Petersburg. Everything was covered with deep snow, only Peter the Great on his horse, gloomy and menacing, stood out sharply against the grey background and the darkness of the night.

> 'And looming black through mists of night
> With stately poise and haughty mien,
> Pointing afar with outstretched hand,
> A warrior on a horse is seen,
> A mighty figure, bold and free.
> The steed is reined. It rears aloft
> And paws the air imperiously,
> So that its lord might further see. . . .'[1]

Why was it the conflict of the 14th of December took place on that Square? Why was it from that pedestal that the first cry of Russian freedom rang out? Why did the revolting troops cling round Peter the First? Was it his reward . . . or his punishment? The 14th of December 1825 was the sequel of the work interrupted on the 21st of January 1725.[2] Nicholas's guns were turned upon the insurrection and upon the statue alike; it is a

[1] Translated by Juliet M. Soskice.
[2] Date of Peter the Great's death.—(*Translator's Note.*)

pity that the grapeshot did not shoot down the bronze Peter. . . .

Returning to my hotel I found one of my cousins awaiting me, and after talking to him of one thing and another, I touched, without thinking, upon St. Isaac's Square and the 14th of December.

'How is uncle?' asked my cousin. 'How did you leave him?'

'Thank God, just as usual; he sends you his greetings.'

My cousin, without changing his expression in the least, telegraphed reproach, advice, warning with his eyes alone; the direction of his eyes made me look round. A man was putting wood into the stove; when he had lighted it up, himself performing the duty of bellows as he did so, and making a pool on the floor from the snow that melted off his boots, he took an oven fork, the length of a Cossack's lance, and went out. My cousin at once fell to scolding me for having touched upon such a 'scabrous' subject, and in Russian too, before the man. As he went away he said to me in an undertone: 'By the way, before I forget it, there is a barber comes here to the hotel, he sells all sorts of rubbish, combs and rotten pomatums, please be on your guard with him. I am certain that he is connected with the police and talks all sorts of nonsense. While I was staying here I bought some trifles from him just to get rid of him.'

'To encourage him. Well, and is the laundress in the ranks of the gendarmes too?'

'You may laugh, you may laugh, you'll come to grief before any one; you're only just back from exile, and they will put a dozen nurses to keep watch on you.'

'Though they say that seven are enough for the child to grow up with one eye.'

Next day I went to see the official who used in old days to look after my father's affairs: he was a Ukrainian, who spoke Russian with an appalling accent, never listened to what was said to him, and showed his surprise at everything by shutting his eyes and holding up his fat little paws in a way that reminded one of a mouse. . . . He could not restrain himself either, and seeing that I had taken up my hat, led me aside to the window, looked about him, and said to me: 'You mustn't be angry. Just for the sake of my old acquaintance with the family of your father and his late brothers, you must not say much about what has happened to you. Upon my word, just think yourself, what use is it? Now it has all passed like smoke. You said something before my cook; she is a Finnish woman. Who can tell what she is, and I was a little . . . more than a little in fact . . . frightened.'

A pleasant town, I thought, as I left the frightened clerk. . . . The soft snow was falling in big flakes, the damp, cold wind penetrated to the very bones, and lifted one's hat and coat. My driver, who could scarcely see a step before him, screwing up his eyes and bending his head before the snow, shouted,' 'Ware, 'ware!' I remembered my father's advice. I thought of my cousin, of the clerk, and of the travelling sparrow in George Sand's fable who asked the half-frozen wolf in Lithuania why he lived in such a horrid climate. 'Freedom,' answered the wolf, 'makes one forget the climate.'

The driver was right—beware, beware! and how I longed to make haste and get away.

My stay was, in fact, brief on my first visit. In three weeks I had finished all my business, and galloped back to Vladimir for the New Year.

The experience I had gained in Vyatka was extremely useful to me in the Promotion Office. I knew already that the Promotion Office was something after the style of old St. Giles 'in London, the den of a gang of officially recognised thieves, which no inspection, no reform could change. To clear St. Giles', they took a pick, pulled down the houses, and razed them to the ground. That is what should be done with the Promotion Office. Moreover, it is utterly useless—a sort of parasitic service, the office of official promotion, a Ministry of grades and ranks, an archaeological society for the investigation of letters of nobility, a secretariat of secretariats. It need hardly be said that the abuses there were bound to be on a higher scale.

My father's agent brought me a faded old man in a uniform, every button of which was hanging by a thread; he was anything but clean, and had already had a drop, though it was early in the day. This was the proof corrector of the Senate Printing Press; after correcting grammatical errors, he used to assist various secretaries in other errors behind the scenes. Within half an hour I had come to terms with him, after bargaining exactly as though we were discussing the purchase of a horse or a piece of furniture. He could not, however, give me a positive answer himself, but ran round to the Senate for instructions, and after getting them at last, asked for a 'deposit.'

'But they will keep their promise?'

'Oh, excuse me, they are not people like that. It never happens that after taking a gratuity they do not discharge a debt of honour,' answered the proof corrector in a tone of so much offence that I thought it necessary to soften him with a slight additional gratuity.

'There used,' he observed, when I had thus propitiated him, 'to be a secretary in the Promotion Office who was a wonderful man. You've maybe heard of him, he used to take bribes recklessly and never got into trouble. Once a provincial official came to the office to talk about his business, and as he said good-bye he gave him a grey note on the sly, under cover of his hat. "But why do you make a secret of it?" the secretary said to him—"upon my word, as though you were giving me a love-letter. If it's a grey one—all the better. Let the other petitioners see it, it will encourage them when they know that I have accepted two hundred roubles and settled your business for it." And smoothing out the note, he folded it up and put it in his waistcoat pocket.'

The press corrector was right. The secretary discharged his debt of honour.

I left Petersburg with a feeling not very far from hatred, and yet there was no help for it. I had to move to that unattractive town.

I was not long in the service. I got out of my duties in every possible way, and so I have not a great deal to tell about the service. The secretariat of the Ministry of Home Affairs had the same relation to the secretariat of the Vyatka government as boots that have been cleaned have to those that have not; the leather is the same, the sole is the same, but the one sort are muddy, while the others are polished. I did not see clerks drunk in Petersburg. I did not see twenty kopecks taken for looking up a reference, but yet I somehow fancied that under those close-fitting dress-coats and carefully combed heads there was such a nasty, black, envious, petty, and cowardly soul that the head-clerk of my table in Vyatka seemed to me more of a man than any of them. As I looked at my new colleagues, I recalled how, on one occasion, after having a drop too much at the supper at the district surveyor's, he played a dance tune on the guitar, and at last could not resist leaping up with his guitar and beginning to join in the dance; but these Petersburg men were never carried away by anything. Their blood never boiled; wine did not turn their heads. In some dancing class, in company with German young ladies, they could walk through a French quadrille, pose as disillusioned, repeat lines from Timofeyev[1] or Kukolnik[2] . . . they

[1] Timofeyev, a sixth-rate writer of forgotten poems.
[2] Kukolnik, Nestor (1805-1868), was a schoolfellow of Gogol's,

were diplomats, aristocrats, and Manfreds. It is only a pity that Dashkov, the Minister, could not train these Childe Harolds not to stand at attention and bow even at the theatre, at church, and everywhere.

The Petersburghers laugh at the costumes seen in Moscow; they are outraged by the caps and Hungarian jackets, the long hair and civilian moustaches. Moscow certainly is a non-military city, rather careless and unaccustomed to discipline, but whether that is a good quality or a defect is a matter of opinion. The harmony of uniformity, the absence of variety, of what is personal and whimsical, a traditional obligatory dress and external discipline are all found on the largest scale in the most inhuman condition in which men live—in barracks. The uniform and a complete absence of variety are passionately loved by despotism. Nowhere are fashions followed so respectfully as in Petersburg, and that shows the immaturity of our culture; our clothes are alien. In Europe people dress, but we dress up, and so are terrified if a sleeve is too full, or a collar too narrow. In Paris all that people are afraid of is being dressed without taste; in London all that they are afraid of is catching cold; in Italy every one dresses as he likes best. If one were to show an Englishman the battalions of fops on the Nevsky Prospect, all wearing exactly similar, tightly buttoned coats, he would take them for a squad of 'policemen.'

I had to do violence to my feelings every time I went to the Ministry. The chief of the secretariat, K. K. von Paul, a *Herrnhuter*,[1] and a virtuous and lymphatic native

and a very popular writer of stories and dramas in the most extreme romantic style—fearfully bombastic and unreal, and hyperpatriotic.

[1] The Moravian Brethren, called *Herrnhuter* from the little town of Herrnhut in Saxony, where they settled in 1722, are a Protestant sect who abjure military service, the taking of oaths, and all distinctions of rank.—(*Translator's Notes*.)

of the Island of Dago, induced a kind of pious boredom in all his surroundings. The heads of the sections ran anxiously about with portfolios and were dissatisfied with the head-clerks of the tables; the latter wrote and wrote and certainly were overwhelmed with work, and had the prospect before them of dying at those tables, or, at any rate, if not particularly fortunate, sitting there for twenty-years. In the Registration Office there was a clerk who had for thirty-three years been keeping a record of the papers and printed parcels that went out.

My 'literary exercises' were of some benefit to me here too; after experience of my incapacity for anything else, the head of the section entrusted me with the composition of a general report on the Ministry from the various provincial secretariats. The foresight of the government had led them to propound certain general deductions beforehand, not leaving them to the chance risks of facts and figures. Thus, for instance, in the sketch of the proposed report appeared the statement: 'From the examination of the number and character of crimes' (neither their number nor their character was yet known) 'your Majesty may be graciously pleased to perceive the progress of national morality, and the increased zeal of the officials for its improvement.' Fate and Count Benckendorf saved me from taking part in this faked report. It happened in this way.

At nine o'clock one morning, early in December, Matvey told me that the superintendent of the local police-station wished to see me. I could not guess what had brought him to me, and bade Matvey show him in. The superintendent showed me a scrap of paper on which was written that I was summoned at ten o'clock in the morning to the Third Section of His Majesty's Own Secretariat.

'Very well,' I answered. 'That is by Tsyepnoy Bridge, isn't it?'

'Don't trouble yourself,' he answered. 'I have a sledge downstairs. I will go with you.'

It is a bad look-out, I thought, and with a pang at my heart I went into the bedroom. My wife was sitting with the baby, who had only just begun to recover after a long illness. 'What does he want?' she asked. 'I don't know, some nonsense. I shall have to go with him. . . . Don't be anxious.'

My wife looked at me and said nothing; she only turned pale as though a dark cloud had passed over her, and handed me the child to say good-bye to it.

I felt at that moment how much heavier every blow is for a man with wife and children; the blow does not strike him alone, he suffers for all, and unconsciously blames himself for their sufferings.

The feeling can be conquered, overcome, concealed, but one must recognise what it costs. I went out of the house in black misery. Very different was my mood when six years before I had set off with the police-master Miller to the Pretchistensky police-station.

We drove over the Tsyepnoy Bridge and through the Summer Garden and turned towards what had been Kotchubey's house; in the lodge there, the secular inquisition founded by Nicholas was installed: people who went in at its back gates, before which we stopped, did not always come out of them again, or, if they did, it was perhaps to be cast away in Siberia or perish in the Alexeyevsky ravelin. We crossed all sorts of courtyards and little squares, and came at last to the office. In spite of the presence of the commissar, the gendarme did not admit us, but summoned an official who, after reading the summons, left the police-superintendent in the corridor and asked me to follow him. He took me to the director's room. At a big table near which stood several armchairs a thin, grey-headed old man, with a sinister face, was sitting in complete solitude. To add to his dignity, he went on reading a paper to the end, then got up and came towards me. He had a star on his breast from which I concluded that he was some sort of commanding officer in the army of spies.

'Have you seen General Dubbelt?'

'No.'

He paused. Then, frowning and knitting his brows, without looking me in the face, he asked me in a sort of threadbare voice (the voice reminded me of the nervous, hissing notes of Golitsyn junior at the Moscow commission of inquiry): 'I think that you have not very long had permission to visit Petersburg or Moscow?'

'I received it last year.'

The old man shook his head. 'And you have made a bad use of the Tsar's graciousness. I believe you'll have to go back again to Vyatka.'

I gazed at him in amazement.

'Yes,' he went on, 'you've chosen a fine way to show your gratitude to the government that permitted you to return.'

'I don't understand in the least,' I said, lost in conjecture.

'You don't understand? That's just what is bad, too! What connections! What pursuits! Instead of showing your zeal from the first, effacing the stains left from your youthful errors, turning your abilities to service —no, indeed, it's nothing but politics and criticisms, and all to the detriment of the government. This is what your talk has brought you to! How is it you've learnt nothing from experience? How do you know that among those who talk to you there is not always some scoundrel[1] who asks nothing better than to come *here* a minute later to give information.'

'If you can explain to me what it all means, you will

---

[1] I declare, on my word of honour, that the word 'scoundrel' was used by this worthy old person.

greatly oblige me. I am racking my brains and cannot understand what your words are leading up to, or at what they are hinting.'

'What they are leading to? Hm. . . . Come, did you hear that a sentry at the Blue Bridge killed and robbed a man at night?'

'Yes, I did,' I answered with great simplicity.

'And perhaps you repeated it?'

'I believe I did repeat it.'

'With comments, I daresay?'

'Very likely.'

'With what sort of comments? There you see the disposition to attack the government. I tell you openly, the one thing that does you credit is your sincere avowal, it will certainly be taken into consideration by the Count.'

'Upon my word' I said, 'what is there to avow? All the town was talking of the story; it was talked of in the secretariat, and in the Ministry of Home Affairs and in the shops. What is there surprising in my having spoken about the incident?'

'The diffusion of false and mischievous rumours is a crime amenable to the law.'

'You seem to be charging me with having invented the story.'

'In the note submitted to the Tsar it is merely stated that you assisted in the propagation of this mischievous rumour, upon which the decision of the Most High concerning your return to Vyatka has been taken.'

'You are simply trying to frighten me,' I answered. 'How is it possible to send a man with a wife and child a thousand miles away for such a trivial matter, and, what's more, to condemn and sentence him without even inquiring whether it is true.'

'You have admitted it yourself.'

'But you say the report was submitted and the matter settled before you spoke to me.'

'Read for yourself.' The old man went up to the table, fumbled among a small heap of papers, coolly pulled out one and handed it to me. I read it and could not believe my eyes; such complete absence of justice, such insolent, shameless disregard of the law was amazing, even in Russia.

I did not speak. I fancy that the old man himself felt that it was a very absurd and extremely silly business, as he did not think it necessary to defend it further, but after a brief silence asked:

'I believe you said you were married?'

'I am married.'

'It is a pity that we did not know that before. However, if anything can be done, the Count will do it. I will repeat our conversation to him. *In any case* you will be banished from Petersburg.'

He looked at me. I did not speak, but felt that my face was burning. Everything I could not utter, everything restrained within me could be seen in my face.

The old man dropped his eyes, paused, and in an apathetic voice, with an affectation of refined politeness, said to me: 'I will not venture to detain you further. I most sincerely hope—however, you will hear later.'

I rushed home. My heart was boiling with a consuming fury—that feeling of impotence, of having no rights, the position of a caged beast at which a scornful street boy mocks, knowing that all the tiger's strength is not enough to break the bars.

I found my wife in a fever; she was taken ill that day, and, having another fright in the evening, was a few days later prematurely confined. The baby only lived a day, and it was three or four years before she fully recovered her strength.

They say that that tender paterfamilias, Nicholas Pavlovitch, shed tears when his daughter died. . . . And what strange passion induces them to raise a hubbub, gallop full-speed, make such a fuss and do everything in tearing haste, as though the town were on fire, the throne were tottering, or the dynasty in danger, and all that without the slightest necessity! It is the sense of romance of the police, the dramatic efforts of the detective, the spectacular setting for the display of loyal zeal. . . . The janissaries, the swashbucklers, the bloodhounds!

On the evening of the day on which I had been to the Third Section, we were sitting sorrowfully at a small table—the baby was playing with his toys on it; we spoke little—and all at once some one pulled the bell so violently that we could not help starting. Matvey rushed to open the door, and a second later an officer of gendarmes, clashing his sabre and jingling his spurs, darted into the room and began in choice language apologising to my wife. He could not have imagined, he had had no suspicion, no idea that there was a lady and children in the case. It was extremely unfortunate. . . . Gendarmes are the very flower of courtesy; if it were not for their duty, for the sacred obligations of the service, they would never make secret reports, or even beat post-boys and drivers at posting-stations. I know that from the Krutitsky Barracks where the *désolé* officer was so deeply distressed at being forced to feel in my pockets. Paul Louis Courier[1] observed in his day that executioners and prosecutors are the most courteous of men. 'My dear executioner,' writes the prosecutor, 'if it is not troubling you too much, you will do me the greatest service if you will kindly undertake to chop off So-and-so's head to-morrow morning.' And the executioner hastens to answer that he esteems himself fortunate indeed that he can by so trifling a service do something agreeable to

[1] Paul Louis Courier (1772-1825), a learned and brilliant writer of political pamphlets and letters, who discovered a complete manuscript of Longus's *Daphnis and Chloe*, of which he published a French translation.—(*Translator's Note*.)

the prosecutor and remains always his devoted and obedient servant the executioner, and the other man, the third, remains devoted without his head!

'General Dubbelt summons you to his presence.'

'When?'

'Upon my word! now, at once, this minute.'

'Matvey, give me my overcoat.'

I pressed my wife's hand—her face was flushed, her hand was burning. Why this hurry at ten o'clock in the evening? Had a plot been discovered? Had some one run away? Was the precious life of Nicholas in danger? I really was unfair to that sentry, I thought. There was nothing to be surprised at in one of the agents of this government murdering two or three passers-by; the sentries of the second and third degree are no better than their comrade on the Blue Bridge. And what about the head sentry of all?

Dubbelt had summoned me in order to tell me that Count Benckendorf commanded my presence at eight o'clock next morning to inform me of the decision of the Most High.

Dubbelt was an original person; he was probably more intelligent than the whole of the Third Section—indeed, of all the three sections of His Majesty's Own Secretariat. His sunken face, shaded by long, fair moustaches, his fatigued expression, particularly the furrows on his cheeks and on his brow, unmistakably betrayed that his breast had been the battlefield of many passions before the pale-blue uniform had dominated, or rather hidden, everything within it. His features had something wolfish and even foxy about them, *i.e.*, they expressed the subtle shrewdness of beasts of prey; there was at once evasiveness and conceit in them. He was always courteous.

When I went into his study, he was sitting in a uniform coat, without epaulettes, and smoking a pipe as he wrote.

He rose instantly, and asking me to sit down facing him, began with the following surprising sentence:

'Count Alexandr Christophorovitch has given me this opportunity of making your acquaintance. I believe you saw Sahtynsky this morning?'

'Yes, I did.'

'I am very sorry that the occasion that has forced me to ask you to see me is not quite an agreeable one for you. Your imprudence has again brought his Majesty's anger upon you.'

'I will say to you, General, what I said to Mr. Sahtynsky, I cannot imagine that I am being exiled simply for having repeated a street rumour, which you, of course, heard before I did, and possibly spoke of just as I did.'

'Yes, I heard the rumour, and I spoke of it, and in that we are alike; but this is where the difference comes in—in repeating the absurd story I swore that there was nothing in it, while you made the rumour a ground for attacking the whole police. It is this unfortunate passion *de dénigrer le gouvernement*—a passion that has developed in all of you gentlemen from the fatal example of the West. It is not with us as in France, where the government is at daggers drawn with the parties—there it is dragged into the mud. Our government is paternal—everything is done as privately as possible. . . . We do our very utmost that everything should go as quietly and smoothly as possible, and here men, who in spite of painful experience persist in a fruitless opposition, alarm public opinion by repeating verbally, and in writing, that the soldiers of the police murder men in the streets. Isn't that true? You have written about it, haven't you?'

'I attach so little importance to the matter that I don't think it necessary to conceal that I have written about it, and I will add to whom—to my father.'

'Of course, it is not an important matter, but see what it has brought upon you. His Majesty at once remembered your name, and that you had been in Vyatka, and commanded that you should be sent back there, and so the Count has commissioned me to inform you that you must come to him to-morrow at eight o'clock and he will announce to you the decision of the Most High.'

'And so it is left that I am to go to Vyatka with a sick wife and a sick child on account of something that you say is not important?. . .'

'Why, are you in the service?' Dubbelt asked me, looking intently at the buttons of my uniform coat.

'In the Ministry of Home Affairs.'

'Have you been there long?'

'Six months.'

'And all the time in Petersburg?'

'All the time.'

'I had no idea of it.'

'You see,' I said, smiling, 'how discreetly I have behaved.'

Sahtynsky did not know that I was married, Dubbelt did not know that I was in the service, but both knew what I said in my own room, what I thought, and what I wrote to my father. . . . What was really wrong was that I was just beginning to be friendly with Petersburg literary men, and to publish articles, and, worse still, had been transferred from Vladimir to Petersburg by Count Strogonov without the secret police having been consulted, and when I arrived in Petersburg had not presented myself either to Dubbelt or to the Third Section, as worthy persons had hinted that I should do.

'To be sure,' Dubbelt interrupted me, 'all the evidence that has been collected about you is to your credit. Only yesterday I was speaking to Zhukovsky and should be thankful to hear my son spoken of as he spoke of you.'

'And yet I am to go to Vyatka?'

'You see it is your misfortune that the secret report

has been handed in already, and that many circumstances had not been taken into consideration. You will have to go, there is no altering that, but I imagine that it might be another town instead of Vyatka. I will talk it over with the Count, he is going to-night to the Palace. We will try and do all that can be done to make things easier; the Count is a man of angelic kindness.'

I got up, Dubbelt escorted me to the door of the study. At that point I could not restrain myself, and stopping, I said to him:

'I have one small favour to ask of you, General. If you want me, please do not send constables or gendarmes. They are noisy and alarming, especially in the evening. Why should my sick wife be more severely punished than any one on account of the sentry business?'

'Oh! good heavens, how unpleasant that is,' replied Dubbelt, 'how tactless they all are! You may rest assured that I will not send a policeman again. And so till to-morrow; don't forget, eight o'clock at the Count's; we shall meet there.'

It was exactly as though we were agreeing to go to Smurov's to eat oysters together.

At eight o'clock next morning I was in Benckendorf's reception room. I found five or six petitioners waiting there; they stood gloomy and anxious by the wall, started at every sound, and then timidly drew themselves in again, and bowed to every adjutant that passed. Among their number was a woman in deep mourning, with tear-stained eyes. She sat with a paper rolled up in her hand, and the roll trembled like a leaf. Three paces from her stood a tall, rather bent old man of seventy, bald and sallow, in a dark-green overcoat, with a row of medals and crosses on his breast. From time to time he sighed, shook his head and murmured something to himself.

Some sort of friend of the family,' a flunkey, or a clerk

on duty, sat in the window, lolling at his ease. He got up when I went in, and looking intently at his face I recognised him; that loathsome figure had been pointed out to me at the theatre as one of the chief street detectives, and his name, I remember, was Fabre. He asked me:

'Have you come with a petition to the Count?'

'I have come at his summons.'

'Your surname?'

I mentioned it.

'Ah,' he said, changing his tone as though he had met an old acquaintance, 'won't you be pleased to sit down? The Count will be here in a quarter of an hour.'

It was horribly still and *unheimlich* in the room, the daylight hardly penetrated through the fog and frozen window-panes, no one said a word. The adjutants ran quickly to and fro, and the gendarme standing at the door sometimes jingled his accoutrements as he shifted from foot to foot. Two more petitioners came in. The clerk on duty ran to ask each what he had come about. One of the adjutants went up to him and began in a half-whisper telling him some story, assuming a desperately roguish air as he did so. No doubt it was something revolting, for they interspersed their talk at frequent intervals with flunkeyish, nioseless laughter, during which the worthy clerk, affecting to be quite helpless, and ready to explode, repeated: 'Do stop, for God's sake stop, I can't bear it.'

Five minutes later Dubbelt came in with his uniform unbuttoned as though he were off duty, glanced casually at the petitioners, whereupon they all bowed, and seeing me at the farther end said: '*Bonjour, Monsieur Herzen. Votre affaire va parfaitement bien* . . . very well indeed.'

They would let me stay, perhaps! I was on the point of asking, but before I had time to utter a word Dubbelt had disappeared. Next there walked into the room a

A MODEL GENERAL

general, polished up and highly decorated, tightly laced and stiffly erect, in white breeches, with a scarf across his breast. I have never seen a finer general. If ever there is an exhibition of generals in London as there now is a Baby Exhibition at Cincinnati, I should advise his being sent from Petersburg. The general went up to the door from which Benckendorf was to enter and became petrified in stiff immobility; with great interest I scrutinised this sergeant's ideal. A lot of soldiers, I expect, he had flogged in his day for falling out of step! Where do these people come from? He was born for rifle drill and army discipline! He was attended by the most elegant cornet in the world, probably his adjutant, a fair-haired youth, with incredibly long legs, a tiny face like a squirrel's, and that simple-hearted expression which often persists in mamma's darlings who have never studied anything, or, at any rate, have never succeeded in learning anything. This eglantine in uniform stood at a respectful distance from the model general.

Dubbelt darted in again, this time looking dignified, with all his buttons done up. He at once addressed the general, and asked him what he had come about. The general, with the perfect correctness with which privates speak when presenting themselves to their superior officers, reported: 'Yesterday I received through Prince Alexandr Ivanovitch the command of the Most High to join the Army at the front at the Caucasus, and esteemed it my duty to present myself to his Excellency before leaving.'

Dubbelt listened with religious attention to this speech, and with a slight bow as a sign of respect went out and returned a minute later.

'The Count,' he said to the general, 'sincerely regrets that he has not time to receive your Excellency. He thanks you and has commissioned me to wish you a good journey.' Whereupon Dubbelt flung wide his arms, embraced the general, and twice touched his cheeks with his moustaches.

The general retreated at a solemn march, the youth with the face of a squirrel and the legs of a crane strode after him. This scene made up to me for a great deal of bitterness that day. The general's attitude, the farewell by proxy, and the sly face of *Reinecke Fuchs* as he kissed the brainless countenance of his Excellency was all so ludicrous that I could scarcely contain myself. I fancied that Dubbelt noticed it and began to respect me from that time.

At last both folds of the double door were flung open and Benckendorf walked in. There was nothing unpleasant in the appearance of the chief of the gendarmes; his exterior was rather typical of a nobleman of the Baltic provinces, and, indeed, of the German aristocracy generally. His face looked creased and tired, he had the delusively good-natured expression which is so often found in evasive and apathetic people.

Possibly Benckendorf did not do all the harm he might have done, being the head of that terrible police, standing outside the law and above the law, having a right to meddle in everything. I am ready to believe it, especially when I recall the insipid expression of his face. But he did no good either, he had not enough will-power, energy, or heart for that. To be timid of saying a word in defence of the oppressed is as bad as any crime in the service of a man so cold and merciless as Nicholas.

How many innocent victims passed through Benckendorf's hands, how many perished through his lack of attention, through his frivolity, because he was engrossed in flirtation perhaps—and how many gloomy images and painful memories may have haunted his mind and tormented him when, prematurely collapsing and growing senile, he sailed off to seek, in betrayal of his own religion, the protection of the Catholic Church with its all-forgiving indulgences. . . .

'It has reached the knowledge of his Imperial Majesty, he said to me,' that you take part in the diffusion of rumours injurious to the government. His Majesty, seeing how little you have reformed, graciously commanded that you should be sent back to Vyatka; but at the request of General Dubbelt, and relying upon information collected about you, I have reported to his Majesty on the subject of your wife's illness, and his Majesty was graciously pleased to alter his decision. His Majesty forbids you to visit Petersburg and Moscow, and you will be under police supervision again, but it is left to the Ministry of Home Affairs to fix the place where you are to reside.'

'Allow me to tell you frankly that even at this moment I cannot believe that there is no other cause for my exile. In 1835 I was exiled on account of a supper-party at which I was not present! Now I am being punished for a rumour about which the whole town was talking. It is a strange fate!'

Benckendorf shrugged his shoulders, and turning out the palms of his hands like a man who has exhausted all the resources of argument, cut short my speech.

'I make known to you the Imperial will, and you answer me with criticisms. What profit will there be from all that you say to me, or that I say to you? It is a waste of words. Nothing can be changed now. What will be later partly depends on you, and since you have referred to your first affair, I particularly recommend you not to let there be a third. You will certainly not get off so easily a third time.'

Benckendorf gave me a gracious smile and turned towards the petitioners. He said very little to them; he took their petition, glanced at it, then handed it to Dubbelt, receiving the petitioners' observations with the same graciously condescending smile. These people had been for whole months thinking about it, and preparing themselves for this interview, upon which their honour, their fortune, their family depended; what effort, what labour had been spent by them before they had succeeded in getting an entrance, how many times they had knocked at the closed door and been turned away by the gendarme or the porter. And how immense, how poignant must the necessity have been that brought them to the head of the secret police; no doubt all legal channels had been exhausted first. And this man got rid of them with commonplaces, and probably some clerk drew up some decision to pass the case on to some other department. And what had he to preoccupy him? What need had he for haste?

When Benckendorf went up to the old man with the medals, the latter dropped on his knees and articulated: 'Your Excellency, enter into my position.'

'How degrading!' cried the Count; 'you are disgracing your medals,' and full of righteous indignation he passed by without taking his petition. The old man slowly got up, his glassy eyes were full of horror and bewilderment, his lower lip quivered, he muttered something.

How inhuman these people are when the whim takes them to be humane!

Dubbelt went up to the old man and said: 'Whatever did you do that for? Come, give me your petition. I'll look through it.'

Benckendorf had gone off to see the Tsar.

'What am I to do?' I asked Dubbelt.

'Settle on any town you choose with the Minister of Home Affairs; we will not interfere. We will send the whole case on there to-morrow. I congratulate you on its having been so satisfactorily settled.'

'I am very much obliged to you.'

From Benckendorf I went to the Ministry. Our director, as I have mentioned, belonged to that class of Germans who have something of the lemur about them, lanky, slow, and long drawn out. Their brains work slowly, they do not catch the point at once, and pass through a long process to reach any sort of conclusion. My story unfortunately arrived before the communication of the Third Section; he had not expected it at all, and so was completely bewildered, uttered incoherent phrases, perceived the fact himself, and to set himself right said to me: '*Erlauben Sie mir deutsch zu sprechen.*' Possibly his remarks were grammatically more correct in the German language, but they were no clearer and more definite in meaning. I perceived distinctly two feelings struggling in him: he grasped all the injustice of it, but thought it his duty as director to justify the action of the government; at the same time, he did not like to appear a barbarian in my eyes, nor could he forget the hostility which invariably existed between the Ministry of Home Affairs and the secret police. So the task of expressing all this jumble was in itself not easy. He ended by declaring that he could say nothing until he had seen the Minister, and going off to see him.

Count Strogonov sent for me, inquired into the matter, listened to the story attentively, and said to me in conclusion: 'It's a police trick, pure and simple—all right, I'll pay them out for it.'

I actually imagined that he was going straight off to the Tsar to explain the position to him; but ministers do not go so far.

'I have received the command of the Most High concerning you,' he went on—'here it is. You see that it is left to me to select the place of your exile and a post in the service for you. Where would you like to go?'

'To Tver or to Novgorod,' I answered.

'To be sure. . . . Well, since the choice of a place is

left to me, and it probably does not matter to you to which of those towns I send you, I will give you the first councillor's vacancy in the provincial government. That is the highest position that you can receive in the regular way of promotion, so order yourself a uniform with an embroidered collar,' he added jocosely.

So that was how I scored, though not on my own play.

A week later Strogonov recommended me to the Senate for an appointment as councillor at Novgorod.

It really is funny to think how many secretaries, assessors, district and provincial officials had been scheming passionately, persistently, for years to get that post; bribes had been given, the most solemn promises had been received, and here, all at once, a Minister, to carry out the commands of the Most High and at the same time to have a slap at the secret police, *punished* me with this promotion and, by way of gilding the pill, flung this post, the object of ardent desires and ambitious dreams, at the feet of a man who accepted it with the firm intention of throwing it up at the first opportunity.

From Strogonov I went to see a lady; I must say a few words about this acquaintance.

Among the letters of introduction given me by my father when I first went to Petersburg was one which I had picked up a dozen times, turned over and thrust back again into the table drawer, putting off my visit until another day. The letter was addressed to a lady of seventy, of high rank and great wealth, whose friendship with my father dated from time immemorial; he had first made her acquaintance when she was at the Court of Catherine 11.; then they had met in Paris, had travelled here and there together, and at last both had come to rest at home some thirty years before.

I disliked persons of consequence as a rule, particularly when they were women, and even more so when they were seventy; but my father had inquired for the second time whether I had called upon Olga Alexandrovna Zherebtsov, so at last I resolved to swallow the bitter pill. A footman led me into a rather gloomy drawing-room, poorly decorated, and looking as though it were darkened and faded; the furniture, the hangings, all had lost their colour, and all had evidently been standing for ages in the same place. I was reminded of the atmosphere of Princess Meshtchersky's house; old age, no less than youth, puts its imprint on all around it. I waited with resignation for the lady to make her appearance, preparing myself for tedious questions, for deafness, for a cough, for attacks on the younger generation, and perhaps moral exhortations.

Five minutes later a tall old woman, with a stern face that bore traces of great beauty, walked in with a firm step; an unswerving will, a strong character, and a strong intellect were apparent in her deportment, in her movements and her gestures. She scanned me from head to foot with a penetrating gaze, went up to the sofa, with one movement of her arm pushed back the table, and said to me: 'Sit in this arm-chair here, nearer to me. I am a great friend of your father's, you know, and I love him.' She opened the letter, and handed it to me, saying: 'Please read it to me; my eyes are bad.'

The letter was written in French and full of all sorts of compliments, reminiscences, and allusions. She listened, smiling, and when I had finished said: 'His mind shows no signs of age, he is just the same as ever; he was very charming and very caustic. And now, I suppose, he keeps his room, wears his dressing-gown, and plays the invalid? Two years ago I was passing through Moscow and then I went to see your father. "I can hardly see any one," he said. "I am breaking up," and then he got into talk and forgot his ailments. It's all nonsense, he is not much older than I am, two or three years at the most, though I doubt if he is that, and I am a woman, yet I still keep on my legs. Yes, yes, much water has flowed by since those days your father talks of. Why, only fancy, he and I were among the leading dancers. The English dances were the fashion in those days; Ivan Alexeyevitch and I used to dance at the late Empress's. Can you imagine your father in a full-skirted light blue French coat, wearing powder, and me in a hoop and *décolletée*? It was very pleasant to dance with him, *il était bel homme*, he was finer looking than you—let me have a good look at you—yes, he really was finer. . . . Don't be angry, at my age I may tell the truth. Besides, I believe you don't care about that—of course, you are literary and learned. Ah, my goodness, by the way, do tell me please what was all that business with you? Your father wrote to me when you were sent to Vyatka. I did try to speak to Bludov, but he did not do anything. They won't say what they exiled you for. They keep that a *secret d'état*.'

There was so much simplicity and genuineness in her manner that, contrary to my expectation, I was at ease and unconstrained with her. I answered between jest and earnest and told her all about our case.

'He makes war on students,' she observed; 'he has nothing in his head but conspiracies, and, to be sure, they are pleased to oblige him; they think of nothing but nonsense. They are such wretched little creatures about him! Where did he get hold of them—no rank and no family. Well, *mon cher conspirateur*, how old were you then?—sixteen, I expect.'

'Just one and twenty,' I answered, laughing genuinely at her utter contempt for our political activities, both mine and Nicholas's, 'but then I was the eldest.'

'Four or five students scared *tout le gouvernement*, you see—what a disgrace!'

After talking in this style for half an hour, I got up to go.

'Stay a little,' said Olga Alexandrovna in a still more friendly tone. 'I have not finished my catechism; how was it you carried off your bride?'

'How do you know?'

'Oh, my dear, the world is full of rumour—youth, *des passions*. I talked to your father at the time. He was still angry with you, but, there, he is a sensible man, he understood. . . . Thank God you live happily. What more does he want? "Well," he said to me, "the boy came to Moscow contrary to the Imperial decree. If he had been caught he would have been sent to the fortress." "But you see he wasn't caught," I said, "so you ought to be thankful for that, and what is the use of talking nonsense and imagining what might have been?" "Oh, you were always fearless," he told me, "and lived recklessly." "Well, my dear sir, I am ending my days no worse than other people," I answered him—"and what's the sense of your leaving the young people without money? That's beyond anything." "Well," he said, "I'll send them some. I'll send them some. Don't be angry." You'll bring your wife to see me, won't you?'

I thanked her, and said that I had not brought her with me to Petersburg yet.

'Where are you staying?'

'At Demouthe's.'

'And do you dine there?'

'Sometimes there; sometimes at Dumais.'

'Why restaurants—it's expensive, and besides it's not nice for a married man. If it won't bore you to dine with an old woman, come here. I am really very glad to have made your acquaintance. I must thank your father for having sent you to me; you are a very interesting young man, and have a good understanding of things though you are young,—so you and I will have a talk about one thing and another, for you know I am bored with these courtiers; they can talk of nothing but the court, and who has received a decoration; it is all so silly.'

In one volume of Thiers' *History of the Consulate* he gives a rather detailed and rather correct account of the murder of Paul. There are two references in his story to a woman, the sister of Count Zubov, who was the last of Catherine's favourites. The beautiful young widow of a general (killed, I believe, during the war), a passionate and vigorous character, spoilt by success, endowed with exceptional intellect and masculine strength of will, she became the centre round which the discontented rallied during the savage and senseless reign of Paul. The conspirators met at her house; she incited them, their relations with the English Embassy were carried on through her. Paul's police suspected her at last, and, warned in time, perhaps by Pahlen himself, she went abroad before it was too late. The plot was by then matured, and while dancing at a ball at the court of the Prussian king she received the news that Paul had been killed. Not concealing her j oy, she rapturously announced the news to every one in the ball-room. This so scandalised the Prussian king that he ordered her to be banished from Berlin within twenty-four hours.

She went to England. Brilliant, spoilt by court life, and devoured by a consuming passion for a great career, she made her appearance as a lioness of the first magnitude in London, and played an important part in the reserved and exclusive society of the English aristocracy. The Prince of Wales, *i.e.*, the future King George iv., was her devoted adorer, and soon more than that. . . . The years of her life abroad were spent amidst noisy magnificence, but they passed, and glory after glory faded. With old age came emptiness, misfortunes, loneliness, and the melancholy life of memory. Her son was killed at Borodino; her daughter died leaving her a grandchild, now Countess Orlov. Every August the old woman went from Petersburg to Mozhaisk to visit her son's grave. Loneliness and misfortune had not broken her strong character, but only made it more austere and angular. Like a tree in winter, she retained the outline of her branches, the leaves had dropped, and the bare twigs were cold and stiff as dry bones, but the gigantic stature and bold proportions were but the more distinctly visible, and the trunk, silvered with hoar-frost, stood proud and gloomy, and no wind, no storm could bend it.

Her long life, so full of movement, the immense wealth of meetings, of contrasts in it, had formed her disdainful view of the world, which had its share of mournful truth. She had her own philosophy, resting upon a profound contempt for her fellow-creatures, though, owing to her active disposition, she could not abandon them altogether.

'You don't know them yet,' she would say to me, nodding her head towards the retreating figures of various stout and thin senators and generals. 'I have seen enough of them. It is not so easy to take me in as they imagine; before I was twenty my brother was in the highest favour, and the Empress was very kind to me, and very fond of me. So then, would you believe it, old men, beribboned and decorated, who could scarcely drag one leg after the other, were falling over one another to reach the vestibule and hand me my pelisse and my warm shoes. The Empress died, and next day my house was deserted. They ran from me as from the plague, in the madman's days, you know, and those the very same persons. I went my way, I had no need of any one, I crossed the sea. After my return the Lord visited me with, great misfortunes, but I met with sympathy from no one. There were two or three old friends who did not desert me, though. Well, then, your reign has come. Orlov, you see, has influence, though indeed I don't know how far that is true . . . they imagine it is, anyway. They know that he is my heir and that my granddaughter loves me; so now they are such friends again—again they are ready to hand me my cloak and my goloshes! Ugh! I know them, but one is sometimes tired of sitting alone; my eyes are bad, it is hard to read, besides one does not always care to, so I let them come, they babble all sorts of nonsense; it amuses me, and serves to pass an hour or two. . . .'

She was a strange, original relic of another age, surrounded by degenerate successors that had sprung up on the mean and barren soil of Petersburg court life. She felt superior to it, and she was right. If she had shared the Saturnalia of Catherine and the orgies of George iv., she had also shared the dangers of the conspirators of Paul's reign.

Her mistake lay not in her contempt for these worthless people, but in her taking this produce of the court kitchen-garden for the whole of our generation. In the reign of Catherine, the court and the Guards really did include all that was cultured in Russia; and this persisted, more or less, until 1812. Since then Russian society has taken immense strides; the war led to an awakening, and that awakening to the Fourteenth of December. Society was divided in two from within: the worst part remained on the side of the court; executions and savage punishments drove away some, while the new tone prevailing drove away others. Alexander carried on the traditions of culture of the reign of Catherine. Under Nicholas the worldly aristocratic tone was replaced by one of frigid formality and ferocious despotism on the one hand and boundless servility on the other—a blend of the abrupt and rude Napoleonic manner with the callousness of bureaucracy. A new society, the centre of which was in Moscow, rapidly developed.

There is a wonderful book which one cannot help recalling when one speaks of Olga Alexandrovna—I mean the *Memoirs of Princess Dashkov*, published twenty years ago in London. To the book are appended the memoirs of the two sisters Wilmot who lived with Princess Dashkov between 1805 and 1810. They were highly cultured Irishwomen, with a great gift of observation. I should very much like their letters and memoirs to be known in Russia.

When I compare Moscow society before 1812 with that which I left in 1847 my heart throbs with joy. We have made tremendous strides forward. In those days there was a society of the discontented—that is, of those who had been left out, dismissed, or laid on the shelf; now there is a society of independent people. The lions of those days were capricious oligarchs, such as Count A. G. Orlov and Ostermann, 'a society of shadows' as Miss Wilmot says, a society of political men who had died fifteen years before in Petersburg, but went on powdering their heads, putting on their ribbons, and appearing at dinners and festivities in Moscow, sulking, giving themselves airs of consequence, and having neither influence nor significance. After 1825 the lions of Moscow were Pushkin, M. Orlov, Tchaadayev, Yermolov. In the earlier days society had flocked with cringing servility to the house of Count Orlov, ladies 'in other people's diamonds,'[1] gentlemen who dared not sit down without permission; the Count's serfs danced before them in masquerade attire. Forty years later I saw the same society crowding about the platform of one of the lecture-rooms of the Moscow University; the daughters of those ladies in other people's jewels, the sons of the men who had not dared to sit down, were, with passionate sympathy, following the profound, vigorous words of Granovsky, greeting with outbursts of

[1] Miss Wilmot's words.

applause sentences that went straight to the heart from their boldness and nobility.

It was just the society that gathered from all parts of Moscow and crowded about the platform on which the young champion of learning delivered his earnest message and deciphered the future from the past—it was just this society of the existence of which Madame Zherebtsov had no suspicion. She was particularly kind and attentive to me because I was the first example of a world unknown to her; she was surprised at my language and at my ideas. She welcomed in me the coming of another Russia, not that Russia whose only light filtered through the frozen windows of the Winter Palace. Thanks to her for that!

I could fill a whole volume with the anecdotes I heard from Olga Alexandrovna; with whom had she not been on friendly terms, from Comte d'Artois[1] and the Comte de Ségur[2] to Canning and Lord Granville, and she looked at all of them independently, from her own point of view, and a very original one. I will confine myself to one small incident which I will try to repeat in her own words.

She lived in the Morskaya. A regiment of soldiers happened one day to pass along the street with a band. Olga Alexandrovna went to the window and looking at the soldiers said to me: 'I have a summer villa not far from Gatchina. I sometimes go there for a rest in the summer. I ordered a big lawn to be made there before the house, in the English style, you know, covered with turf. Last year I went down there; only fancy: at six

[1] The Comte d'Artois—afterwards Charles x.

[2] The Comte de Ségur (1753-1830) was French ambassador in Petersburg and a favourite of Catherine II. He was a man of action as well as a spirited writer, served in the American War of Independence, welcomed every movement on the side of liberty, and wrote a charming account of his times in his *Galerie Morale et Politique*, and his *Mémoires*.—(*Translator's Notes*.)

o'clock in the morning I hear a dreadful beating of drums. I lie in bed more dead than alive; it keeps coming closer and closer. I ring the bell, my Kalmyk girl runs in. "What has happened, my good girl?" I ask; "what is this noise?" "Oh, that," says she, "Mihail Pavlovitch[1] is pleased to be drilling his soldiers." "Where is that?" "On our lawn." He liked our lawn, it was so smooth and green. Only fancy, with a lady living there, old and ill, he came with the drums at six o'clock in the morning. Well, I thought, that won't do. "Call the steward," I said. The steward came and I said to him: "Have the cart got out at once, drive into Petersburg, hire as many White Russians as you can find, and let them begin digging a pond to-morrow." Well, I thought, I hope they won't hold a Naval Review before my windows. They are all such ill-bred creatures!'

It was natural that I should go straight from Strogonov to Olga Alexandrovna and tell her all that had happened.

'Good heavens! What folly; they go from bad to worse,' she observed when she heard my story. 'How can a man with a family be dragged off to exile for such nonsense? Let me talk to Orlov. I hardly ever ask him to do anything, they all dislike it; but there, once in a way he may do something for me. Come and see me in a couple of days, and I'll tell you his answer.'

Two days later she sent for me. I found several visitors with her. She had a white batiste kerchief round her head instead of a cap; this was usually a sign that she was out of spirits; she screwed up her eyes and hardly took any notice of the privy councillors and generals who had come to pay their respects to her.

One of the visitors with a very complacent air took a document out of his pocket and, handing it to Olga Alexandrovna, said: 'I have brought you yesterday's

[1] The Grand Duke, brother of Nicholas i., is meant.—(*Translator's Note.*)

Imperial letter to Prince Pyotr Mihailovitch. Perhaps you have not yet read it.'

Whether she had heard him or not I do not know, but she took the paper, opened it, put on her spectacles and, frowning, read with great effort: 'Pri—nce Pyo—tr Mi—hailo—vitch!'

'What's this you have given me? It's not for me, is it?'

'I told you it's an Imperial letter.'

'Good heavens, my eyes are bad, I can't always read the letters addressed to me, and you make me read other people's letters.'

'Allow me, I'll read it . . . I didn't think.'

'You needn't; why trouble yourself for nothing? What have I to do with their correspondence? I am getting through my last days somehow, and my head is full of something very different.'

The gentleman smiled as people smile when they have made a blunder, and put the Imperial letter into his pocket.

Seeing that Olga Alexandrovna was in a bad humour, in a very warlike one, indeed, the visitors one after another took leave. When we were left alone she said to me: 'I asked you to come here to tell you that I have made a fool of myself in my old age. I gave you a promise, and I have done nothing; you know the peasants' proverb: "Don't step into the water till you know how deep it is." I spoke to Orlov about your case yesterday and you've nothing to expect. . . .'

At that moment a footman announced that Countess Orlov had arrived.

'Well, never mind, one of ourselves. I'll tell you the rest directly.'

The Countess, a beautiful woman, still in the bloom of her age, went up to kiss her hand and inquire how she was, to which Olga Alexandrovna answered that she felt very poorly, then mentioning my name, added, 'Come, sit down, sit down, my dear. How are the children—quite well?'

'Quite well.'

'Well, thank God—excuse me, I am just talking about what happened yesterday. Well, you see, I told her husband to speak to the Tsar about you, and ask what they are about with this nonsense. Not a bit of it! He wouldn't move hand or foot: "That's Benckendorf's affair," he told me. "I'll talk to him if you like, but as for reporting on it to the Tsar, I can't, he doesn't like it—besides, it isn't done!" "What is there," I said, "in talking to Benckendorf? I can do that myself. Besides, he is in his dotage; he doesn't know what he is doing; his head is full of actresses, though I should have thought his flirting days were over; some wretched little secretary gives him all sorts of secret reports and he hands them on. What would he do? No!" I said, "you had better not demean yourself asking favours of Benckendorf, the whole nasty business is his doing." "It is the rule with us," he said to me, and began telling me all about it. . . . Well, I saw that he was simply afraid to go to the Tsar. . . . "Whatever is he—a wild beast, or what, that you are afraid to approach him, though you see him half a dozen times a day?" I said, and turned away in disgust; it is no use talking to them. Look,' she added, pointing to Orlov's portrait. 'What a conquering hero he is there; yet he is afraid to say a word!'

I could not resist looking at Countess Orlov instead of at the portrait; her position was not very agreeable. She sat smiling, and sometimes glanced at me as though to say: 'Age has its privileges, the old lady is irritated,' but meeting my eyes, which did not assent, she pretended not to notice me. She did not enter into the conversation, and that was very wise of her. It would not have been easy to suppress Olga Alexandrovna, the old woman's cheeks were flushed, she would have given back more than she got. There was nothing for it but to lie low and wait for the storm to pass over one's head.

'Why, I suppose down there where you've been, in that Vologda, the clerks imagine Count Orlov is a man in favour, that he has power. . . . That's all nonsense. I'll be bound it is his subordinates who spread that rumour. None of them have any influence, they don't behave so as to have influence, and they are not on that footing. . . . You must forgive me for meddling in what isn't my business. Do you know what I advise you? What do you want to go to Novgorod for? You had better go to Odessa; it is farther away from them and almost like a foreign town, besides, if Vorontsov isn't corrupted, he is a man of a different stamp.'

Olga Alexandrovna's confidence in Vorontsov, who was at that time in Petersburg and came to see her every day, was not fully justified. He was willing to take me with him to Odessa *if* Benckendorf would give his consent.

Meanwhile the months passed, the winter was over, no one reminded me about going away. I was forgotten and I gave up being *sur le qui-vive*, particularly after the following meeting. Bolgovsky, the military governor of Vologda, was at that time in Petersburg; being a very intimate friend of my father, he was rather fond of me, and I was sometimes at his house. He had taken part in the killing of Paul, as a young officer in the Semyonovsky Regiment, and was afterwards mixed up in the obscure and unexplained Speransky affair in 1812. He was at that time a colonel in the army at the front. He was suddenly arrested, brought to Petersburg, and then sent to Siberia. Before he had time to reach his place, of exile Alexander pardoned him, and he returned to his regiment.

One day in the spring I went to see him; a general was sitting in a big easy-chair with his back towards the door so that I could not see his face, but only one silver epaulette.

'Let me introduce you,' said Bolgovsky, and then I recognised Dubbelt.

'I have long enjoyed the pleasure of Leonty Vassilyevitch's attention,' I said, smiling.

'When are you going to Novgorod?' he asked me.

'I thought I ought to ask you that.'

'Oh! not at all! I had no idea of reminding you. I simply asked the question. We have handed you over to Count Strogonov, and we are not trying to hurry you, as you see. Besides, with such a legitimate reason as your wife's illness. . . .'

He really was the politest of men!

At last, at the beginning of June, I received the Senate's decree, confirming my appointment as councillor in the Novgorod Provincial Government. Count Strogonov thought it was time for me to set off, and about the 1st of July I arrived in the 'City in the keeping of God and of Saint Sophia'—Novgorod—and settled on the bank of the Volhov, opposite the very barrow from which the Voltaireans of the twelfth century threw the wonder-working statue of Perun[1] into the river.

[1] Perun was the God of sky and of thunder, the chief God of the ancient Slavs.—(*Translator's Note.*)

Chapter 27

THE PROVINCIAL GOVERNMENT—I AM UNDER MY OWN SUPERVISION—THE DUHOBORS AND PAUL—THE PATERNAL RULE OF THE LANDOWNERS—COUNT ARAKTCHEYEV AND THE MILITARY SETTLEMENTS—A FEROCIOUS INVESTIGATION—RETIREMENT

BEFORE I went away Count Strogonov told me that the military governor of Novgorod, Elpidifor Antihovitch Zurov was in Petersburg, that he had spoken to him about my appointment, and advised me to call upon him. I found him a rather friendly and good-natured general, short, middle-aged, and of very military appearance. We talked for half an hour, he graciously escorted me to the door, and there we parted.

When I arrived in Novgorod I went to see him and the change of scene was amazing. In Petersburg the governor had been a visitor, here he was at home; he actually seemed to me to be taller in Novgorod. Without any provocation on my part, he thought fit to inform me that he would not permit councillors to give their opinions and put their views in writing, that it delayed business, and that, if anything were not right, they could talk it over, but that if it came to giving opinions, one or the other would have to take his discharge. I observed, smiling, that it was hard to frighten me with that prospect, since the sole object of my service was to get my discharge from it, and added that while bitter necessity forced me to serve in Novgorod I should probably have no occasion for giving my opinion.

This conversation was quite enough for both of us. As I went away I made up my mind to avoid getting into closer contact with him. So far as I could observe, the impression I made on the governor was much the same as that which he made upon me, *i.e.*, we disliked each other as much as we possibly could on so brief and superficial an acquaintance.

When I looked a little into the work of the provincial government I saw that my position was not only extremely disagreeable but very risky. Every councillor was responsible for his section and shared the responsibility for all the rest. To read the papers in all the sections was absolutely impossible, one had to sign them on trust. The governor, in accordance with his theory that a councillor should never give counsel, put his signature, contrary to the law and good sense, next after that of the councillor in whose section the case was. This was excellent for me personally; in this signature I found some guarantee, as he shared the responsibility, and because he often with a peculiar expression talked of his lofty honesty and Robespierre-like incorruptibility. As for the signatures of the other councillors they were very little comfort to me. They were hardened old clerks who by dozens of years of service had worked their way up to being councillors, and lived only by the service, that is, by bribes. It is useless to blame them for that; a councillor, I remember, received twelve thousand paper roubles a year; a man with a family could not possibly exist in comfort on that. When they perceived that I was not going to share with them in dividing the booty, nor going to plunder on my own account, they began to look upon me as an uninvited guest and dangerous witness. They did not become very intimate with me, especially when they had discovered that between the governor and me there existed an affection of a very lukewarm character. They stood by one another and watched over one another's interests, but they did not care what became of me. Moreover, my worthy colleagues were not afraid of getting into trouble, or of being fined or of having to refund even large sums of money, because they had nothing. They could risk it, and the more readily the more important the case was; whether the deficit was of five hundred roubles or of five hundred thousand did not matter to them. In case of a deficit, a fraction of their salary went to the reimbursement of the Treasury, and the repayment could be spread over two or three hundred years if the official lasted so long. Usually either the official died or the Tsar did, and then in the rejoicings at his accession the heir forgave the debts. Manifestoes remitting such debts were also published on occasions such as a Royal birth or coming of age; the officials reckoned upon them. In my case, on the contrary, they would have taken my money and the part of the family estate which my father had assigned to me.

If I could have relied on my own head-clerks, things would have been easier. I did a great deal to gain their attachment, treated them politely and helped them with money, but my efforts only resulted in their ceasing to obey me—they only stood in awe of the councillors who treated them as though they were schoolboys—and they took to coming to the office half-drunk. They were very poor men with no education and with no expectations. All the imaginative side of their lives was confined to wretched little taverns and strong drink. So I had to he on my guard in my own section too.

At first the governor gave me Section Four, in which all business dealing with contracts and money matters took place. I asked him to make a change, he would not, saying that he had no right to make a change without the consent of the other councillor. In the governor's presence I asked the councillor in charge of Section Two, he consented and we exchanged. The new section was less alluring; its work was concerned with passports, circulars of all sorts, cases of the abuse of power by landowners, of dissenters, forgers of counterfeit coin, and people under the supervision of the police.

Anything sillier and more absurd cannot be imagined;

I am certain that three-fourths of the people who read this will not believe it,[1] and yet it is the bare truth that I, as councillor of the provincial government, in control of the Second Section, every three months signed the report of the police-master upon myself as a man under police supervision. The police-master from politeness made no entry under the heading 'behaviour,' and under that of 'occupation' wrote: 'Engaged in the government service.' Such are the prodigies of absurdity that can be reached by having two or three police departments antagonistic to each other, official formalities instead of laws, and a field corporal's conception of discipline in place of a governing intelligence.

This absurdity reminds me of an incident that occurred at Tobolsk some years ago. The civil governor was on bad terms with the vice-governor, a quarrel was carried on on paper, they wrote each other all sorts of biting and sarcastic things in official form. The vice-governor was a ponderous pedant, a formalist, a good-natured specimen of the divinity student; he composed his malignant answers himself with immense labour and, of course, made this feat the object of his life. It happened that the governor went away to Petersburg for a time. The vice-governor took over his duties and in the character of governor received an impudent document from himself sent the day before; without hesitation he ordered the secretary to answer it, signed the answer and, receiving it as vice-governor, set to work again, racking his brains and scribbling an insulting letter to himself. He regarded this as a proof of his disinterested honesty.

For six months I was in harness in the provincial government. It was disagreeable and extremely tedious.

[1] This is so true that a German who has abused me a dozen times in the *Morning Advertiser* adduced as proof that I had never been exiled the fact that I had the post of councillor in the provincial government.

Every morning at eleven o'clock I put on my uniform, buckled on my civilian sword, and went to the office. At twelve o'clock the military governor arrived; taking no notice of the councillors, he walked straight to the corner and put down his sabre there. Then, looking out of the window and straightening his hair, he went towards his easy-chair and bowed to those present. Scarcely had the sergeant with fierce, grey moustaches that stood up at right angles to his lips solemnly opened the door and the clank of the sabre become audible in the office, when the councillors got up and remained standing with backs bent until the governor had bowed to them. One of my first actions, by way of protest, was taking no part in this collective rising and reverential expectation, but sitting quietly and only bowing when he bowed to us.

There were no great discussions or heated arguments; it rarely happened that a councillor asked the governor's opinion, still more rarely that the governor put some business question to the councillors. Before every one lay a heap of papers and every one signed his name, it was a signature factory.

Remembering Talleyrand's celebrated injunction, I did not try to distinguish myself by my zeal and attended to business only so far as was necessary to escape reprimand or avoid getting into trouble. But there were two classes of work in my section towards which I considered I had no right to take so superficial an attitude; these were matters relating to the dissenters and to the abuse of power by the landowners.

Dissenters are not consistently persecuted in Russia, but something comes over the Synod, or the Ministry of Home Affairs, all of a sudden, and they make a raid on some dissenting convent, or some community, plunder it, and then subside again. The dissenters usually have intelligent agents in Petersburg who warn them of coming danger; the others at once collect money, hide their

THE DUHOBORS AND PAUL

books and their ikons, stand drink to the orthodox priests, and stand drink to the orthodox police-captain and buy themselves off; with that, the matter rests for ten years or so.

In the reign of Catherine there were a great many Duhobors[1] in the Novgorod Province. Their leader, the old head of the posting drivers, in Zaitsevo, I think it was, enjoyed immense respect.

When Paul was on his way to his coronation at Moscow he ordered the old man to be summoned before him, probably with the idea of converting him. The Duhobors, like the Quakers, do not take off their caps, and the grey-headed old man went up to the Emperor of Gatchina with head covered. This was more than the Tsar could put up with. A petty and meticulous readiness to take offence was a particularly striking characteristic of Paul and is, indeed, of all his sons except Alexander; having a monstrous power in their hands, they have not even the wild beast's sense of power which keeps the big dog from attacking the little one.

'Before whom are you standing in your cap?' shouted Paul, puffing and showing every sign of frenzied rage: 'do you know me?'

'I do,' answered the dissenter calmly, 'you are Pavel Petrovitch.'

'Put him in chains: to penal servitude with him! to the mines!' the chivalrous Paul exclaimed.

The old man was seized and the Tsar ordered the village to be set fire to on four sides and the inhabitants to be sent to exile in Siberia. At the next station some one in attendance on the Tsar threw himself at his feet and said that he had ventured to delay the carrying out of the will of the Most High, and was waiting for him to repeat it. Paul was somewhat more sober and perceived that setting fire to villages and sending men to the mines

[1] I am not certain whether these dissenters were Duhobors.

without a trial was a queer way of recommending himself to the people. He commanded the Synod to investigate the peasants' case and ordered the old man to be incarcerated for life in the Spasso-Yefimyevsky Monastery; he thought that the orthodox monks would torment him worse than penal servitude; but he forgot that our monks are not merely good orthodox Christians but also men who are very fond of money and vodka; while the dissenters drink no vodka and are not sparing of their money.

The old man had the reputation of a saint among the Duhobors. They came from all parts of Russia to do homage to him and paid with gold for admission to see him. The old man sat in his cell, dressed all in white, and his friends draped the walls and the ceiling with linen. After his death they gained permission to bury his body with his kindred and carried him in triumph upon their shoulders from Vladimir to the province of Novgorod. Only the Duhobors know where he is buried. They are persuaded that he had the gift of working miracles in his lifetime and that his body is untouched by decay.

I heard all this partly from the governor of Vladimir, I. E. Kuruta, partly from the post-drivers in Novgorod, and partly from a lay-brother in the Spasso-Yefimyevsky Monastery. Now there are no more political prisoners in the monastery, though the prison is full of priests and church servants of all kinds, disobedient sons of whom their parents have complained, and so on. The archimandrite, a tall, broad-shouldered man in a fur cap, showed us the prison yard. When he went in, a non-commissioned officer with a gun went up to him and reported: 'I have the honour to report to your Reverence that all is well in the prison and that the prisoners are so many.' The archimandrite in answer gave him his blessing—what a mix-up!

RULE OF THE LANDOWNERS

The business relating to the dissenters was of such a nature that it was best not to raise the subject again. I looked through the documents referring to them and left them in peace. . . . On the other hand, those relating to the abuse of the landowners' power needed a thorough overhauling. I did all I could and scored a few victories in that boggy path; set one young girl free from persecution and put one naval officer under arrest. These I believe were the only things I can boast of in my official career.

A certain lady was keeping a servant-girl in her house without any documentary evidence of ownership; the girl petitioned that her claims to freedom should be inquired into. My predecessor had very sagaciously thought fit to leave her until her case was decided in complete bondage with the lady who claimed her. I had to sign the documents; I turned to the governor and observed that the girl would not be in a very enviable position in her mistress's house after lodging this petition.

'What's to be done with her?'

'Keep her in the police-station.'

'At whose expense?'

'At the expense of the lady, if the case is decided against her.'

'And if it is not?'

Luckily at that moment the provincial prosecutor came in. A prosecutor from his social position, from his official relations, from the very buttons on his uniform, is bound to be an enemy of the governor, or at least to thwart him in everything. I purposely continued the conversation in his presence. The governor began to get angry and said that the whole question was not worth wasting a couple of words on. The prosecutor cared not a straw what became of the girl or how she was treated, but he immediately took my side and advanced a dozen different points from the code of laws in support of it. The governor, who in reality cared as little, said to me, smiling ironically, that it was much the same whether she went to her mistress or to the prison.

'Of course she will be better off in prison,' I observed.

'It will be more consistent with the intention expressed in the code,' observed the prosecutor.

'Let it be as you like,' the governor said, laughing more than ever. 'You've done a service to your protegée: when she has been in prison for a few months she will thank you for it.'

I did not continue the argument, my object was to save the girl from domestic persecution; I remember that two months later she was released and received her legal freedom.

Among the unsettled questions in my department there was a complicated correspondence lasting over several years, concerning the acts of violence of a retired naval officer called Strugovshtchikov and his various misdeeds in the management of his estate. The question was raised on the petition of his mother, afterwards the peasants made complaints. He had come to some arrangement with his mother, and himself charged the peasants with intending to kill him, without, however, adducing any serious proofs. Meanwhile it was clear from the evidence of his mother and his house-serfs that the man was guilty of all sorts of lawless violence. The business had been sleeping the sleep of the just for more than a year; it is always possible to drag a case out with inquiries and unnecessary correspondence and then, recording it settled, to file it on the archives of the office. A recommendation had to be made to the Senate that he should be put under restraint, but for this purpose the assent of the Marshal of Nobility was necessary. As a rule, the Marshal of Nobility evades giving it, being disinclined to lose a vote. It rested entirely with me whether

THE NAVAL OFFICER'S CASE

the case was pushed forward, but a *coup de grâce* from the marshal was essential.

The marshal of the Novgorod Province, a nobleman with a Vladimir medal who had served in the militia in 1812, tried to show that he was a well-read man when he met me, by talking in the bookish language of the period before Karamzin; on one occasion, pointing to a monument which the nobility of Novgorod had raised *to itself* in recognition of its patriotism in 1812, he alluded with feeling to the severe and sacred character of a marshal's duties, and the flattering honour of so weighty a trust.

All that was to the good. The marshal came to the office in connection with certifying the insanity of some church servitor; after all the presidents of all the courts had exhausted their whole store of foolish questions, from which the lunatic might well have concluded that they too were a little deranged, and had finally certified him as insane, I drew the marshal aside and described the case to him. The marshal shrugged his shoulders, assumed an air of horror and indignation, and ended by referring to the naval officer as an arrant scoundrel 'who cast a black shadow on the stainless reputation of the nobility of Novgorod.'

'You would, of course,' said I, 'give us the same answer in writing, if we appealed to you?'

The marshal, caught unawares, promised to answer conscientiously, adding that 'honour and uprightness were the invariable attributes of the nobility of Russia.'

Though I had some doubts of the invariability of those attributes, I pushed the case forward and the marshal kept his word. The case was brought before the Senate, and I well remember the sweet moment when the decree of the Senate reached my section, appointing trustees to superintend the naval officer's estate and putting him under the supervision of the police. The naval officer was persuaded that the case had been shelved, and, thunderstruck at the decree, came to Novgorod. He was at once told how it had happened; the infuriated officer threatened to fall upon me from behind a corner, to engage ruffians and lie in wait, but, being unaccustomed to strategy on land, quietly disappeared from sight in some distant town.

Unfortunately the 'attributes' of brutality, debauchery, and violence with house-serfs and peasants appear to be more 'invariable' than those of 'honour and uprightness' among the nobility of Russia. Of course there is a small group of cultured landowners who are not knocking their servants about from morning to night, are not thrashing them every day, but even among them there are 'Pyenotchkins'[1]; the rest have not yet advanced beyond the stage of 'Saltytchiha'[2] and the American planters.

Rummaging about, I found the correspondence of the provincial government of Pskov concerning a certain Madame Yaryzhkin. She flogged two of her maids to death, was tried on account of a third, and was almost completely acquitted by the Criminal Court, who based their verdict among other things on the fact that the third one did not die. This woman invented the most surprising punishments, beating with a flat iron, with gnarled sticks, or with a washing bat.

I do not know what the girl in question had done, but her mistress surpassed herself. She made the girl kneel down on some boards into which nails had been driven; in this position she beat her about the back and the head

[1] The landowner in 'The Agent,' one of Turgenev's 'Sportsman's Sketches.'
[2] Saltytchiha was a lady notorious in the reign of Catherine for her cruelty to her serfs. She was eventually brought to justice.—(*Translator's Notes.*)

with a washing bat, and when she was exhausted, called the coachman to take her place; luckily he was not at hand and she went out to find him, while the girl, half frantic with pain and covered with blood, rushed out into the street with nothing on but her smock and ran to the police-station. The police-inspector took her evidence and the case went its regular course. The police and the department of justice were busy over it for a year; finally the court, obviously bribed, very sagaciously decided to call the lady's husband and to admonish him to restrain his wife from such punishments, while, leaving her under suspicion of having brought about the death of two servants, they forced her to sign an undertaking not to punish the maids for the future. On this understanding the unfortunate girl, who had been kept somewhere else while the case was going on, was handed over to her mistress again.

The girl, in terror of the future, began writing one petition after another; the matter reached the ears of the Tsar; he ordered it to be investigated, and sent an official from Petersburg. Probably the Yaryzhkins' means were not equal to bribing the Petersburg gendarmes and officials from the various Ministries, and the case took a different turn. The lady was exiled to Siberia, her husband was put under restraint. All the members of the Criminal Court were sent for trial; how their trial ended I don't know.

In another place[1] I have told the story of the man flogged to death by Prince Trubetskoy and of the *Kammerherr* Bazilevsky who was thrashed by his own servants. I will add one more story of a lady.

A serf-girl in the family of a colonel of gendarmes at Penza was carrying a kettle full of boiling water. Her mistress's child ran against the servant, who spilt the boiling water, and the child was scalded. The mistress

[1] *Property in Serfs.*

to suit the punishment to the offence ordered the servant's child to be brought and scalded its hand from the samovar. . . .

Pantchulidzev, the governor, hearing of this monstrous incident, expressed his heartfelt regret that he was in somewhat strained relations with the colonel of the gendarmes and consequently felt it improper to take proceedings which might seem to be instigated by personal motives!

And then sensitive hearts wonder at the peasants murdering their landowners with their whole families, or at the soldiers of the military settlement of Staraya Russa massacring all the Russian Germans and all the German Russians.

In the servants 'quarters and in the maids' rooms, in the villages and the police-cells, perfect martyrologies of terrible crimes lie buried; the memory of them haunts the soul and in course of generations matures into bloody and merciless vengeance *which it is easy to prevent* now, but it will hardly be possible to stop when it has begun.

Staraya Russa, the military settlements! Terrible words! Can it be that history (bought beforehand by Araktcheyev's bribe[1]) will never pull away the shroud under which the government has concealed the series of crimes coldly and systematically perpetrated in establishing the military settlements. There have been plenty of horrors everywhere, but in that case they were marked by the peculiar imprint of Petersburg and Gatchina, of German and Tatar influence. The beating with sticks and scourging with lashes for the insubordinate went on for months together . . . the blood was never dry on the floors of the rural offices . . . every crime

[1] Araktcheyev left, I believe, a hundred thousand roubles to be paid a hundred years later, together with the accumulated interest, to the man who should write the best history of the reign of Alexander 1.

that may be committed by the people against their torturers on that tract of land is justified beforehand.

The Mongolian side of the Moscow period which distorted the Slav character of the Russians, the inhumanity of army discipline which distorted the Petersburg period, are embodied in the full perfection of their hideousness in Count Araktcheyev. Araktcheyev was undoubtedly one of the most loathsome figures that rose to the surface of the Russian government after Peter the Great. That 'flunkey of a crowned soldier,' as Pushkin said of him, was the model of an ideal corporal as seen in the dreams of the father of Frederick the Second; he was made up of inhuman devotion, mechanical accuracy, the exactitude of a chronometer, routine and energy, a complete lack of feeling, as much intelligence as was necessary to carry out orders, and enough ambition, spite, and envy to prefer power to money. Such men are a real treasure to Tsars. Only the petty resentment of Nicholas can explain the fact that he made no use of Araktcheyev, but only employed his underlings.

Paul discovered Araktcheyev through sympathy. So long as Alexander's sense of shame lasted he kept him at some distance; but, carried away by the family passion for discipline and drill, he entrusted him with the secretariat of the army. Of the victories of this general of artillery we have heard little[1]; for the most part he performed civilian duties in. the military service, his battles were fought on the soldiers' backs, his enemies were brought him in chains, they were already conquered. In the latter years of Alexander 1. Araktcheyev governed all Russia. He interfered in everything, he had a blank

[1] Araktcheyev was a pitiful coward, as Count Toll tells us in his memoirs, and the Secretary of State Martchenko in a little story of the Fourteenth of December published in the *Polar Star*. I have heard that he was in hiding during the Staraya Russa rising, and was in deadly terror of Reihel the general of Engineers.

cheque giving him a right to everything. As Alexander grew feebler and sank into gloomy melancholy, he hesitated a little between Prince A. N. Golitsyn and Araktcheyev and in the end naturally inclined towards the latter.

At the time of Alexander's Taganrog visit the house-serfs on Araktcheyev's estate in Gruzino killed the Count's mistress; this murder gave rise to the investigation of which to this day, *i.e.*, seventeen years later, the officials and inhabitants of Novgorod speak with horror. The mistress of Araktcheyev, an old man of sixty, was one of his serf-girls; she oppressed the servants, quarrelled and told tales, while the Count thrashed them according to the stories she brought him. When their patience was completely exhausted, the cook killed her. The crime was so cleverly carried out that no clue to the guilty party could be found.

But a guilty party was essential for the vengeance of the doting old man; he laid aside the affairs of the Empire and galloped off to Gruzino. In the midst of tortures and blood, in the midst of groans and dying shrieks, Araktcheyev, with the blood-stained kerchief which had been taken from his mistress's body tied round him, wrote touching letters to Alexander, and Alexander replied: 'Come and find rest from your unhappiness in the bosom of your friend.' Alexander's doctor must have been right when he declared that the Emperor had water on the brain before his death.

But the guilty parties were not discovered. The Russian has a wonderful power of holding his tongue.

Then, utterly infuriated, Araktcheyev made his appearance in Novgorod, where a crowd of victims was brought. With his face yellow and livid, with frenzied eyes, and still wearing the blood-stained kerchief, he began a new investigation and the affair began to assume monstrous proportions. Eighty persons were seized

A FEROCIOUS INVESTIGATION

again, people were arrested in the town on the strength of one word, on the slightest suspicion, for a remote rumour. Persons passing through the town were seized and flung into prison. Merchants and clerks were kept waiting for weeks to be questioned. . . . The inhabitants hid in their houses and were afraid to go out into the streets; no one dared to refer to the case.

Kleinmihel, who served under Araktcheyev, took part in this investigation. . . .

The governor transformed his house into a torture chamber; people were tortured near his study from morning till night. The police-captain of Staraya Russa, a man accustomed to horrors, broke down at last, and when he was ordered to question under the rods a young woman who was several months gone with child he was not equal to the task. He went in to the governor (it took place before old Popov, who told me about it) and told him that the woman could not be flogged, that it was directly contrary to the law; the governor leapt up from his seat and, mad with fury, rushed to the police-captain brandishing his fist: 'I order you to be arrested at once, I will have you brought to trial, you are a traitor.' The police-captain was arrested and resigned his commission; I am truly sorry I do not know his surname, but may his previous sins be forgiven him for the sake of that minute—I say it in all seriousness—of heroism; in dealing with these ruffians it was no trifling matter to show human feeling.

The woman was put to the torture, she knew nothing about the crime . . . but she died.

And Alexander 'of blessed memory' died too. Not knowing what was coming, these monsters made one last effort, and succeeded in finding the guilty party; he, of course, was condemned to the knout. In the midst of this judicial triumph came a command from Nicholas putting them all under arrest and stopping the whole case.

Orders were given that the governor[1] should be tried by the Senate . . . even by them he could not be acquitted. Nicholas issued a gracious manifesto remitting sentences after his coronation. The friends of Pestel and Muravyov were not included under it, but this scoundrel was. Two or three years later, he was condemned at Tambov for the abuse of power on his own property.

At the beginning of the year 1842 I was hopelessly weary of provincial government and was trying to invent an excuse to get out of it. While I was hesitating between one means and another, a quite external chance decided for me.

One cold, winter morning as I reached the office I found a peasant woman about thirty standing in the vestibule; seeing me in uniform, she fell on her knees before me and bursting into tears besought my protection. Her master, Mussin-Pushkin, was sending her with her husband to a settlement, while their son, a boy of ten, was to remain behind; she implored permission to take the child with her. While she was telling me this, the military governor came in; I motioned her towards him and repeated her petition. The governor explained to her that children of ten or over may be kept by the landowners. The mother, not understanding the stupid law, went on entreating him; he was bored, while the woman, sobbing, clutched at his legs, and, roughly pushing her away, he said: 'What a fool you are, don't I tell you in plain Russian that I can do nothing? Why do you persist?' After that he went with a firm and resolute step to the corner, where he put down his sabre.

And I went too. . . I had had enough. . . . Did not that woman take me for one of *them*? It was high time to end the farce.

'Are you unwell?' asked a councillor called Hlopin,

[1] I am extremely sorry that I have forgotten the Christian name of the worthy gentleman. I remember his surname was Zherebtsov.

who had been transferred from Siberia for some shortcoming or other.

'I am ill,' I answered, and I got up, made my bows and went out. The same day I sent in a declaration that I was ill, and never set foot again in the office of the provincial government. Then I asked for my discharge on the ground 'of illness.' The Senate gave me my discharge accompanying it with promotion to the grade of Court Councillor; but Benckendorf at the same time informed the governor that I was forbidden to visit Petersburg or Moscow and required to live in Novgorod.

When Ogaryov returned from his first tour abroad, he did his utmost in Petersburg to procure permission for us to return to Moscow. I had little faith in the success of such a patron and was fearfully bored in the wretched little town with the great historical name. Meanwhile Ogaryov managed our business for us. On the 1st of July 1842 the Empress, on the occasion of some family festivity, besought the Tsar's permission for me to live in Moscow in consideration of my wife's illness and her desire to return there. Nicholas gave his consent, and three days later my wife received from Benckendorf a letter in which he informed her that I was permitted to accompany her to Moscow in consequence of the Tsarina's intervention. He concluded the letter with the agreeable announcement that I should remain under police supervision there also.

I felt no regret at leaving Novgorod and made haste to get away as soon as possible. Before I left it, however, almost the only agreeable incident of my sojourn there occurred.

I had no money! I did not want to wait for a remittance from Moscow and so I commissioned Matvey to try and borrow fifteen hundred roubles for me. Within an hour Matvey returned with an innkeeper called Gibin, whom I knew, and at whose hotel I had stayed for a week.

Gibin, a stout merchant with a good-natured expression, handed me a roll of notes with a bow.

'What rate of interest do you ask?' I inquired.

'Well, you see,' answered Gibin, 'I am not a money-lender and I won't take interest, but since I heard from Matvey Savelyevitch that you are in want of money for a month or two, and we are very much pleased with you, and thank God have the money to spare, I have brought it along.'

I thanked him and asked him if he would like a simple receipt for the money or an I O U, but to this, too, Gibin answered: 'That is quite unnecessary, I trust your word more than a piece of stamped paper.'

'Upon my word, but I may die you know.'

'Well then, in my distress at your decease I shouldn't worry much about the loss of the money.'

I was touched and pressed his hand warmly instead of giving him a receipt. Gibin embraced me in the Russian fashion and said: 'We see it all of course, we know you were not serving of your own will and didn't behave yourself like the others, God forgive them, but stood up for us and for the ignorant people, so I am glad of a chance to do you a good turn too.'

As we were driving out of the town late in the evening our driver pulled up the horses at the inn and Gibin gave me a cake the size of a cart-wheel as provision for the journey....

That was my 'medal for good service.'

Chapter 28

GRÜBELEI—MOSCOW AFTER EXILE—POKROVSKOE—
THE DEATH OF MATVEY—FATHER IOANN

OUR life in Novgorod had not been a happy one. I had gone there not in a spirit of self-sacrifice and determination, but with my heart full of annoyance and exasperation. This second exile, with the vulgarity of its attendant circumstances, irritated more than it distressed me; it was not enough of a calamity to rouse the spirit, but was merely a worry, without the interest of novelty or the stimulus of danger. The mere sight of the provincial government office with its Elpidifor Antihovitch Zurov, its councillor Hlopin, and its vice-governor Pimen Arapov, was enough to poison my existence.

I was ill-humoured; Natalie sank into melancholy. Her sensitive nature, accustomed from childhood to tears and sadness, gave way again to brooding depression. She dwelt on painful ideas and readily let slip everything bright and joyful. Life was becoming more complex; there were more chords in it and with them more anxiety. After Sasha's illness had come the shock of the secret police, her premature confinement, and the loss of the baby. The death of a baby is scarcely felt by the father, anxiety over the mother makes him almost forget the little creature that has flitted away almost before it had time to cry and take the breast. But to the mother the new-born child is something close and familiar already; for months she has been *feeling* him; there has been a physical, chemical, nervous connection between them; moreover, the baby makes up to the mother for the burden of pregnancy, for the sufferings of childbirth; without him her agonies are motiveless and resented, without him the unwanted milk affects the brain.

After Natalie's death. I found among her papers a note which I had quite forgotten. It consisted of a few lines I had written an hour or two before Sasha's birth. It was a prayer, a blessing, a dedication of the unborn creature to 'the service of humanity,' his 'consecration to the path of hardship.'

On the other side was written in Natalie's hand: '*January* 1, 1841.—Yesterday Alexandr gave me this; he could not have made me a better present, those lines at once called up the whole picture of our three years of unbroken, boundless happiness, resting on love alone. So we have passed into a new year; whatever awaits us in it, I bow my head and say for both of us, Thy Will be done! We welcomed the New Year at home, in solitude, only A. L. Vitberg was with us. Little Alexandr was missing from our party, he was so sound asleep, neither past nor future exists for him yet. Sleep, my angel, free from care, I pray for you—and for you too, my child unborn, whom I love with all a mother's love. Your movements, your tremors mean so much to my heart, and may your coming into the world be glad and blessed!'

But the mother's hope was not fulfilled: the babe was sentenced by Nicholas. The deadly hand of the Russian autocrat intervened here also—and here also destroyed a life!

The baby's death left its ma rkupon her soul.

With sadness and rankling resentment we went to Novgorod.

The *truth* of that period, as it was seen at the time, without the artificial perspective given by distance, without the cooling effect of years, and the different light thrown on it by a series of other events is preserved in a diary of the period. I had meant to keep a diary, had begun it many times, but had never kept it up. On my birthday in Novgorod Natalie gave me a white book in which I sometimes wrote down what was in my heart, or my head.

This book has been preserved. On the first page Natalie wrote: 'May all the pages of this book, and of all your life be bright and joyous!'

Three years later she added on the last page: 'In 1842 I hoped that all the pages of your diary might be bright and untroubled; three years have passed since then, and looking back I do not regret that my hope has not been fulfilled; both joy and suffering are essential for a full life, and you will find peace in my love, in the love with which my whole being, my whole life is filled. Peace to the past and a blessing for the future! March 25th, 1845, Moscow.'

This was what was written on the 4th of April 1842:

'Oh Lord, what unbearable misery! Is it weakness or have I a right to feel it? Must I reckon my life finished? Is all my readiness for work, all my craving for self-expression to be crushed, till my yearnings are stifled and I am ready for a life of emptiness? It might be possible to exist with no object but one's own inner development, but the same awful depression comes over me in the midst of study. I must express myself—perhaps from the same necessity as the grasshopper churrs . . . and for years to come I have to drag this weight.'

And as though frightened at my own words, I followed this with Goethe's lines:—

> 'Gut verloren—etwas verloren,
> Ehre verloren—viel verloren,
> Musst Ruhm gewinnen,
> Da werden die Leute sich anders besinnen.
> Mut verloren—alles verloren,
> Da ware es besser nicht geboren';

and later:—

'My shoulders are breaking but still they will bear!'

'Will those who come after us understand, will they appreciate all the horror, all the tragic side of our existence? And meanwhile our sufferings are the soil from which their happiness will develop; will they understand what makes us slothful, makes us seek all sorts of pleasure, drink and so on? Why do we not lift our hands to great tasks, why at the moment of rapture do we not forget our despondency? Let them stop with musing and sadness before the stones under which we slumber: we have deserved their mournful thoughts!

'I cannot go on for long in my position, I shall be stifled—and I don't care how I get out of it, if only I get out of it. I have written to Dubbelt (I asked him to try and get leave for me to return to Moscow). Writing that letter made me ill, *on se sent flétri*. I expect it is what prostitutes feel when first they begin selling themselves.'[1]

And it was just this vexation, this impatient cry of revolt, this fretting for free activity, this feeling of fetters on the limbs that Natalie misunderstood.

Often I found her with tear-stained eyes by Sasha's cot; she assured me that it was nothing but nerves, that I had better not notice it, not question her.... I believed her.

One evening I returned home late; she was in bed when I went in, I was feeling sick at heart. F——had asked me to go and see him in order to tell me that he Suspected that one of our common acquaintances was in relations with the police. That sort of thing usually sends a pang to the heart, not so much from the possible danger as from the feeling of moral repulsion.

I walked up and down the room in silence, turning over what I had just heard, when all at once I fancied that Natalie was weeping; I took her handkerchief, it was soaked with tears.

'What is it?' I asked, alarmed and distressed.

---

[1] These extracts are inserted here by the author in a slightly altered form.— *Note to Russian edition*.

She took my hand and in a voice full of tears said:

'My dear, I will tell you the truth; perhaps it is self-love, egoism, madness, but I feel, I see, that I cannot distract your mind, you are bored,—I understand it, I don't blame you, but it hurts me, it hurts me, and I cry. I know that you love me, that you are sorry for me, but you don't know what makes you depressed, what gives you that feeling of emptiness, you feel the poverty of your life—and, indeed, what can I do for you?'

I was like a man suddenly roused in the middle of the night and told something terrible before he is quite awake: he is frightened and trembling, though he doesn't yet understand what is wrong. I was so completely at peace, so sure of our deep, perfect love, that I never spoke about it; it was the great assumption upon which all our life rested; a serene consciousness, a boundless conviction of it excluding doubt, even distrust of myself, was the fundamental basis of my happiness. Peace, tranquillity, the aesthetic side of life, all that—as before our meeting in the graveyard on the 9th of May 1838, as at the beginning of our life in Vladimir—rested on her, on her, on her!

My deep distress and my astonishment at first dissipated these clouds, but in a month or two they began to return. I soothed and comforted her; she smiled herself at the dark phantoms, and again the sunshine brightened our corner; but as soon as I had forgotten them they raised their heads again for no reason whatever, and when they had passed I began to be afraid of their return.

Such was the state of mind in which in July 1842 we moved to Moscow.

Moscow life, at first too full of distractions, could have no beneficial nor soothing effect. Far from helping her at that time I gave only too much cause for her *Grübelei* to grow deeper and more intense.[1]

---

[1] Here Herzen describes how, returning late one evening after a festive supper party with his friends, he was tempted by a maid-

. . . . . .

Natalie became absorbed in melancholy, more and more her faith in me wavered, her idol was shattered. It was a crisis, the painful transition from youth to maturity. She could not get over the thoughts that fretted her heart, she was ill, and grew thin—while terrified and reproaching myself I stood beside her and saw that I had no longer the boundless power with which I had once been able to exorcise the spirits of gloom. It wounded me to see it, and I was immensely sorry for her.

They say that children grow in illness; in this spiritual illness which brought her to the verge of consumption she made colossal strides in growth. From the slanting rays and glow of dawn she passed by this sorrowful path into the clear bright light of midday. Her health was equal to the strain and that was all that mattered. Without losing one iota of her womanliness she developed intellectually with extraordinary boldness and depth. Gently and with a smile of self-sacrifice she left behind what was lost beyond recall, without sentimental repining, without a sense of personal grievance, and on the other hand without conceited satisfaction.

It was not in a book, nor through a book, that she found her freedom, but through living and clearness of vision. Unimportant incidents, bitter experiences, which for many would have passed without a trace, left a deep imprint on her soul and were enough to arouse her mind to immense activity. A slight hint was sufficient for her to pass from one deduction to another, till she reached that fearless grasp of the truth which is a heavy burden even for a man to bear. Mournfully she parted from her shrine in which had stood so many holy things, bathed in, tears of grief and joy; she left them without blushing

servant, who, half undressed, opened the door to him. This transgression came to the knowledge of Natalya Alexandrovna.— *Note to Russian edition.*

as big girls blush at the sight of their doll of yesterday. She did not turn away from them, she let them go with anguish, knowing that she would be the poorer, the more defenceless for the loss, that the soft light of the glimmering ikon lamp would be followed by the grey dawn, that she must make friends with harsh, callous forces, deaf to the murmur of prayer, deaf to the hopes of immortality. She gently put them from her bosom like a dead child, and gently laid them in the grave, respecting in them her past life, their poetry and the comfort they had given at some moments. Even later she disliked touching them coldly, just as we avoid wantonly stepping on a grave.

With this intense mental activity, with this shattering and rebuilding of all her convictions, she naturally needed rest and solitude.

We went away to my father's estate near Moscow.

And as soon as we found ourselves alone surrounded by trees and fields, we breathed freely and looked clearly at life again. We stayed in the country until late autumn. From time to time we had visitors from Moscow. Ketscher stayed a month with us, all our friends arrived for the 26th of August, Natalie's nameday; then again peace and stillness and the woods and the fields—and no one but ourselves.

Pokrovskoe, standing solitary, surrounded by immense forest estates, was of quite a different and much more serious character than Vassilyevskoe, lying so sunnily with its villages on the bank of the Moskva. This difference was even noticeable in the peasants. The Pokrovskoe peasants, hemmed in by woods, were less like people living within reach of Moscow than those of Vassilyevskoe, although as a fact they were fifteen miles nearer the city. They were quieter, more unsophisticated, and hung together very closely. My father moved a wealthy family of peasants from Vassilyevskoe to Pokrovskoe, but the peasants of the latter place never considered the family as belonging to their village, but always called them 'the settlers.'

With Pokrovskoe, too, I had been closely connected throughout my childhood; I used to stay there when I was too young to remember, and from the year 1821 we used to spend a few days there almost every summer on our way to and from Vassilyevskoe. There lived old Kashentsov, paralysed and in disgrace since 1813, who dreamed of seeing his master, the Senator, in all his finery and regalia; there lived—and later in the cholera of 1831 died—the venerable grey-headed corpulent village elder, Vassily Yakovlyev, whom I remembered at all his stages with his beard first dark brown and afterwards quite grey; there lived my foster-brother Nikifor, who prided himself on the fact that he had for my benefit been robbed of the milk of his mother, who died later on in a madhouse. . . .

The little village of some twenty or twenty-five homesteads stood at some distance from our rather large house. On one side lay a semicircular meadow that had been cleared and fenced in, on the other there was a view of the river, dammed up for the sake of a mill which they had intended to build fifteen years before, and of an ancient wooden church all on the slant, which my uncle the Senator and my father, who owned the estate in common, had also been intending to repair for the last fifteen years.

The house which had been built by the Senator was a very good one; there were lofty rooms, big windows, and on both sides porches that were like verandahs. It was built of choice thick logs, not covered with anything either outside or in, but with the crevices stuffed up with tow and moss. The walls smelt of resin, which oozed out here and there like drops of amber. Before the house there was a small field and beyond that began a dark forest of large trees, through which ran a track to Zvenigorod; in the other direction a side-path ran like a thin, dusty ribbon by the village and was lost in the rye, coming out through the Maikovsky factory and going on to the Mozhaisk road. There was the forest stillness and the forest sound, the incessant buzzing of flies, bees, and insects, . . . and the fragrance . . . that fragrance of grass and forest, made up of the scents of plants, of leaves, but not of flowers . . . which I have so eagerly sought in Italy and in England, both in spring and in hot summer, but scarcely ever found. Sometimes one gets a whiff of it in the hay-field, or when the sirocco is blowing, or before a storm . . . and it brings back the little place before the house, on which, to the great distress of the village elder and the house-serfs, I would not have the grass clipped close; on the grass a boy of three, rolling in the clover and the dandelions among the grasshoppers and ladybirds, and we ourselves and youth and friendship!

The sun has set, it is still very warm, we don't want to go home, we still sit on the grass. Ketscher sorts out the mushrooms and scolds me for no reason. Can that be the tinkle of a bell? Is it something for us? Perhaps— it is Saturday. 'It must be the police-captain going off somewhere,' says Ketscher, suspecting that it is not. The troika rattles through the village, rumbles over the bridge, disappears behind a knoll, and the only road is towards us. While we run to meet it, it drives up to the house; Shtchepkin has already rolled off it like an avalanche, smiling, kissing his hand, and roaring with laughter, while Byelinsky, cursing the distance from Pokrovskoe and the way that Russian carts and Russian roads are made, is still alighting and stretching himself, and already Ketscher is scolding them: 'What devil has brought you at eight o'clock in the evening, couldn't you have come sooner, it is all that perverse Byelinsky, he can't, get up early, what were you thinking about?'

'Why, he is more of a savage than ever,' says Byelinsky, 'and what a head of hair he has grown! You would do for the moving forest in *Macbeth*, Ketscher. Wait a bit, don't exhaust all your abuse, there are villains coming later still.'

Another troika is already turning into the yard, Granovsky and Yevgeny Korsh.

'Have you come to stay long?'

'Two days.'

'Splendid!' and Ketscher himself is so pleased that he greets them almost as Tarass Bulba greeted his sons.

Yes, that was one of the happy periods of our life. Of past storms nothing remained but a trace of vanishing cloud; at home among our friends there was perfect harmony.

But a senseless fatality very nearly spoilt it all.

One evening Matvey, showing Sasha something on the dam where we too were standing, slipped and fell into the water on the shallow side. Sasha was terrified, he rushed up to him as he got out, held him tight in his little arms and repeated tearfully: 'Don't go there, you'll be drowned!' No one imagined that the child's embrace was the last Matvey would receive and that Sasha's words were indeed a terrible prophecy.

Drenched and covered with mud, Matvey went to bed and we never saw him again.

At seven o'clock next morning I was standing on the verandah when I heard voices growing louder and louder, confused screams, and then peasants came into sight running at full speed. 'What has happened?' 'Oh, something dreadful,' they answered, 'your man is drowning . . . they pulled one out in time but they can't get the other.' I rushed to the river, the village elder was there with his boots off and his breeches tucked up; two peasants were throwing a net from a canoe. Five minutes later they shouted: 'We have got him, we

DEATH OF MATVEY

have got him!' and dragged Matvey's dead body to the bank. The young man, so blooming, handsome, and rosy-cheeked, lay with wide-open eyes in which there was no trace of life, and already the lower part of his face was beginning to swell. The village elder laid the body on the bank, sternly bade the peasants not to touch it, threw a coat over it, set a man to watch it, and sent for the rural police. . . .

When I returned home I met Natalie; she knew already what had happened and ran to me sobbing.

We were sorry, very sorry to lose Matvey. He had played so intimate a part in our little family, he was so closely bound up with all the chief events of its last five years, and he loved us so truly that we could not easily get over his loss.

'Perhaps,' I wrote at the time, 'death may have been a blessing for him, life had terrible blows in store for him and he had no way of avoiding them. But it is dreadful to witness such a way of escape from the future. He had developed under my influence, but in too great a hurry; his development was a worry to him through its one-sidedness.'

The melancholy side of Matvey's life lay precisely in the gulf which the haphazard character of his education had brought with it, and in his incapacity for filling it up, his lack of strength of will for overcoming it. In him generous feelings and a tender heart were stronger than intellect or character. Rapidly, like a woman, he assimilated a great deal, especially of our outlook on life; but he was incapable of going humbly back to the first elements, to the ABC, and filling in the blanks and empty places by study. He did not like his calling and, indeed, he could not like it. Social inequality is nowhere apparent in so degrading and humiliating a form as in the relations between master and servant. Rothschild in the street is far more on an equality with the beggar who stands with a broom and sweeps away the mud before him than with his valet in silk stockings and white gloves.

The complaints made of servants, which we hear every day, are quite as just as the servants' complaints against their masters, and that not because either class has grown worse than it was, but because they are growing more and more conscious of their mutual relation. It is oppressive to the servant and corrupting to the master.

We are so accustomed to our aristocratic attitude to servants that we do not notice it at all. How many good-natured and sensitive young ladies there are in the world, ready to weep over a frozen puppy and to give their last farthing to a beggar, who will yet drive through severe frost to a fancy dress ball for the benefit of the destitute in Syria, or a concert given for burnt-out villagers in Abyssinia, and will ask their mother to stay for one more quadrille without a thought of the little postillion boy on horseback with the blood freezing in his veins in the night frost.

The attitude of masters to their servants is loathsome. The workman at any rate knows what his job is; he does something; he can do it more quickly and then be free, besides he can dream of becoming his own master. The servant can never finish his work, he is like a squirrel in a wheel; life makes dirt, it makes dirt incessantly, and the servant is incessantly cleaning up after it. He is obliged to take upon himself all the petty discomforts of life, all its dirty and tedious aspects. He is put into a livery to show he is not his own man but some one else's. He waits upon a man who is twice as strong and healthy as himself, he must step into the mud that the other may go dry-shod, he must be cold that the other may be warm.

Rothschild does not make the starving Irishman look on at his feasts of Lucullus, he does not send him to pour out Clos-de-Vougeot for twenty persons, with the unspoken understanding that if he pours out a glass for himself he will be turned away as a thief. The Irish peasant is luckier too than the indoor slave because he does not know what soft beds and fragrant wines are like.

Matvey was fifteen when he came to me from Sonnenberg, with him I lived in exile and with him in Vladimir; he was our servant at the time when we were without money. He looked after Sasha like a nurse, and had a boundless faith in me and a blind devotion to me, which came from his understanding that I was not really a master. His relation to me was more like that which existed in old days between the pupils of the Italian artists and their *maestri*. I was often vexed with him, but not in the least as a servant. . . . I felt worried about his future; oppressed by his position and unhappy about it, he did nothing to escape from it. At his age if he had cared to work he might have begun a new life; but to do so needed persevering hard work, often tiresome and often childish. His reading was confined to novels and poetry. His understanding and appreciation of them was sometimes very correct, but serious reading wearied him. He was slow and inaccurate in reckoning, and his writing was bad and illegible. How often have I insisted on his working at arithmetic and handwriting, but never could get him to do it: instead of Russian grammar, he would at one time take up the French alphabet, at another German dialogues; of course, that was waste of time and only discouraged him. I used to scold him vigorously for it; he would be mortified, sometimes shed tears and say that he was an unlucky man and that it was too late to study; sometimes he would come to such depths of despair as to wish for death, would fling up all his pursuits and would spend weeks, even months in idleness and boredom.

With modest abilities and not too wide an aim, all might yet have been well. But unhappily in those spiritually sensitive but soft characters the energy is mostly wasted on rushing ahead in spurts, and there is no energy left for going forward steadily. From the distance they have a vision of education and culture on their poetical side, they would like to grasp them, forgetting their lack of technical equipment, of the fingering without which no instrument is mastered.

I often asked myself whether his half-education was not a poisoned gift; what awaited him in the future?

Fate cut the Gordian knot.

Poor Matvey! Even his funeral was surrounded with all the gloomy oppressiveness and horrible accompaniments which were yet typically Russian. At midday the police-sergeant arrived together with his clerk and our village priest, a very old man and a great drunkard. They saw the body, asked questions and sat down to write the answers. The priest, who was neither writing nor reading, put on a big pair of silver-rimmed spectacles and sat in silence sighing, yawning, and making the sign of the cross over his mouth, then suddenly turned to the village elder and making a movement as though he had an insufferable pain in his back, asked him: 'I say, Savely Gavrilovitch, will there be a little bit of lunch?'

The village elder, a dignified peasant, promoted to his position by the Senator and my father, because he was a good carpenter, did not belong to the village (consequently he knew nothing of what went on in it). He was very handsome in spite of being sixty. He stroked his beard, which was combed out like a fan, and as though he had nothing whatever to do with the matter, answered in a deep bass, looking at me from under his brow: 'About that we can give no information!'

'There will,' I answered, and called a servant.

'Thanks be to Thee, O Lord! and indeed it is high time; I get up early, Alexandr Ivanovitch, and I am sick with hunger.'

The police-sergeant laid down his pen and, rubbing his

hands, said, preening himself: 'I fancy Father Ioann is hungry; a good thing too, if our host doesn't mind, we might have a snack.'

The servant brought a cold lunch with sweet vodka, home-made liqueurs, and sherry.

'Say a blessing, Father, since you are shepherd; set the example and we sinners will follow you,' observed the police-sergeant.

With great haste and with an extremely condensed grace, the priest took a wineglass of sweet vodka, put a bit of crumb of bread into his mouth, munched it, and at the same time drank off another glassful, and then quietly and persistently set to work on the ham.

The police-sergeant, too—and this is vividly impressed on my memory—was particularly pleased with the sweet vodka, and after taking a second glass, he turned to me with the air of a connoisseur and observed: 'I expect your *Doppelkümmel* came from widow Rouget's?'

I had no idea where the vodka had been bought, and told them to bring the bottle; the vodka really had come from widow Rouget's. What practice a man must have had to be able to tell the name of the maker from the bouquet of a vodka!

When they had finished, the village elder put a bundle of oats and a sack of potatoes in the police-sergeant's cart; the clerk, who had had a good deal to drink in the kitchen, got on the box, and he and the police-sergeant drove away. With unsteady footsteps the priest set off homewards, picking his teeth with a shaving. I was giving orders to the servants about the funeral when suddenly Father Ioann stopped and began waving his hands: the village elder ran up to him and then back to me.

'What has happened?'

'Oh, the Father bade me ask your honour,' answered the elder, not concealing a smile, '"Who," says he, "will arrange a memorial feast for the dead man?"'

'What did you tell him?'

'I told him not to be anxious; there will be pancakes all right, I said.'

Matvey was buried, pancakes and vodka were given to the priest, and it all left a long, dark shadow behind it. I still had a terrible task before me—telling his mother.

I cannot part from this worthy priest of the Church of the Veil of Our Lady in the village of Pokrovskoe without saying a little more about him.

Father Ioann was not a fashionable priest from the seminary; he did not know the Greek declensions nor the Latin syntax. He was over seventy, and he had spent half his life as a deacon in a big village belonging to Elisaveta Alexeyevna Golohvastov, who induced the Metropolitan to ordain him priest and appoint him to a vacancy in my father's village. Though he had tried all his life to accustom himself to taking an immense quantity of strong drink, he could never get over its effect, and hence was invariably drunk after midday. He drank to such an extent that often after a wedding or a christening in neighbouring villages, which formed part of his parish, the peasants would carry him out dead-drunk, lay him like a sheaf of corn on his cart, tie the reins to the bar in front and send him off under the sole supervision of his horse. The nag, who knew the road well, brought him home without fail. His wife, too, got drunk every time the Lord sent her the means. But what is more remarkable is that his daughter at fourteen could toss off a whole teacupful of vodka without turning a hair.

The peasants despised him and all his family; on one occasion, they even complained against him to the Senator and to my father, who asked the Metropolitan to inquire into the matter. The peasants charged him with being very extortionate in asking for money, with refusing for over three days to bury a man without payment beforehand, and declining to perform weddings altogether

THE VILLAGE PRIEST

until he had been paid. The Metropolitan or the Consistory found the peasants' complaint a just one and sent Father Ioann for two or three months to humbler duties. The priest returned from this correction not only twice as drunken, but a thief as well.

Our servants used to tell us that on the dedication day of the church an old peasant, drinking with the priest when both were drunk, said: 'You are such a disgrace we had to bring it before his Reverence! You wouldn't mend your ways so they clipped your wings for you.' The offended priest is said to have replied: 'Well, I pay you out, you rascals, for whether I marry you or whether I bury you, it is the very worst prayers I say for you.'

A year later, that is in 1844, we were again spending the summer in Pokrovskoe. The grey-headed, thin, old priest was still drinking in the same way, and still as unable to resist the effect of vodka. He got into the habit of coming after service on Sundays to see me, drinking too much vodka and sitting for two hours or more. I got sick of this. I told them to tell him I was not at home, and actually hid in the wood to escape from him. But even this did not settle him. 'The master not at home?' he said, 'but the vodka is at home, surely? I'll be bound he did not take it with him?' My servant brought him out into the vestibule a large glass of sweet vodka, and the priest, after drinking it and having a snack of caviare, meekly went his way.

At last our acquaintance was broken off completely.

One morning the sacristan, a tall, lanky fellow with his hair done like a woman's, arrived to see me, together with his freckled young wife; they were both in great excitement, both talked at once, both shed tears simultaneously and wiped them away at the same moment.

The sacristan in a sort of flat falsetto, his wife with a terrible lisp, vied with each other in telling me that their watch had been stolen a few days before and also a box in which there were fifty roubles, that the sacristan's wife had found the 'fief' and that this 'fief' was no other than our worthy pastor and Father in Christ, Ioann.

The proofs were conclusive; the sacristan's wife had found a piece of the lid of the stolen box amongst the rubbish swept out of the priest's house. They came to beg me to take their part. Although I explained to them several times over the distribution of authority between the spiritual and the secular powers, the sacristan still persisted and his wife still wept; I did not know what to do. I felt sorry for them; they valued their loss at ninety roubles. After thinking a little I ordered the cart to be got ready and sent the village elder with a letter to the police-captain; I asked him for the advice which the sacristan hoped to get from me. Towards evening the village elder returned, the police-captain had told him to give me a verbal message: 'Drop the thing or the Consistory will intervene and make a bobbery. Tell your master not to interfere with the long-haired gentry if he does not want his hands to stink.' This answer, and the last observation particularly, Savely Gavrilovitch delivered with great satisfaction.

'But that the Father stole the box,' he added, 'that is as sure as that I am standing here.'

I regretfully repeated to the sacristan the answer of the secular authority. The elder, on the contrary, said to him reassuringly: 'Come, why are you so downhearted already? Wait a bit, we'll be even with him yet. Are you an old woman or a sacristan?'

And the elder with the help of others did get even with him.

Whether Savely Gavrilovitch was a dissenter or not I do not know for certain, but the peasants of the family brought from Vassilyevskoe when my father sold it were all Old Believers. Sober, shrewd, and hard-working people, they all hated the priest. One of them whom the peasants called the corn-chandler had his own shop in Neglinny Street in Moscow. The story of the stolen watch reached him at once; making inquiries, the corn-chandler discovered that a deacon out of a place, a son-in-law of the Pokrovskoe priest, had offered to sell or pawn a watch, and that this watch was at the money-changer's; the corn-chandler knew the sacristan's watch, he went to the money-changer's and at once saw that it was the very watch. Not sparing his horses in his delight, he arrived himself in Pokrovskoe with the news.

Then with the complete proofs in his hand, the sacristan went to the head-priest of the district. Three days later I heard that the priest had paid the sacristan a hundred roubles and they were reconciled.

'How was that?' I asked the sacristan.

'The head-priest, as your honour heard, graciously sent for our Herod. He kept him a long time and what passed I don't know. Only afterwards he was pleased to summon me and said to me sternly: "What is this silly quarrel? For shame, young man, anything may happen in drink. The old man, as you see, is old, he might be your father. He will give you a hundred roubles to make it right. Are you satisfied?" "I am satisfied, your Reverence." "Well, if you are satisfied, then keep your jaw shut, there is no need to set the bells ringing, he is over seventy, anyway; if you don't, mind I'll make you smart too."

And this drunken thief, unmasked by the corn-chandler, came back to perform his sacred duties before the same village elder who had so confidently told me that he had stolen the box; with in the choir the same sacristan in whose pocket the celebrated watch was now for ever and ever marking the fleeting hours; and—before the very same peasants!

That happened in 1844, about thirty-five miles from Moscow, and I was an eye-witness of it all!

It would be no wonder if at the summons of Father Ioann the Holy Ghost, as in Beranger's ballad, refused to come down.

> 'Non, dit l'esprit saint, je ne descends pas.'

How was it they did not dismiss him?

A minister of the Church, our sages of Orthodoxy will tell us, can like Caesar's wife never be suspected.

Chapter 29

OUR FRIENDS

THE MOSCOW CIRCLE—TABLE TALK—THE WESTERNERS
(BOTKIN, RYEDKIN, KRYUKOV, AND VEVGNY KORSH)
—ON THE GRAVE OF A FRIEND

I

WITH our visit to Pokrovskoe and the quiet summer we spent there begins the harmonious, mature, and active part of our Moscow life, which lasted till my father's death and perhaps until we went abroad.

Our nerves, overstrained in Petersburg and Novgorod, had recovered, our spiritual storms had subsided. The agonising analysis of ourselves and of each other, the useless reopening of recent wounds, the incessant going back to the same painful subjects was over; and our shaken faith in our own infallibility gave a truer and more earnest character to our lives. My article *On a Drama* was the last word of the sickness we had passed through.

On the external side, the only restriction we suffered from was police supervision; I cannot say it was very oppressive, but the unpleasant feeling of a Damocles' cane wielded by the local police-constable was very distasteful.

Our new friends received us warmly, far more warmly than two years before. Foremost among them stood Granovsky, he took the leading place in those five years. Ogaryov was almost all the time abroad. Granovsky filled his place for us. To him we are indebted for the happiest moments of that period. There was a wonderful power of love in his nature. With many I was more in agreement in opinion, but to him I was nearer—deep down, somewhere in the soul.

Granovsky and all of us were very busy, all hard at work, one lecturing in the university, another contributing to reviews and magazines, another studying Russian history; the first beginnings of all that was done afterwards date from this period.

By now we were far from being children; in 1842 I was thirty; we knew only too well where our work was leading us, but we went on. We went along our chosen path, no longer rashly but deliberately, with the calm, even step to which experience and family life had trained us. This did not mean that we had grown old, no, we were still young, and that is how it was that some coming from the university lecture-room, others publishing articles or editing newspapers were every day in danger of being arrested, dismissed, exiled.

Such a circle of talented, cultured, many-sided, and pure-hearted people I have met nowhere since, neither in the highest ranks of the political nor on the summits of the literary and aristocratic world. Yet I have travelled a great deal, I have lived everywhere and with all sorts of people. I have been brought by the revolution into contact with all that was foremost in culture, and I am honestly bound to say the same thing.

The finished, self-contained personality of the Western European, which surprises us at first by its specialisation, surprises us later by its one-sidedness. He is always satisfied with himself, his self-sufficiency offends us. He never forgets his personal views, his position is altogether cramped and his morals only appropriate to paltry surroundings.

I do not imagine that men were always like this here; the Western European is not in a normal condition, *he is moulting*. Unsuccessful revolutions have turned inwards, none of them have transformed him, but each has left its trace and confused his ideas, while the natural historical process has left in the foreground the slimy stratum of the petty-bourgeois, under which the fossilised aristocratic classes are buried and the rising masses submerged. Petty-bourgeoisdom is incompatible with the Russian character—and thank God for it!

Whether it is due to our carelessness, or our lack of moral stability and of definite work, or our youth in the matter of culture, or the aristocratic character of our bringing-up, any way we are on the one hand far more artists in life, and on the other far simpler than Western Europeans; we have not their specialised knowledge, but on the other hand we are far more many-sided than they. Persons of culture are not common amongst us, but their culture is richer, wider in its scope, free from hedges and barriers. It is quite different in Western Europe.

Talking to the nicest people here[1] you immediately reach contradictions where there is nothing in common, and it is quite impossible to convince. In this stubborn obstinacy and instinctive lack of comprehension you seem to be knocking your head against the limits of a completed world.

Our theoretical differences, on the contrary, brought more living interest into our lives, more craving for active exchange of opinions, kept our minds more vigorous and helped us to progress; we grew in this friction against each other, and in reality were the stronger for this co-operation which Proudhon has so superbly described in the sphere of mechanical labour.

I love to dwell on that time of work in unison, of a full, throbbing pulse, of harmonious order and manly struggle, on those years in which we were young for the last time! . . .

Our little circle met frequently, sometimes at the house of one, sometimes of another, most often at mine. Together with chat, jests, supper, and wine, there was the most active, the most rapid exchange of ideas, of news, and of knowledge; every one handed on what he had read or learned. Views came out in argument and what

[1] Written in England.—(*Translator's Note.*)

had been worked out by each became the property of all. There was nothing of significance in any sphere of knowledge, in any literature, or in any art, which did not come under the notice of some one of us, and was not at once communicated to all.

It was just this character in our gatherings that dull pedants and tedious scholars failed to understand. They saw the meat and the bottles, but they saw nothing else. Feasting goes with fullness of life, ascetic people are usually dry, egoistic people, we were not monks, we lived on all sides, and, sitting round the table, gained more in culture and did no less than those fasting toilers who grub in the backyards of science.

I will not have anything said against you, my friends, nor against that bright, splendid time; I think of it with more than love, almost with envy. We were not like the emaciated monks of Zurbaran,[1] we did not weep over the sins of the world, we only sympathised with its sufferings, and were ready with a smile for anything, and not depressed with forebodings of our sacrifices in the future. Ascetics who are for ever austere have always excited my suspicion; if they are not pretending, either their mind or their stomach is out of order.

'You're right, my friend, you're right. . . .'

Yes, you were right, Botkin—and far more so than Plato—when you sometimes taught us, not in gardens and porticos (it is too cold in Russia without a roof on) but round the friendly dinner-table, that a man may find 'pantheistic enjoyment' alike in contemplating the dance of the sea-waves and of Spanish maidens, in listening to the songs of Schubert and in sniffing the fragrance of turkey stuffed with truffles.

[1] Zurbaran, a Spanish painter of religious subjects. A well-known picture of his is of a monk castigating himself before an effigy of the Madonna.—(*Translator's Note.*)

Listening to your sage words, I appreciated for the first time the democratic spirit of our language which talks of 'hearing an odour,' putting smell on a level with sound.

It was not for nothing that you left your lodging in Moroseika and learned in Paris to respect the culinary art, and from the banks of the Guadalquivir the religion not only of feet, but of calves, supreme and sovereign, *soberana pantorrilla*!

Yet Ryedkin was in Spain—but what good did he get from it? He went to that land of historical lawlessness for the sake of making juridical commentaries on Puchta[1] and Savigny.[2] Instead of looking at the fandango and the bolero, he looked at the rising in Barcelona (which ended exactly in the same way as every *cachucha*—that is in nothing) and talked so much about it afterwards that the curator Strogonov shook his head and began looking at Ryedkin's lame leg and muttering something about barricades, as though doubtful whether the radical jurist had really hurt his leg falling out of the diligence on to the pavement in loyal Dresden.

'What disrespect for learning! You know I don't like such jokes,' says Ryedkin severely, not in the least vexed.

'That m—m—m—ay be so,' observes Korsh, stammering, 'but why is it you so identify yourself with learning that one can't make fun of you without insulting it?'

'Come now, there will be no end to it,' says Ryedkin, and with the determination of a man who has read the whole of Roteck[3] attacks the soup, pelted lightly with

[1] Puchta, a German professor and authority on Roman law.
[2] Savigny, a German university teacher, of French origin, and an authority on modern jurisprudence.
[3] Roteck, a German university teacher and authority on Roman law.—(*Translator's Notes.*)

Kryukov's jests—elegantly modelled on an antique pattern.

But the attention of all has already abandoned them; it is bent upon the sturgeon, which is expounded by Schtchepkin himself, who has studied the flesh of contemporary fish more thoroughly than Agassiz did the bones of antediluvian ones. Botkin glances at the sturgeon, screws up his eyes and gently shakes his head, not from side to side but backwards and forwards; only Ketscher, indifferent on principle to the splendours of this world, lights his pipe and speaks of something else. Do not be angry with these lines of nonsense; I will not go on with them, they dropped almost unconsciously from my pen when I thought of our Moscow dinners; for a minute I forgot both the impossibility of repeating jokes and the fact that these sketches are living only for me, and for few, very few, survivors. I feel terrified when I think how short a time ago the path seemed so long, so very long before us all! . . .

And now those who have gone rise up before my eyes, not with the cloud of death about them, but young, full of strength. One of them, like Stankevitch, died far away from home—I mean E. P. Galahov.

How we used to laugh at his stories! It was not merry laughter, though, but more like that which Gogol sometimes excites. Jests and witticisms flashed from Kryukov and from Yevgeny Korsh like sparkling wine, from their exuberance. There was nothing bright in Galahov's humour, it was the humour of a man out of harmony with himself and with his surroundings, thirsting for peace and serenity, but with no great hope of finding them.

Having been brought up in the aristocratic fashion, Galahov very early got into the Izmailovsky Regiment and also left it very early, and then set to work to educate himself in earnest. With a vigorous, but more impulsive and passionate than dialectic mind, he tried with petulant impatience to wring out the truth, and the practical truth too, immediately applicable to life. He did not notice, as the greater number of Frenchmen do not, that truth can only be reached by method and remains inseparable from it; truth as a result is but a truism, a commonplace. Galahov sought not with modest self-abasement what was to be found, but sought for a truth that was to be comforting, and it is no wonder that it eluded his capricious pursuit. He was vexed and angry. People of that type cannot live in negation, in analysis; dissection is hateful to them, they seek for something ready-made, complete, creative. What could our age, and in the reign of Nicholas too, give Galahov?

He rushed hither and thither, knocking at every door, even at the Catholic Church, but his living soul was revolted by the gloomy twilight, the damp, grave-like, prison atmosphere of her comfortless crypts. Leaving the old Catholicism of the Jesuits and the new of Buchez,[1] he was beginning to approach philosophy, but her cold, inhospitable portals repelled him, and for several years he found rest in Fourierism.

The ready-made organisation, the obligatory regulations and almost barrack-like discipline of the phalanstery, though the critical may find little to like in it, has undoubtedly great attractions for those tired people who beg almost with tears for Truth to take them in her arms and lull them to sleep. Fourierism offers a definite aim —work, and work in common. Men are very often ready to give up their own will for the sake of being rid of hesitation and uncertainty. This occurs over and over again in the most ordinary daily affairs. 'Would you like to go to the theatre to-day, or drive out of town?' 'As you like,' answers the other; they don't know what

[1] Buchez, Philippe (1796-1865), a French philosopher and political writer; at first a follower of Saint Simon, afterwards an advocate of what he called Christian Socialism.—(*Translator's Note*.)

to do and wait with impatience for some circumstance to decide for them. This was the groundwork upon which Cabet's [1] settlement, the communistic convent, the Stauropigalian and Icarian communities were formed in America. The restless French workmen, educated by two revolutions and two reactions, began at last to be exhausted and to be assailed by doubts, frightened by them; they were glad of something new, renounced their aimless freedom, and submitted in Icaria to a strict discipline and subordination which was certainly no less severe than the monastic rule of the Benedictines.

Galahov was too cultured and independent to be completely lost in Fourierism, but for some years it attracted him. When I met him in Paris in 1847 the feeling he cherished for the phalanstery was more like the tenderness we feel for the school at which we have studied, for the house in which we have spent some peaceful years, than that which believers have for their church.

In Paris Galahov was even more charming and original than in Moscow. His aristocratic character, his generous, chivalrous ideas were wounded at every step; he looked at the petty-bourgeois world surrounding him there with the disgust with which fastidious people look at something dirty. Neither the French nor the Germans impressed him, and he rather looked down on many of the heroes of the day—with extreme simplicity pointing out their petty triviality, mercenary views, and insolent conceit. In his disdain for these people he even displayed a national haughtiness, really quite foreign to him. Speaking, for instance, of a man whom he greatly disliked, he would by his expression, by his smile and the screwing up of his

[1] Cabet, Étienne (1788-1856), was a French communist, one of the leaders of the Carbonari, and author of a philosophical and social romance *Voyage en Icarie*, describing a Communist Utopia. In 1848 a band of French workmen went out to found an 'Icarian colony' in Texas.— (*Translator's Note.*)

eyes, compress into the one word 'German' a whole biography, a whole physiology, a regular series of the petty, coarse, clumsy failings especially characteristic of the German race.

Like all nervous people Galahov was very variable; he was sometimes silent and dreamy, but *par saccades* would talk freely and with heat, would carry his listeners away by serious subjects on which he had felt deeply, and sometimes made them roar with laughter at the unexpected freakishness of phrase or startling aptness of the pictures he sketched in two or three strokes.

To repeat the things he said is almost impossible. I will recall as best I can one of his stories, and that in a brief extract. In Paris conversation somehow turned on the unpleasant feeling with which we cross our frontier. Galahov began describing how he had travelled for the last time to his estate; it was a *chef-d'œuvre*.

'I drive up to the frontier; rain, sleet, a log painted black and white lying across the road; we wait, they won't let us through. I look out: a Cossack with a pike on horseback comes riding down upon us. "Your passport, please." I give it to him and say, "I'll come to the guard-house with you, brother, it is very wet here." "You can't go there, sir." "Why so?" "Kindly wait." I turned towards the Austrian guard-house, but that was no good either: another Cossack with the face of a Chinaman seemed to spring out of the earth. "You can't go there, sir!" What had happened? "Kindly wait!" And the rain was pouring and pouring. . . . All at once a sergeant shouts from the guard-house: "Lift it up!" There is a clanking of chains and the striped guillotine begins rising; we drive under it, the chains clank again and the beam descends. There, I thought, I am caught. In the guard-house a military clerk is copying out my passport: "Is this yourself?" he asks. I promptly give him a *zwanziger*. Then the sergeant comes in; he says nothing, but I make haste and give him a *zwanziger*. "Everything is correct, you can go on to the Customs." I get in, drive off . . . only I still fancy they are pursuing me. I look round—a Cossack with a pike—trot, trot, after me. . . . "What is it, brother?" "I am escorting your honour to the Customs." At the Customs a clerk in spectacles looks through my books. I give him a *thaler* and say, "You needn't trouble, the books are all scientific, medical!" "To be sure they are: hey! porter, lock up the box again!" Again a *zwanziger*.

'They let me go at last. I take a *troika*, we drive past endless fields; suddenly there is a glow in the distance, it grows redder and redder . . . a fire. "Look," I say to the driver, "how dreadful!" "It is no matter," he answers, "it must be a cottage or a barn burning. Come, come, look alive, get on!" Two hours later the sky is red on the other side; this time I do not even ask, comforted by the reflection that it is a hut or a barn on fire.

'I came to Moscow from the country in Lent. The snow had almost melted, the sledge-runners grated on the cobbles, the street lamps were dimly reflected in the dark pools, and the trace-horse flung up the frozen mud in large clods straight into one's face. And what is very queer, as soon as the spring comes and there are four or five fine days, clouds of dust appear instead of the mud; the police-master coughs, and standing anxiously on his droshky points with dissatisfaction at it, while the policemen bustle about and scatter powdered brick by way of laying the dust!'

Galahov was extremely absent-minded, and in him absent-mindedness was as charming a defect as stuttering was in Yevgeny Korsh; sometimes he was a little vexed, but as a rule he laughed himself at the extraordinary mistakes into which he was continually falling.

Madame H—— once invited him to an evening party.

Galahov went with us to hear 'Linda di Chamonix'; after the opera he went to Chevalier's, and after spending an hour and a half there drove home, changed his clothes, and went off to Madame H——'s. There was a candle burning in the vestibule and some baggage was lying about. He went into the dining-room—there was no one there; he went into the drawing-room, there he found Madame H——'s husband, who had just come from Penza and was still in his travelling clothes. He looked with surprise at Galahov, who inquired what sort of a journey he had had and quietly sat down in an armchair. He said that the roads were very bad and that he was very tired. 'And where is Marya Dimitryevna?' asked Galahov. 'She has been asleep for hours.' 'Asleep? Why, is it so late?' he asked, beginning to suspect the truth. 'Four o'clock,' answered H——. 'Four o'clock!' repeated Galahov 'Excuse me, I only wanted to congratulate you on your safe arrival.'

Another time he came to an evening party at the same house; all the men were in swallow-tails and the ladies in evening dress. Galahov either had not received an invitation or had forgotten it, anyway he entered the drawing-room in his overcoat; he sat down, took a candle, lighted a cigar, and began talking without observing the visitors or their costumes. Two hours later he asked me: 'Are you going anywhere?' 'No.' 'But you are in evening dress?' I burst out laughing. 'Ough, how absurd!' muttered Galahov, snatched up his hat and went away.

When my son was five years old, Galahov brought him for the Christinas tree a wax doll as tall as the child himself. Galahov sat the doll at the table and awaited the effect of the surprise. When the Christmas tree was ready and the doors were opened, Sasha, breathless with joy, moved slowly about, casting fascinated eyes on the tinsel and candles, but suddenly he stopped—stood stock still, flushed crimson, and with a roar rushed back. 'What's the matter, what 's the matter?' we all asked; bathed in bitter tears he only repeated: 'There is a strange boy there, I don't want him, I don't want him.' He saw in Galahov's doll a rival, an *alter ego*, and was deeply mortified at it, but Galahov was even more deeply mortified; he caught up the unlucky doll, went home, and for a long time disliked speaking about it.

The last time I met him was in the autumn of 1847 in Nice. The Italian movement was working up just then: he was carried away by it. In spite of his ironical attitude he kept romantic hopes and still eagerly ran after convictions. Our long conversations, our arguments led me to think of recording them. *From the Other Shore* begins with one of our conversations. I read the beginning of it to Galahov; he was then very ill, visibly wasting away and on the brink of the grave. Not long before his death he sent me in Paris a long letter full of interest. It is a pity that I have not got it, I would have published extracts from it.

From his grave I pass to another, fresher and even more dear.

II

On the Grave of a Friend

*'Generous and pure in spirit with a heart
Tender as a caress . . . And friendship with him
Lives in my memory like a fairy tale.'*

. . . In 1840 when I was passing through Moscow I met Granovsky[1] for the first time. He had only just

---

[1] Readers of *The Possessed* may be interested to know that Dostoevsky is supposed (I cannot say whether on sufficient evidence) to have modelled the character of Stepan Trofimovitch in the earlier chapters of that novel on Granovsky.—(*Translator's Note.*)

come back from foreign parts and been appointed to the Chair of History in the university. He attracted me by his noble, thoughtful appearance, his melancholy eyes under overhanging brows, and mournfully good-natured smile; in those days his hair was long, and he was wearing a dark blue Berlin overcoat of a peculiar cut, with velvet revers and cloth fastenings. His features, dress, dark hair—all gave so much grace and elegance to his figure as he stood at the dividing line between youth and a richly developing manhood, that even a man not easily enthusiastic could not have remained indifferent to him I have always respected beauty, and looked upon it as a talent and a strength.

I had but a passing glimpse of him then, and carried away with me to Vladimir a noble image, and a conviction, perhaps founded on it, that he would one day be my friend. My presentiment did not deceive me. Two years later, after I had been in Petersburg and, at the end of my second exile, returned to live in Moscow, a close and deep friendship was formed between us.

Granovsky was gifted with an amazing tact of the heart. His whole nature was so remote from the irritability of diffidence, from pretentiousness, so clear, so candid, that he was extraordinarily easy to get on with. He did not oppress me with his friendship, and his love was deep and equally free from jealous exactingness and unconcerned indifference. I do not remember that Granovsky ever touched roughly or awkwardly upon those delicate 'capillary tissues' that shrink from light and noise and exist in every man who has really lived. That was why one was not afraid to speak to him of the things of which it is hard to speak even with those most near and dear, whom one trusts completely though some scarcely audible chords in them are not tuned to the same pitch.

In contact with his loving, serene, and indulgent spirit

all the angular discords vanished, the voice of oversensitive vanity was almost mute. He was a uniting link for many things and many people among us, and often brought together in their sympathy with him whole circles mutually hostile, and friends on the brink of separation. Granovsky and Byelinsky, completely unlike each other, were among the noblest and most remarkable figures of our circle.

Towards the end of the oppressive period from which Russia is now emerging, when everything was crushed to the earth, when only the voice of official infamy dared make itself heard, when literature had been brought to a standstill, and instead of humane learning a theory of slavery was taught, when the censorship shook its head over the parables of Christ and blotted out Krylov's *Fables*—in those days, if one saw Granovsky on the lecture platform one's spirit was comforted. 'All is not lost yet if he still goes on speaking,' every one thought, and breathed more freely.

And yet Granovsky was not a fighter like Byelinsky, nor a dialectician like Bakunin. His strength lay not in keen polemic nor in bold denunciation, but just in positive moral influence, in the absolute confidence which he inspired, in the artistic completeness of his nature, the calm serenity of his spirit, the purity of his character, and in his constant and profound protest against the existing order in Russia. Not only his words were effective but also his silence; his thought, denied free utterance, came out so plainly in his face that it was hard not to read it, especially in a land in which a narrow despotism has trained us all to guess and to divine the hidden word. In the gloomy years of persecution from 1848 down to the death of Nicholas, Granovsky succeeded, not only in keeping his chair in the university, but also his independent views—and that because a feminine delicacy, a softness of expression, and the reconciling power of which we have spoken were harmoniously combined with chivalrous courage and the complete devotion of passionate conviction.

Granovsky reminds me of a number of the reflectively calm preachers and revolutionaries of the reformation—not those fierce, turbulent spirits who 'feel their life fully in their wroth' like Luther, but the serene, mild reformers who put the crown of glory on their heads as simply as the crown of thorns. Their gentleness nothing can ruffle, they go forward with firm step but with no loud tramping of feet; judges fear these men, they are ill at ease with them; their smile of reconciliation leaves a sting in their torturer's conscience.

Such was Coligny himself, such were the best of the Girondists; and certainly Granovsky in all the harmonious moulding of his soul, in his romantic bent, in his dislike of extremes, might more readily have been a Huguenot or a Girondist than an Anabaptist or a follower of the Montagnards.

Granovsky's influence on the university, and on the whole of the younger generation, was immense, and outlived him; he left a long streak of light behind him. I look with peculiar tenderness at the books dedicated to his memory by his former students, at the warm, enthusiastic lines about him in their prefaces and in magazine articles, at the good, youthful desire to connect their new work with the spirit of that friend, to touch gently on his grave as they begin, to claim their intellectual pedigree from him.

Granovsky's development had been different from ours. Educated in Oryol, he went to the Petersburg University. As he received but little money from his father he was obliged from a very early age to write 'to order' for the papers. He and his friend Yevgeny Korsh, whom he met in his university days and with whom he maintained the closest friendship up to his death, used to work for

Senkovsky, who needed fresh energies and inexperienced lads in order to transform their conscientious work into the effervescing wine of 'The Library of Good Reading.'

There was no tempestuous period of passion and dissipation in his life. When he had taken his degree the Institute of Pedagogy sent him to Germany.

In Berlin Granovsky met Stankevitch, and that was the most important event of his youth.

Any one who knew them both would understand how immediately Granovsky and Stankevitch must have rushed at each other. There was in them so much that was similar, in character, in tendency, in age . . . and each bore within him the fatal seed of premature death. But mere resemblance is not enough to give men this close intimacy, this enduring sense of kinship. Only that love is deep and lasting in which each completes the other: for active love difference is as necessary as resemblance; without it the feeling is lifeless and passive and passes into a mere habit.

There was a vast difference in the abilities of the two young men and in the direction of their energies. Stankevitch, from early years trained by the Hegelian dialectic, had a conspicuous talent for speculative thought, and if he brought the aesthetic element into his thinking, he certainly brought philosophy as much into aesthetics. Granovsky, who had deep sympathy with the intellectual tendencies of the day, had neither love nor talent for abstract thought. His choice of history as his chief pursuit showed a clear understanding of his own vocation. He would never have made either a metaphysician or a remarkable naturalist. He could never have endured the passionless impartiality of logic, nor the passionless objectivity of nature; he could not have renounced everything for the sake of thought, nor have renounced himself for the sake of observation; the doings of men, on the contrary, interested him keenly. And, indeed, is not history the same thought and the same nature expressed in a different form? Granovsky thought in history, learned from history, and later on made propaganda through history, while Stankevitch in a natural and poetic way communicated to him, not only the theory of contemporary learning but also its method.

Pedants who estimate the value of thought by the sweat and labour it has cost will doubt this. . . . But, we would ask them, what about Proudhon and Byelinsky? Had not they a better grasp even of Hegel's method than all the scholastics who studied it until they went bald and wrinkled? And yet neither of them knew German, neither of them had read one of Hegel's works, nor one of the dissertations of his followers of the left or right wing, but had only talked sometimes about his method with his disciples. . . . Granovsky's life in Berlin with Stankevitch was, to judge from the stories of the one and the letters of the other, one of the most radiant periods of his existence, in which the exuberance of youth, of energy, of the first passionate impulses, of fun and irony without malice, went hand in hand with earnest intellectual work, all warmed and fostered by a deep, ardent friendship such as is only found in youth.

Two years later they were separated. Granovsky went to Moscow to take the Chair of History at the university; Stankevitch went to Italy for his health and died of consumption. The death of Stankevitch was a great shock to Granovsky. Long afterwards in my presence he received a medallion of his dead friend; I have rarely seen such quiet, speechless, overwhelming sorrow.

It happened soon after his marriage. The harmony that surrounded his new life with peace and calm was overcast with mourning. It was long before the traces of it passed away—indeed, I do not know whether they ever passed entirely.

His wife was very young and hardly yet formed; she retained that peculiar element of youthful awkwardness, even of the apathy which is not infrequently met with in young girls with flaxen hair, especially if they are of German descent. These natures, often gifted and strong, cannot readily come to full consciousness when they awaken. The shock that had awakened the young girl had been so tender and so free from pain and conflict, had come so early that she had scarcely noticed it. Her blood still flowed slowly and serenely.

Granovsky's love for her was a quiet, gentle affection, rather deep and tender than passionate. There was something serene and touchingly calm in the atmosphere of their youthful household. It did the heart good to see at times beside Granovsky engrossed in his work the tall, willowy figure of his silent companion, deeply in love and happy. Looking at them, I used to think of the serene chaste families of the early Protestants who fearlessly sang forbidden psalms, ready to go hand in hand, calmly and firmly, to face the inquisitor.

They seemed to me like brother and sister, the more so as they had no children.

We quickly became friends and saw each other almost every day; we sat through the nights until dawn talking of one thing and another. . . . It is in those wasted hours and through them that people grow together inseparably and irrevocably.

It is dreadful and painful to me to think that later on Granovsky and I were for a long time at variance over theoretical convictions. To us they were not something extraneous but the real foundation of our lives. But I hasten to add that if time proved that we could think differently, could fail to understand and could wound each other, time has also proved with redoubled force later on that we could neither part nor cease to be friends, that even death could not divide us.

It is true that, much later, a streak of bitterness was added to a theoretical difference between Granovsky and Ogaryov, who loved each other ardently and deeply, but we shall see that it too was, though late, completely effaced.

As for our disputes Granovsky himself put an end to them; he concluded a letter from Moscow to me in Geneva on August 25th., 1849, with the following words. With pride and reverence I repeat them: 'What was best and strongest in my soul has gone into my affection for you two (that is Ogaryov and me). There is in it something of passion which set me weeping in 1846 and blaming myself for being unable to break a tie which apparently could not last. Almost with despair I discovered that you were bound fast to my soul with threads which I could not cut without tearing away the living flesh. This interval has not been profitless to me. I have come out of it victorious over the *worse side of* myself. Of *the romanticism for which you blamed me not a trace is left*. On the other hand, all that was romantic in my very nature has gone into my personal attachments. Do you remember my letter about your *Krupov*? It was written on a night that I well remember. A black shroud dropped off my soul, your image rose up before me in all its brightness, and I stretched out my hand to you in Paris as lightly and lovingly as I held it out in the happy holy minutes of our life in Moscow. It is not your talent only that had so great an effect on me. That play brought all of you back to me with a rush. Once you wounded me by saying: "Don't build anything on the personal, believe only in the universal," while I always laid so much stress on the personal. But for me personal and universal are blended in you, that is why I love you so warmly and completely.'

Let these lines be remembered when my account of our difference is read....

At the end of 1843 I published my articles on 'Dilettantism in Learning.' Their success was a source of childlike pleasure to Granovsky. He used to go from house to house with *Notes of the Fatherland*, used to read them aloud himself with comments, and was seriously vexed if anybody did not like them. After that it was my lot to see Granovsky's success, and a success of a very different order. I am speaking of his first public lectures on the 'Mediaeval History of France and England.'

'Granovsky's lectures,' Tchaadayev said to me as we came away from the third or fourth, out of a lecture-hall packed to overflowing with ladies and all the aristocratic society of Moscow, 'are of historical significance.' I entirely agreed with him. Granovsky turned the lecture-hall into a drawing-room, a place for meeting, for social intercourse of the *beau monde*. To do this he did not deck out history in lace and gauze, quite the contrary; his language was severe, extremely grave, full of force, daring, and poetry, which roused his hearers and had a powerful effect on them. His boldness passed without provoking interference, not from any compromises he made but from the mildness of expression which was natural to him, from the absence of sentences *à la française*, putting big dots on tiny i's like the moral after a fable. As he laid the events of history before his audience, grouping them artistically, he spoke *in them* so that the thought unuttered, but perfectly clear, was the more readily assimilated by his hearers that it seemed to be their own thought.

The end of the first lecture was the scene of a regular ovation, a thing unheard of in Moscow University. When at the end, deeply moved, he thanked the audience, every one leapt up in a sort of delirium, ladies waved their handkerchiefs, others rushed to the platform, pressed his hands, asked for his portrait. I myself saw young men with flushed cheeks shouting through their

A GREAT OVATION

tears: 'Bravo! Bravo!' There was no possibility of getting out. Granovsky, pale as a sheet, stood with his arms folded and his head a little bent; he wanted to say a few words more but could not. The applause, the shouting, the fury of approbation was redoubled, the students ranged themselves on each side of the stairs and left the general public to make a noise in the lecture-room. Granovsky made his way, exhausted, to the council-room; a few minutes later he was seen leaving it, and again there was endless applause; he turned with a deprecating gesture, and, ready to drop with emotion, went into the office. There I flung myself on his neck and we wept in silence. . . .

Tears as happy flowed down my cheeks when the hero Ciceruacchio,[1] in the Coliseum, glorified by the last rays of the setting sun, dedicated his youthful son to the Roman people, who had risen in armed insurrection, a few months before they both fell shot without trial by the armed assassins of the graceless youth[2] who wore the crown!

Yes, those were precious tears; the first, born of my faith in Russia, the second, of my faith in the Revolution!

Where is that Revolution? Where is Granovsky? Gone together with the boy with the black curls, and the broad-shouldered *popolano*, and the others who were so near and dear. Faith in Russia is still left. Surely it will not be my lot to lose that also?

And why did a blind chance carry off Granovsky, that noble worker, that deeply suffering spirit, on the very threshold of a new age for Russia, as yet obscure but

[1] Ciceruacchio, a popular leader (his real name was Angelo Brunetti) in Rome, who had great influence from 1847, supporting the reforms of Pius ix., and active in bringing about the proclamation of a republic in February 1849. He was captured and shot with his sons the following July.

[2] The late Emperor of Austria, Francis Joseph.—(*Translator's Notes*.)

different, anyway? Why did not fate let him breathe that fresh air of which we have a breath and which does not smell so strongly of the torture-chamber and the barracks?

The news of his death was a terrible blow to me. I was on my way to the railway station at Richmond when the letter was given me. I read it as I walked along and literally did not at first understand it. I got into the railway carriage. I did not want to read the letter again, I was afraid of it. Strangers with stupid, ugly faces kept coming in and going out, the engine whistled, I looked at it all and thought: 'But it is absurd! What? That man in all the flower of his age, he whose smile, whose glance is before my eyes now—he no more? . . .' I was overcome by a heavy torpor and I felt horribly cold. In London I met A. Talandier; after greeting him I said I had a letter with bad news, and as though I had only just heard it, I could not restrain my tears.

We had had little intercourse in later days, but I needed to know that there, far away in our native land, that man was living!

Without him Moscow was empty, another tie was snapped! . . . Shall I alone, far away from all, ever be able to visit his grave—it has hidden as much strength, as much of the future, as many thoughts, as much love and life, as another, not quite unknown to him, which I have visited!

Here I add some lines of mournful reconciliation which are so precious to me that I have begged them as a gift for our memoirs.

TO A DEAD FRIEND

'Amid the burial urns and stones
Upon that gloomy Autumn day,
Uneven, damp, and freshly strewn
The new-made grave before me lay.

TO A DEAD FRIEND

The gifts of love, the gifts of grief,
Placed by thy pupils' hands were seen:
Fresh wreaths bestowed with tender care
Of fragrant flowers and foliage green,
Above it, stretching, dark and grim,
Reflecting the Autumnal mood,
The ancient guardians of the graves,
The pine-trees, cold, indifferent, stood.
The river, lapping at the banks
With trackless waves went, flowing, by,
Without a pause, without an end,
On, on,—into eternity.

. . . . . .

Thy tenderness was lost to me:
For years our lives were spent apart,
And the last greeting from thy lips
I did not hear, to rend my heart.
Our angry silence kept so long
Perchance was bitter grief to thee,
And I was powerless to forget
Thy deep, unmeant offence to me.
My error I could not confess,
We each were sure that we were wronged,
And when I hastened to thy side,
To bare my heart before thee, longed,
That my repentance thou should'st learn
And grant me pardon in return,
It was too late. . . .
                Upon that day
In gloomy Autumn did I grieve
Beside thy new-made grave alone,
And could not make myself believe . . .
And shall I see my friend no more?
And shall thine eyes be closed for aye?
Thy voice be hushed in sorrow's hour?
Shall no word speed me on my way,
No fond embrace, when I depart?
And will thy loving heart not learn
The true devotion of my heart?
'Tis over now, for ever gone—
The fearful truth I cannot flee,
Some words distracted, vague and wild
Fall from my lips, unmeaningly,

> My body trembles like a leaf,
> Some words of sad reproach I hear,
> With bitter sobs my breast is rent,
> My heart is numb with grief and fear,
> The blood is freezing in my veins,
> Oh, let me breathe! Oh, give me light!
> What fearful dream oppresses me?
> What frenzied vision haunts my sight?
>
> . . . . . .
>
> But I survived. Mid work and leisure
> From day to day my life I spend,
> But in my heart the grief still lingers,
> And tears with laughter closely blend.
> One souvenir alone is left me:
> His picture as he lay at rest,
> I gaze upon it: Oh, my brother,
> Thine image lives within my breast!
> And suddenly the thought arrests me:
> 'Tis but a passing dream, this pain,
> He does but sleep, serenely smiling,
> To-morrow he will wake again.
> His noble voice, upraised, will newly
> The sacred gifts to youth impart,
> The spirit free, the faith undaunted,
> To stir the mind and fire the heart.
> But once again, that sad remembrance . . .
> The funeral urns, thy new-made bed,
> The flowers and foliage strewn upon it,
> The grim custodians at its head . . .
> The river lapping at the banks
> With trackless waves, that passes by,
> Without a pause, without an end,
> On, on—into eternity. . . .'[1]

Granovsky was not persecuted; the lawless cruelty of Nicholas's agents halted before his glance of mournful reproach. He died surrounded by the love of the younger generation, the sympathy of all cultivated Russia, recognised even by his enemies. Nevertheless I adhere to my expression, yes, he knew great suffering. Not chains of

[1] Translated by Juliet M. Soskice.

iron alone wear life away; in the one letter Tchaadayev wrote to me abroad (July 1851), he speaks of the way he is perishing, growing feeble and with rapid steps approaching the end—'not from the oppression against which men revolt, but from that which they endure with a touching resignation, and which for that very reason is even more fatal.'

Before me lie three or four letters which I received from Granovsky in later years; what a consuming deadly sadness there is in every line!

'Our position,' he writes in 1850, 'grows more insufferable every day. Every progressive movement in Western Europe is followed by some repressive measure here. People are being denounced by thousands. They have twice been getting up a case against me during the last three months. But what does personal danger matter in comparison with the universal oppression and suffering? It has been proposed to shut the universities, but for the present they have confined themselves to the following measures: they have raised the students' fees, and diminished their number by a law according to which no more than three hundred must be attending a university. In Moscow there are fourteen hundred university students, so we must expel twelve hundred to have the right to admit a hundred new ones. The Institute of Nobility is closed; many institutions are threatened with the same fate, the Lyceum for instance. Despotism is crying aloud that it cannot make terms with enlightenment. New programmes have been drawn up for the Cadet Schools. The Jesuits might envy the military pedagogue who drew up the programme. The priest is instructed to instil into the cadets that the greatness of Christ lies pre-eminently in submission to authority. He is depicted as a model of submission and discipline. The teacher of history is to unmask the trumpery virtues of the ancient republics and to bring out the grandeur—

not yet grasped by historians—of the Roman Empire, which lacked but one thing, the hereditary character! . . .

'It is enough to drive one mad. It is a blessing for Byelinsky that he died in time. Many decent people have sunk into despair and look with blank apathy at what is being done—when will this world fall to pieces?

'I have made up my mind not to resign, but to wait at my post what the fates bring me. I can do a little; let them turn me out themselves.

'. . . Yesterday the news came of Galahov's death, and the other day there was a rumour that you were dead too. When they told me that I almost burst out laughing. Though after all why shouldn't you die? It would be no more stupid than the rest.'

In the autumn of 1853 he writes:

'My heart aches at the thought of what we were in old days' (*i.e.*, when I was there) 'and what we have become now. We drink our wine from old habit, but there is no gladness in our hearts; only at the thought of you my spirit renews its youth. My best, most comforting dream now is to see you once again—and even that is not likely to come true.'

He ends one of his last letters like this: 'On all sides a low vague murmur can be heard, but where is there strength? where is there resistance? It is bitter, brother, —and there is no escape in this life.'

In our North the savage autocracy wears men out quickly. With a pang of dread I look back—it is like a battlefield, there lie the dead and the maimed. . . .

Granovsky was not alone, he was one of a group of young professors who came back from Germany while we were in exile. They did a great deal for the advancement of the Moscow University. History will not forget them. Men of conscientious erudition, they were pupils of Hegel, Gantz, Ritter, and others, just at the period when the dry bones of dialectic began to be clothed with flesh, when learning ceased to consider itself antagonistic to life, when Gantz used to come to his lectures not with an ancient folio in his hand, but with the latest number of a review from Paris or London. They were trying at that time to solve historical questions of the day by the dialectic method; it was an impossible task, but it put the facts in a clearer light.

Our professors brought with them their cherished dreams, their ardent faith in learning, and in men; they preserved all the fire of youth, and the lecturer's chair was for them a sacred lectern from which they were called to preach the truth. They took their stand in the lecture-room not as mere professional savants, but as missionaries of the religion of humanity.

And what has become of that Pleiades of young professors, including the best of them, Granovsky? Dear Kryukov, brilliant, intelligent, learned, died at thirty-five. Petcherin, the Hellenistic scholar, struggled and Struggled in the terrible conditions of Russian life, till, unable to endure it, he went away without aim, without means, ill and shattered, to foreign lands, wandered homeless and forlorn, became a Jesuit priest and is burning Protestant Bibles in Ireland. Ryedkin became a secular monk, serves in the Ministry of Home Affairs, and writes divinely inspired articles, interspersed with texts. Krylov —but enough. *La toile! La toile!*

Chapter 30

OUR 'OPPONENTS'

THE SLAVOPHILS AND PANSLSVISM — HOMYAKOV — THE
KIREYEVSKYS—K. S. AKSAKOV—P. Y. TCHAADAYEV

'Yes, we were their opponents, but very strange ones. We had the same love, but not the same way of loving—and like Janus or the two-headed eagle we looked in opposite directions, though the heart that beat within us was but one.'—'The Bell,' p. 90. (On the death of K. S. Aksakov.)

I

BESIDE our circle were our opponents, *nos amis les ennemis*, or more correctly, *les ennemis nos amis* —the Moscow Slavophils.

The conflict between us ended long ago and we have held out our hands to each other; but in the early 'forties we could not but be antagonistic—without being so we could not have been true to our principles. We might not have quarrelled with them over their childish homage to the childhood of our history; but accepting their orthodoxy as meant in earnest, seeing their ecclesiastical intolerance on both sides—in relation to learning and in relation to sectarianism—we were bound to take up a hostile attitude to them. We saw in their doctrines fresh oil for anointing the Tsar, new chains laid upon thought, new subordination of conscience to the slavish Byzantine Church.

The Slavophils are to blame for our having so long failed to understand the Russian people and its history; their ikon-painter's ideals and incense smoke hindered us from seeing the realities of the people's existence and the foundations of village life.

The orthodoxy of the Slavophils, their historical patriotism and over-sensitive, exaggerated feeling of nationality were called forth by the extremes on the other side. The importance of their outlook, what was true and essential in it, lay not in orthodoxy, and not in exclusive nationalism, but in those elements of Russian life which they unearthed from under the manure of civilisation.

The idea of nationality is in itself a conservative idea—the demarcation of one's rights, the opposition of self to another; it includes both the Judaic conception of superiority of race, and the aristocratic claim to purity of blood, and right to ascendancy. Nationalism as a standard, as a war-cry, is only surrounded with the halo of revolution when a people is fighting for its independence, when it is throwing off a foreign yoke. That is why national feeling with all its exaggerations is full of poetry in Italy and in Poland, while it is vulgar in Germany.

For us to display our nationalism would be even more absurd than it is for the Germans; even those who abuse us do not doubt it; they hate us from fear, but they do not refuse to recognise us, as Metternich did Italy. We have had to set up our nationalism against the Germanised government and its renegades. This domestic struggle could not be raised to the epic level. The appearance of Slavophilism as a school, and as a special doctrine, was quite in place; but if the Slavophils had found no other standard than the banner of the church, no other ideal than the *Domostroy*,[1] and the very Russian but cumbrously tedious life before Peter the Great, they would have passed away as an eccentric party of changelings and cranks belonging to another age. The strength and future of the Slavophils lay elsewhere. Their treasure may have been hidden in church vessels of old-fashioned

[1] The *Domostroy* was a sixteenth-century book of moral precepts and practical advice written by the priest Sylvester, the adviser of Ivan the Terrible.—(*Translator's Note*.)

workmanship, but its value lay not in its form, though at first they did not separate what was precious from what was external.

To their own historical traditions were added the traditions of all the Slav peoples. Our Slavophils took sympathy with the western Panslavists for identity of cause and policy, forgetting that their exclusive nationalism was at the same time the cry of a people oppressed by a foreign yoke. Western Panslavism on its first appearance was taken by the Austrian government itself for a conservative movement. It developed at the melancholy epoch of the Congress of Vienna. It was a period of restorations and resurrections of all sorts, a period when every kind of Lazarus, fresh and decayed, rose up from the dead. Together with Teutschthum,[1] which looked for the renaissance of the *happy days* of Barbarossa and the Hohenstaufens, Czech Panslavism made its appearance. The governments were pleased with this movement and at first encouraged the development of international hatreds; the masses rallied again round the idea of racial kinship, the bond of which was drawn tighter, and were again turned aside from general demands for the improvement of their lot. Frontiers became more impassable, ties and sympathies between peoples were broken. It need hardly be said that only among apathetic and feeble peoples was nationalism allowed to develop, and only so long as it confined itself to archaeological and linguistic disputes. In Milan and in Poland where nationalism was not confined to grammar, a tight rein was kept upon it.

The Czech Panslavism provoked Slavonic sympathies in Russia.

Slavism, or Russianism, not as a theory, not as a doctrine,

[1] Deutschthum was the nationalist movement in Germany. It was considered more patriotic to spell it Teutschthum.—(*Translator's Note.*)

but as a wounded national feeling, as an obscure tradition and a true instinct, as antagonism to an exclusively foreign influence, has existed ever since Peter the Great cut off the first Russian beard.

There has never been any interval in the resistance to the Petersburg forcible imposition of culture; it reappears in the form of the mutinous Stryeltsi, punished, quartered, hanged on the walls of the Kremlin and there shot by Menshikov and other favourites of the Tsar, in the form of the Tsarevitch Alexis poisoned in the dungeon of the Petersburg fortress, as the party of the Dolgorukys in the reign of Peter II., as the hatred for the Germans in the time of Biron, as Pugatchov in the time of Catherine II., as Catherine herself, the Orthodox German in the reign of the Russian Holsteiner Peter III., as Elizabeth who ascended the throne through the support of the Slavophils of those days (the people in Moscow expected all the Germans to be massacred at her coronation).

All the dissenters are Slavophils.

All the clergy, both white and black, are Slavophils of another sort.

The soldiers who demanded the removal of Barclay de Tolly[1] on account of his German name were the precursors of Homyakov and his friends. The war of 1812 greatly developed the national consciousness and love for the Fatherland. But there was nothing of the Old Believers' Slavonic character in the patriotism of 1812 which we see in Karamzin and Pushkin, and in the Emperor Alexander himself. Practically it was the expression of that instinct of strength which all powerful nations feel when they are attacked by others; afterwards it was the triumphant feeling of victory, the proud sense

[1] Barclay de Tolly was one of the ablest of the Russian generals of 1812. He was, as a matter of fact, of Scottish not of German descent.—(*Translator's Note*.)

of successful resistance. But it was weak on the theoretical side; to show their love of Russian history the patriots adapted it to European manners; they translated Greek and Roman patriotism from French into Russian and did not go beyond the line '*Pour un cœur bien né que la patrie est chère!*' Shishkov[1] was raving even then, it is true, about the restoration of archaic forms of language, but his influence was limited. As for the real speech of the people, the only person who showed a knowledge of it was the Frenchified Count Rostoptchin in his proclamations and manifestoes.

As the war was forgotten, this patriotism subsided and finally degenerated on the one hand into the mean cynical flattery of the *Northern Bee*, on the other into the vulgar patriotism of Zagoskin's calling Shuya Manchester, and Shebuev[2] Raphael, and boasting of the bayonets and the spears from the ices of Torneo to the mountains of the Crimea.

In the reign of Nicholas patriotism became something associated with the knout, with the police, especially in Petersburg, where the savage government ended, in harmony with the cosmopolitan character of the town, by the invention of a national hymn after Sebastian Bach[3] and in Prokopy Lyapunov[4]—after Schiller![5]

To cut himself off from Europe, from enlightenment,

---

[1] Shishkov, born 1754, began his career as a naval officer and attained the rank of vice-admiral, but, disapproving of the reforms of the early years of Alexander's reign, left the navy. From 1812 he became prominent as a writer and president of the Academy, and from 1824 to 1828 was Minister of Public Instruction. Intensely conservative and patriotic, he bitterly opposed every new movement in literature and politics.

[2] Shebuev (1776-1855) was a well-known painter of historical pictures in the pseudo-classical style.—(*Translator's Notes.*)

[3] At first the national hymn was very naively sung to the tune of 'God save the King,' and indeed it was scarcely ever sung. It was among the innovations of Nicholas. From the time of the Polish War the national hymn composed by Colonel Lvov of the

from the revolution of which he had been terrified since
the Fourteenth of December, Nicholas on his side raised
the banner of orthodoxy, autocracy, and nationalism,
remodelled after the fashion of the Prussian standard and
supported by anything that came to hand—the barbaric
romances of Zagoskin, barbaric ikon-painting, barbaric
architecture, by Uvarov, by the persecution of the

Corps of gendarmes was, by Imperial command, sung at all the royal
festivities and at large concerts.

The Emperor Alexander was too well educated to like crude
flattery; he listened with disgust in Paris to the Academicians
'despicable speeches grovelling at the feet of the Conqueror. On
one occasion meeting Chateaubriand in his vestibule he showed him
the last number of the *Journal des Débats*, and added:' I assure you
I have never once seen such dull abjectness in any Russian paper.'
But in the time of Nicholas there were literary men who fully
justified his Imperial confidence, and outdid all the journalists of
1814 and even some of the prefects of 1852. Bulgarin wrote in
the *Northern Bee* that among the other advantages of the railway
between Moscow and Petersburg, he could not think without
emotion that the same man would be able to hear a service for the
health of his Imperial Majesty in the morning in the Kazan
Cathedral, and in the evening in the Kremlin! One would have
thought it difficult to excel this awful absurdity, but there was
found a literary man in Moscow who surpassed its author. On
one of Nicholas's visits to Moscow a learned professor wrote an
article in which, speaking of the immense mass of the people
crowding before the palace, he added that the Tsar had but to
express the faintest desire—and those thousands rushing to carry
it out would gladly fling themselves into the river Moskva. The
sentence was erased by S. G. Strogonov, who told me this charming
anecdote.

4 'Lyapunov, a national hero who fought the Poles in the' Time
of Trouble.' Several plays were written about him—one by
Gedebnov, on which Turgenev wrote a criticism. Kukolnik's
play is meant here.—(*Translator's Note.*)

5 I was at the first performance of Lyapunov in Moscow and
saw the hero tuck up his sleeves and say something like, 'I'll wash
my hands in Polish blood.' A hollow moan of repulsion broke
from the whole body of the theatre; even the gendarmes, policemen, and people in stalls, the numbers on whose seats had somehow
been rubbed off, could not summon up the pluck to applaud.

Uniats[1] and by 'The Hand of the Most High saved the Fatherland.'[2]

The existence of the Petersburg Slavophilism of Nicholas was very unfortunate for the Moscow Slavophils. Nicholas was simply flying to nationalism and orthodoxy to escape from revolutionary ideas. The Slavophils had nothing in common with him but words. Their extremes and absurdities were disinterestedly absurd, and had no connection with the secret police, or the Committee of Security, which of course did not prevent their absurdities from being excessively absurd.

Thus, for instance, there was staying in Moscow towards the end of the 'thirties the Panslavist Gaj who afterwards played an ambiguous part as a Croatian agitator and was at the same time closely connected with the Ban of Croatia, Jellachich.[3] Moscow people as a rule put implicit trust in a foreigner; Gaj was more than a foreigner, more than one of themselves; he was both at once. He had no difficulty in touching the hearts of our Slavophils with the fate of their suffering and orthodox brothers in Dalmatia and Croatia; an immense subscription was raised in a few days, and moreover Gaj was given a banquet in honour of all Serbian and Ruthenian sympathies. At the banquet one of the mildest (both in voice and pursuits) of the Slavophils, a man of the *reddest* orthodoxy, probably a little elevated by the toasts to the Montenegrin Bishop and to all sorts of great Bosnians, Czechs and Slovaks, improvised a poem in

[1] The Uniats are members of the Greek Church who accept the supremacy of the Pope.

[2] 'The Hand of the Most High saved the Fatherland' is the title of a play by Kukolnik.

[3] Baron Joseph Jellachich, an Austrian general, who was also a poet and politician. In 1848 he was appointed Ban of Croatia, and took part in suppressing the revolt of the Hungarians.— (*Translator's Notes*.)

which the following not quite Christian expression occurred:

'I will feast on the blood of the Magyar and German.'

All who were not a little deranged heard this phrase with horror. Fortunately the witty statistician Androssov rescued the bloodthirsty poet; he jumped up from his chair, clutched a dessert knife, and said: 'Excuse me, gentlemen, I'll leave you for a moment: it occurs to me that my landlord Dietz, an old piano-tuner, is a German. I'll just run and cut his throat and be back directly.'

A roar of laughter drowned the indignation.

It was while I was in exile and living in Petersburg and Novgorod that the Moscow Slavophils formed themselves into this party so bloodthirsty in its toasts.

Their passionate and polemical character was particularly marked after the appearance of Byelinsky's critical articles; though even before that they had to close their ranks and take a definite stand on the appearance of Tchaadayev's letter and the commotion it caused.

That letter was in a sense the last word, the dividing point. It was a shot that rang out in the dark night; whether it was something perishing that proclaimed its end, whether it was a signal or a cry for help, whether it heralded the dawn or foretold that it would never be— anyway, it forced all to awake.

What, one may wonder, is the significance of two or three pages published in a monthly review? And yet such is the strength of utterance, such is the power of the spoken word in a land of silence, unaccustomed to free speech, that Tchaadayev's letter shook all thinking Russia. And well it might. There had been nothing written since *Woe from Wit* which made so powerful an impression. Between that play and the letter there had been ten years of silence, the Fourteenth of December, the gallows, penal servitude, Nicholas. It was the first break in the national development since the period of Peter the Great. The empty place left by lie strong men who had been exiled to Siberia was not filled up. Thought languished, men's minds were working, but nothing was reached. To speak was dangerous, and indeed there was nothing to say; all at once a mournful figure quietly rose and asked for a hearing in order calmly to utter his *lasciate ogni speranza.*

In the summer of 1836 I was calmly sitting at my writing table in Vyatka when the postman brought me the latest number of the *Telescope*, One must have lived in exile and in the wilds to appreciate a new book. I abandoned everything, of course, and set to work to cut the *Telescope*. I saw 'Philosophical Letters Written to a Lady,' unsigned. In a footnote it was stated that these letters had been written by a Russian in French, that is, that it was a translation. This rather put me against them, and I proceeded to read the criticisms and other matter.

At last the turn came for the letters; from the second or third page I was struck by the mournfully earnest tone. Every word breathed of prolonged suffering, by now grown calm, but still bitter. It was written as only men write who have been thinking for years, who have thought much and learned much from life and not from theory. . . . I read further, the letter grew and developed, it turned into a gloomy denunciation of Russia, the protest of one who for all he has endured longs to utter some part of what is accumulated in his heart.

Twice I stopped to take breath and collect my thoughts and feelings, and then again I read on and on. And this was published in Russian by an unknown author. . . . I was afraid I had gone out of my mind. Then I read the letter to Vitberg, then to S——, a young teacher in the Vyatka High School, then read it again to myself.

It is very likely that exactly the same thing was happening in all sorts of provincial and distant towns, in Moscow and Petersburg and in country gentlemen's houses. I learned the author's name a few months later.

Long cut off from the people, part of Russia had been suffering in silence under the most stupid and prosaic yoke, which gave them nothing in return. Every one felt the oppression of it, every one had something weighing on his heart, and yet all were silent; at last a man had come who in his own way told them what it was. He spoke only of pain, there was no ray of light in his words, nor indeed in his view. Tchaadayev's letter was a merciless cry of reproach and bitterness against Russia; it deserved the indictment; had it shown pity or mercy to the author or any one else? Of course such an utterance was bound to call forth opposition, or Tchaadayev would have been perfectly right in saying that Russia's past was empty, its present insufferable, and that there was no future for it at all, that it was a blank sheet, a terrible lesson given to the nations of the plight to which a people can be brought by isolation and slavery. This was both penitence and accusation; to know beforehand the path of reconciliation is not the task of penitence, nor the task of protest—or consciousness of guilt becomes a jest, and expiation insincere.

But it did not pass unnoticed; for a minute all, even the drowsy and the crushed, were roused, alarmed by this menacing voice. All were astounded, most were offended, a dozen men loudly and warmly applauded its author. Talk in the drawing-rooms anticipated government measures, provoked them. The Russian patriot of German origin Vigel (well known from Pushkin's unflattering epigram) set them going.

The review was at once prohibited; Boldyrev, the censor, an old man, and the Rector of the Moscow University, was dismissed; Nadyezhdin the editor was sent to Ust-Sysolsk; Nicholas ordered Tchaadayev himself to be declared insane, and made to sign an undertaking to write nothing. Every Saturday he was visited by the doctor and the police-master; they interviewed him and made a report, that is, gave out over his signature fifty-two false statements in accordance with the command of the Most High—an intelligent and moral proceeding. It was they of course who were punished. Tchaadayev looked with profound contempt on these tricks of the truly insane caprice of power. Neither the doctor nor the police-master ever hinted what they had come for.

I had seen Tchaadayev once before my exile. It was on the very day of Ogaryov's arrest. I have mentioned already that on that day there was a dinner party at M. F. Orlov's. All the visitors were gathered together when a man, bowing coldly, walked into the room. His original appearance, handsome with a striking air of independence, was bound to attract every one's attention. Orlov took me by the hand and introduced me, it was Tchaadayev. I remember little of that first meeting, I had no thoughts to spare for him; he was as always, cold, grave, clever, and malicious. After dinner Madame Rayevsky, Orlov's mother-in-law, said to me: 'How is it you are so melancholy? Oh you young people! I don't know what has come over you!' 'Then you do think,' said Tchaadayev, 'that there still are young people?'—that is all that has remained in my memory.

On my return to Moscow I made friends with him and from that time until I went away we were on the best of terms.

Tchaadayev's melancholy and original figure stood out sharply like a mournful reproach against the faded and dreary background of Moscow 'high life.' I liked looking at him among the tawdry aristocracy, flighty Senators, grey-headed rascals, and venerable nonentities. However dense the crowd, the eye found him at once. The years did not mar his graceful figure; he was very scrupulous in his dress, his pale delicate face was completely motionless when he was silent, as though made of wax or of marble,— 'a head like a bare skull,'—his grey-blue eyes were melancholy and at the same time there was something kindly in them, though his thin lips smiled ironically. For ten years he stood with folded arms, by some column, by some tree on the boulevard, in drawing-rooms and theatres, at the club and, an embodied veto, a living protest, gazed at the vortex of faces senselessly twisting and turning about him. He became whimsical and eccentric, held himself aloof from society, yet could not leave it altogether, then uttered his message, quietly concealing it, just as in his features he concealed passion under a layer of ice. Then he was silent again, again showed himself whimsical, dissatisfied, irritated; again he was an oppressive influence in Moscow society, and again he could not leave it. Old and young alike were awkward and ill at ease with him; they, God knows why, were abashed by his immobile face, his direct glance, his gloomy mockery, his malignant condescension. What compelled them to invite him . . . still more to visit him? It is a very difficult question.

Tchaadayev was not wealthy, particularly in later years; he was not of high rank—a retired captain with the iron Kulm cross on his breast. It is true, as Pushkin writes, that he would

> 'In Rome have been a Brutus,
> In Athens Pericles,
> But here, under the yolk of Tsars,
> Was only Captain of Hussars.'

Acquaintance with him could only compromise a man in the eyes of the police. To what did he owe his influence? Why did the 'swells' of the English Club, and the patricians of the Tversky Boulevard flock on Mondays to his modest little study in Old Basmanny

Street? Why did fashionable ladies peep into the cell of the morose thinker? Why did generals who knew nothing about civilian aflairs feel obliged to call upon the old man, to pretend awkwardly to be people of culture, and brag afterwards, distorting some phrase of Tchaadayev's, uttered at their expense? Why did I meet at Tchaadayev's the savage Tolstoy, 'the American,' and the savage Adjutant-General Shipov who destroyed culture in Poland?

Tchaadayev not only made no compromise with them, but worried them and made them feel very clearly the difference between him and them.[1] Of course these people went to see him and invited him to their gatherings from vanity, but that is not what matters; what is important is the involuntary recognition that thought had become a power, that it had its honoured place in direct opposition to the authority of the Most High. In so far as the authority of the 'insane captain' Tchaadayev was recognised, the 'insane' power of Nicholas was diminished.

Tchaadayev had his eccentricities, his weaknesses, he

[1] Tchaadayev was often at the English Club. On one occasion Menshikov, Minister of Naval Affairs, went up to him with the words: 'How is it, Pyotr Yakovlevitch, you don't recognise your old acquaintances?' 'Oh, it is you,' answered Tchaadayev, who really had not recognised him, 'but how is it you are wearing a black collar? I fancy that you used to wear a red one.' 'Why, don't you know I am Minister of Naval Affairs?' 'You! why, I imagine you have never steered a boat.' 'You don't need much wit to bake a pot, you know,' answered Menshikov, a little bit displeased. 'Oh well, if it is on that principle . . .' answered Tchaadayev.

A Senator was making great complaints of being very busy. 'With what?' asked Tchaadayev. 'Upon my soul, the mere reading of the notes and papers!' and the Senator made a gesture indicating a pile a yard from the floor. 'But you don't read them?' 'Oh yes, sometimes I do, and besides, it is often necessary to give my opinion on them.' 'Well, I don't see the necessity,' answered Tchaadayev.

was embittered and spoilt. I know no society less indulgent, or more exclusive than that of Moscow; it is just that which gives it a provincial flavour and reminds one that its culture is of recent growth. How could a solitary man of fifty who had been deprived of almost all his friends, who had lost his property, who lived a great deal in thought, and had suffered many mortifications, fail to have his whims and habits?

Tchaadayev had been Vassiltchikov's adjutant at the time of the celebrated Semyonovsky affair. The Tsar was at the time, if I remember right, at Verona or Aachen for a Congress. Vassiltchikov sent Tchaadayev to him with a report and he was somehow or other an hour behind time, and arrived later than a courier sent by the Austrian ambassador Lebzekern. The Tsar, annoyed at the news, and at that time completely influenced towards reaction by Metternich, who was delighted at the news of the Semyonovsky affair, received Tchaadayev very harshly, reprimanded him, lost his temper, and then recovering himself, directed that he should be offered the post of an Imperial adjutant; Tchaadayev declined the honour and asked only one favour—his discharge. Of course this was not liked, but he received his discharge.

Tchaadayev was in no haste to return to Russia; on relinquishing his gold lace uniform he devoted himself to study. Alexander died—the Fourteenth of December came—Tchaadayev's absence saved him from almost certain persecution[1]—about 1830 he returned.

In Germany Tchaadayev made friends with Schelling; the acquaintance probably did a great deal to turn him towards mysticism. In his case it developed into revolutionary Catholicism to which he remained faithful all his life. In his letter he attributes half the calamities

[1] We now know for certain from Yakushkin's *Diary* that Tchaadayev was a member of the Decembrist society.—(*Translator's Note*.)

of Russia to the Greek Church, to its severance from the all-embracing unity of the West.

Strange as such a view is to us, we must not forget that Catholicism has great power of attraction. Lacordaire preached Catholic Socialism while remaining a Dominican monk; he was supported by Chevé,[1] while remaining a contributor to the *Voix du Peuple*. In reality neo-Catholicism is not worse than rhetorical deism, that rationalised theology of the cultured bourgeois which is neither religion nor science, but atheism surrounded by the institutions of religion.

If Ronge[2] and the followers of Buchez were still possible after 1848, after Feuerbach and Proudhon and Pius ix. and Lamennais; if one of the most energetic parties in the movement set a mystic formula on its banner; if to this day there are men like Mickiewicz,[3] like Krasinski,[4] who continue Messianists, there is no cause for wonder in Tchaadayev's bringing a similar doctrine from the Europe of the 'twenties. We have a little forgotten what it was like: one has but to recall the aflair of Volabella, the Letters of Lady Morgan,[5] the memoirs of Andryane,[6] of Byron, and of Leopardi, to realise that it was one of the most oppressive periods in history. The revolution had turned out a failure, crude monarchy boasted cynically of its power, while crafty monarchy

[1] Charles François Chevé (1813-1875) was a political writer, at one time a follower of Proudhon, but afterwards a Catholic.

[2] Ronge was the founder of a school of Liberal Catholicism.

[3] Mickiewicz (1798-185 5), the great Polish poet, author of *Pan Tadeusz*, spent some time in Russia and was a friend of Pushkin and his circle.

[4] Sigismund Krasinski (1812-1859), a Polish poet, author of *Nieboska Komedeja, the Undivine Comedy*.

[5] Lady Morgan (*née* Sydney Owenson) (1789-1859), a lively Irish authoress (and something of an adventuress), published many novels as well as entertaining memoirs.

[6] *Mémoires d'un Prisonnier d'Ètat au Spitzberg*, by Alexandre Andryane, is probably the work here referred to.—(*Translator's Notes*.)

chastely hid itself behind the parties; at most and at rare intervals one heard the songs of the Greeks fighting for their liberty or a vigorous speech from Canning or Royer-Collard.[1]

In Protestant Germany a Catholic party was being formed at that time. Schlegel[2] and Leo[3] changed their faith at that time, old Jahn[4] and others were raving of a popular and democratic Catholicism. People took refuge from the present in the Middle Ages, in mysticism, read Eckartshausen, studied magnetism and the miracles of Prince Hohenlohe[5]; Hugo, the enemy of Catholicism, did as much to assist its revival as did Lamennais at that period, when he was horrified at the soulless indifference of his time.

On the Russian such Catholicism was bound to have an even stronger effect. It formally contained all that was lacking in Russian life, left to itself, oppressed only by the material power, and seeking a way out by instinct alone. The stern discipline and proud inde-

[1] Royer-Collard, Pierre Paul (1763-1845), was in 1811 Professor of Philosophy in Paris, opposed materialism, supported the Scottish School of Reid and Stewart, and originated the 'Doctrinaire' School of which Jouffroy and Cousin were afterwards representative.

[2] Fried rich Schlegel, German critic, author of *Lectures on the Philosophy of History*, and *History of Literature*, joined the Roman Catholic Church.

[3] Heinrich Leo (1799-1878), originally a Radical, went over to the reactionary side on hearing of the murder of Kotzebue. He was much influenced by Herder, and was suspected of leanings towards Catholicism.

[4] Friedrich Ludwig Jahn (1778-1852), commonly called' Vater Jahn,' is chiefly known for his advocacy of gymnastic clubs. He was also connected with the formation of the Burschenschaft, a students' association persecuted by the government authorities. He was in prison from 1819 to 1825.

[5] Prince Hohenlohe, nicknamed the 'miracle-worker,' was brought up by Jesuits, became a priest, preached in Munich and other towns, and set out to heal diseases. He was checked in his activities both by the Pope and the police.—(*Translator's Notes*.)

pendence of the Western Church, its finished definiteness, its practical applications, its unassailable confidence and supposed removal of all contradictions by its higher unity, its eternal *fata Morgana*, its *urbi et orbi*, its contempt for the temporal power, might easily dominate an ardent mind which only began its education after reaching maturity.

When Tchaadayev returned to Russia he found there a different society and a different tone. Young as I was, I remember how conspicuously aristocratic society deteriorated and became baser and more servile with the accession of Nicholas. The brilliance and recklessness of the officers of the Guards, the aristocratic independence of the reign of Alexander, had all vanished from 1826 onwards. There were germs of a new life springing up, young creatures, not yet conscious of themselves, still wearing a lay-down collar *à l'enfant*, at boarding schools, or in Lyceums. There were young literary men beginning to try their strength and their pen, but all that was still hidden, and not in the world in which Tchaadayev lived.

His friends were in penal servitude; at first he was the only one left in Moscow, then he was joined by Pushkin, and later on by Orlov too. Often after the death of both these friends Tchaadayev used to show two small patches on the wall above the sofa-back where they used to lay their heads!

It is infinitely sad to set side by side Pushkin's two epistles to Tchaadayev, separated not only by their life but by a whole epoch, the life of a generation, racing hopefully forward and coarsely flung back again. Pushkin as a youth writes to his friend:

> 'Comrade, have faith. That dawn will break
> Of deep intoxicating joy;
> Russia will spring from out her sleep
> And on the fragments of a fallen tyranny
> Our names will be recorded,'[1]

---

[1] Translated by Juliet Soakice.

TCHAADAYEV'S PESSIMISM

but the dawn did not rise; instead Nicholas rose to the throne, and Pushkin writes:

> 'Tchaadayev, dost thou call to mind
> How in the past, by youthful ardour prompted,
> I dreamt to add that fatal name
> Unto the rest of those that lie in ruins?
> ... But now within my heart by tempests chastened
> Silence and lassitude prevail, unchallenged,
> And with a glow of tender inspiration
> Upon the stone by friendship sanctified
> I write our names ...'[1]

Nothing in the world could be more opposed to the Slavophils than the hopeless pessimism which was Tchaadayev's vengeance on Russian life, the deliberate curse wrung out of him by suffering, with which he summed up his melancholy existence through a whole period of Russian history. He could not but awaken intense opposition in them; with bitterness and weary malice he insulted all that was precious to them, from Moscow downwards.

'In Moscow,' Tchaadayev used to say, 'every foreigner is taken to look at the great cannon and the great bell—the cannon which can never be fired and the bell which fell down before it was rung. It is a strange town in which the objects of interest are distinguished by their absurdity; or perhaps that great bell without a tongue is a hieroglyph symbolic of that immense dumb land, inhabited by a race calling themselves Slavs[2] as though surprised at the possession of human speech.'[3]

Tchaadayev and the Slavophils alike stood facing the unsolved Sphinx of Russian life, the Sphinx sleeping under

---

[1] Translated by Juliet Soskice.

2 The name Slav is derived from Slovo, tvord, *language*.—(*Translator's Note.*)

[3] 'Moreover,' he said to me in the presence of Homyakov, 'they boast of speech, but in the whole race Homyakov is the only one who speaks.'

the overcoat of the soldier and the watchful eye of the Tsar; they alike were asking: 'What will come of it? To live like this is impossible: the oppressiveness and absurdity of the present position is obvious and unendurable—where is the way out?'

'There is none,' answered the man of the Petersburg period of exclusively Western civilisation, who, in Alexander's reign, had believed in the European future of Russia. He mournfully pointed out to what the efforts of a whole age had led. Culture had only given new methods of oppression, the church had become a mere shadow under which the police lay hidden; the people bore all, endured all, the government crushed all, oppressed all. 'The history of other nations is the story of their emancipation. Russian history is the development of serfdom and autocracy.' Peter the Great's upheaval had made us into the worst that men can be made into— enlightened slaves. We had suffered enough, in this oppressive, troubled moral state, misunderstood by the people, struck down by the government—it was time to find rest, time to find peace for the soul, to find support in something . . . this almost meant 'time to die,' and Tchaadayev thought to find in the Catholic Church the peace promised to all who are weary and heavy-laden.

From the point of view of Western civilisation in the form in which it found expression at the time of the restoration, from the point of view of the Russia of the Petersburg period, this attitude was completely justified.

The Slavophils solved the question in a different way.

Their solution implied a true recognition of the living soul in the people; their instinct was more penetrating than their reasoning. They saw that the existing condition of Russia, however oppressive, was not a moral disease. And while Tchaadayev had a faint glimmer of the possibility of saving individuals but not the people, the Slavophils had a clear perception of the ruin of

BACK TO THE OLD WAYS

individuals in the grip of the existing order and faith in the salvation of the people.

'The way out is with us,' said the Slavophils, 'the way out lies in renouncing the Petersburg period, in going back to the people from whom we have been cut off by foreign education and foreign government; let us return to the old ways!'

But history does not turn back; life is rich in materials, it has no need to remake old clothes. All renaissances, all restorations have been masqueraders. We have seen two; the Legitimists did not go back to the days of Louis XIV. nor the Republicans to the 8th of Thermidor. What has once happened is stronger than anything written; no axe can hew it away.

Moreover, we have nothing to which to go back. The political life of Russia before Peter the Great was grotesque, poor, savage, yet it was to this that the Slavophils wanted to return, though they did not admit the fact; how else are we to explain all their antiquarian revivals, their worship of the manners and customs of old days, and their attempts to return, not to the existing (and excellent) dress of the peasants but to the old-fashioned and clumsy costumes?

In all Russia no one wears the *murmolka* but the Slavophils. K. S. Aksakov wore a dress so national that the peasants in the street took him for a Persian, as Tchaadayev used to tell as a joke.

They took the going back to the people in a very crude sense too, as the majority of Western democrats did also, accepting the people as something complete and finished. They imagined that to share the superstitions of the people meant being at one with them, that it was a great act of humility, to sacrifice one's reason instead of developing reason in the people. This led to an affectation of devoutness, the observance of rites which are touching when there is a naive faith in them and insulting where an ulterior motive can be discerned. The best proof of the lack of reality in the Slavophils' return to the people lies in the fact that they did not arouse the slightest sympathy in the people. Neither the Byzantine Church nor the Granovitaya Palata[1] will do anything more for the future development of the Slav world. To go back to the village, to the workmen's guild, to the meeting of the mir, to the Cossack system is a different matter; but we must return to them not in order to strengthen them in immovable Asiatic crystallisations but to develop and set free the elements on which they were founded, to purify them from all that is extraneous and distorting, from the rank growths with which they are overgrown —that, of course, is what we are called to do. But we must make no mistake, all this lies outside the sphere of the State: the Moscow period is of as little use here as the Petersburg, indeed it was at no time better. The Novgorod[2] bell which used to call the citizens to their ancient mote was merely melted into a cannon by Peter, but had been taken down from the belfry by Ivan III.; serfdom was only confirmed by the census under Peter but was introduced by Boris Godunov; in the *Ulozhenie*[3] there is no mention of sworn witnesses, and the knout, the rods, and the lash made their appearance long before the day of *Spitzruten and Fuchteln*.

The mistake of the Slavophils lies in their imagining that Russia once had an individual culture, obscured by

[1] Granovitaya Palata, the hall in the Kremlin in which the Tsar and his councillors used to meet before the time of Peter the Great.

[2] Novgorod, the most famous city in the earliest period of Russian history, was to some extent a republic under the rule of its princes from Rurik upwards. It was almost destroyed and was deprived of its liberties by Ivan III. in 1471.

[3] The Ulozhenie is the code of laws of Tsar Alexis Mihailovitch (father of Peter the Great), compiled in the seventeenth century.— (*Translator's Notes*.)

FOUNDATIONS OF OUR LIFE 275

various events and finally by the Petersburg period. Russia never had this culture, never could have had it. That which is only now reaching our consciousness, that of which we are beginning to have a presentiment, a glimmer in our thoughts, that which existed unconsciously in the peasants' hut and in the open country, is only now beginning to grow in the fields of history, enriched by the blood, the tears, the sweat of twenty generations.

The foundations of our life are not memories, they are the living elements, existing not in chronicles but in the actual present; but they have merely survived under the hard historical process of building up a single state and under the yoke of the state they have only been preserved not developed. I doubt, indeed, whether the inner strength for their development would have been found without the Petersburg period, without the period of European culture.

The primitive foundations of our life are insufficient. In India there has existed for ages and exists to this day a village commune very like our own and founded on a division of fields; yet the people of India have not gone very far, even with it.

Only the mighty thought of the West to which all its long history has led up is able to fertilise the seeds slumbering in the patriarchal mode of life of the Slavs. The workmen's guild and the village commune, the sharing of profits and the division of fields, the mir meeting and the union of villages into self-governing *volosts*, are all the corner-stones on which the temple of our future, freely communal existence will be built. But these corner stones are only stones . . . and without the thought of the West our future cathedral will not rise above its foundations.

This is what happens with everything truly *social*, it inevitably draws the nations into mutual interdependence.

. . . Holding themselves aloof, cutting themselves off, some remain at the barbaric stage of the commune, others get no further than the abstract idea of communism, which, like the Christian soul, hovers over the decaying body.

The receptive character of the Slavs, their femininity, their lack of initiative, and their great capacity for assimilation and adaptation, make them pre-eminently a people that stands in need of the other peoples; they are not fully self-sufficing. Left to themselves the Slavs readily 'lull themselves to sleep with their own songs' as a Byzantine chronicler observed. Awakened by others they go to the furthest consequences; there is no people which could more deeply and completely absorb the thoughts of other peoples while remaining true to itself. The persistent misunderstanding which exists to-day, as it has for a thousand years, between the Germanic and the French peoples does not exist between them and the Slavs. The craving to give itself up and be carried away is innate in their sympathetic, readily assimilative, receptive nature.

To be formed into a princedom, Russia needed the Varangians[1]; to be formed into a kingdom, the Mongols.

Contact with Europe developed the kingdom of Muscovy into the colossal empire ruled from Petersburg.

'But for all their receptiveness, have not the Slavs Shown everywhere a complete incapacity for developing a modern European political order without continually falling into the most absolute despotism, or hopeless disorganisation?'

This incapacity and this incompleteness are great *talents* in our eyes.

All Europe has now reached the inevitability of despotism in order to preserve the existing political order

[1] The Varangians were Scandinavian and Norman tribes, whose rulers were, according to tradition, summoned in 862 by the Northern Slavs to rale over them.— (*Translator's Note*.)

against the pressure of social ideas striving to create a new order, towards which Western Europe, for all its terror and resistance, is being carried with incredible force.

There was a time when the half-free West looked proudly at Russia crushed under the throne of the Tsars, and cultivated Russia, sighing, gazed at the happiness of its elder brothers. That time has passed. The equality of slavery prevails.

We are present now at an amazing spectacle; even those lands in which free institutions have survived are striving for despotism. Humanity has seen nothing like it since the days of Constantine when free Romans sought to become slaves to escape civic burdens.

Despotism or socialism—there is no other alternative. Meanwhile, Europe has shown a surprising incapacity for social revolution.

We believe that Russia is not so incapable of it, and in this we are at one with the Slavophils. On this our faith in its future is founded, it is the faith which I have been preaching since the end of 1848.

Europe has chosen despotism, has preferred Imperialism. Despotism means military discipline, Empires mean war, the Emperor is the commander-in-chief. Every one is under arms, there will be war, but where is the real enemy? At home—down below in the depths —and yonder beyond the Niemen.

The war now beginning[1] may have intervals of truce but will not end before the beginning of the general revolution which will shuffle all the cards and begin a new game. It is impossible that the two great historical powers, the two veteran champions of all West European history, representatives of two worlds, two traditions, two principles—of state and of personal freedom—should not crush the third, which, dumb, nameless, and bannerless, comes forward so opportunely with the rope of slavery

[1] Written at the time of the Crimean War.

on its neck and rudely knocks at the doors of Europe and the doors of history, with an insolent claim to Constantinople, with one foot on Germany and the other on the Pacific Ocean.

Whether these three will try their strength and crush each other in the trying; whether Russia breaks up into pieces or Europe, enfeebled, sinks into Byzantine decay; whether they are reconciled and go hand in hand forward into a new life or slaughter each other endlessly—one thing we have discovered for certain and it will not be rooted out of the consciousness of the coming generations; that is: that the *free and rational development of Russian national existence is at one with the ideas of Western Socialism*.

II

On my return from Novgorod to Moscow I found both parties at the barrier. The Slavophils were in full fighting formation, with their light cavalry under the leadership of Homyakov and extremely heavy infantry under that of Shevyryov[1] and Pogodin, with their sharpshooters, chasseurs, ultra-Jacobins who renounced everything later than the Kieff period, and moderate Girondists who renounced nothing but the Petersburg period; they had their chairs in the university and their monthly review, which was always two months late in appearing but still did appear. The main body was reinforced by orthodox Hegelians, Byzantine theologians, mystic poets, a great number of women, and so on.

Our warfare greatly interested the literary drawing-rooms of Moscow, which was at that time just entering the period of enthusiasm over intellectual subjects when,

[1] Shevyryov, professor of literature in Moscow University and author of a *History of Poetry*, in which he advances many fantastic theories. Pogodin was professor of history, and they were co-editors of the Moskvltyanin.—(*Translator' s Note.*)

political questions being impossible, literary ones become the problems of life. The appearance of a remarkable book, for instance, *Dead Souls*, was an event. Criticisms favourable and unfavourable were read and commented upon with the attention with which parliamentary debates used to be followed in England or France. The suppression of all other spheres of human activity threw the cultured section of society into the world of books, and only in it was heard in muffled undertones the protest against the yoke of Nicholas, the protest which we heard more loudly and openly the day after his death.

In the person of Granovsky Moscow society welcomed Western thought breaking its way to freedom, the idea of intellectual independence and the struggle for it. In the persons of the Slavophils it protested against the outrage done to its feelings of nationalism by the Biron-like arrogance of the Petersburg government.

Here I must make a digression.

I knew two circles in Moscow, the two opposite poles of its social life, and can only speak of them. At first I was lost in the society of old people, officers of the Guards of the time of Catherine, comrades of my father, and other old gentlemen who had found a quiet haven in that almshouse, the Senate, comrades of his brother. Afterwards I knew only the young literary and social Moscow and I speak only of it. I knew nothing and cared to know nothing of what lived or vegetated between the veterans of the pen and the sword who were awaiting their funerals in order of rank, and their sons and grandsons who sought no rank and cared only for books and ideas. That world that stood between them, the real Russia of Nicholas, was colourless and vulgar, without the originality of the times of Catherine, without the dash and daring of the men of 1812, without our strivings and interests. It was a pitiful, crushed generation in which a few martyrs struggled, were suffocated, and perished. When I speak of the Moscow drawing-rooms and dining-rooms, I speak of those in which Pushkin once reigned supreme; in which up to our own day the Decembrists set the tone; in which Griboyedov laughed; in which M. F. Orlov and A. P. Yermolov met a friendly welcome because they were under the ban; in which Homyakov argued from nine in the evening until four o'clock in the morning; in which K. S. Aksakov[1] with a *murmolka* in his hand fiercely defended Moscow though no one had attacked it, and never took a glass of champagne in his hand without secretly repeating a prayer and a toast which every one knew; in which Ryedkin logically deduced a personal God *ad* majorem *gloria*m *Hegelii*; in which Granovsky appeared with his firm and gentle speech; in which every one remembered Bakunin and Stankevitch; in which Tchaadayev with his delicate wax-like face, scrupulously dressed, enraged the nonplussed aristocrats and orthodox Slavophils by biting sarcasms, always cast in original form and carefully iced; in which A. I. Turgenev,[2] young in spite of his age, gossiped charmingly about all the celebrities of Europe, from Chateaubriand and Recamier to Schelling and Rahel Varnhagen; in which Botkin and Kryukov *pantheistically* enjoyed M. S. Shtchepkin's stories; and into which Byelinsky sometimes fell like Congreve's rocket, setting fire to everything he touched. Life in Moscow is more like life in the country than in the town, the only difference is that the houses are

[1] Konstantin and Ivan Aksakov were the sons of Sergey Timofeyevitch Aksakov (1791-1859), a writer of the first rank, some of whose charming pictures of the country and old-fashioned Russian life are now accessible in excellent translations by J. D. Duff.

[2] Alexandr Ivanovitch Turgenev, a distinguished person in hia own day, now chiefly remembered for having been a very good friend to Pushkin, was one of the Turgenevs of Simbirsk, and not related to the famous Turgenev, who has left among his critical articles an obituary notice of this Alexandr Ivanovitch.— (*Translator's Notes.*)

nearer each other. Everything in it is not on the same pattern, but specimens of different ages, cultures, social strata, of the length and breadth of Russia, live after their own fashion. In it the Larins[1] and the Famussovs calmly live out their days; and not only they but Vladimir Lensky and our eccentric Tchatsky, and indeed there are even too many Onyegins. With little to do they all live without haste, without special anxieties, without pulling up their sleeves. The easy-going ways of the Russian country gentleman are, we must own, dear to our hearts; there is a breadth about them which we do not find in the petty-bourgeois life of the West. The servile dependence on the rich and powerful, of which Miss Wilmot speaks in the *Memoirs of Princess* Dashkov, and which I myself remember, did not exist in the circles of which I am speaking. The rank and file of this society was composed of landowners not in the service, or serving not on their own account but to pacify their relations, of young literary men and professors. This society had the freedom and fluidity of relations and habits that had not been reduced to a rigid tradition, a freedom which is not found in the old European life, and at the same time it retained the traditions of Western politeness instilled into us by education and now vanishing in the West; this courtesy, blended with the Slav *laisser aller*, and at times with riotous merriment, made up the special Russian character of Moscow society, to its great regret, because it was desperately anxious to be Parisian and probably still is so.

We still only know of Europe as it was in the past; we are still haunted by the days when Voltaire reigned supreme over the Parisian salons and people were invited to hear Diderot arguing, as to partake of a sturgeon; when

[1] The Larins and Lensky are characters in Pushkin's *Yevgeny Onyegin*. Tchatsky is the hero of Griboyedov's *Woe from Wit*, and Famussov is a character in the same play.—(*Translator's Note.*)

the arrival of David Hume in Paris was an epoch and all the countesses and viscountesses hung about him and flirted with him till another spoilt darling, Grimm, sulked and thought it quite out of place. We still think of the soirées of Baron d'Holbach[1] and the first performance of *Figaro*, when all the aristocracy of Paris stood in a queue for whole days, and fashionable ladies missed their dinner and ate dry buns to get a seat and see the revolutionary play, which was to be performed a month later at Versailles with the Count de Provence, *i.e.*, the future Louis XVIII., in the part of Figaro and Marie Antoinette in the part of Suzanne!

Tempi passati . . . past are not only the salons of the eighteenth century, those marvellous salons in which under powder and lace aristocrats dandled and fed on aristocratic milk the young lion from whom sprang a titanic revolution. There are not even such salons as those, for instance, of Madame de Staël or Récamier, in which all the celebrities of aristocracy, literature, and politics gathered. Literature is feared, and indeed there is none, while the parties have drifted so far apart that people of different shades of opinion cannot meet with civility under the same roof.

One of the last attempts at a salon, in the old sense of the word, failed and flickered out together with its hostess. Delphine Gay[2] exhausted all her talents and brilliant intelligence in the attempt to preserve a decorous peace between guests who suspected and hated each other. Can there be any pleasure in a strained, uneasy state of truce, in which the host as soon as he is alone throws

[1] Baron d'Holbach (1723-1789), of German origin, one of the French encyclopaedists, was the social centre round which all the leading literary and philosophic celebrities of Paris gathered. He was a passionate atheist, and an extremely good-hearted man, giving shelter to his worst enemies, the Jesuits, when they were persecuted.

[2] Delphine Gay (Mme. de Girardin) wrote witty verses, novels, and plays.—(*Translator's Notes*.)

himself exhausted on the sofa and thanks heaven that the evening has passed off without unpleasantness?

Indeed, Western Europe (and particularly France) has no thought to spare for literary gossip, for *bon ton* and elegant manners. Covering the terrible gulf with the bee-embroidered Imperial mantle, bourgeois generals, bourgeois bankers, bourgeois ministers are carousing, piling up millions, losing millions, while they await the Nemesis of liquidation. . . . They need not light *causerie* but heavy orgies and colourless wealth, in which, as in the first Empire, art is driven out by gold, the lady by the *lorette*, the literary man by the stock-exchange gambler.

This dissolution of society was not confined to Paris. George Sand was the living centre of all her neighbourhood at Nohant. Acquaintances of all sorts visited her with no great ceremony whenever they liked, and spent the evening extremely elegantly. There would be music, reading, and dramatic improvisations, and above all there was George Sand herself. From the year 1852 the tone began to change, the good-natured neighbours no longer came to rest and laugh, but with malice in their eyes, brimming over with spite, attacked one another openly and secretly; some displayed their new livery, while others dreaded being denounced to the government; the lack of restraint which had made jest and gaiety light and charming had vanished. The continual effort to appease, to soften and to part the combatants, so harassed and wearied George Sand that she made up her mind to give up her evenings at Nohant and reduced her circle to two or three old friends. . . .

They say that Moscow—young Moscow—has grown old, has not survived Nicholas, that even the university has become petty, and that the landowning temper has come out in too strong relief in face of the question of emancipation; that its English club has become less

English than ever, that in it Sobakevitches[1] are clamouring against emancipation and Nozdryovs noisily maintaining the natural and inalienable rights of the nobility. Perhaps! . . . But the Moscow of the 'forties was not like that, and it was that Moscow that took active sides for and against the *murmolka*; girls and ladies read very boring essays, listened to very long arguments, and argued themselves in defence of K. S. Aksakov or Granovsky, only regretting that Aksakov was too Slavophil and Granovsky not sufficiently patriotic.

The arguments were renewed at every literary and non-literary evening at which we met, and that was two or three times a week. On Monday we assembled at Tchaadayev's, on Tuesday at Sverbeyev's, on Sundays at Madame A. P. Yekgin's. . . . Besides those who took part in the arguments, besides the people who had opinions, men and even women would come to these evenings and sit until two o'clock in the morning to see which of the matadors would dispatch the other, and how he would be dispatched himself; they came as in old days people used to go to prize fights, and to the amphitheatre behind the Rogozhsky Gate.

The champion who impressed all on the side of orthodoxy and Slavophilism was Alexey Stepanovitch Homyakov, 'Gorgias the immemorial questioner of the world,' to use the expression of the half-crazy Moroshkin. Gifted with a powerful and mobile intelligence, a good memory, and power of rapid reflection, rich in resources and indiscriminate in the use of them, he spent his whole life in heated and inexhaustible argument. An unwearying and unresting fighter, he dealt blows and thrusts, attacked and pursued, pelted with witticisms and quotations, terrified and drove into a maze from which there was no escape without prayer—in short, if he attacked a con-

[1] Sobakevitch and Nozdryov are characters in Gogol's *Dead Souls.—(Translator's Note.)*

viction the conviction was lost, if he attacked a man's logic his logic was gone.

Homyakov really was a dangerous opponent; a hardened old duellist of dialectics, he took advantage of the slightest inadvertence, the slightest concession. An extraordinarily gifted man, with formidable stores of erudition at his disposal, he was like the mediaeval knights who guarded the Madonna and slept fully armed. At any hour of the day or the night he was ready for the most intricate argument, and to secure the triumph of his Slavophil views turned everything in the world to use, from the casuistry of Byzantine theologians to the subtleties of a tricky lawyer. His refutations, often only apparent, always dazzled and confounded his opponent.

Homyakov was very well aware of his strength, and played with it; he pelted people with words, intimidated them by his learning, mocked everything, made a man laugh at his own theories and convictions, leaving him in doubt whether he really had anything left which was sacred. In masterly fashion he caught those who had halted half-way and roasted them on the dialectical gridiron, terrified the timid, reduced the dilettante to despair, and, with all that, laughed, *as it seemed*, simply and candidly. I say 'as it seemed,' because there was in his somewhat Oriental features a look as of something concealed and a sort of simple-hearted Asiatic cunning together with the Russian canniness. As a rule he rather confused his opponent than convinced him.

His philosophical contentions rested on rejecting the possibility of attaining truth by reason; he attributed to reason a formal faculty only, the faculty of developing rudiments received in other ways and relatively complete (*i.e.*, imparted by revelation or accepted through faith). If reason is left to itself, then, wandering in empty space, and building category after category, it may throw light on its own laws, but will never reach the conception of the spirit, nor the conception of immortality—and so on. On this basis Homyakov confuted people who halted between religion and science. However they struggled in the fetters of the Hegelian method, whatever deductions they made, Homyakov went with them step by step and in the end blew down the house of cards built of logical formulas or gave them a kick and sent them falling into 'materialism' which they shamefacedly renounced, or into 'atheism 'of which they were simply afraid. Homyakov triumphed!

As I had several times been present while he was arguing, I noticed this device, and the first time that it was my lot to try my strength with him I myself drew him to these deductions. Homyakov screwed up his slanting eyes, shook his pitch-black curls, and smiled in anticipation. 'Do you know,' he said suddenly, as though surprised by a new idea, 'it is not merely impossible by reason alone to arrive at a rational spirit developing nature, but by reason alone you can reach no other interpretation of nature than that of a simple, uninterrupted ferment which has no aim and may either go on or come to a stop? And if that is so, you cannot even prove that history will not be cut short to-morrow, will not perish together with the human race, together with the planet.'

'I didn't say,' I answered, 'that I undertook to prove it. I know very well that it is impossible.'

'What?' said Homyakov, somewhat surprised, 'you can accept these terrible results of the theory of immanence pushed to this ferocious extreme and nothing in your soul is revolted?'

'I can, because the deductions of reason are independent of whether I desire them or not.'

'Well, you at any rate are consistent. But what violence a man must do to his soul to resign himself to these gloomy deductions of your science, and to accustom himself to them.'

'Prove that your non-science is more true, and I will accept it as frankly and fearlessly, whatever it may lead me to, even to the Iversky Madonna.'

'For that you must have faith.'

'But, Alexey Stepanovitch, you know the saying: "If you haven't got a thing, it's not your fault."'

Many people thought—indeed I sometimes did myself—that Homyakov argued from an artistic pleasure in argument, that he had no deep convictions; and his manner, his everlasting laugh, and the superficiality of his critics were responsible for that idea. I don't think that any one of the Slavophils did more to gain acceptance for their theories than Homyakov. His whole life—and he was a very wealthy man and not in the service—was devoted to propaganda. Whether he laughed or wept was a question of his nerves, of the cast of his mind, of the way he had been formed by his environment and had reflected it; it had nothing to do with depth of conviction.

Perhaps in continual preoccupation with the trivial activity of discussion and the busy idleness of polemic Homyakov stifled the feeling of emptiness which, on the other hand, stifled everything joyous in his comrades and nearest friends, the Kireyevskys.

That these people were crushed and crippled by the age of Nicholas was unmistakable. In the heat of argument one might sometimes forget it—to do so now would be weak and pitiful.

The two Kireyevsky brothers stand like melancholy shades at the dividing line of the national renaissance; not recognised by the living, not sharing their interests, they never dropped the shroud.

The prematurely aged face of Ivan Kireyevsky bore unmistakable traces of the suffering and conflict which had been followed by the gloomy calm of the sea rippling above a foundered ship. His life was a failure. He threw himself with ardour—in 1833, if I remember right—into a monthly review, *The European*. The two numbers that appeared were excellent, but on the publication of the second *The European* was prohibited. He inserted an article upon Novikov[1] in the *Dennitsa*. The *Dennitsa* was seized and the censor, Glinka, was put under arrest. Kireyevsky, who had lost a great deal of his fortune over *The European*, retired despondently into the wilderness of Moscow life: there was nothing for him to do there; he could not endure it, and went away to the country, burying in his heart profound unhappiness and a painful yearning for activity. This man, too, firm and true as steel, was consumed by the rust of that terrible period. Ten years later he went back to Moscow from his seclusion, a mystic and a believer in the church.

His position in Moscow was a hard one. He found no complete intimacy or sympathy either in his friends ox in us. Between him and us stood the barrier of the church. A worshipper of liberty and of the great age of the French Revolution, he could not share the disdain of the new 'Old Believers' for everything European. He once said with intense sadness to Granovsky: 'In heart I am closer to you, but I do not share many of your convictions; I am nearer in belief to our party, but just as far from them on the other side.' And he really was fading out of life, lonely in his own family.[2] Beside him stood his brother and friend, Pyotr. Both the brothers took part in conversations sadly, as though their tears were

[1] Novikov, a man of letters and mystic of the time of Catherine, was imprisoned and exiled for advocating the emancipation of the serfs.

[2] The Kireyevskys' mother did not share their views. This is the only explanation I can discover for his being described as 'lonely in his own family.'—(*Translator's Notes.*)

IVAN KIREYEVSKY

not yet dried, as though misfortune had visited them the day before. I looked at Ivan Kireyevsky as at a widow, as at a mother who had lost her son; life had cheated him, all was emptiness in the future and the only consolation:

> 'Wait a little,
> Thou too shalt rest!'[1]

One was sorry to disturb his mysticism. I used to feel the same scruple in the old days with Vitberg. The mysticism of both was aesthetic; it was as though the truth had not disappeared altogether behind it, but was hidden in fantastic outlines and monastic cassocks. One only feels a ruthless desire to shake a man out of his theories when his madness takes a polemical form or when he is so near one that any dissonance rends the heart and gives one no peace.

And what argument could one use to a man who said things like this: 'I once stood at a shrine and gazed at a wonder-working ikon of the Mother of God, thinking of the childlike faith of the people praying before it; some women and infirm old men knelt, crossing themselves and bowing down to the earth. With ardent hope I gazed at the holy features, and little by little the secret of their marvellous power began to grow clear to me. Yes, this was not simply a painted board . . . for whole ages it had absorbed these streams of passionate aspiration, the prayers of the afflicted and unhappy; it must have been filled with power which emanates from it, is reflected from it, upon the believing. It had become a living organism, a meeting-place between the Creator and men. Thinking of this, I looked once more at the old men, at the women and children prostrate in the dust, and at the holy ikon—then I myself saw the features of the Mother of God suffused with life, she looked with love and mercy

[1] From Lermontov's translation of Goethe's poem.—(*Translator's Note.*)

at these simple folk . . . and I sank on my knees and meekly prayed to her.'

Pyotr Kireyevsky was even more incorrigible and went to even greater lengths in orthodox Slavophilism; his was perhaps a less gifted nature, but he was single-minded and strictly consistent. He did not, like his brother Ivan or the Slavophil Hegelians, try to reconcile religion with science, and the Western civilisation with nationalism; on the contrary he rejected all compromises. Firmly and independently he stood his ground, neither seeking arguments nor avoiding them. He had nothing to fear: he was so entirely devoted to his idea and so bound up with it in sorrowful sympathy for the Russia of his day that his position was easy. It was as impossible to agree with him as with his brother; but it was easier to understand him, as it is easier to understand every ruthless extreme. He had discerned (and this I only realised long afterwards) some part of the bitter, crushing truths concerning the social condition of Western Europe which we only came to see after the upheavals of 1848. He perceived them with melancholy clear-sightedness, divined them through hatred and resentment for the evil wrought by Peter the Great in the name of Western civilisation. That is why Pyotr Kireyevsky had not, as his brother had, together with his orthodoxy and Slavophilism, yearnings towards some humane and religious philosophy in which his lack of faith in the present would be resolved. No, his austere nationalism involved complete, final estrangement from all that was Western.

It was their common misfortune that they had been born either too early or too late; the Fourteenth of December found us children, but them young men. That made a great difference. At that time we were at our lessons, knowing nothing at all of what was really being done in the practical world. We were full of theoretical dreams, we were Gracchi and Rienzi in the nursery;

OUR PREDECESSORS

afterwards confined to a small circle we spent our academic years together; as we passed out of the gates of the university we entered the gates of prison. Prison and exile in youth, in the grey and stifling days of persecution, are extremely beneficial; they are a hardening process; only feeble organisms are subdued by prison, those in whom resistance was the passing impulse of youth and not a talent, not a spiritual necessity. To be the object of open persecution strengthens the desire for resistance, increased danger trains to endurance and moulds conduct. All this provides an interest, a distraction, and excites irritation and anger; with the prisoner or the exile moments of fury are more frequent than the exhausting hours of listless, impotent despair of men in freedom but helpless in vulgar and oppressive surroundings.

When we came back from exile a new spirit was already stirring in the university, in literature, in society itself. Those were the days of Gogol and Lermontov, of Byelinsky's articles, the lectures of Granovsky and the young professors.

It was very different with our predecessors; they were coming of age when the bell tolled for the execution of Pestel and pealed for the coronation of Nicholas; they were too young to take part in the conspiracy of December the Fourteenth, and not young enough to be at school after it. They were faced with the ten years which ended in Tchaadayev's gloomy letter. Of course they could not grow old in those ten years, but they were crushed and stifled, surrounded by a society with no living interests, paltry, cowardly, cringing. And those were the first ten years of manhood! Inevitably a man was driven, like Onyegin, to envy the paralysis of the Tula assessor, to go to Persia like Lermontov's Petchorin, to become a Catholic like the real Petchorin, or to throw himself into desperate orthodoxy or violent Slavophilism, if he had no desire to get drunk, to flog peasants, or to play cards.

When first Homyakov was conscious of this emptiness he went for a tour in Europe, during the dull and sluggish reign of Charles x.; after finishing in Paris his forgotten tragedy, *Yermak*, and talking to various Czechs and Dalmatians on the way home, he returned. Everything was dull! Fortunately the Turkish war broke out; he, quite superfluously, quite aimlessly, joined a regiment and went to Turkey. The war ended, and another forgotten tragedy, *Dmitri the Pretender*, was finished. Dullness again!

In this boredom, in this depression, in the midst of terrible environment and terrible emptiness a new thought flashed upon him: it was greeted with derision as soon as it was uttered; that only made Homyakov fly the more furiously to defend it, and made it enter the more deeply into the very flesh and blood of the Kireyevskys.

The seed was scattered; their energies all went into the sowing and the guarding of the young crops. Men were needed of another generation, not warped and distorted, by whom their thought could be accepted and inherited, not come to by suffering and sickness as they themselves had reached it. Young men responded to their summons, men of Stankevitch's circle joined them, and among them were such powerful personalities as K. Aksakov and Yury Samarin.

Konstantin Aksakov did not laugh like Homyakov and was not engrossed in hopeless grieving like the Kireyevskys. He threw himself with energy into the work, as a youth on the threshold of manhood. There was no uncertain testing of his ground, no melancholy sense of being a voice crying in the wilderness, no gloomy sighing, no faint hope about him, but a fanatical faith, intolerant, narrow, one-sided, that faith which paves the way to victory. Aksakov was one-sided like every fighter; a calmly balanced eclecticism is no equipment for battle.

He was surrounded by hostile elements, powerful elements, that had great advantages over him, he had to fight his way through a succession of all sorts of enemies, and to hoist his flag. How could he be tolerant!

His whole life was an uncompromising protest against the Russia of officialdom, against the Petersburg period, in the name of the unrecognised, oppressed Russian people. His dialectical powers were inferior to those of Homyakov, and he was not a poet and thinker like Ivan Kireyevsky, but he was ready to go out into the market-place for his faith; he would have gone to the stake, and when that is felt behind a man's words they become terribly convincing. Early in the 'forties he was preaching the village commune, the mir, and the workmen's guild. He taught Haxthausen[1] to understand them, and, consistent to the point of childishness, was the first to put his trousers inside his high boots, and to wear a shirt with a collar fastened at the side.' Moscow is the capital of the Russian people,' he used to say, 'while Petersburg is only the residence of the Emperor.' 'And observe,' I answered, 'to what lengths the distinction goes—in Moscow they invariably put you in the lock-up, while in Petersburg they take you to the *Hauptwacht*.'

To the end of his days Aksakov remained an everlastingly enthusiastic and boundlessly generous youth; he carried away and was carried away, but was always perfectly single-hearted. In 1844 when our differences had reached such a point that neither the Slavophils nor we cared to go on meeting, I was walking along the street when I saw K. Aksakov in a sledge. I bowed to him in a friendly way. He was on the point of driving by, but he suddenly stopped the coachman, got out of his sledge, and came towards me. 'It hurts me too much,' he said,

---

[1] Baron Haxthausen was a learned German who after a visit to Russia at this period wrote an account of the Russian system of land tenure.—(*Translator's Note*.)

'to pass you and not say good-bye. You understand that after all that has happened between your friends and mine I am not coming to see you; I am sorry, very sorry, but there is no help for it.' He went rapidly towards his sledge, but suddenly turned round. I was standing still; I was sad; he rushed up to me, threw his arms round me and kissed me warmly. I had tears in my eyes. How I loved him at that moment of strife!

The quarrel in question was the result of the discussions of which I have spoken.

Granovsky and I still managed to get on with them somehow, without giving up our principles; we did not make a personal question of our difference of opinion. Byelinsky, passionate in his intolerance, went further and bitterly reproached us. 'Iama Jew by nature,' he wrote to me from Petersburg,' and cannot eat at the same table with the Philistines. . . . Granovsky wants to know whether I have read his article in the *Moskvityanin*. No, and I am not going to read it; tell him I am not fond of meeting my friends in improper places, and I don't make appointments with them there.'

On the other hand, the Slavophils were ruthless in their treatment of him. The *Moskvityanin*, irritated by Byelinsky, by the success of the *Notes of the Fatherland* and of Granovsky's lectures, used any weapon that came to hand in self-defence, and spared Byelinsky least of all, speaking of him in so many words as a dangerous man who thirsted for destruction and rejoiced at the sight of the conflagration.

The *Moskvityanin*, however, was pre-eminently the organ of the university doctrinaire section of the Slavophils. This section might be described not merely as the university, but to some extent as the government party. That such a party should find expression was a great novelty in Russian literature. Among us servility either keeps quiet, takes bribes, and can barely read or write, or, disdainful of prose, strikes chords on the lyre of loyalty and patriotism.

Bulgarin and Gretch[1] are in no way typical, no one was deceived by them, no one mistook the cockade of their livery for the badge of any shade of opinion.

Pogodin and Shevyryov, the editors of the *Moskvityanin*, were on the contrary conscientiously servile: Pogodin from hatred of the aristocracy, Shevyryov I do not know why, possibly influenced by the example of his ancestor, who, in the midst of the tortures and agonies of the reign of Ivan the Terrible, sang psalms and almost prayed for the ferocious old man's days to be prolonged.

There are periods at which thinkers are on the side of authority, but that is only when authority is progressive, as in the days of Peter the Great, is defending the country as in 1812, or is healing its wounds and letting it rest as in the reign of Henry iv. of France and perhaps of Alexander 11. But to select the most arid and narrow epoch of Russian autocracy and, leaning upon the Little Father the Tsar, take up arms against the individual misdeeds of the aristocracy, which is developed and supported by the power of that same Tsar, is absurd and harmful.

I shall be told that under the aegis of devotion to the Imperial power the truth can be spoken more boldly. Why then did they not speak it?

Pogodin was a useful professor who appeared, with energy that was new and a Guerin that was not, on the debris of Russian history, which had been whittled away and turned to smoke and ashes by Katchenovsky.[2] But as

---

[1] Both were authors of a very low order; Gretch, a trifle more stupdi and less unscrupulous than Bulgarin, who was scurrilous in his attacks on Pushkin, and commonly believed to be in the pay of the police.—(*Translator's Note*.)
[2] Katchenovsky, Mihail Trofimovitch (1775-1842), of humble origin and largely self-educated, became editor of the *Vyestnik*

a writer he was of little importance in spite of the fact that he wrote everything, even *Götz von Berlichingen*, in Russian. His unswept and unpolished style, coarse manner of throwing out gnawed and ragged remarks and undigested thoughts, inspired me in old days, and I wrote a parody of him, a little fragment of *Vedrin's Notes of Travel*. Strogonov (the Director of Moscow University), after reading it, said: 'Pogodin will certainly imagine that he wrote it himself.'

It is doubtful whether Shevyryov did anything at all as a professor. As for his literary articles, I do not remember a single original idea or a single independent opinion in anything he wrote. His style was quite the opposite of Pogodin's, being windy, spongy, rather like too limp a blancmange in which the almond flavouring has been forgotten, although under his treacle a vast amount of jaundiced, conceited irritability was masked. As one reads Pogodin one feels as though he were swearing and looking round to see whether there are ladies in the room. Reading Shevyryov one slumbers and keeps dreaming of something quite different.

Speaking of the style of these Siamese twins of Moscow journalism inevitably reminds one of George Foster the celebrated companion of Captain Cook in the Sandwich Islands and of Robespierre in the Convention of the one and indivisible Republic. Being professor of botany in Vilna and listening to Polish so rich in consonants, he remembered his friends in Otaheite who spoke almost entirely in vowel sounds and observed: 'If those two languages were mixed what a smooth and sonorous tongue it would make!'

However, badly as they wrote, the co-editors of the

Yevropi, and professor of Fine Arts, of Literature, and later on of History in Moscow University. His sceptical attitude on historical subjects gave offence, and he was superseded in the Chair of History by Pogodin.—(*Translator's Note*.)

A RECONCILIATION BANQUET

Moskvityanin began attacking not only Byelinsky but also Granovsky for his lectures, and always with the same unhappy lack of tact which set all decent people against them. They accused Granovsky of partiality for Western culture, for a certain 'order of ideas' for which Nicholas from 'an idea of order' clapped men in fetters and sent them to Nertchinsk.

Granovsky took up their challenge, and his bold and noble reply put them to shame. He asked his accusers publicly from the lecturer's platform why he ought to hate Western Europe, and if he did hate Western culture what inducement would he have to lecture on its history.

'I am accused,' said Granovsky, 'of using history merely as a means of expressing my own views. That is partly true; I have convictions and I bring them forward in my lectures. If I had none I should not appear before you in public simply in order, more or less interestingly, to describe a succession of events.'

Granovsky's answers were so simple and manly, and his lectures so attractive, that the Slavophil doctrinaires subsided, while the young people applauded no less than we. At the end of the course an effort was even made at reconciliation. We gave Granovsky a dinner after his final lecture. The Slavophils wanted to join us in it, and Yury Samarin was chosen by them (as I was by our side) as steward.

The banquet was a success; at the end of it, after many toasts, not only unanimous but drunk with zest, we embraced the Slavophils and kissed them in the Russian, style. Ivan Kireyevsky only begged me one thing, that I would alter the spelling of my name, and by changing the e into a Slavonic vowel make it more Russian to the ear. But Shevyryov did not even insist on that, on the contrary as he embraced me he repeated in his soprano: 'He is a good man even with an e, he is a Russian even with an e.' On both sides the reconciliation was genuine and without reservations, which, of course, did not prevent us from disagreeing more than ever a week later.

Reconciliations as a rule are only possible when they are unnecessary, *i.e.* when personal exasperation is over, or when opinions have approximated and when people see themselves that they have nothing to quarrel about. Otherwise every reconciliation involves weakening on both sides, they both fade, that is, lose their distinctive colouring. The efforts of our peace conference very soon turned out to be impracticable, and the conflict raged with fresh exasperation. On our side it was impossible to rope in Byelinsky; he sent us threatening letters from Petersburg, excommunicated and anathematised us, and wrote more angrily than ever in the *Notes of the Fatherland*. At last he pointed a triumphant finger at the 'dodges' of Slavophilism and repeated reproachfully,' there you have them,' while we hung our heads in contrition. Byelinsky was right!

A poet,[1] at one time a favourite, who became a' Slavophil through family connections and a sanctimonious bigot through illness, tried with his dying hand to have a lash at us; but unluckily the police whip was again the means chosen for the purpose. In a play entitled Our *Opponents*, he called Tchaadayev a renegade from orthodoxy, Granovsky a false teacher corrupting the young, me a footman wearing the gorgeous livery of Western culture, and all three of us traitors to our country. Of course, he did not mention our names; those were put in by the readers who enthusiastically carried this spy's report in verse from drawing-room to drawing-room. K. Aksakov indignantly answered him also in verse, branding with emphatic disapproval his spiteful attacks, and saying that their real opponents were the Slavophils who played the gendarmes in the name of Christ.

[1] Yazykov, a friend of Pushkin's.—(*Translator's Note*.)

This incident added much bitterness to our relations. The poet's name, the name of the man who recited the poem, the circle in which he lived, the circle which was enthusiastic over it—all helped to increase the irritation caused by it.

Our dissensions very nearly led to a terrible calamity, to the ruin of the two purest and best representatives of the two parties. All the efforts of their friends were needed to patch up the quarrel between Granovsky and Pyotr Kireyevsky which very nearly came to a duel.

In the midst of these circumstances Shevyryov, who could never resign himself to the colossal success of Granovsky's lectures, had the happy thought of trying to beat him in his own field, and announced a course of public lectures. He lectured on Dante, on Nationalism in Art, on Orthodoxy and Culture, and so on; his audience was numerous, but it remained cold. He displayed boldness at times and this was very much appreciated, but the general effect was negligible. One lecture has remained in my memory, the one in which he talked of Michelet's *Le Peuple* and George Sand's story *La Mare au Diable*, because in it he touched vividly on a living and contemporary interest. It was difficult to arouse sympathy when talking of the charms of the ecclesiastical writers of the Eastern Church and lauding the Greco-Russian Church. Only Fyodor Glinka[1] and his wife Yevdokia, who wrote of 'the milk of the Holy Virgin,' usually sat side by side in the front row, modestly casting down their eyes when Shevyryov was immoderate in his praises of the Orthodox Church.

Shevyryov spoilt his lectures, just as he spoilt his articles, by sallies against ideas, books, and persons, whom

[1] This Glinka, one of the founders of the League of Public Welfare, out of which the Decembrist movement developed, was exiled in 1826, but allowed to return later. He was a literary character of the mild and pious type.—(*Translator's Note*.)

one could hardly have defended without being clapped in prison.

Meanwhile, 'in spite of all the devices invented to make a success' of the *Moskvityanin,* it was definitely a failure. To make a polemical journal living one must have the instinct of modernity, one must have that delicate sensitiveness of the nerves which is at once stimulated by all that stimulates society. The editors of the *Moskvityanin* were entirely destitute of this intuitive vision and, however they turned and twisted poor Nestor and poor Dante, they were at last themselves convinced that in our depraved age you could have no success, either with the roughly chopped phrases of Pogodin or the sing-song suavity of Shevyryov's eloquence. After much consideration they determined to offer the editorship to Ivan Kireyevsky. The choice of Kireyevsky was a particularly happy one, not only because of his intelligence and talents, but also on the financial side. There is no one in the world with whom I should so much like to transact business as with Kireyevsky.

To give an idea of his commercial philosophy I will relate the following anecdote. He had a stud-farm from which horses were brought to Moscow, valued, and sold. On one occasion a young officer came to buy a horse to which he had taken a great fancy; the coachman, seeing this, put up the price. After some bargaining the officer agreed to his terms and went to Kireyevsky. The latter after receiving the money looked in the list and observed to the officer that the horse was priced at eight hundred roubles, not at a thousand, and that the coachman must have made a mistake. This so dumbfounded the officer that he asked permission to look at the horse again, and after examining it refused to buy it, saying: 'It must be a nice sort of horse, if the owner is ashamed to take the price agreed on for it. . . .' Where could one find a better editor?

He set to work zealously, wasted a great deal of time and moved to Moscow on account of it, but for all his talent he could do nothing with the magazine. The *Moskvityanin* did not respond to any living widely diffused demand, and therefore could not have any circulation except in its own coterie. Its failure must have been a great disappointment to Kireyevsky.

The *Moskvityanin* did not recover after its second breakdown, and the Slavophils themselves perceived that they could not make much headway on that boat. They began to think of another magazine.

This time it was not they who came off victorious. Public opinion clamorously decided in our favour. In the dark night when the *Moskvityanin* was sinking and the *Lighthouse* was no longer lighting it up from Petersburg, Byelinsky, who had fed the *Notes of the Fatherland* with his own blood, set their illegitimate offspring on its feet and gave them both such a shove that they were able for some years to keep on their way with no staff but proof-correctors, printers, and the publicans and sinners of literature. Byelinsky's name was enough to make the fortune of two shops and to concentrate all that was best in Russian literature in the publications in which he took part, while Kireyevsky's talent and Homyakov's contributions could bring neither circulation nor readers to the *Moskvityanin*.

Such was the field of battle when I left it and went away from Russia. Both sides expressed themselves fully once more,[1] and all the questions have been thrown into a new light by the great events of 1848.

Nicholas is dead; a new life has drawn the Slavophils and us beyond the limits of our feud. We have stretched out our hands to them, but where are they? Gone!

[1] K. Kavélin's article, and Yury Samarin's reply to it. They are dealt with in the *Développement des* Idees Révolutionnaires *en* Russie.

And K. Aksakov is gone, and those 'opponents' who were dearer to us than many of our own side are no more.

It was a hard life that burnt men away like a candle set in the wind of autumn.

They were all living when I wrote this chapter the first time. This time let it end with the following lines spoken on the death of Aksakov:

'The Kireyevskys, Homyakov, and Aksakov have done their work; whether their lives were short or long, they could, as they closed their eyes, say to themselves with full conviction that they had done what they meant to do, and, though they could not stop the express troika which Peter the Great had sent flying on its way and in which Biron sat urging the driver with blows to drive over cornfields and crush the people, they did bring public opinion to a halt and made all earnest people reconsider their position.

'With them a new era of Russian thought begins and, when we say that, it seems impossible to suspect us of partiality.

'Yes, we were their opponents, but very strange ones. We had the same love, but not the same way of loving.

'Both they and we had been from earliest years possessed by one unaccountable, physiological, passionate feeling, which they took as memory and we as prophecy—a feeling of boundless, absorbing love for the Russian people, Russian manner of life, Russian mode of thought. And like Janus, or the two-headed eagle, we looked in different directions while one heart throbbed within us.

'They laid all their love, all their tenderness at the feet of their oppressed mother. In us, brought up away from home, the tie was weaker. We had been in the charge of a French governess, and only learned later on that not she was our mother but a downtrodden peasant woman, and we ourselves divined it from the likeness in our features and because her songs were dearer to us than the vaudevilles. We loved her dearly, but her life was too narrow. We were stifled in her narrow dwelling with everywhere tarnished faces behind the silver setting, where she lived terrified by priests and church servitors, and bullied by soldiers and clerks. Even her everlasting wailing for her lost happiness rent our hearts, we knew she had no bright memories, we knew something else too, that her happiness lay in the future, that the new life was stirring under her heart, our younger brother, to whom without the mess of pottage we would yield our heritage. And meanwhile:

> "Mutter, Mutter, lass mich gehen
> Schweifen auf die wilden Höhen!"

'Such were our family dissensions fifteen years ago. Much water has flowed away since then, and we have met the *mountain spirit* that has checked our flight, while they have stumbled out of a world of relics on to living Russian problems. It would be strange for us to adjust accounts, we have no monopoly of understanding; time, history, and experience have brought us nearer, not because we have drawn them to us, nor they us to them, but because both they and we are nearer to a true outlook now than we were then, when we attacked each other unsparingly in magazine articles, though even then I do not remember that we ever doubted the warmth of their love for Russia, nor they ours.

'This faith in one another, this common love gives us, too, the right to do homage at their tombs and to throw our handful of earth upon their dead, in the sacred hope that on their graves and ours, young Russia may blossom into light and power.'

Chapter 31

My Father's Death—My Heritage—The Partition—Two Nephews

FROM the end of the year 1845, my father's strength grew steadily less; he changed unmistakably after the loss of the Senator, whose death was completely in keeping with his whole life, taking place casually and almost in his carriage. In 1839 he spent one evening as usual with my father; he had come from some School of Agriculture, brought with him a model of some agricultural machine, the use of which I imagine could have very little interest for him, and at eleven o'clock in the evening he went home.

It was his habit to take a very light repast and to drink a glass of red wine on reaching home; that evening he declined to take anything and told my old friend Calot that he was rather tired and would go to bed. Calot helped him undress, put a candle by his bedside and went out; he had scarcely reached his room and taken off his coat when the Senator rang the bell; Calot ran, the old man was lying dead on the floor by the bed. This was a great shock to my father and very much alarmed him. His solitude was even more complete, his own turn was terribly near, his three elder brothers were in their graves; he was gloomier, and though, as his habit was, he concealed his feelings and maintained his frigid pose, yet his muscles failed him; I say muscles intentionally, for his brain and his nerves remained unchanged to the very end.

In April 1845, the old man's face looked as though he were near his death, his eyes had lost their lustre; he was by now so thin that sometimes, showing me his hands, he would say:

'The skeleton is quite ready, you have only to take off the skin.'

His voice was weaker, he spoke more slowly; but his mind, his memory, and his will were the same as ever, there was the same irony, the same continual dissatisfaction with every one.

'Do you remember,' one of his old friends asked ten days before his death, 'who was our *chargé d'affaires* in Turin after the war? You used to know him abroad.'

'Syeverin,' answered the old man after thinking a few seconds.

On the 3rd of May I found him in bed, his cheeks were flushed with fever, which had scarcely ever happened to him before; he was restless and said that he could not get up; then he ordered leeches to be applied and, as he lay in bed, continued his biting remarks during that operation.

'So you are here,' he said, as though I had only just come in; 'you had much better go off somewhere and amuse yourself, my dear fellow, it is a very melancholy spectacle to watch a man's dissolution, *cela donne des pensées noires*, but first give the lad ten kopecks for vodka.'

I fumbled in my pocket and found nothing less than a twenty-five-kopeck piece and would have given it, but the sick man saw it and said: 'How tiresome you are, I said ten kopecks.'

'I haven't got it.'

'Give me my purse out of the bureau,' and after a long search he found a ten-kopeck piece.

Golohvastov, my father's nephew, came in; the old man did not speak. In order to say something, Golohvastov observed that he had just come from the governor-general's; at that word my father put his finger to his black velvet skull-cap, like a soldier saluting. I had studied all his gestures so thoroughly that I knew at once what was wrong; Golohvastov ought to have said: 'From Shtcherbatov's.'

'Only fancy, how strange,' the latter went on, 'it turns out that he has gallstones.'

'Why is it strange that the governor-general should have gallstones?' the invalid asked slowly.

'Well, *mon oncle*, he is over seventy, and it is the first time he has suffered in that way.'

'Well, but here am I, though I am not governor-general, still it is just as strange; I am seventy-six and it is the first time I am dying.'

He was fully aware of his position and that gave his irony a *macabre* character, which made one smile while petrified with horror. His valet, who always reported on small domestic matters to him in the evenings, told him that the bridle was in a very bad condition and that they would have to buy a new one.

'What a queer fellow you are,' my father answered; 'a man is passing away and you talk to him about a bridle. Wait a day or two till you have put me on the drawing-room table, then tell him (pointing to me), he'll bid you buy a saddle and reins as well, though they are not wanted.'

On the 5th of May his temperature was higher, his features were more sunken and began to look black, the old man was visibly wasting away from the burning fever. He spoke little but with perfect collectedness. In the morning he asked for coffee and for broth, and frequently drank some sort of tisane. In the dusk, he called me to him and said: 'It is over,' passing his hand over the quilt like a sword or a scythe as he spoke. I pressed his hand to my lips, it was burning. He tried to say something, was beginning . . . and, without having said anything, ended: 'But there, you know.' And he turned to G——I—— who was standing on the other side of the bed: 'Very bad,' he said to him and rested his weary eyes upon him.

G——I——, an extremely honest man who at that

time was managing my father's business affairs and was more trusted by him than any one, bent down to him and said: 'All the measures you have tried hitherto have been useless, allow me to advise you to resort to another remedy.'

'What remedy?' asked the sick man.

'Won't you send for the priest?'

'Oh,' said my father, turning to me, 'I thought G——I——, really had some remedy to advise.'

Soon afterwards he fell into a sleep which lasted till next morning; I suppose it must have been a state of unconsciousness. His illness made fearful progress during the night; the end was near, at nine o'clock I sent a horse messenger for Golohvastov.

At half-past ten my father asked to be dressed. He could not stand up nor hold anything securely in his hand, but he noticed at once that the silver buckle with which his trousers were fastened was missing and asked for it. When he was dressed he moved, supported by us, into his study. There was a big Voltairian armchair and a hardy narrow couch in the room; he bade us lay him down on the latter and at once uttered a few unintelligible and incoherent words, but five minutes later opened his eyes, and meeting Golohvastov's gaze asked him: 'Why have you come so early?'

'I happened to be close by, uncle,' answered Golohvastov, 'so I looked in to ask how you are.'

The old man smiled as though he would say, 'You don't take me in, my dear fellow!' Then he asked for his snuff-box. I handed it him and opened it, but, though he made great efforts, he could not control his fingers sufficiently to take a pinch; this seemed to strike him, he looked gloomily around him, and again his brain seemed clouded, he uttered a few inarticulate words, then asked: 'What do you call those pipes that are smoked through water?'

'Hookahs,' observed Golohvastov.

'Yes, yes . . . my hookah'—and that was all.

Meanwhile Golohvastov outside the door was getting the priest ready with the sacrament. He asked the sick man in a loud voice whether he would receive him; my father opened his eyes and nodded. K—— opened the door and the priest walked in . . . my father was unconscious again, but a few words intoned by the priest and still more the smell of the incense aroused him, and he crossed himself; the priest went up to him; we moved away.

After the ceremony my father saw Dr. Levental zealously writing a prescription.

'What are you writing?' he asked.

'A prescription for you.'

'What prescription, musk or something? You ought to be ashamed, you had better prescribe opium to help me off peacefully. . . . Lift me up, I want to sit in the armchair . . .' he added, turning to us. Those were almost the last coherent words he uttered. We lifted up the dying man and sat him in the chair. 'Push me up to the table.' We did so. He looked feebly at all. 'Who's that?' he asked, indicating M——K——. I mentioned his name.

He wanted to rest his head on his hand, but his arm gave way and fell as though lifeless on the table; I put mine in its place. Twice he bent a weary sick glance on me as though asking for help, a more and more peaceful and serene expression came into his face . . . there was a sigh—another sigh, and the head that was so heavy on my arm began to grow stiff. . . . Everything in the room preserved for some minutes a deathly silence.

This was on the 6th of May 1846, about three o'clock in the afternoon.

He was buried in the Dyevitchy Monastery with great pomp and ceremony; two families of peasants who had been set free by him came from Pokrovskoe to bear the coffin. We followed them, with torches, choristers, priests, archimandrites, bishops . . . and the heart-rending 'With thy Saints give rest,' and then the grave and the heavy falling of the earth on the coffin lid, and with that was ended the long life of the old man who had so obstinately and powerfully maintained his authority over his household, who had so weighed on all who surrounded him; and now all at once his authority had vanished, his power was removed, he was gone, utterly gone!

Earth was scattered on the grave, the priests and monks were taken off to dinner. I did not join them, but went home. The carriages drove away, the beggars pressed round the monastery gates, the peasants stood in a group, wiping the sweat from their faces; I knew them all well, said good-bye to them, thanked them and drove away.

Before my father's death we had almost entirely moved out of the little house into the big one in which he was living; and so it was natural that in the bustle of the first few days I had not had time to look round. But what I saw now on returning from the funeral sent a strange pang to my heart; in the courtyard and in the porch I was met by the servants, men and women, begging my favour and protection (why, I will explain at once). There was a smell of incense in the drawing-room. I went into the room in which my father's bed used to stand, it had been carried out; the door, which had for so many years been approached with cautious steps, not only by the servants but even by myself, was wide open, and the maid was setting a small table in the corner. Every one turned to me for orders. My new position was detestable, revolting to me—this house and everything in it belonged to me because some one was dead, and that some one was my father. It seemed to me that in this coarse taking possession there was something unclean, as though I were robbing the dead man.

There is something profoundly immoral in inheritance; it distorts the legitimate grief at the loss of one near to us by entering into possession of his belongings. Fortunately we avoided other revolting consequences—the savage recriminations and hideous quarrelling of those who share the booty. The division of all the property was complete in a couple of hours, during which no one raised his voice or uttered a single cold word, and after which all present separated with increased respect for one another. This fact, the chief credit for which is due to Golohvastov, deserves a few words of explanation.

During the lifetime of the Senator, he and my father made wills bequeathing the ancestral estate to each other, on condition that the survivor would leave it to their nephew Golohvastov. Part of his own estate my father sold and assigned the sum he received from it to us. Afterwards he gave me a little estate in the province of Kostroma, doing so because Olga Alexandra Zherebtsov insisted upon it. The government sequestered this estate contrary to the law before any inquiry was made of me whether I intended to return. My father sold, after the Senator's death, the latter's Tver estate. So long as my father's own estates covered what he sold of the property belonging to his brother, Golohvastov said nothing. But when the idea occurred to the old man to give me the estate in the Moscow province on condition that I should, in accordance with his instructions, pay a sum of money for it, partly to my brother and partly to other persons, then Golohvastov observed that this was inconsistent with the wishes of the Senator who had intended the estate to pass to him. The old man, who could not endure the slightest opposition, especially in plans which he had long cherished and therefore considered beyond all criticism, heaped sarcasms upon his nephew. Golohvastov refused to have anything to do with his affairs, above all to act as his executor. The misunderstanding was at first so acute that they broke off all relations.

This was a serious blow to my father. There were few people in the world that he really liked and Golohvastov was one of them. He had grown up before his eyes, the whole family was proud of him. My father put great trust in him, and always held him up to me as a model, and now, all of a sudden, 'Mitya, sister Lizaveta's son,' was on bad terms with him, was refusing to carry out his arrangements, was putting his veto on his plans, and already he could see behind him the ironical eyes of 'the Chemist,' as with a smile he rubbed his nose with fingers burnt with acid.

As his habit was, my father showed not the faintest sign of his mortification; he avoided talking about Golohvastov, but became perceptibly more morose and uneasy and talked more often of 'this awful age in which all ties of relationship have grown lax, and age no longer meets with the respect with which it was surrounded in happier days,' I suppose when Catherine 11. was the representative of all the domestic virtues!

At the beginning of the quarrel I was at Sokolovo and scarcely heard of it, but the day after my return to Moscow Golohvastov called upon me early in the morning. Being an extremely pedantic and formal person, he told me all about it at very great length and in fine and correct language, adding that he had made haste to come to me expressly to warn me what was wrong before I should hear anything of the quarrel.

'I may well be called Alexander,' I said jocosely, 'I will cut the Gordian knot for you at once. Whatever happens, you must be reconciled, and, to remove all subject of dispute, I tell you plainly and directly that I refuse to accept Pokrovskoe; and the forest there alone will be enough to cover the loss of the Tver estate.'

Golohvastov was a little embarrassed and therefore

proceeded to prove to me even more circumstantially all that I had thoroughly grasped from his first few words. We parted on the best of terms.

One evening a few days later my father began of his own accord speaking of Golohvastov. As his way was, when he was displeased with any one, he did not leave him a leg to stand on. The ideal which he had held up to me since I was ten years old, the model son, the exemplary brother, the best of nephews, and the man who dressed so well that the knot of his cravat was never too large or too small, appeared now, as though in some photographic negative, with all the hollow places prominent and all the white spots black.

The change to simple abuse would have been too abrupt and conspicuous without all sorts of fine shades, transitions, and connections. My father was too clever to be so inconsequent.

'Oh, tell me, by the way, I keep forgetting to ask you, have you seen Dmitry Pavlovitch' (he had always called him 'Mitya') 'since you came back?'

'Yes, once.'

'Well, how is his Excellency?'

'Oh, he is quite well.'

'It's quite right that you should see him; one ought to stick to such people. I like him and have always liked him and, indeed, he deserves to be liked. Of course he, too, has many absurd failings. . . . But God alone is without sin. Making his career so rapidly has turned his head. . . . Well, he is young for the Anna ribbon; besides he has such duties; he as curator goes to scold the schoolboys and so he has got into the way of talking to people as though they were inferiors . . . he lectures and the pupils stand at attention and listen to him . . . he imagines that he can talk in that tone to every one. I don't know whether you have noticed it, but his voice even is different. I remember under the late Empress,

Prince Prozorovsky used to give commands to his orderlies in just that harsh voice. Ridiculous as it seems, he came here to give me a lecture. I listened to him and thought, "What if my sister Lizaveta could have seen it!" I gave her away to Pavel Ivanovitch on their wedding day, and here was her son shouting: "Well, uncle, if that is how it is, you had better apply to Alexey Alexandrovitch, but I beg you to excuse me." I have one foot in the grave, as you know, and no end of worries and infirmities; I am a long-suffering Job, in fact. And he shouts at me and gets crimson in the face. . . . *Quel siècle!* I know that he is accustomed to *décastères*. Why, he never goes anywhere, but likes to sit at home giving orders to his elders and stable-boys, and then those wretched little clerks with "your Excellency this," and "your Excellency that!" Why, it has turned his brain. . . .'

In short, just as by slightly changing the features in the portrait of Louis Philippe you can finally get from a finelooking old man to a rotten pear, so the model Mitya passed point by point into a Cartouche[1] or a Shemyaka.

When the last touches had been put in, I told him all my conversation with Golohvastov. The old man listened attentively, scowled, and then, after deliberately, carefully, methodically taking pinches of snuff, said to me:

'Pray don't imagine, my dear fellow, that you are troubling me by refusing Pokrovskoe. . . . I am not bowing down and begging any one to take my estate, and I am not going to beg you to. There are plenty who would be glad of it. Every one thwarts my plans; I am sick of it; I will give everything to a hospital—the patients will be glad to have it. As though Mitya were not enough, here are you teaching me what to do with my

[1] The famous chief of a band of robbers whose feats have passed into a legend. He flourished in France during the early part of the eighteenth century.—(*Translator's Note.*)

property, and it is only the other day that Vera was washing you in a tub. No, I am tired of it, it is time I was out of the way; I had better go to the hospital myself.'

So the conversation ended.

At eleven o'clock next morning my father sent his valet for me. This happened very rarely; as a rule, I went in to see him before dinner or, if I were not dining with him, went round to tea.

I found the old man at his writing-table with his spectacles on and some papers in front of him.

'Come here and, if you can spare me an hour, help me to put some of these papers in order. I know you are busy, you are for ever writing your articles, you are a literary man. . . . I saw your article in the *Post of the Fatherland*, I couldn't make anything of it. It is full of such learned expressions. I don't know what literature is coming to. . . . In old days Derzhavin and Dmitriev used to write, but nowadays it is you . . . and our cousin Ogaryov. Though, after all, it is better to stay at home and write nonsense than to be always driving about, going to Yar's and drinking champagne.'

I listened and could not imagine what this *captatio benevolentiae* was leading up to.

'Sit down here, read this document and tell me your opinion.'

It was his will and a few codicils added to it. From his point of view this was the greatest mark of confidence he could have shown me.

A strange psychological fact. From what I read and from what he said I drew two conclusions: first, that he was longing to be reconciled to Golohvastov, and secondly, that he greatly appreciated my refusing to take the estate; and, indeed, from that time, that is, from October 1845 up to the time of his death, he not only put confidence in me in every case, but sometimes asked my advice and on two occasions even acted upon it.

Yet what would a man have thought who had overheard our conversation the day before? I have not altered one word of my father's answer about Pokrovskoe, I remember it well.

The will in itself was clear and simple; he left all his real property to Golohvastov, all his personal belongings, money, and houses to my mother, my brother, and me, to be divided equally among us. On the other hand, the codicils, written on all sorts of scraps of paper and undated, were far from being simple. The responsibility he laid upon us, and especially upon Golohvastov, was extremely unpleasant. These codicils contradicted each other and had that character of indefiniteness which commonly leads to ugly quarrels and recriminations.

For instance, the following words occurred in one: 'I set free all the house-serfs who have served me well and zealously and I charge you to give them rewards and money according to their deserts.'

In one the old brick house was left to G——I——. In another the house was disposed of differently, and money was left to G——I——, but it was nowhere stated that this money was to be instead of the house. In one codicil my father left a certain sum of ten thousand silver roubles to a cousin, while in another he left this cousin's sister a small estate on condition that she paid her brother out of it this ten thousand roubles.

I must observe that I had heard beforehand from him of half of these arrangements, and not I alone. The old man had, for instance, spoken several times before me of leaving the house to G——I——, and had even advised him to move into it.

I suggested to my father that he should invite Golohvastov and commission him and G——I——to put all these notes together into one codicil.

'Of course,' he said, 'Mitya might be of use, but then he is very busy. You know these political gentlemen.

. . . What does he care about his dying uncle? He is always inspecting seminaries.'

'He'll be sure to come,' I observed, 'it's a matter of so much consequence for him.'

'I am always glad to see him. Only my head is not always strong enough to talk business. Mitya, *il est très verbeux*—talks my head off, and my thoughts will be in a whirl directly; you had better take him all these papers and let him first make his comments on the margin.'

Two or three days later Golohvastov came himself; being extremely methodical, he was more alarmed by the confused state of the will than I was, and being a classical scholar he expressed his feelings thus: '*Mais, mon cher, c'est le testament d'Alexandre le Grand.*'

My father, as he always did in such circumstances, affected to be twice as ill as usual, aimed indirect shafts of sarcasm at Golohvastov, then embraced him, touched his cheek with his own, and the family Campo Formio[1] was concluded.

So far as we could, we persuaded the old man to revise his supplementary notes and to turn them into a single codicil. He meant to write this himself, and in six months had not finished it.

After the division of the property, the question naturally arose who were to receive their freedom and who not. As for the money gratuities, I had persuaded my father to fix a definite sum; after long discussions he had fixed three thousand silver roubles. Golohvastov told the servants that, not knowing which of them had served in the house and how they had served, he left the selection to me. I began by putting on the list all who were serving in the house. But when news of my list spread abroad, a perfect stream of serfs of past generations burst upon me from all parts—old men with grey unshaven

[1] The peace between France and Austria in 1797 was concluded at Campo Formio, a village in Italy,—(*Translator's Note.*)

chins and bald heads, clad in rags, with that tremulous shaking of the head and hands which is the fruit of twenty or thirty years of drunkenness; wrinkled old women wearing caps and huge flounces; and children to whom I had stood godfather by proxy though I had no conception of their existence. Some of these people I had never seen at all, others I remembered faintly as in a dream; finally some turned up who had, I knew for a fact, never served in our house, but had always lived away with a passport, and others who had once lived not in our house but in the Senator's, or had spent all their days in the country. If these hobbling old men and old women, shrunken and blackened with age, had wanted freedom for themselves, they would have been no great loss; but on the contrary they were quite ready to end their days in the service of Dmitry Pavlovitch, but each of them had sons, daughters, grandchildren. I pondered and pondered, and in the end put down all their names. Golohvastov was perfectly aware that half of these strangers had never been in our service, but, seeing my list, he gave orders that deeds of freedom should be drawn up for all of them; as we signed them, he passed his finger through his hair and said to me, smiling: 'I fancy we have set free several serfs belonging to other people.'

Golohvastov too was an original person in his own way, like all my father's family.

My father's younger sister had been married to Pavel Ivanovitch Golohvastov, an old, old-fashioned, and very wealthy Russian gentleman of ancient lineage. There are glimpses of Golohvastovs here and there in Russian history from the days of Ivan the Terrible; their names are met with in the days of the False Dmitri and in the Time of Trouble. Avraamy Palitsyn[1] brought upon

[1] In the Time of Trouble at the beginning of the seventeenth century the famous Troitse-Sergievsky Monastery made an heroic resistance against the Poles. Avraamy Palitsyn, the Father Super-

himself first the anger of Dmitry Pavlovitch and afterwards a very long critical article through having incautiously referred to one of the latter's ancestors in his account of the Siege of the Troitse-Sergievsky Monastery.

Pavel Ivanovitch was a morose and niggardly but extremely honest and business-like man. I have described already how he hindered my father from getting out of Moscow in 1812 and how he died afterwards in the country from a stroke.

He left two sons and a daughter. They lived with their mother in the very same big house on the Tversky Boulevard the fire in which had so astonished their old father. The rather strict, niggardly, and oppressive tone characteristic of the old father survived him.

An elaborate, solemn dullness and affectation of courteousness and benevolence always reigned in their house, together with a sense of their own dignity which, *à la longue,* was excessively boring. The spacious and well-kept rooms were too empty and silent. The daughter would sit in silence at her work; the mother, who preserved traces of great beauty and was still a youngish woman, forty-five or thereabouts, was in failing health and usually lay on the sofa; both spoke in a drawling, rather sing-song tone, as Moscow ladies generally did in those days. Dmitry Pavlovitch at eighteen was like a man of forty. The younger brother was livelier, but then he scarcely ever put in an appearance. . . .

And all that has passed away . . . while I still remember Dmitry Pavlovitch's mother making a solemn presentation to him of a horse and droshky for his exclusive use. Their former tutor, Marshal, an excellent man, who served me as the model for Joseph in *Who is to Blame?* used to give me lessons after Bouchôt left us.

intendent, together with the Abbot, issued manifestoes calling on the people to drive out the Poles and elect a Tsar,—(*Translator's Note.*)

However one may try to evade or disguise them, however cleverly one may settle these agitating questions of life and death and destiny, there is still no escaping them with their funeral crosses and with that smile on the grinning jaws of the dead face that seems so inappropriate!

Though indeed, on second thoughts, one sees that there is nothing for it but to smile. Take the fate of those two brothers, for instance—thinking about them leads one to strange reflections!

The difference between my father and the Senator pales before the sharp contrast between the Golohvastovs, though they grew up in the same room, had the same tutor, the same teachers, the same surroundings.

The elder brother had fair hair with a British shade of red in it, light grey eyes which he was fond of screwing up and which were suggestive of the steely imperturbability of his soul. With advancing years his figure became more and more expressive of a feeling of complete respect for himself and of a comfortable digestion in a spiritual sense. By that time he had begun not merely to screw up his eyes, but also his nostrils, which were of a peculiar, rather attractive cut. As he talked, he used to pass the third finger of his left hand through the hair on his temples, which was always curled and carefully arranged, while he kept his lips perpetually curved in a benevolent smile; the latter trick he inherited from his mother and from Lampi's[1] portrait of Catherine 11. His regular features together with his graceful and rather tall figure, his carefully rounded movements, and his neckerchief, the knot of which 'was never too big nor too small,' gave him the somewhat majestic comeliness of the man who gives the bride away at a wedding, of an honourable witness, of a man who has to distribute prizes to the best

[1] Lampi, J. B., was an Austrian painter who came to Petersburg in 1792, and painted portraits of Catherine, Potyomkin, and various distinguished persons.—(*Translator's Note*.)

schoolboys, or at the very least of a man who has come to congratulate, to wish one a happy Christmas or New Year. But for the daily round, for workaday life, he was too elegant.

His whole life was a series of rewards for success and morality. He fully deserved them. Marshal, whose hair had been turned white by his younger brother, could not find words strong enough for Dmitry Pavlovitch's merits and had absolute confidence in the impeccability of his French syntax. He did in fact speak French with that inapproachable correctness with which Frenchmen never speak the language (probably because the sense of the immense importance of knowing the French grammar is not so highly developed in them). At fourteen he not only took part in the management of the estate, but translated the whole of Heraskov's *Rossiad* into French prose by way of an exercise in style. Most likely his old father in the other world was more delighted at hearing of this than the 'Swan on the waters of the Meander.' But Golohvastov did not merely speak French and German correctly and know Latin well, he knew Russian and spoke it well and correctly.

Just as Marshal considered him his best pupil, so his mother considered him her best son, his uncles thought him their best nephew, and Prince Dmitry Vladimirovitch Golitsyn, whose department he entered, esteemed him the best of his subordinates. And what is still more important, all this really was true. Yet, strange to say . . . one felt the absence of something in him. He was an intelligent, competent man, he had read and remembered a great deal—what more, one may say, could one ask?

I have since more than once met these characters, these 'level' minds, these brains so clearly comprehending— in a certain sphere and to a certain depth. They are so intelligent in their judgments, never deviating from their data; they are still more intelligent in their conduct, never stepping aside from the beaten track; they are the true contemporaries of their age, of their circle. Everything they say is true, but they might say something different; everything they do is good, but they might do something else. They are usually moral, but the evil spirit whispers in one's ear: 'But are they capable of being immoral?' The Germans would call such people 'reasonable'; you find them among the Whigs in England, of whom the genius and highest representative now is Macaulay and in old days was Sir Walter Scott, among the followers of the practical philosophy of the 'hermit *de la Chausseé d' Antin*'[1] and of the philosophical disquisitions of Weiss.[2] Everything in these gentlemen is correct, decorous, distinguished, in place; they very properly love virtue and avoid vice; everything about them has the charm of a grey summer day—free from rain and sun; but something is lacking, a trifle, a nothing, as with the daughters of Tsar Nikita . . . but

> 'That was just what was missing,'

and without it all the rest is no use.

Golohvastov's younger brother was born a cripple; this circumstance alone deprived him of the possibility of attaining the antique pose and Versailles deportment of his elder brother. Moreover he had black hair and big black eyes which he never screwed up. This vigorous and handsome exterior was all there was; within, rather unbalanced passions and confused ideas strayed at random. My father, who thought nothing of him, would say when

[1] The popular writer Victor Joseph Étienne de Jouy (1754-1846) was known as the 'hermit of the Chausseé d'Antin,' the name of his most widely read prose work.
[2] Weiss, Bernhard (1827-1892), a learned German, who became adviser to the government in spiritual concerns, and author of many theological works.—(*Translator's Notes.*)

he was particularly displeased with him: '*Quel jeu intéressant de la nature* to see on Nikolasha's shoulders'—and the old man shrugged his own—'the head of the Shah of Persia!'

While his elder brother could never find a minute's leisure and was continually doing something, Nikolay Pavlovitch did absolutely nothing all his life. In his youth he did not study; at twenty-three he was married, and in a very amusing fashion. He eloped with himself. Having fallen in love with a poor girl of no rank, who was like an extremely charming Greuze head or elegant Sevres china doll, he asked permission to marry her, and at that I am not surprised. His mother, who was filled with aristocratic prejudices and imagined that no one less than a Rumyantsov or an Orlov would be a fitting bride for one of her sons—and even such a bride would have had to bring a whole population of the province of Voronezh or Ryazan as a dowry—of course refused her consent. But in spite of his brother's persuasions and his uncles 'and aunts' admonitions, the young girl's bright eyes gained the upper hand. Our Werther, seeing that he could not alter the decision of his relations, one night let down from his bedroom-window a box, some linen, and his valet Alexandr, then let himself down, leaving his door locked on the inner side. By the time the door was opened at the dinner hour next day he was already married. His mother was so distressed at the secret marriage that she took to her bed and died, laying her life as a sacrifice on the altar of etiquette and decorum.

A deaf and grumbling old lady with a little moustache, the widow of an officer who had been in command of the fortress of Orsk in the time of the plague and of Pugatchov, lived in their house. She often used to tell me afterwards about the terrific incident of the elopement, and every time added: 'My good sir, ever since he was a little boy I have seen that Nikolay Pavlovitch would never come to any good and would never be a comfort to Elizaveta Alexeyevna. He was twelve years old, you know, when he came running to me—I shall never forget it—laughing till the tears came into his eyes, and saying, "Nadyeshda Ivanovna, Nadyeshda Ivanovna, make haste, look out of the window and see what has happened to our cow!" I ran to the window and fairly groaned. Why, only fancy, sir, the dogs, I suppose it was, had torn her tail off, anyway the poor darling was left without a tail. . . . It was a Tyrolese cow. . . . I couldn't help saying, "So this is how you laugh at your mamma's cow, and your own property! Well, you will come to no good!" And I gave up all hope of him from that day.'

The prediction so strangely based upon a cow's tail not being in its proper place was quickly fulfilled. The brothers divided the property and the younger one proceeded to waste his in riotous living.

Every one knows the series of sketches in which Hogarth represents side by side the lives of the industrious man and the idler. The industrious man yawns in church while the idler is playing knuckle-bones; the industrious man reads an edifying book in the family circle while the idler is drinking gin, and so on. Except for the difference in social position, the parallel was true of the two brothers. One of Hogarth's heroes begins by stealing and ends on the gallows, while the other spends his whole life in dullness and lectures his friends to death. Thieving was a *hors-d' œuvre*, it was not the thief's fault that his mother did not leave him two thousand souls in the Kaluga province and half a million of money, as Elizaveta Alexeyevna did her son. He would hardly in that case have put himself to so much trouble and effort, for thieving is far from a recreation, it is a very unpleasant and extremely risky pursuit.

On dividing the property, both brothers set zealously to work, one to improve his estate, the other to ruin his;

I do not know whether Dmitry Pavlovitch added a hundred roubles to his fortune by his unflagging efforts, but within ten years Nikolay Pavlovitch had debts of more than a million.

Soon after his mother's death Dmitry Pavlovitch, after establishing his sister, that is, marrying her off, went to Paris and London to see Europe; while Nikolay Pavlovitch set about showing himself to Moscow: balls, dinners, entertainments followed one another; his house was packed from morning to night with gourmands fond of a good dinner, connoisseurs of good wine, young people fond of dancing, interesting Frenchmen, officers of the Guards—wine flowed, bands played, and he even sometimes fêted local divinities of the first magnitude, such as Prince D. V. Golitsyn and Prince Yussupov.

Meanwhile Dmitry Pavlovitch, still unmarried, after duly inspecting Europe and learning English, returned, furnished with plans of Devonshire farms and Cornwall stud-stables and accompanied by an English groom and two immense thoroughbred Newfoundland dogs of incredible stupidity with long hair and shaggy paws. Sowing and winnowing machines, extraordinary ploughs, and models of all sorts of agricultural devices were brought by sea.

While Dmitry Pavlovitch was studiously introducing the four-field system of husbandry, which does not suit our soil, and sowing our orthodox meadows with clover, while he was giving English training to colts of Russian parentage and studying Thiers, Nikolay Pavlovitch—and this I consider the worst and silliest part of his conduct—managed to get tired of his wife and, as though he thought balls and dinner-parties not a sufficiently rapid means for reaching ruin, took as a mistress a stage-dancer who was certainly not worthy to tie his wife's stay-lace. From that moment everything went like wildfire; an inventory was made of the estate, his wife pined and grieved over the fate of her children and herself, caught a cold and died after a few days' illness—the family was ruined.

Seeing this, Dmitry Pavlovitch took vigorous measures to prevent his estate, too, going to his brother's creditors—he made up his mind to get married. He carefully selected a sensible and careful wife, his marriage was not the fruit of unbridled passion; from dynastic considerations he desired direct heirs in order to secure the property of his ancestors.

His brother's marriage bitterly chagrined Nikolay Pavlovitch. He had not expected such a surprise from him; they were destined, it seemed, to astonish each other by their matrimonial alliances. To console himself he was wilder than ever in his debauchery. Slow as such processes are with us, at last the day came when his estate was to be sold by auction. I do not imagine that Dmitry Pavlovitch would have been greatly concerned over his brother's fate, but here again dynastic considerations came in and led him, with the assistance of his uncles, to attempt to save his brother. They began buying up all sorts of bills, paying forty kopecks in the rouble, that is practically threw a large sum of money into the fire, and only saw afterwards that it was quite useless, for the bills were so many. One episode in this story has remained in my memory. At the division of the family property Nikolay Pavlovitch had received his mother's diamonds, and these too he had in the end pawned. To see the diamonds that had once decked the majestic form of Elizaveta Alexeyevna sold to some merchant's wife was more than Dmitry Pavlovitch could stand; he represented to his brother all the iniquity of his conduct; the latter wept and swore that he was penitent; Dmitry Pavlovitch gave him an I O U and sent him to the pawnbroker's to redeem the diamonds. Nikolay Pavlovitch asked his permission to bring the diamonds to him that he might keep them in safety as the sole heritage of his daughters. He did redeem the diamonds and was taking them to his brother, but probably changed his mind on the way; for instead of taking them to his brother, he went to another pawnbroker and pawned them again. The reader must imagine the amazement of the Senator, the annoyance of Dmitry Pavlovitch, and my father's abundant reflections on the subject to understand how heartily I laughed over this extremely comic incident.

When all his resources were completely exhausted, when the estate was sold and the house was for sale, the servants scattered in all directions, and the diamonds not redeemed a second time, when Nikolay Pavlovitch had actually given orders for his garden to be cut down for firewood to heat his stove, the same kindly fate that had spoiled him all his life came to his help again. He drove over to his cousin's summer villa and there went out for a walk, stopped in the middle of a conversation, put his hand to his head, fell down and died.

In those latter years the *diligent* [1] Dmitry Pavlovitch had left his plough like Cincinnatus and was administering the republic of learning in Moscow. This is how it came to pass. The Emperor Nicholas, assuming that Major-General Pissarev had cropped the students' hair sufficiently and trained them to button up their uniforms, wished to replace the military rule of the university by civilian control. On the road between Moscow and Petersburg he appointed Prince Sergiey Mihailovitch Golitsyn director of the university—on what grounds it would be difficult to say, probably he could not have explained even to himself why he did it. Possibly he appointed him in order to prove that the post of director was altogether superfluous. Golitsyn, whom the Tsar had taken with him, half-dead already at being driven at break-neck speed, was so terrified at his new appointment

---

[1] English in the original.—(*Translator's Note.*)

that he tried to refuse it. But in these cases it was impossible to argue with Nicholas; his obstinacy was like the morbid persistence of pregnant women when they have a craving for something.

When Vrontchenko was made Minister of Finance he flung himself at the Tsar's feet protesting his incapacity for the position. Nicholas made him the profound answer: 'That's all nonsense; I never governed an empire before, but here you see I have learned and you will learn too.' And Vrontchenko willy-nilly remained Minister to the great delight of all the 'protected females'[1] of Myestchansky Street, who illuminated their windows, saying, 'Our Vassily Fyodorovitch has become a Minister!'

After galloping another hundred versts Golitsyn, still more crushed, determined to enter upon negotiations and announced that he would only accept the post if he should have a trustworthy colleague who could help him to shepherd the university flock. Fifty versts farther on the Tsar told him to find a colleague for himself; so they reached Petersburg without disaster.

After taking a month's rest to recover from the journey, Golitsyn drove slowly to Moscow and set to work to find a colleague. He had an assistant in the university, Count A. Panin, the most exalted of mortals next to his own brother and the drum-major of the Preobrazhensky Regiment; but he was really too exalted for the little old gentleman to select him. After looking about him in Moscow, Golitsyn's eye fell upon Dmitry Pavlovitch. From his own point of view he could have made no better choice. Dmitry Pavlovitch had all the qualities which those in power seek in a man of our day without the defects for which they persecute him—education, good family, wealth, knowledge of scientific agriculture, and a complete absence, not merely of 'unsound ideas' but

[1] English in the original.—(*Translator's Note.*)

any sort of incident in his life. Golohvastov had had no single love intrigue, had never fought a duel, had never played a game of cards in his life, and had never once been drunk, while on the other hand he frequently went to mass on Sundays—and not to mass just anywhere, but to mass in Prince Golitsyn's private chapel. To this distinction must be added a masterly knowledge of the French language, polished manners, and only one passion, a perfectly innocent one—a passion for horses. No sooner had Golitsyn thought of him than Nicholas raced headlong to Moscow again. There Golitsyn caught him before he sped on to Tula and presented to him Dmitry Pavlovitch. The latter left the Tsar's presence assistant director.

From that day Dmitry Pavlovitch began to grow perceptibly fatter, his deportment was still more expressive of dignity. He took to speaking through his nose more than ever and began to wear a more ample dresscoat, with no star as yet but with an unmistakable anticipation of one.

Until his university appointment we were as intimate as the difference of our years permitted (he was sixteen years older than I). At this point I almost quarrelled with him, at least for ten years we looked on each other with chilly hostility.

There was no private reason for this. His behaviour to me was always full of delicacy, equally free from unnecessary intimacy and mortifying aloofness. This deserves to be noted, since my father in his efforts to bring us together did everything that was calculated to make us dislike each other.

He was continually impressing upon me that the Senator and Dmitry Pavlovitch were my *natural protectors*, that I ought to *cling* to them, that I ought to appreciate the kindness they showed me as relations. To this he would add that of course all their attentions were really for his sake and not for mine. As regards the old Senator, to whom I was almost as much used as to my father, with the difference that I was not afraid of him as of my father, these words had no effect upon me, but they did tend to make me avoid Golohvastov, and that they did not succeed in doing so was thanks to the tact with which Golohvastov always behaved.

My father used to say these things to me not in moments of vexation but when he was in his very best humour, and he said them because in the days of Catherine patronage was the regular thing; subordinates dared not resent familiarity from a superior, and every one in the world openly sought patrons and protectors.

When Dmitry Pavlovitch received his university appointment I thought, like Golitsyn, that it would be a very good thing for the university; it turned out quite the other way. If Golohvastov had become a governor or a chief prosecutor it may be presumed that he would have been better than many governors or many chief prosecutors. The post in the university was not at all the right one for him; his frigid formalism, his pedantry led him into making petty regulations and treating the students like schoolboys; there had not been so much interference in the life of the lecture-room and so much discontent even under Pissarev. And what made it worse was that Golohvastov was on the moral side what Panin and Pissarev had been only in regard to hair and buttons.

Till then, in spite of all his Toryism of the Russian provincial stamp, there had always been something cultured and liberal about him—a love for legality, an indignant resentment of arbitrary tyranny and official plundering. When he received his university post he ranged himself *ex officio* on the side of every oppressive measure; he considered this inevitable in his position. My time as a student was the period of the greatest political enthusiasm; could I remain on good terms with so zealous a servant of Nicholas?

His pedantry and the everlasting ceremonial solemnity, the *mise en scène* of himself, sometimes brought him into the most amusing situations from which, everlastingly occupied with keeping up his dignity and invariably self-satisfied, he could never extricate himself adroitly.

As president of the Moscow censorship committee he was, of course, an oppressive burden upon it and was the cause of books and articles being sent for censorship to Petersburg. There was an old fellow in Moscow called Myasnov, a great amateur of horseflesh, who had compiled some sort of genealogy of pedigree horses, and anxious to gain time asked leave to send to the censor the proofs instead of the manuscript, in which he wanted probably to make corrections. Golohvastov made difficulties, delivered a long speech in which he very verbosely expounded the arguments for and against granting permission, and ended by saying that he might, however, sanction the proofs being sent for censorship if the author would guarantee that there was nothing in his book opposed to the government, religion, or morality.

Myasnov, a choleric and irritable old man, got up and said with a grave face: 'Since the responsibility rests upon me, I think it is essential to explain that there is of course not one word opposed to the government in my book, nor opposed to morality, but as regards religion I am not so certain.'

'You don't say so?' said Golohvastov, surprised.

'Well, you see, there is a text in the Book of Moral Precepts that says: "They that swear over earthen pots, they that plait their hair and that go to the coursing of steeds shall be accursed"; and since I say a very great deal in my book about the coursing of steeds, I really don't know——'

'That can be no obstacle,' observed Golohvastov.

'I humbly thank you for setting my mind at rest,' said the sarcastic old man, bowing himself out.

When I came back from my second exile Golohvastov's position in the university was not the same. The post that had been filled by Prince *Sergiey* Mihailovitch Golitsyn was by then held by Count *Sergeyey* Grigoryevitch Strogonov. Strogonov's ideas, though confused and not clear, were still incomparably more cultured. He wanted to raise the significance of the university in the eyes of the Tsar, he defended its rights, protected the students from police raids, and was liberal so far as it was possible to be liberal while wearing the epaulettes of an adjutant-general on his shoulders and being the humble possessor of the Strogonov estates. In such cases one must not forget *la difficulté vaincue*.

'What a terrible story that is of Gogol's, *The Overcoat*,' Strogonov said once to Yevgeny Korsh.' That ghost on the bridge, you know, simply pulls the greatcoat off the shoulders of nearly every one of us. Put yourself in my place and then look at that story.'

'That's v—very d—difficult for me,' answered Yevgeny Korsh. 'I am not used to looking at things from the point of view of a man who has thirty thousand souls.'

Indeed, with two such blind spots in the eye as the estates and the adjutant-general's epaulettes it is hard to look clearly at the light of day, and Count Strogonov did sometimes step over the traces and behave like a regular adjutant-general, that is, with stupid coarseness, particularly when his liver was out of order; but he could not keep up the deportment of a general, and in that again the good side of his nature was apparent. To explain what I mean I will quote an example.

On one occasion a student from among those educated at government expense who had finished his studies very successfully and had afterwards received a post as a senior master in a provincial high school, hearing that there was a vacancy in one of the Moscow high schools for a junior master in his subject, came to beg the Count to transfer him. The young man's object was to continue his studies, for which he had not the means in the provincial town; but unluckily Strogonov came out of his room as yellow as a church candle.

'What right have you to this post?' he asked.

'I ask for the post, Count, because there is a vacancy.'

'Yes, and there is another vacancy,' the Count interrupted, 'that of the Russian ambassador to Constantinople. Wouldn't you like that?'

'I did not know that it was in your Excellency's gift,' answered the young man. 'I will accept the post of ambassador with genuine gratitude.'

The Count looked more jaundiced than ever but asked him civilly into his study.

My personal relations with him were very curious; our very first interview was not without the peculiar flavour typically Russian.

One evening in Vladimir I was sitting at home; all at once the German teacher at the high school, a doctor of the Jena University called Delitch, called upon me, wearing his uniform. He informed me that the director of the university, Count Strogonov, had arrived from Petersburg that morning, and had sent him to invite me to call upon him at ten o'clock next day.

'It's impossible; I don't know him at all and you must have made a mistake.'

'That is not possible. *Der Herr Graf geruhten aufs freundiichste sich bei mir zu beurkunden über ihre Lage hier*. You will go?'

Being a Russian, I went on arguing with Delitch, convinced myself still more thoroughly that it was quite unnecessary to go, and went next morning.

Alfieri, not being a Russian, acted differently when the French marshal who had taken Florence, and to whom he was a stranger, invited him. He wrote to him that if this was simply a private invitation he was very much obliged for it but begged to be excused, as he never visited persons with whom he was unacquainted; but if it were a command, then knowing the military position of the town he *se constituent prisonnier* at eight o'clock in the evening without fail.

Strogonov invited me as a curiosity connected in the past with the university, as a reprobate graduate. He simply wanted to see me, and, moreover, such is the weakness of the heart of man even under the finery of a general, to boast to me of his reforms in the university.

He gave me a very good reception. He paid me a lot of compliments and quickly reached the point desired: 'It is a pity you can't be in Moscow, you would not recognise the university now; from the buildings and the lecture-rooms to the professors and the curriculum, everything is changed,' and so on, and so on.

To show that I was listening attentively and that I was not a vulgar fool I very modestly observed that I supposed the curriculum was so changed because many new professors had returned from foreign parts.

'No doubt,' answered the Count, 'but besides that, there is the spirit of the administration, the unity, you know, the moral unity....'

To give him his due, however, he did more good to the university with his 'moral unity' than Zemlyanika[1] to his hospital by 'honesty and discipline.' The university was very much indebted to him, but still one cannot but smile at the thought that he boasted of it to a man who was under police supervision for political offences. It is just as absurd that a man exiled for political offences should have gone with no sort of necessity at the summons

[1] A character in Gogol's *Inspector General.*—(*Translator's Note.*)

of an adjutant-general. Oh, Russia! . . . It is no wonder that foreigners can make nothing of us!

I saw him for the second time in Petersburg, just at the moment when I was being exiled to Novgorod. Sergeyey Grigoryevitch was staying with his brother, the Minister of Home Affairs. I went into the drawing-room just as he was going out. He was in white breeches and in all his court finery, with a ribbon across his shoulder; he was going to the palace. Seeing me, he stopped and drawing me aside began questioning me about my case. His brother and he were revolted at the iniquity of my exile.

This was at the time of my wife's illness, a few days after the birth of a baby who died. I suppose great indignation or irritability was apparent in my eyes and my words, for he suddenly began persuading me to bear my trials with Christian meekness.

'Believe me,' he said, 'it falls to the lot of every man to bear a cross.'

'A good many sometimes indeed,' I thought, looking at the crosses of all sorts and sizes that covered his breast, and I could not help smiling.

He divined my thought and flushed crimson.

'I daresay you think,' said he, 'that it is very well for me to preach. Believe me that *tout est compensé*.'

Besides preaching to me he joined Zhukovsky in actively exerting himself on my behalf, but the jaws of the bulldog that had me in its grip would not readily loose their hold.

When I settled in Moscow in 1842 I visited Strogonov from time to time. He was well disposed to me but was sometimes sulky. I very much liked these ebbs and flows in him. When he was in a liberal frame of mind he used to talk of books and magazines, extol the university, and was continually comparing its present state with the pitiful condition in which it had been in my day. When he was in a conservative mood he reproached me for not being in the service and for having no religion, abused my articles, saying that I was corrupting the students, abused the young professors and declared that they were more and more set on forcing him to be false to his oath or to close their lecture-rooms.

'I know what an outcry that would excite; you will be the first to call me a vandal.'

I bowed my head in assent and added: 'You will never do that, and so I can thank you most sincerely for your good opinion of me.'

'I certainly shall,' muttered Strogonov, pulling his moustaches and turning yellower. 'You will see.'

We all knew that he would never do anything of the sort and so could let him threaten it periodically, especially when we remembered his enormous estates, his rank, and his liver.

Once he was so carried away in talking to me that, abusing everything revolutionary, he told me how on the Fourteenth of December Trubetskoy left the square, ran distracted to his father's house and, not knowing what to do, went to the windows and began drumming on the panes; and so spent some time. 'A Frenchwoman who was governess in their family could not refrain from saying to him aloud, "For shame! Is this your place when the blood of your friends is flowing in the square? Is this how you understand your duty?" He snatched up his hat and went—where do you think?—to hide in the Austrian embassy.'

'Of course he ought to have gone to the police and given information,' I said.

'What!' cried Strogonov amazed, and he almost drew back in horror.

'Why, do you think like the Frenchwoman,' I said, 'that it was his duty to go to the square and shoot at Nicholas?'

'You see,' observed Strogonov, shrugging his shoulders and looking instinctively towards the door, 'what an unfortunate turn of mind you have. . . . I am only saying that with these people . . . when there are no true moral principles based on faith, when they leave the straight path . . . everything is in a tangle. You will see all that as you get older.'

That age I have not yet reached, but this lack of readiness in Strogonov at which Tchaadayev used often to mock maliciously is to my mind greatly to his credit.

They say that during the time when the spirit of our Saul of the Neva was completely darkened, after the February revolution, Strogonov too was carried away. He is said to have insisted in the new censorship committee on prohibiting everything written by me. I take that as a genuine sign of his goodwill to me; when I heard of it I set up a Russian printing press. But our Saul went much further. The reaction overtook and outstripped the Count, he would not take part in strangling the university and resigned his position as director. But that is not all. Two or three months after Strogonov's resignation Golohvastov too resigned, horrified by a series of senseless measures dictated to him from Petersburg.

So ended the public career of Dmitry Pavlovitch, and having cast off the burden of state affairs he settled down to dignified repose like a true Muscovite, busying himself with looking after his land and surrounded by his family, his trotting horses, and his well-bound books.

In his private life all had gone well during the period of his curatorship, that is, children had come into the world in due season and had cut their teeth in due season. His estate was provided with lawful heirs. Moreover, the last ten years of his life were soothed and delighted by another personage. I mean Bytchok the trotter, who for speed, beauty, muscles, and hoofs was the champion not only of Moscow but of all Russia. Bytchok furnished the poetic side of Dmitry Pavlovitch's serious existence. Several portraits of Bytchok in oils and in water-colours hung in his study. Just as Napoleon is represented first as a thin consul with long, damp locks; then as a fat emperor with a tuft of hair on his forehead and little short legs, sitting astride on a chair; then as an emperor retired from business, standing, his hands folded behind his back, on a rock in the midst of the splashing ocean— so Bytchok was represented at the various moments of his brilliant career: in the stall in which he spent his youth; in the fields, free, with only a little bridle on; and finally in light hardly visible harness with a minute box on runners and beside him a coachman in a velvet cap and a blue, full coat, with a beard combed as regularly as an Assyrian bull god—the very coachman who had won upon him I do not know how many goblets of Sazin workmanship which stood under glass cases in the drawing-room.

One would have thought that, free from the tedious cares of his university work, with an immense estate and an immense income, Dmitry Pavlovitch might well have lived and lived long. Fate decreed otherwise; soon after his retirement he, a strong, healthy man, a little over fifty, began to ail, got worse and worse, developed consumption of the throat, and after a painful illness died in 1849.

And here I cannot help pausing to reflect over those two graves, and the series of strange questions to which I have referred already rise up in my mind again.

Death brought the two unlike brothers to the same level. Which of them made the best use of his interval between the two mute and blank abysses? One wasted both himself and his property, but he had his brief time of honey of the best lime-flower flavour. Let us admit that he was a useless man, but he did no intentional harm to any one. He left his children in poverty; that was bad, but still they received an education and were bound to get something from their uncle. And how many men who have worked hard all their lives breathe their last with bitter tears in their eyes, looking at their children for whom they could secure neither education nor provision. Carlyle, to comfort people who are too much touched at the fate of the luckless son of Louis xv., tells them: 'It is true that he was trained as a shoemaker, that is, he received the poor education which millions of children of poor villagers and workmen have received and are receiving now.'

The other brother did not live at all, he 'served' life just as priests serve the mass, that is, with extraordinary dignity performed an accustomed ritual, more ceremonial than profitable. He no more paused to consider why he was performing it than his brother. If from Dmitry Pavlovitch's life two or three things, such as Bytchok, races, the goblets, and two or three entrances and exits —for instance when he entered the university with consciousness that he was in control of it, when he went out of the room for the first time wearing his star, when he was presented to his Imperial Majesty and when he led his Imperial Majesty through the lecture-rooms—all that is left is prose: nothing but a stiff and constrained official business morning. No doubt the thought of the importance of his share in the affairs of state afforded him satisfaction: etiquette is a poetry of a sort, an artistic gymnastic of a sort like parades and dances; but what a poor sort of poetry. compared with the sumptuous feasts in which his brother spent his life after secretly marrying a pretty girl with enchanting eyes.

And to complete it all, Dmitry Pavlovitch's regular life, his exemplary behaviour in the moral, the official, and the hygienic sphere, did not even win him health or length of years and he died as suddenly as his brother, only with far greater suffering.[1]

Well, and *all right* [2] too!

---

[1] I think while I am speaking of Dmitry Pavlovitch I ought not to omit to mention his last action in regard to me. After my father's death he was left owing me forty thousand silver roubles. I went abroad without claiming this money. When he died, he directed his executors that I should be the first of his debtors to be paid, because I could officially claim nothing. I received the money by the next post after that by which I heard of his death.

[2] English in the original.—(*Translator's Note.*)

Chapter 32

THE LAST VISIT TO SOKOLOVO—THE THEORETICAL
RUPTURE—A STRAINED POSITION—DAHIN! DAHIN!

AFTER the reconciliation with Byelinsky in 1840 our little group of friends went on without any important disagreement: there were shades of opinion, personal views, but what was of most importance and common to all was based on the same principles. I do not think it could have gone on like that for ever. We were bound to reach a line, a limit at which some would halt while others would pass over it.

Three or four years later I began with profound regret to notice that though we started from the same first principles we were reaching different conclusions—and not because we interpreted them differently but because not all of us *liked* them. At first these disputes were half in jest. We used to laugh, for instance, at the Little Russian obstinacy with which Ryedkin tried to deduce a logical proof of a personal soul. I remember one of the last jests of dear, kind-hearted Kryukov about it. He was very ill and Ryedkin and I were sitting by his bedside. It had been a dull, cloudy day, and all at once there was a flash of lightning followed by a loud clap of thunder. Ryedkin went to the window and let down the blind. 'Will that do any good?' I asked him. 'Why,' Kryukov answered for him, 'Ryedkin believes in *die Persönlichkeit des absoluten Geistes*, and so covers the window that He may not see where to aim if He should think fit to shoot at us.'

But it may well be imagined that such an essential difference in outlook would not long remain a jesting matter.

I find in a diary of that period the following sentence

written with evident *arrière-pensée*: 'Personal relations are very bad for straightforward thinking. Through respect for the excellent qualities of individuals we sacrifice the sharp clarity of thought for their sakes. It needed great strength to weep and yet be able to sign the death-warrant of Camille Desmoulins.'

The germs of the angry dissensions of 1846 were already latent in this envy of Robespierre's strength.

The questions upon which we came in collision were not casual ones; like fate, there was no escaping them. They are the stumbling-blocks on the road of knowledge which have been the same in all ages, terrifying men and alluring them. And just as liberalism carried out consistently inevitably brings a man face to face with the social question, so philosophy—if only a man trusts himself to it without anchorage—inevitably beats him with its waves upon the grey rocks upon which all who have had the temerity to think—from the seven wise men of Greece up to Kant and Hegel—have been cast. Instead of simple explanations almost all have tried to get round them and have only covered them with fresh layers of symbols and allegories, and that is how it is that even now they stand as menacingly, while navigators are afraid to make straight for them and to convince themselves that they are not rocks at all but only fog seen in a fantastic light.

This step is not easy, but I believed both in the strength and in the will of our friends; they had not to seek anew the way out as Byelinsky and I had. He and I had spent weary hours struggling in the squirrel's wheel of dialectic repetition and had leapt out of it in the end at our own risk. They had our example before their eyes and Feuerbach in their hands. For a long time I could not believe it, but at last I reached the conviction that though our friends did not share Ryedkin's method of proof they were yet in reality more in agreement with him than with me, and that, for all the independence of their minds, there were still truths of which they were frightened. I differed from all except Byelinsky, even from Granovsky and Yevgeny Korsh.

This discovery filled me with deep regret; the limit at which they hesitated, once recognised in words, could no longer be ignored. Discussions arose from the inner need to reach the same standard again; to do so we had, so to speak, to call to each other to find out where each one stood.

Before we ourselves brought our theoretical split into the light of day it had been noticed by the younger generation, who stood much nearer to my standpoint. Not only in the university and the Lyceum but even in the clerical schools young people were eagerly reading my articles on 'Dilettantism in Philosophy' and my letters on the 'Study of Nature.' This last fact I learned from Count S. Strogonov to whom Filaret complained of it, threatening to take precautionary measures against such pernicious spiritual fare.

About the same time I learned of their success among seminarists from a different source. This incident gives me so much pleasure that I cannot pass it over.

The son of a priest of our acquaintance living in the Moscow province, a young man of seventeen, came several times to me for the *Notes of the Fatherland*. He was shy, scarcely spoke, blushed, was confused, and in haste to get away. His open and intelligent face was eloquent in his favour, and at last I overcame his youthful diffidence and began talking to him about the *Notes of the Fatherland*. It was the philosophical articles that he read with great attention and assiduity. He told me how eagerly the seminary students in the higher course read my historical exposition of the philosophical systems and how it astonished them after the philosophic manuals of Burmeister and Wolf.

A SEMINARIST

The young man took to coming to see me sometimes, and I had ample opportunity for gauging his ability and capacity for work.

'What do you intend doing when you have finished your studies?' I asked on one occasion.

'Enter the priesthood,' he answered, blushing.

'Have you thought seriously of the life that awaits you if you go into the priesthood?'

'I have no choice, my father definitely objects to my taking up any secular calling. I shall have leisure enough for my studies.'

'You must not be angry with me,' I replied, 'but I cannot help telling you my opinion openly. Your conversation, your way of thinking, which you have not concealed from me, and the liking you have for my work —all that, and besides the sincere interest I take in your future together with my age, gives me the right to speak. Think again a hundred times before you put on the cassock. It will be far more difficult to take it off afterwards, and perhaps it will be hard for you to breathe in it. I will ask you one very simple question: Tell me, is there in your soul faith in any one dogma of the theology you are being taught?'

The young man, dropping his eyes, said after a pause: 'I am not going to lie to you—no!'

'I knew that. Only think now of your future position. You will have every day for the whole of your life to lie aloud in the face of the people, to be false to truth; why, that is the sin against the Holy Spirit, conscious, premeditated sin. Will you be able to face such duplicity? Your whole social position will be a falsehood. How will you look into the eyes of one who is praying in earnest; how will you comfort the dying with heaven and eternal life; how will you absolve men's sins. And you will be forced to convert heretics too, and to condemn them for their heresy.'

'That is awful! awful!' said the young man, and he went away perturbed and agitated.

He came back the next evening.

'I have come to tell you,' said he, 'that I have thought a great deal about what you said. You are perfectly right, the priestly calling is out of the question for me and I assure you that I would sooner go for a soldier than allow myself to be made a priest.'

I pressed his hand warmly and promised that when the time came I would do my utmost to persuade his father to agree to his wishes.

So I in my time have saved a soul alive or have at least assisted in its salvation.

I was able to get a nearer view of the bent of the students for philosophy. Through the whole academic year of 1845 I attended the lectures on comparative anatomy. In the lecture-room and the dissecting theatre I became acquainted with a new generation of young people. Their prevailing tendency was absolutely realistic, *i.e.*, that of positive science. It is remarkable that this was the tendency of almost all the students who came from the Tsarskoe-Syelo Lyceum. The Lyceum, turned by the suspicious and petrifying despotism of Nicholas out of its beautiful park, was still the same great nursery of talent; Pushkin's bequest, the poet's blessing, survives the coarse blows of ignorant force.[1]

[1] The story of how one of the students got into the university is so full of the native flavour of the Nicholas period that I cannot resist telling it. The anniversary day with which we are all familiar from Pushkin's superb verses was celebrated annually in the Lyceum. As a rule, on this day of parting from companions and seeing again former schoolfellows the young people were allowed to make merry. On one of these anniversaries a youth who had not yet finished his studies in a light-hearted moment flung a bottle at the wall; unluckily, the bottle struck a marble slab on which was inscribed in gold letters: 'His Imperial Majesty the Emperor graciously deigned to visit us on such and such a date . . .' and broke a piece off it. A superintendent ran up, fell upon the culprit

With joy I welcomed a new, vigorous generation in these Moscow students from the Lyceum.

Well, it was these young university students, devoted with all the impatience and fire of youth, with all the flush of health, to the world of realism that was opening before them, who discerned, as I have said, the point of difference between us and Granovsky. Passionately as they loved him, they were beginning to revolt against his 'romanticism.' They urgently desired that I should bring him over to our side, regarding Byelinsky and me as the representatives of their philosophical opinions.

This was the position in 1846. Granovsky was beginning a new course of public lectures. Again all Moscow gathered round his platform, again his plastic,

with terrible abuse, and tried to remove him. The youth, insulted before his comrades and exhilarated by the wine, tore the cane out of his hand and struck him with it. The superintendent promptly reported the incident; the youth was arrested and kept in detention on the terrible charge not merely of striking a superintendent but also of sacrilegious disrespect for a slab on which the sacred name of the monarch was inscribed.

He might very easily have been sent for a soldier had not another calamity saved him. At that very time his elder brother died. His mother, overwhelmed with grief, wrote to him that he was now her only hope and support, and urged him to make haste and finish his studies and come to her. The principal of the Lyceum, General Bronevsky I believe it was, was touched on reading this letter and resolved to save the youth without bringing it to the knowledge of Nicholas. He told the Grand Duke Michael of the incident, and the latter directed that he should be expelled from the Lyceum privately, and that that should end the matter. The youth left the Lyceum with a certificate on which he could not enter any educational institution, that is, almost every career was barred to him for he was not at all wealthy, and all this for damaging a slab adorned with the Imperial name! And even this was only thanks to the peculiar favour of Providence which killed his brother at the right moment, to a tenderness unheard of among generals, and an indulgence almost incredible in a grand duke! Being a young man of exceptional talent, he succeeded long afterwards in obtaining the right to attend lectures in the Moscow University, dreamy eloquence set all hearts quivering; but the completeness, the enthusiasm there had been in his first course was lacking, as though he were tired or as though some idea with which he could not cope were absorbing and hindering him. That was just how it was, as we shall see later.

At one of these lectures in March one of our common acquaintances ran in headlong to tell us that Ogaryov and S—— had arrived from foreign parts.

We had not met for several years and very rarely corresponded. . . . What would they be like? . . . How would they stand? . . . With beating hearts Granovsky and I dashed off to Yar's where they were staying. And here they were at last—and how changed, and what a beard—and we had not seen each other for some years; we fell to looking at trifles and talking of trifles though we felt that we wanted to talk of something else.

At last our little circle was almost all assembled—now we would have a life!

We had spent the summer of 184 5 at a villa in Sokolovo. It is a beautiful corner of the Moscow district, some fifteen miles from the town on the Tver road. There we took a little country house standing almost in the park which sloped away downhill to a little river. On the one side stretched our Great Russian ocean of cornfields; on the other there was a wide view into the distance, for which reason the owner of the house had not failed to call the arbour placed there 'Belle Vue.'

Sokolovo belonged at one time to the Rumyantsovs. The wealthy landowners and aristocrats of the eighteenth century with all their faults were possessed of a breadth of taste which they have not transmitted to their heirs. The old-fashioned villages and homesteads on the banks of the river Moskva are exceptionally fine, especially those in which the last two generations have made no reforms and no changes.

We had spent our time happily there. No serious cloud darkened the summer sky; we lived in our park, working hard and going for long walks. Ketscher grumbled less, though he did sometimes lift his eyebrows very high and utter weighty sayings with vivid mimicry. Granovsky and E—— used to come for the night almost every Saturday and sometimes used to stay till Monday. Shtchepkin had taken another villa a little way off. He often walked over, wearing a broad-brimmed hat and a white coat like Napoleon at Longwood, with a basket of gathered mushrooms; he made jokes, sang Little Russian songs, and was almost the death of us with his stories, which I do believe would have made Ioann the Sorrowful, who spent his life weeping over the sins of this world, shed tears of laughter. . . .

Sitting in a friendly group in a corner of the park under a big lime tree, we used to regret nothing but Ogaryov's absence. Well, here he was, and in 1846 we went again to Sokolovo and he with us; Granovsky took a little lodge for the whole summer, and Ogaryov was installed in the entresol over the steward, a naval officer who had lost one ear.

And for all that, two or three weeks later an undefined feeling was whispering to me that our *villeggiatura* would not be a success and that there was no help for it. Who has not had the experience of preparing some festivity, rejoicing at the coming gaiety of his friends, and when they arrive everything goes well, there is nothing amiss, yet the expected gaiety does not come off. Life only passes well and briskly when one does not feel the blood circulating in one's veins and does not think how the lungs rise and fall. If every shock is felt, you may be sure there will be pain, a disharmony which one cannot always overcome.

The first days after our friends' arrival were spent in the enthusiasm and cordiality of festivities; before they were over my father was taken ill. His death and all the worries and business that followed distracted us from theoretical questions. In the peace of our life at Sokolovo our divergencies were bound to come to the surface.

Ogaryov, who had not seen me for four years, was absolutely of the same tendency as I was. We had moved over the same ground by different paths and found ourselves together. Natalie, too, was with us. Our serious and at first sight overwhelming deductions did not alarm her; she gave a special poetical turn to them.

Arguments became more frequent and came back in a thousand variations. One day we were dining in the garden. Granovsky was reading in the *Notes of the Fatherland* one of my letters on the study of nature (it was the one on the Encyclopaedists, I remember) and was delighted with it.

'But what is it you like?' I asked him. 'Can it be only the method of exposition? You cannot possibly agree with the underlying implications of it.'

'Your opinions,' answered Granovsky,' are just as much an historical moment in the study of thought as the writings of the Encyclopaedists themselves. I like in your articles just what I like in Voltaire or Diderot; they stir vividly and sharply questions which rouse a man and urge him forward, and as for the one-sidedness of your views I don't want to go into that. Does any one talk of Voltaire's theories nowadays?'

'Do you mean to say that there is no standard of truth and that we rouse men only to talk nonsense to them?'

The conversation continued for some time on these lines. At last I observed that the development of science, its contemporary condition, *obliges us* to accept certain truths apart from whether we like them or not; that, once recognised, they cease to be historical problems and become simply irrefutable facts of knowledge like the theories of Euclid, like the laws of Kepler, like the con-

THE THEORETICAL DIFFERENCE

nection of cause and effect and the indivisibility of spirit and matter.

'All that is so far from being obligatory,' answered Granovsky with a slight change in his face, 'that I never shall accept your dry, cold idea of the unity of soul and body; with it the immortality of the soul disappears. You may not need it, but I have buried too much to give up that belief. Personal immortality is essential for me.'

'Life would be a splendid affair,' I said, 'if anything any one wants were always true at once as in fairy tales.'

'Only think, Granovsky,' added Ogaryov, 'why, it's a sort of running away from unhappiness.'

'Listen,' answered Granovsky, turning pale and assuming the air of a disinterested outsider, 'you will greatly oblige me if you will never speak to me again on these subjects; there are plenty of interesting things oi which we can talk with far more profit and pleasure.'

'Certainly, I shall be delighted,' I said, feeling a cold chill on my face. Ogaryov said nothing, we all glanced at one another and that glance was quite enough; we all loved one another too much not to gauge to the full what had happened. Not a word more was said. The discussion was not resumed. Natalie tried to cover up the incident and set things right. We came to her help. Children, who always come to the rescue in such cases, served as a subject of conversation, and the dinner ended so peacefully that no outsider coming in would have noticed anything wrong. . . .

After dinner Ogaryov jumped on his horse Kortik while I mounted the gendarme's discarded nag and we rode out into the open country. We were as sad as though some one near and dear were dead; for till then Ogaryov and I had expected that we should come to an agreement, that our friendship would blow away our differences like dust, but the tone and meaning of Granovsky's last words had revealed a distance between us such as we had never imagined. So here was the boundary line, the limit, and with it the censorship. Neither he nor I spoke all the way. As we came home, we shook our heads sadly and both said with one voice: 'And so it seems we are alone again.'

Ogaryov took a chaise and three horses and drove to Moscow; on the way he composed a little poem from which I extract the following lines:

> '. . . For neither grief nor tedium can exhaust me,
> The truth I've spoken fearlessly in gatherings of my friends,
> And friends have fled from me in childish terror.
> He too has gone, whom like a brother
> Or like a sister, haply, I fondly loved and cherished . . .
>
> .   .   .   .
> .   .   .   .
>
> Once more we will set out alone upon our cheerless journey,
> Speaking of truth, unwearied and undaunted,
> And let the dreams and people pass us by.'[1]

I met Granovsky the next day as though nothing had happened, a bad sign on both sides. The pain was still so keen that it could find no words; and dumb pain that has no outlet like a mouse in the stillness gnaws away thread after thread. . . .

Two days later I was in Moscow. Ogaryov and I went to see Korsh. He was as solicitously gracious and mournfully sweet with us as though he were sorry for us, but, hang it all, had we committed some crime? I asked Korsh straight out, had he heard of our discussion. He had; he said that we had all been too hot over abstract subjects; pointed out that the perfect identity between people and between opinions of which we dreamed did not exist, that people's sympathies, like chemical affinity, have their limit of saturation which

[1] Translated by Juliet M. Soskice.

could not be exceeded without stumbling upon aspects on which men were strangers again. He jested at our being so young when over thirty, and he said all this with friendliness and delicacy, one could see that he did not find it easy.

We parted peacefully. Blushing a little I thought of my 'naïveté,' and afterwards when I was left alone I felt as I lay in bed that another bit of my heart had been torn away—skilfully, painlessly, but it was gone!

Nothing further happened . . . only everything seemed clouded over with something dark and colourless; the freedom from constraint, the complete *abandon* had vanished from our circle. We became more careful, we edged round certain questions, that is, we really did retire at 'the limit of chemical affinity'—and all this gave us the more pain and bitterness because we had great and genuine love for one another.

I may have been too intolerant, may have argued conceitedly and answered sarcastically . . . perhaps so . . . but in reality I am convinced even now that for really intimate relations it is essential to have the same religion, to be at one in the theoretical convictions that really matter. Of course theoretical agreement alone is not enough for intimacy between men; I was nearer in sympathy, for instance, to Ivan Kireyevsky than to many of my own set. What is more, one may be a good and faithful ally agreeing in some definite cause and differing in opinions. I was on such terms with men for whom I had the greatest respect, though I differed from them on many subjects—for instance, with Mazzini and with Worcell. I did not try to convince them nor they me, we had enough in common to go the same way together without quarrelling. But between us brothers of one family, who had been so near and had lived one life together, it was impossible to differ so deeply.

If only we had had some inevitable work which would

have absorbed us completely; but as it was, all our activity lay precisely in the sphere of thought and the propaganda of our convictions . . . how was compromise possible in that realm? . . .

The little rift in one of the walls of our temple of friendship grew wider, as is always the case, through trifles, misunderstandings, unnecessary openness where it would have been better to be silent and harmful silence where it was essential to speak; these things are decided only by the tact of the heart, there are no rules to guide one.

Soon afterwards everything was at sixes and sevens among the ladies too. . . .

There was no help for it at the moment.

To go away, far away, for years, only to go! But it was not easy to go. The fetters of police supervision were on my legs, and without permission from Nicholas a foreign passport could not be got.

Chapter 33

A Police-Officer in the Part of a Valet—The Police-master Kokoshkin—'Disorder in Order'—Dubbelt Once More—The Passport

A FEW months before my father's death Count Orlov was appointed to succeed Benckendorf. I wrote at the time to Olga Alexandrovna to ask whether she could procure me a passport for abroad or permission on some pretext or other to visit Petersburg in order to get one for myself. My old friend answered that the latter was easier to manage, and a few days later I received from Orlov the 'Most High' permission to visit Petersburg for a short time to arrange my affairs. My father's illness, his death, arranging my affairs in reality, and some months spent in the country delayed me till winter. At the end of November I set off for Petersburg, having first sent a petition for a passport to the governor-general. I knew that he could not grant it because I was still under *strict* police supervision, all I wanted was that he should send on the petition to Petersburg.

On the day of my departure I sent in the morning to get a permit from the police, but instead of a permit a policeman came to say that there were certain difficulties and that the local police-superintendent himself would come to me. He did come, and asking me to see him alone he mysteriously informed me that five years ago I had been forbidden to visit Petersburg and without the 'Most High' orders he could not sign the permit.

'That won't stand in our way,' I said, laughing, and took the letter out of my pocket.

The police-superintendent, greatly astonished, read it, asked permission to show it to the police-master, and two hours later sent me my permit and the letter.

I must mention that my police-superintendent carried

on half the conversation in extraordinarily polished French. How mischievous it is for a police-superintendent, or indeed any Russian policeman, to know French, he had learnt by very bitter experience.

Some years previously a French traveller, the legitimist Chevalier Preaux, arrived in Moscow from the Caucasus. He had been in Persia and in Georgia, had seen a great deal, and was so incautious as to criticise severely the military operations in the Caucasus, and still more severely the administration of government there. Afraid that Preaux would say the same thing in Petersburg, the governor-general of the Caucasus prudently wrote to the Minister of War that Preaux was a very dangerous military agent of the French government. Preaux was living quite happily in Moscow and was very well received by Prince D. V. Golitsyn, when suddenly the latter received orders to send the Frenchman from Moscow to the frontier accompanied by a police-officer. To do anything so stupid and so rude is always more difficult to an acquaintance, and so Golitsyn after two days of hesitation invited Preaux to his house, and beginning with an eloquent introduction told him at last that reports of some sort about him, probably from the Caucasus, had reached the Tsar, who had ordered that he should leave Russia, that they would, however, give him an escort. . . .

Preaux, incensed, observed to Golitsyn that, seeing that the government had the right to eject him, he was prepared to go, but that he would not accept an escort, since he did not consider himself a criminal who needed to be guarded.

Next day when the police-master came to Preaux the latter met him with a pistol in his hand and told him point-blank that he would not permit a police-officer to enter his room or his carriage, and that he would send the bullet through his head if he attempted to enter by force.

Golitsyn was a very decent man, which made it the more difficult for him; he sent for Veiller, the French consul, to ask his advice. The latter found a way out of the difficulty; he asked for a police-officer who spoke French well and promised to present him to Preaux as a traveller who begged Preaux for a place in his carriage on condition of paying half the travelling expenses.

From the consul's first words Preaux guessed what it meant.

'I don't sell seats in my carriage,' he said to the consul.

'The man will be in despair.'

'Very well,' said Preaux,' I will take him for nothing, but he must undertake a few little services in return; he's not an ill-humoured fellow I suppose, if he is I will leave him on the road.'

'The most obliging man in the world; he will be entirely at your disposition. I thank you on his behalf.' And the consul galloped off to Prince Golitsyn to announce his success.

In the evening Preaux and the *bona fide* traveller set off. Preaux did not speak all the way; at the first station he went indoors and lay down on the sofa. 'Hey,' he shouted to his companion, 'come here and take off my boots.' 'Upon my word, what next?' 'I tell you, take off my boots, or I will turn you out on the road; I am not going to keep you.' The police-officer took off the boots. 'Brush them and polish them!' 'That's really too much!' 'Very well, you can stay here.' The officer polished the boots.

At the next station there was the same story with his clothes, and so Preaux went on tormenting him till they reached the frontier. To console this martyr of the secret service, the Sovereign's special attention was drawn to him and in the end he was made a police-superintendent.

The third day after my arrival in Petersburg the house

porter came to ask me from the local police: 'With what papers had I come to Petersburg?' The only paper I had, the decree concerning my retirement from the service, I had sent to the governor-general with my petition for a passport. I gave the house-porter my permit, but he came back with the remark that it was valid for leaving Moscow but not for entering Petersburg. Then a police-officer arrived with a summons to the police-master's office. I went to Kokoshkin's office, which was lighted by lamps though it was daytime, and within an hour he arrived. Kokoshkin more than other persons of the same order was a servant of the Tsar, a man in favour, ready to do any dirty job, with no distinct aims, no conscience, no reflection. He served and made his pile as naturally as birds sing.

Pokrovsky told Nicholas that Kokoshkin was a terrible bribe-taker. 'Yes,' answered Nicholas, 'but I sleep soundly at night knowing that he is police-master in Petersburg.'

I looked at him while he was talking to other people. . . . What a battered old decrepitly dissolute face he had; he was wearing a curled wig which was glaringly incongruous with his sunken features and wrinkles.

After conversing with some German women in German and with a familiarity showing that they were old acquaintances, which was evident, too, from the way the women laughed and whispered, Kokoshkin came up to me, and looking down asked in a rather gruff voice: 'Why, are not you forbidden to enter Petersburg by the "Most High"?'

'Yes, but I have a permit.'

'Where is it?'

'I have it here.'

'Show it. How's this? You are using the same permit twice.'

'Twice?'

'I remember that you came before.'

'I didn't.'

'And what is your business here?'

'I have business with Count Orlov.'

'Have you been to the Count, then?'

'No, but I have been to the secret police.'

'Have you seen Dubbelt?'

'Yes.'

'Well, I saw Orlov himself yesterday and he told me that he had sent you no permit.'

'You have it in your hand.'

'God knows when that was written, and the time has passed.'

'It would be strange on my part to come without permission and begin with a visit to General Dubbelt.'

'If you don't want to get into trouble you will kindly go back, and no later than within the next twenty-four hours.'

'I was not proposing to remain here long . . . but I must wait for Count Orlov's answer.'

'I cannot give you leave to do so, besides Count Orlov is much displeased at your coming without permission.'

'Kindly give me my permit and I will go at once to the Count.'

'It must remain with me.'

'But it is a letter to me, addressed to me personally, the only document on the strength of which I am here.'

'The document will remain with me as a proof that you have been in Petersburg. I seriously advise you to go to-morrow that nothing worse may befall you.'

He nodded and went out. Much good it is talking to them!

The old General Tutchkov had a lawsuit with the Treasury. His village elder undertook some government contract, he did something dishonest and made away with the money entrusted to him. The court ordered that the money should be paid by the landowner who had given the village elder the authorisation. But no authorisation in regard to the undertaking ever had been given and Tutchkov stated this in his answer. The case was brought before the Senate, and the Senate again decided:

'Inasmuch as retired Lieutenant-General Tutchkov gave an authorisation . . .' and so on. To which Tutchkov again answered: 'Inasmuch as retired Lieutenant-General Tutchkov gave no authorisation . . .' and so on. A year passed, again the police appeared with a stern repetition: 'Inasmuch as retired Lieutenant-General, etc.,' and again the old man wrote the same answer. I don't know how this interesting case ended. I left Russia without waiting for the conclusion.

All that is not at all exceptional but quite the normal thing. Kokoshkin holds in his hands a document of the genuineness of which he has no doubt, on which there is a number and date so that it can be easily verified, in which it is written that I am permitted to visit Petersburg, and says: 'Since you have come without permission you must go back,' and puts the document in his pocket.

Tchaadayev was right indeed when he said of these gentry: 'What rogues they all are!'

I went to the Third Section and told Dubbelt what had happened. He roared with laughter. 'What a muddle they always make of everything! Kokoshkin told the Count you had come without permission and the Count said you were to be sent away, but I explained the position to him afterwards; you can stay as long as you like. I'll have the police written to at once. But now about your petition; the Count does not think it would be of any use to ask permission for you to go abroad. The Tsar has refused you twice, the last time it was Count Strogonov who interceded for you; if he refuses a third time, you won't get to the waters during this reign, for certain.'

'What am I to do?' I asked in horror, for the idea of travel and freedom had taken deep root in my heart.

'Go to Moscow: the Count will write a private letter to the governor-general telling him that you want to go abroad for the sake of your wife's health, assuring him that he knows nothing but what is good of you, and asking him whether he thinks it would be possible to relieve you from police supervision. He can make no answer but "yes" to such a question. We will report to the Tsar the removal of police supervision, and then you take a passport for yourself like anybody else, and you can go to any watering-place you like, and good luck to you.'

All this seemed to me extremely complicated, and indeed I fancied it was a device simply to get rid of me. They could not refuse me point-blank, it would have brought down upon them the wrath of Olga Alexandrovna, whom I visited every day. When once I had left Petersburg I could not come back again; corresponding with these gentry is a difficult business. I communicated some part of what I was feeling to Dubbelt; he began frowning, that is, grinning more than ever with his lips and screwing up his eyes.

'General,' I said in conclusion, 'I do not know, but the fact is I do not feel certain that Strogonov's representation reached the Tsar.'

Dubbelt rang the bell and ordered the papers relating to my case to be brought, and while waiting for them said to me good-naturedly: 'The Count and I are suggesting to you the course of proceeding by which we think you most likely to get your passport; if you have better means at your disposal, make use of them, you may be sure that we will not hinder you.'

'Leonty Vassilyevitch is perfectly right,' observed a sepulchral voice. I turned round; beside me, looking older and more grey-headed than ever, stood Sahtynsky, who had received me five years before in the same Third

Section. 'I advise you to be guided by his opinion if you want to go.' I thanked him.

'And here's the case,' said Dubbelt, taking a thick manuscript from the hands of a clerk (what would I not have given to read the whole of it! In 1850 I saw my 'dossier' in Carlier's office in Paris; it would have been interesting to compare them). Turning the pages, he handed it to me open; there was Benckendorf's entry after Strogonov's letter petitioning for permission for me to go for six months to a watering-place in Germany. On the margin was written in big letters in pencil: 'Too soon.' The pencil marks were glazed over with varnish, and below was written in ink: '"Too soon," written by the hand of his Imperial Majesty.—Count A. Benckendorf.'

'Do you believe now?' asked Dubbelt.

'Yes, I do,' I answered, 'and I believe in your advice so fully that I will go to-morrow to Moscow.'

'Well, you can stay and amuse yourself here a little, the police will not worry you now, and before you go away, look in and I will tell them to show you the letter to Shtcherbatov. Good-bye. *Bon voyage*, if we don't meet again.'

'A pleasant journey,' added Sahtynsky.

We parted, as you see, on friendly terms.

On reaching home I found a summons from the superintendent of the Second Admiralty Police-Station I believe it was. He asked me when I was going.

'To-morrow evening.'

'Upon my word, but I believe, I thought . . . the general said to-day. His Excellency will put it off, of course. But will you allow me to make certain of it?'

'Oh yes, oh yes; by the way, give me a permit.'

'I will write it in the police-station and send it to you in two hours' time. By what diligence are you thinking of going?'

'The Serapinsky, if I can get a seat.'

'Very good, and if you do not succeed in getting a seat kindly let us know.'

'With pleasure.'

In the evening the policeman turned up again; the superintendent sent to tell me that he could not give me the permit, and that I must go at eight o'clock next morning to the chief police-master's.

What a plague and what a bore! I did not go at eight o'clock, but in the course of the morning I looked in at the office of the chief police-master. The police-station superintendent was there; he said to me: 'You cannot go away, there is an order from the Third Section.'

'What has happened?'

'I don't know. The general gave orders you were not to be given a permit.'

'Does the office-manager know?'

'Of course he knows,' and he pointed out to me a colonel in a uniform and wearing a sword sitting at a big table in another room; I asked him what was the matter.

'To be sure,' he said, 'there was an order concerning you, and here it is.' He read it through and handed it to me. Dubbelt wrote that I had a perfect right to come to Petersburg and could remain as long as I liked.

'And is that why you won't let me go? Excuse me, I can't help laughing; yesterday the chief police-master was sending me away against my will, to-day he is keeping me against my will, and all this on the ground that the document gives me leave to remain as long as I like.'

The absurdity was so evident that even the colonel-manager laughed.

'But why should I pay for a place in the diligence twice over? Please tell them to write me a permit.'

'I cannot, but I will go and inform the general.'

Kokoshkin told them to write me a permit, and as he walked through the office said to me reproachfully: 'It's beyond anything. First you want to stay, then you want to go; why, you have been told that you can stay.'

I made no answer.

When we had driven out of the city gates in the evening and I saw once more the endless plain stretching in all directions, I looked at the sky and vowed with all my heart never to return to that city of the despotism of blue, green, and variegated police, of official muddle, of flunkeyish insolence, of gendarme romance, in which the only civil man was Dubbelt, and he a chief of the secret police.

Shtcherbatov answered Orlov somewhat reluctantly. He had at that time a secretary who was not a colonel but a pietist, who hated me for my articles as an 'atheist and Hegelian.' I went myself to talk to him. The pious secretary, in an oily voice and with Christian unction, told me that the governor-general knew nothing about me, that he did not doubt my lofty moral qualities, but that he would have to make inquiries of the head policemaster. He wanted to drag the business out; moreover, this gentleman did not take bribes. In the Russian service disinterested men are the most terrible of all; the only ones who do not take bribes in all simplicity are Germans; if a Russian does not take money he will take it out in something else and be a villain and a terror into the bargain. Fortunately the head police-master Luzhin gave me a good character.

Ten days later on returning home I stumbled upon a gendarme at my door. The appearance of a police-officer in Russia is as bad as a tile falling upon one's head, and therefore it was not without a particularly unpleasant feeling that I waited to hear what he had to say to me; he handed me an envelope. Count Orlov informed me that his Imperial Majesty commanded that I should be relieved from police supervision. With that I received the right to a foreign passport.

FREE AT LAST

'Rejoice with me, for I am free at last!
Free to set forth to foreign lands at will!
But is it not a dream, deceiving me?
Not so! To-morrow come the post-horses,
And then "vom Ort zu Ort" I'll gallop on,
Paying for passports what the price may be. . . .
Well, I'll set forth! And then—what shall I find?
I know not! I have faith! And yet—and yet—
God knows alone what still may be my fate. . . .
With fear and doubt I stand before the gate
Of Europe. And my heart is full
Of hope, of troubled shadowy dreams. . . .
I am in doubt, my friend, you see,
I shake my head despondingly. . . .'
OGARYOV: Humorous Verse.[1]

Six or seven sledges accompanied us as far as Tchorny Gryaz. There for the last time we clinked glasses and parted, sobbing.

It was evening, the covered sledge crunched through the snow . . . you looked mournfully after us but did not guess that it meant a funeral and eternal separation. All were there, only one was missing, the nearest of the near: he was ill, and by his absence, as it were, washed his hands of my departure.

It was the 21st of January 1847. . . .

The sergeant gave me back our passports: a small, old soldier in a clumsy casque covered with American leather, carrying a gun of disproportionate size and weight, lifted the barrier; an Ural Cossack with narrow little eyes and broad cheek-bones, holding the reins of his little, shaggy, dishevelled nag, which was covered all over with little icicles, came up to wish me a happy journey; the pale, thin, dirty little Jewish driver with rags twisted four times round his neck clambered on the box.

'Good-bye I Good-bye!' said our old acquaintance, Karl Ivanovitch, who was seeing us as far as Taurogen,

---

[1] Translated by Juliet M. Soskice.

while Tata's wet nurse, a handsome peasant woman, dissolved in tears as she said farewell.

The little Jew whipped up his horses, the sledges moved off. I looked back, the barrier had been lowered, the wind swept the snow from Russia on to the road and blew the tail and mane of the Cossack's horse to one side.

The nurse in a sarafan and a sleeveless jacket was still looking after us and weeping; Sonnenberg, that symbol of the parental home, that comic figure from the days of childhood, waved his silk handkerchief—all around was the endless plain of snow.

'Good-bye, Tatyana! Good-bye, Karl Ivanovitch!'

Here was a milestone and on it, covered with snow, a thin and single-headed eagle with outspread wings . . . and it is so much to the good that it is one head less.

Appendix

(To **Chapter 29**)

I

N.H. KETSCHER

(1842—1847)

I MUST speak of Ketscher again, and this time in far more detail. On my return from exile I found him as before in Moscow—though, indeed, he had become so rooted in Moscow and so much a part of the life there that I cannot imagine Moscow without him, or him in any other city. He did try moving to Petersburg, he could not stand six months of it, threw up his position and reappeared on the banks of the Neglinny in Bazhanov's café to preach free-thought to officers as they played billiards, to teach actors dramatic art, to translate Shakespeare, and to love and worry his old friends. It is true that he had now a new circle, *i.e.*, the circle of Byelinsky and Bakunin; but though he lectured them day and night, he was still heart and soul with us.

He was then going on for forty, but he remained absolutely an old student. How did that happen? It is just that that we must investigate.

Ketscher is a perfect example of the class of strange personalities that were developed in the stagnant swamp of the Russia of the Petersburg period, especially after 1812, who were the consequence of it, the victims of it, and indirectly the stepping-stones from it to other things. These people broke away from the wearisome and ignoble common track and never found one of their own, spent their lives in seeking it and got no farther than the search. The characteristics of these victims are very varied; they are not all like Onyegin or Petchorin, they are not all idle and superfluous people; there are people who work hard and yet accomplish nothing, people who are failures: I have been tempted a thousand times to describe a whole series of original figures, to draw striking portraits taken from life, but I have stopped short, overwhelmed by my material. There is nothing of the herd, of the rank and file about them; they are of all shapes and figures, but one common feature or rather one *common misfortune* connects them all. Looking into the dark grey background, they see soldiers under the stick, serfs under the lash, faces that betray a stifled moan, carts on their way to Siberia, prisoners trudging in the same direction, shaven heads, branded faces, helmets, epaulettes, plumes . . . in short, the Russia of Petersburg. It is that that torments them; they have neither the strength to accept it nor to tear themselves away nor to alter things. They try to escape from that background and cannot— they have no ground under their feet; they try to cry out against it—they have no voice, nor are there ears to hear them.

It is no wonder that with this loss of balance there are among them more original and eccentric than practically useful and perseveringly industrious people, that there is as much that is inharmonious and senseless in their lives as there is good and humane.

Ketscher's father was a scientific instrument-maker. He was famed for his surgical instruments and extreme honesty. He died early, leaving his widow a large family to bring up and business afikirs in confusion. Consequently there could be in Ketscher's case no question of real contact, that is, of direct contact with the simple people such as is, even in a wealthy household, absorbed with one's foster-mother's milk, with one's earliest games. The foreign manufacturers and traders, craftsmen and their employers, make up a narrow circle, cut off by habits, interests, and everything else both from the lower and the upper classes of Russia. Often in those circles the family life is pure and moral in comparison with the savage tyranny and hidden vice of our merchants, with the sad and dreary drunkenness of our workmen, and with the narrow, filthy life of our government clerks which rests entirely on thieving. It is, nevertheless, entirely alien to the world surrounding it, it is foreign, and from the very first gives a different *pli* and different fundamental principles.

Ketscher's mother was a Russian, and I imagine that it was owing to that fact that Ketscher did not grow up a foreigner. I do not think she took any part in the children's education, but what was of the greatest consequence was that they were baptized into the Orthodox Church, which meant that they had no religion whatever. Had they been Lutherans or Catholics they would have been drawn in the German direction. They would have gone to one or other *Kirche*, and would insensibly have passed into its *Gemeinde*, with its alienating and isolating influence, with its rival coteries and its parochial interests. No one sent Ketscher to the Russian Church, of course; besides, even if he had been in the habit of going to it sometimes as a child, it has not the spider-like character of its sister churches, especially with foreigners.

It must be remembered that the period of which I am speaking knew nothing of hysterical orthodoxy. The Church, like the State, did not fly to any weapon for its defence and was not jealous of its rights, perhaps because no one was attacking them. Every one knew what these two beasts were like and no one put a finger in the jaws of either. They, for their part, did not snatch at the strangers within their gates, being doubtful of their orthodoxy or of their loyalty. When the Chair of Theology was founded in the Moscow University, old Professor Heym, famous for his lexicons, said with horror in the university hall: '*Es ist ein Ende mit der grossen Hochschule Ruthenias.*' Even Magnitsky's and Runitch's savage epidemic of bigotry, senseless, flagrant as it was, and (as always with us) carried out by spies and policemen, passed over like a malignant storm-cloud, broke over the people who happened to be on the road, and vanished in the shape of diverse Fotys and countesses.[1] In the high schools and boarding-schools the catechism was taught as a form and for the examinations, which always began with 'Scripture.'

In due time Ketscher entered the Academy of Medicine and Surgery. That was also a purely foreign institution and also not particularly orthodox. One of the lecturers there was Just Christian Loder, the friend of Goethe and the teacher of Humboldt, one of the pleiades of free and vigorous thinkers who have raised Germany to a height of which she never dreamed. For these men science was still a religion and propaganda a warfare; freedom from the fetters of theology was new for them; they still remembered the struggle for it, they had faith in their conquest of it and were proud of it. Loder would never have consented to teach anatomy according to the catechism of Filaret. Beside him stood Fischer of Waldheim and the surgeon Hildebrandt, of whom I have spoken in another place. There was never one word of Russian nor one Russian face in the Academy, but there were various other German laboratory assistants, demonstrators, and chemists: everything Russian was thrust into the background. There is only one exception that we remember, *i.e.*, Detkovsky. Ketscher cherished his memory, and he probably had a good influence on the students. The medical students, however, made up of two species, Germans and seminarists, did not even in later days take part in the common life of the universities, but confined themselves to their own affairs.

[1] See p. 335, Vol. i.—(*Translator's Note.*)

Those affairs seemed of little account to Ketscher, which is the best proof of his not being a genuine German and not putting his profession before everything.

His own family circle could have no special attraction for him, and from early years he had preferred to live apart. The rest of his surroundings could only repel and jar upon him. He set to reading and re-reading Schiller.

In later years Ketscher translated the whole of Shakespeare, but Schiller left indelible traces upon him.

Schiller was exactly the right author for our students. Posa and Max, Karl Moor and Ferdinand were students, robber-students: it is all the protest of the first dawn, of the first revolt. More swayed by his heart than his intellect, Ketscher understood and absorbed the poetical theorising of Schiller, the revolutionary philosophy in his dialogue, and there he stopped. He was satisfied: criticism and scepticism were utterly alien to him.

A few years after his first reading of Schiller he came upon another gospel and his moral life was determined for ever. Everything else interested him little and passed without leaving a trace. The revolution of the 'nineties, that vast, colossal tragedy in the style of Schiller, with its bloodshed and its side issues, with its gloomy virtues and its bright ideals, with the same character of dawn and protest, absorbed him entirely. In this, too, Ketscher did not attempt to analyse. He accepted the French Revolution as though it were a biblical legend, he believed in it, he loved its leading figures, he had his personal preferences and dislikes among them; nothing drew him behind the scenes.

Such he was when I met him at Passek's in 1831, and such he was when I parted from him in 1847 on the high road at Tchorny Gryaz.

This—not romantic, but so to speak ethico-political—dreamer could hardly have found the surroundings he was seeking in the Academy of Medicine and Surgery of those days. A worm was gnawing at his heart and medical science could not stifle it. Withdrawing from the persons surrounding him, he took to living more and more in one of the characters with which his imagination was filled. Continually coming into contact with very different interests and petty people, he began to shun society, got into the way of scowling, telling bitter truths that were uncalled for, and truths that every one knew, and tried to live like La Fontaine's 'Sonderling,' or 'Robinson Crusoe' in Sokolniky. In the little garden of their house there was an arbour, and here 'the apothecary Ketscher took refuge to translate the apothecary Schiller' as N. A. Polevoy used to jest in those days. The door of the arbour had no lock and there was hardly room to turn round in it, but that was just right for him. In the morning he used to dig in the garden, plant and transplant flowers and shrubs, treat the poor of his district gratis, correct the proofs of 'The Robbers' and of 'Fiesco,' and instead of evening prayers would recite speeches of Marat and of Robespierre. In fact, if he had worked less with books and more with his spade, he would have been just what Rousseau wished every man to be.

Ketscher made our acquaintance through Vadim in 1831. In our circle, which consisted in those days of Sazonov, the elder Passeks, and two or three other students, besides Ogaryov and me, he saw the first promise of the accomplishment of his cherished dreams, the first signs of new growth on the fields that had been mown so thoroughly in 1826, and so he attached himself to us. Being older than we, he soon acquired 'the rights of censorship' and would not let us take a step without comments and sometimes reproofs. He believed that he was a practical man and more experienced than we; moreover, we liked him, liked him very much in fact.

If any one fell ill, Ketscher was like a sister of mercy, and never left the invalid till he recovered. When Kolreif, Antonovitch and the others were arrested, Ketscher was the first to get into the barracks to see them, did his best to entertain them, lectured them, and went so far that Lissovsky, the general of the gendarmes, sent for him and impressed upon him that he must be more careful and must remember his position (he was an army doctor). When Nadyezhdin, who was theoretically in love, wanted to be secretly married to a young lady whose parents forbade her to think of him, Ketscher undertook to assist him and arrange a romantic elopement, and, wrapped in his celebrated black cloak lined with red, sat on a seat in the Rozhdestvensky Boulevard with Nadyezhdin waiting for a secret signal. For a long time they waited in vain; Nadyezhdin grew weary and disheartened. Ketscher stoically consoled him; despair and his consolations had a singular effect on Nadyezhdin, he fell asleep. Ketscher scowled and strode gloomily up and down the boulevard. 'She isn't coming,' said Nadyezhdin, half asleep, 'let us go home to bed.' Ketscher scowled more than ever, shook his head gloomily, and led the sleepy Nadyezhdin home. When they had gone, the girl came out into the porch of her house and the signal agreed upon was repeated not once but a dozen times, and she waited an hour or two; all was quiet and she more quietly still returned to her room, probably shedding tears but completely cured of her love for Nadyezhdin. It was a long time before Ketscher could forgive Nadyezhdin his sleepiness; he would shake his head, while his lower lip quivered, and say: 'He did not love her.'

The sympathy Ketscher showed at the time of our imprisonment and at the time of my marriage has been described already. For the five years from 1834 to 1840, in which he was almost the only one of our circle left in Moscow, he represented it with pride and glory, preserving our tradition, and not changing it in a single detail. So we found him, some of us in 1840 and some of us in 1842. In us exile, contact with a different world, reading, and work had made many changes. Ketscher, our irremovable representative, remained the same as ever. Only instead of Schiller he was translating Shakespeare.

One of the first things which Ketscher, who was extremely delighted at having his old friends gathered together again in Moscow, did was to renew his censorship *morum*—and this was the occasion of the first signs of friction, which for a long time he failed to notice. His scolding sometimes angered us, which had never happened in old days, and sometimes bored us. In the past we had lived at such high pressure and so much in common that no one had paid attention to little stumbling-blocks in the pathway. Time, as I have said, had made many changes; character had developed in different directions —and the part of a kind but fault-finding uncle was often worse than absurd. Every one tried to turn it into a jest, to cloak his superfluous candour and critical love under his friendliness and good intentions, and they made a great mistake. Yes, what was amiss was that it was necessary to cloak, to explain away, to practise restraint. If he had been checked from the very first, those unhappy misunderstandings with which our Moscow life ended at the beginning of 1847 would never have arisen.

Our new friends, however, were not quite so indulgent as we were, and even Byelinsky, as intolerant of injustice as Ketscher himself, would sometimes lose all patience and, though he was very fond of him, would give him severe lessons, refusing to argue with him for months together. Cold or indifferent Ketscher never was. He was invariably either violently aggressive or ardently affectionate, passing rapidly from being the warmest of friends into being the sternest of judges; this, of course, made coldness and silence harder for him to bear than anything.

Immediately after a quarrel or a series of violent attacks Ketscher's attention was distracted, his anger passed without leaving a trace, probably he was inwardly dissatisfied with himself, but he never admitted it; on the contrary, he tried to turn everything into a joke and again overstepped the limit beyond which a joke ceases to be amusing. It was the everlasting repetition of the famous 'gander' in the reconciliation of Ivan Ivanovitch with Ivan Nikiforovitch.[1] Every one must have seen children who once they have yielded to temptation are nervously unable to stop short of any naughtiness, the conviction that they will be punished seems to intensify the temptation. Feeling that he had again succeeded in irritating some one into cold and biting replies, he returned to an utterly gloomy frame of mind, raised his eyebrows, strode about the room, became a tragic figure from some play of Schiller's, a juryman from the court of Fouquier-Tinville,[2] in a ferocious voice brought out a series of accusations against all of us, accusations for which there was not the slightest foundation, convinced himself in the end of their truth, and, overwhelmed with grief that his friends were such scoundrels, went morosely home, leaving us dumbfoundered and furious, until wrath gave way to mercy and we laughed like lunatics.

Early next morning, Ketscher, mild and mournful, was pacing up and down his room, savagely smoking his pipe, waiting for one of us to come to scold him and be reconciled. He would make it up, always, of course, preserving his dignity as of an old, though exacting, uncle. If no one appeared, Ketscher, concealing a mortal dread in his heart, would go mournfully to a café in Neglinny

[1] One of Gogol's Mirgorod stories.
[2] Public prosecutor of the revolutionary tribunal under the Terror.— (*Translator's Notes*.)

Street, or to the bright, peaceful haven in which he was always met by a good-natured laugh and a friendly greeting, *i.e.*, to M.S. Shtchepkin's, and there stay till the storm he had raised abated. He complained of us, of course, to Schtchepkin. The kind-hearted old man gave him a good scolding, told him that he talked nonsense, that we were not such miscreants as he made out, and offered to take him at once to see us. We knew that Ketscher was miserable after his outbursts, and understood, or rather forgave, the feeling which prevented him from saying simply and directly that he was wrong and so efiacing at the first word all traces of discord. The ladies, who almost always took his part, were foremost in making approaches to him. They liked his open simplicity, which went as far as rudeness (he never spared them), and regarded it as eccentricity. Their support convinced Ketscher that that was the way to behave, that it was charming and was, moreover, his duty.

Our quarrels and disputes at Pokrovskoe were sometimes full of absurdity, and at the same time whole days were overshadowed by them.

'Why is the coffee not nice?' I asked Matvey.

'It has not been properly made,' answered Ketscher, and suggested that his method should be tried. The coffee so made was just the same.

'Bring the spirit-lamp and coffee here. I will make it myself,' said Ketscher, and set to work. The coffee was no better, as I observed to Ketscher. He tried it and, fixing his eyes upon me from under his spectacles, asked in a voice already a little bit excited: 'So in your opinion this coffee is no better?'

'No.'

'Well, it is really amazing that even in such a trifle you refuse to change your opinion.'

'It is not I, but the coffee.'

'Really it is beyond anything, this miserable vanity.'

'Upon my word, I didn't make the coffee and I didn't make the coffee-pot. . . .'

'I know you, anything to prove your point; what pettiness over the beastly coffee—it's hellish vanity!' He could say no more; heartbroken at my despotism and vanity in matters of taste, he thrust his cap down on his head, snatched up a bark basket and went off into the woods. He came back towards evening, having walked fifteen miles; a successful search for edible fungi had dispelled his gloomy mood. I, of course, made no reference to coffee, but paid various civilities to the fungi.

Next morning he tried to raise the coffee question again, but I declined to take up the challenge.

One of the chief subjects of our disputes was the education of my son. Education shares the fate of medicine and philosophy: on those subjects every one in the world has positive and sharply defined opinions, except the few who have devoted a long and serious study to them. Ask about the building of a bridge or draining of a swamp, and a man will tell you frankly that he is not an engineer or an agricultural expert. Begin talking about dropsy or consumption, he will suggest a remedy, one that he remembers, has heard spoken of, or that has benefited his uncle. But in questions of education he goes farther still. 'That is my principle' he tells you, 'and I never depart from it; I don't like trifling in matters of education, it is a subject I feel too keenly about.'

What ideas Ketscher was bound to have about education may be gathered to the minutest detail in the sketch we have given of his character. In this he was consistent, which is more than can be said of people who discourse on education as a rule. Ketscher's ideas were those of Rousseau's 'Émile,' and he firmly believed that the negation of everything which is done with children now would of itself be excellent education. He wanted to wrest the child from artificial life and consciously restore him to a savage condition, to that primitive independence in which equality is carried so far as to wipe out the distinction between man and the monkey.

We were ourselves not so very far removed from this view, but in him, like everything that he had once assimilated, it was a fanatical creed which admitted neither of doubt nor argument. A very real and genuine need is felt for something very different from the old-fashioned theological, scholastic, aristocratic education in which dogmatism, formalism, strained pedantic classicism, and external discipline are considered of more importance than moral development. Unluckily, in education as in everything else, the violent and revolutionary method, while breaking down the old, has given us nothing to replace it. The wild assumption of the 'normal man,' which the followers of Jean Jacques adopted, cut the child off from his historical surroundings, made him a foreigner in them, as though education were not the development of the life of the race in the individual.

The arguments about education were rarely confined to the theoretical field, the application was too near at hand. My son, at that time seven or eight years old, was a delicate child, very liable to attacks of fever and dysentery. This weakness lasted until our visit to Naples, or rather till we met at Sorrento a doctor of whom we knew nothing, who altered the whole system of diet and treatment. Ketscher wanted to harden him all at once like tempered steel. I would not allow it, and he was furious: 'You are a conservative,' he shouted angrily, 'you are ruining the unfortunate child, you are turning him into an effeminate little gentleman and at the same time a slave.'

The child was naughty and shouted when his mother was ill. I checked him: apart from the plain necessity of doing so, it seemed to me perfectly right to make him restrain himself for the sake of somebody else, for the sake of his mother who loved him beyond measure; but Ketscher said to me gloomily:

'What right have you to check his shouting? He ought to shout, it is no life at all. The accursed authority of parents!'

These discussions, however lightly I took them, made our relations difficult and threatened a serious estrangement between Ketscher and his friends. If this had come about, he would have been more severely punished than any one, both because he was very much devoted to us all and because he did not know how to live alone. His character was eminently expansive and not at all self-centred. Some one was necessary to him. His very work was a continual conversation with some one else, that some one else was Shakespeare. After working the whole morning he felt dull. In the summer he could walk in the country or work in his garden; but in winter there was nothing left for him but to put on his famous cloak or his rough, camel-coloured overcoat and go from near Sokolniky to us, to Arbat, or to Nikitsky Street.

His captious intolerance was due to the fact that he never had the intellectual exercise of verifying, analysing, and making problems clear: for him there were no problems; all was settled and he went straight forward without looking back. Perhaps if he had been engaged in practical work this might have been a good thing, but he had none. Active participation in active affairs was impossible, only the three uppermost grades in the service take part in them in Russia. And he transferred his thirst for activity to the private life of his friends. We were spared by theoretical work from the emptiness which gnawed at his heart. Ketscher settled all questions summarily, straight off, in one way or another—which did not matter; having once settled them, he went on without hesitating at anything, remaining obstinately faithful to his conviction.

For all that there was no serious estrangement between us till 1846. Natalie was very fond of Ketscher, he was inseparably connected with the memory of the 9th of May 1838. She knew that a tender affection lay hid under his hedgehog-like prickles and was unwilling to see that the prickles were growing and sending their roots farther and farther down.

A quarrel with Ketscher seemed to her something sinister; she fancied that if time could file away, and with such a tiny file, one of the links that had held so firmly throughout our youth, it would next attack another, and the whole chain would be broken. In the midst of sullen words and harsh answers I used to see her turn pale and entreat me with her eyes to stop, she would shake off her momentary vexation and hold out her hand. Sometimes this touched Ketscher, but he made tremendous efforts to show that he did not really care, that he was ready to make it up, but that he would perhaps go on quarrelling.

The dreadful fluctuating relation of bullying affection and yielding affection might have been prolonged at this stage for years. But new circumstances which complicated Ketscher's life brought things to a head.

He had a love affair, as queer as everything else in his life, which made him settle down quickly in rather clammy domesticity. Ketscher's life, which was based on the utmost simplicity, on the elementary requirements of a student's Bohemian existence among his comrades, was suddenly transformed. A woman appeared in his home, or to be more correct a home appeared because in it there was a woman. Till then no one had conceived of Ketscher as a domestic character, for in his *chez soi* he liked to be irregular in everything, to walk about as he lunched, to smoke between the soup and the beef, to sleep in any bed but his own, so that Konstantin Aksakov observed jestingly 'that Ketscher was distinguished from the human species by the fact that men dine while Ketscher feeds.' All at once he had a dwelling, a domestic hearth, a roof of his own!

This was how it happened.

A few years before, Ketscher, as he walked every day between Sokolniky and Basmanny Street, used to meet a poor, almost destitute little girl. She used to return that way, tired out and depressed, from some workshop. She was plain, shy, scared, and pathetic. No one noticed her existence, no one pitied her. Without parents or relations she had been taken for the sake of Christian charity into some dissenting community, there grew up, and left it to go to hard work with no defence or support, alone in the world. Ketscher got into conversation with her and taught her not to be afraid of him, questioning her about her sorrowful childhood and wretched existence. He was the first person in whom she found sympathy and warmth, and she attached herself to him body and soul. His life was lonely and cheerless; behind all the noise of suppers with his friends, of first nights at the Moscow theatres, and of the Bozhanovsky coffee-house, there was an emptiness in his heart which he would, of course, not have admitted to himself, but which made itself felt. The poor, colourless flower fell of itself on his bosom—and he accepted it, not thinking much about the consequence and probably not attaching special importance to the incident.

In the best and most progressive men there still exists something akin to the property qualification for the franchise in their attitude to women, and there are classes below it which are regarded as naturally destined to be victims. We have all treated them as of no account, so there is hardly any one who can dare to throw a stone.

The orphan was passionately devoted to Ketscher. Being brought up in a dissenting community had left its traces on her: she had gained from it a capacity for blind faith, for idol-worship, a capacity for persistent, concentrated fanaticism and boundless devotion. Everything that she had loved and worshipped, everything she had feared, everything she had obeyed, Christ and the Mother of God, the holy saints and the wonder-working ikon—all that she found now in Ketscher, the man who was the first to pity her, the first to be kind to her. And all this was half-hidden, half-buried, dared not express itself.

She had a child; she was very ill, the baby died. . . . The bond which should have strengthened the tie between them broke it. Ketscher grew colder to S——, went to see her less often, and then abandoned her altogether. That this child of nature would not 'cease to love him easily' might have been confidently predicted. What had she left in all the wide world but her love? There was nothing else but to throw herself in the river Moskva. The poor girl used to go out when her day's work was done, scantily clothed in her poor garments, regardless of rain or cold, along the road leading to Basmanny Street, and would wait for hours together to meet him, to watch him pass, and then to weep, to weep the whole night through; as a rule she hid herself, but sometimes she bowed and spoke. If he answered kindly, S—— was happy and ran home in good spirits. Of her 'misfortune,' of her love she dared not speak, she was ashamed. Two years or more passed like this. In silence, without repining, she endured her fate. In 1845 Ketscher moved to Petersburg. This was too much for her. Not to see him even in the street, not to observe him from a distance and watch him pass, to know that he was hundreds of miles away among strangers and not to know whether he was well or whether any trouble had befallen him—this she could not bear. Entirely without means and without assistance, S—— began saving up her kopecks, devoted all her efforts to this one object, worked for months, then vanished and made her way somehow or other to Petersburg. There, tired, thin, and hungry, she went to Ketscher, imploring him not to spurn her but to take her, telling him that she wanted nothing, that she would find a corner for herself, would find work and live on bread and water, if only she could stay in the city where he was and might sometimes see him. Only then Ketscher fully understood what a heart beat in her bosom. He was shattered, overwhelmed. Pity, remorse, the consciousness of being so loved changed his attitude: now she should remain there with him, this should be her home, he would be her husband, her friend, her protector. Her dreams had come true; forgotten were the cold autumn nights, forgotten the terrible journey and the tears of jealousy and bitter sobs: she was with him and would certainly never be parted from him living. Before Ketscher came back to Moscow no one knew all this story except Mihail Semyonovitch Shtchepkin, now it was neither possible nor necessary to conceal it; we two and all our circle received with open arms this child of nature who had performed so heroic a feat. And this girl, full of love for him as she was, did Ketscher an infinite amount of harm with her absolute devotion and submission. On her lay all the blessing and all the curse that lies upon the proletariat, especially upon ours.

We in our turn did her almost as much harm as she did Ketscher.

And in both cases it was done in complete ignorance and with the purest intentions. She completely ruined Ketscher's life as a child may ruin a fine engraving with his paint-brush, supposing that he is adorning it. Between Ketscher and S——, between S—— and our circle, lay a vast, terrible chasm, steep and precipitous, and with no bridge, no pass to cross it. We and she belonged to different ages of mankind, to different geological formations, to different volumes in the history of the world.

We were the children of New Russia fresh from the university and the academy, we were fascinated by the political splendour of the West and religiously cherished our infidelity, openly denying the Church, while she had been brought up in a dissenting community, in a Russia of the days before Peter, in all the bigotry of sectarianism, with all the superstitions of a hidden religion, with all the legendary marvels of old-world Russian life.

Having by an extraordinary effort of will fastened the severed ties again, she kept tight hold of the knot. Ketscher could not escape now. But indeed he did not wish to. Blaming himself for the past, he strove sincerely to efface it; S——'s stupendous effort had won him. Yielding before it, he knew that he too was making a sacrifice, but, being an extremely pure and generous nature, he was glad to make it as an atonement. But he knew only the material side of the sacrifice: the practical restriction of his freedom. The incongruity of an old student with Schilleresque dreams living with a woman for whom not merely the world of Schiller but even the world of reading and writing, of all secular education, did not exist, never entered his head.

People may say what they like, but the saying *inter pares amicitia* is perfectly true and every *mésalliance* is foredoomed to unhappiness. A great deal that is stupid, supercilious, and bourgeois is implied in the saying, but in essence it is true. In the worst of all forms of inequality, the inequality of culture, there is one salvation: the education of one person by the other; but for that two rare gifts are needed: one must know how to educate and the other must know how to be educated; one must be able to lead, the other to follow.

Far more often the companionship of an undeveloped personality, confined to the pettiness of personal life with no other interests to engross the heart, weighs the other down, induces foolishness and fatigue; imperceptibly he grows petty and narrow, and though he feels ill at ease, yet, entangled in nets and meshes, he reconciles himself to it. Sometimes it happens that neither of them yields, and then the marriage turns into a permanent war, an everlasting duel in which they grow set and remain for ever in fruitless efforts on the one side to lift up, on the other to drag down: that is, both trying to defend their several positions. When their strength is equal, this conflict swallows up their whole life and the strongest natures are exhausted and sink helpless by the way. The more cultured nature is the first to succumb, the aesthetic feelings are deeply wounded by the difference of level. The best moments, which should be bright and musical, are poisoned by it: expansive natures passionately desire that all who are near and dear to them should be near to their thoughts, to their religion; this is taken for intolerance. For them the proselytism of the home is the continuation of their apostolic work, their propaganda; their happiness is limited where they are not understood . . . and most often there is no wish to understand them.

To educate a mature woman is a very difficult task; it is especially difficult in those marriages which are the consequence and not the commencement of intimate relations. Ties that have been lightly, frivolously begun rarely rise above the level of the bedroom and the kitchen. The common roof comes too late for education under it to be possible; only now and then some misfortune will rouse a soul that sleeps but is capable of awakening. For the most part *la petite femme* never becomes a full-sized one, never becomes wife and sister together; she either remains mistress and courtesan, or becomes cook and mistress.

Living under the same roof is in itself a terrible thing over which half the marriages come to ruin. Living cramped up together, people come too close to each other, see each other too minutely, too much in deshabille, and gradually petal by petal tear away all the flowers of the wreath that crowned each with grace and poetry. But similarity of culture goes a long way to smooth things over. If it is absent and there is idle leisure, one cannot be for ever babbling nonsense, talking of housekeeping or paying compliments; and what is to be done with a woman when she is something between an odalisque and a servant, a creature bodily near and intellectually remote. She is not wanted by day and she is for ever on the spot; a man cannot share his interests with her and she cannot share her gossip with him.

Every uneducated woman living with an educated husband reminds me of Delilah and Samson, she cuts off his strength and there is no guarding oneself from her. Between dinner, even if it is late, and bed, even if one goes to it at ten o'clock, there is an endless period in which one does not want to go on working and yet is not ready for sleep, when the linen has been counted and expenses reckoned up. It is in those hours that the wife drags the husband down into the narrow circle of her trivialities, into the world of irritable resentments, tittle-tattle, and spiteful insinuations. This is bound to leave its traces. Relations of cohabitation between a man and a woman without equality of culture are sometimes enduring when they rest on convenience, on common housekeeping, I had almost said on hygiene. Sometimes these working associations are a mutual help combined with mutual satisfaction; for the most part a wife is taken as a nurse, as a good housewife *pour avoir un bon pot-au-feu* as Proudhon said to me. The formula of the old jurisprudence is very clever, *a mensa et toro*; destroy the common bed and common board and they will separate with untroubled conscience.

These business-like marriages are scarcely better. The husband is continually at his work, professional or commercial, at his office, his counting-house, or his shop.

His wife is continually busy with the linen and the stores. The husband returns tired; everything is ready for him, and everything goes with the same little even trot, to the gates of the cemetery to which their parents have preceded them. This is a purely town phenomenon and it is more often met with in England than anywhere; this is the petty-bourgeois happiness preached by the moralists of the French stage and dreamt of by the Germans [1]; different stages of culture can live together more easily within a year after the man leaves the university; there is a division of work and precedence given to the man. The husband, particularly if he has money, becomes what the popular sense calls him, *mon bourgeois* of his wife. By this path and, thanks to the laws of inheritance, it is a path that never gets overgrown with grass, every woman remains perpetually a *kept woman*, her husband's if not some other man's. She knows this.

> 'Dessen Brot man isst,
> Dessen Lied man singt."

But these marriages have a moral unity of their own, they have a similarity of outlook, a similarity of object. Ketscher himself had no object and was incapable of being either the 'bourgeois' or the tutor. He could not even struggle with S——, she always gave way. He frightened her with his loud voice and his grumbling temper. Though her heart was developed she had a heavy, stubborn intelligence, that stagnancy of brain which we often meet with in those who are quite unaccustomed to abstract thought, and which is one of the distinguishing traits of the period before Peter the Great. United to the man she loved so intensely, so devotedly, she desired nothing and feared nothing. And indeed what had she

[1] There is no difference of culture between husband and wife among the proletariat or the peasants, but there is a terrible equality of slavery and terrible inequality of power between the husband and the wife.

to fear? Poverty? but had she not been poor all her life, had she not suffered destitution, that humiliating poverty. Work? but she had toiled from morning till night in a workroom for a few coppers. Quarrelling, separation? Yes, that last had terrors, and great terrors too; but she so utterly abandoned all personal will that it was really difficult to quarrel with her, and ill-humour she would put up with, maybe she would have put up with blows even, so long as she were satisfied that he loved her a little and did not want to part with her. And that he did not want, and there was a fresh reason for not wanting it on the top of everything else. With the instinct of love S—— understood it very well. Dimly aware that she could not fully satisfy Ketscher, she took to making up for what she lacked by continual waiting upon him and solicitude for him.

Ketscher was over forty. He had not been spoilt in regard to domestic comfort. He had spent all his life at home as the Kirghiz in his cart, with no property and no desire to possess it, with no conveniences of any sort and no craving for them. By degrees everything was changed; he was surrounded by a network of attention and services, he saw a childish delight when he was pleased with anything, alarm and tears when he raised his eyebrows, and this went on every day from morning till night. Ketscher took to staying at home more often; he was sorry to leave her continually alone. Besides, it was hard for him not to be struck by the difference of her absolute submission and our growing opposition. S—— endured his most unjust outbursts with the gentleness of a daughter who, concealing her tears, smiles to her father and waits *sans rancune* till the storm is over. S——, submissive, slavishly meek, trembling, ready to weep and kiss his hand, had an immense influence on Ketscher. Intolerance is fostered by giving way to it.

Did not Rousseau's Thérèse, poor, stupid Thérèse, turn the prophet of equality into a petty vulgarian, perpetually absorbed in preserving his own dignity?

S——'s influence on Ketscher showed itself in the way Diderot describes when he complains of Thérèse. Rousseau was suspicious; Thérèse developed his suspiciousness into a petty readiness to take offence, and with no intention of doing so estranged him from his best friends. Remember that Therese could not read properly and could never be taught to read the time on the clock—which did not prevent her from fostering Rousseau's hypochondria till it passed into gloomy madness. In the morning Rousseau would go to see Baron d'Holbach. A servant would bring in lunch and set places for three—Holbach, his wife, and Grimm; engaged in conversation, no one would notice it but Jean Jacques. He would pick up his hat.' But you must stay to lunch,' Madame d'Holbach would say and order another place to be laid; but by then it was too late to set things right. Rousseau, livid with vexation and gloomily cursing the whole human race, would run home to Thérèse and tell her that no plate was set for him as a hint for him to go. Such tales were just to her taste, she could take warm interest in them, they put her on a level with him and indeed a little above him, and she herself began talking scandal, sometimes against Madame d'Houdetot, sometimes against David Hume, sometimes against Diderot. Rousseau would rudely break off all relations, would write senseless and insulting letters, sometimes calling forth terrible replies (for instance, from Hume), and withdrew to Montmorency abandoned by every one, and for lack of human beings cursing the sparrows and the swallows to whom he threw grain.

Once more:—without equality there can be no real marriage. The wife who is excluded from all the interests that occupy her husband, who is apart from them and does not share them, may be a concubine, a housekeeper, a nurse, but not a wife in the full, honourable sense of the word. Heine said of his 'Thérèse' that she 'does not know and never will find out what he wrote about.' This was thought charming, amusing, and it never occurred to any one to ask: 'Why, then, was she his wife?' Moliere, who read his comedies aloud to his cook, was a hundred times more humane, but Madame Heine quite unintentionally paid her husband back. During the last years of his martyred existence she surrounded him with her own friends, faded *dames aux camellias* of a past season, grown moral as they grew wrinkled, and their washed-out, grey-headed adorers.

I do not mean to say that a wife must necessarily do and like what her husband does and likes. The wife may prefer music and the husband painting, that does not disturb their equality. I have always thought that the official trailing of husband and wife about together was dreadful, absurd, and senseless, and the higher placed they are the more ludicrous it is. Why should the Empress Eugénie appear at cavalry drill, and why should Victoria draw her husband to the opening of parliament with which he had nothing to do? Heine did well not to take his better-half to the receptions at the Court functions of Weimar. The prose of their marriage did not lie in that, but in the absence of any common ground, any common interest to unite them apart from sexual attraction.

I will pass to the harm which we did to poor S——. The mistake we made was again the mistake of all Utopias and idealisms. When one side of a question is correctly grasped, no attention is commonly paid to that to which that side adheres and whether it can be separated from it, no attention to the vast network of veins connecting the raw flesh with the whole organism. We still think like Christians that we have but to say to the lame man: 'Take up thy bed and walk.'

At one stroke we flung the solitary and half-savage S——, who had seen no one, from her loneliness into our circle. We liked her originality, we wanted to preserve it, and we destroyed the last chance of her developing by removing all desire for improvement, assuring her that she was all right as she was. But she did not herself care to remain simply as she was. What was the result? We—revolutionaries, socialists, champions of the emancipation of women—turned a naïve, devoted, simple-hearted creature into a Moscow petty-bourgeoise!

Did not the Convention, the Jacobins, and the Commune itself turn France into a petty-bourgeoise, turn Paris into an *épicier*?

The first house that was opened with love and warm-heartedness to S—— was ours. Natalie went to see her and forcibly brought her to us. For a year S—— behaved quietly and was shy of strangers; timid and reserved as before, she was full of the poetical charm of the peasant in a way. There was not the faintest desire to attract attention by her strangeness; on the contrary there was the desire to be unnoticed. Like a child or a weak little wild animal she took refuge under Natalie's wing; her devotion in those days knew no bounds. She loved playing with Sasha for hours together and used to tell him and us details of her childhood, her life among the *raskolniks*, her suffering as an apprentice, *i.e.*, in the workroom.

She became the plaything of our circle; that, of course, she liked; she saw that her position, that she herself was original, and from that time she was lost; no one could have saved her. Natalie alone thought seriously of her education. S—— did not belong to the common herd; she had escaped a number of mean defects; she was not fond of fine clothes, did not care for luxury, for expensive things, nor for money—so long as Ketscher was satisfied and found nothing wanting she did not mind about anything else. At first S——loved to have long, long talks with Natalie and trusted her, meekly listened to her advice, and tried to follow it. . . . But after she had looked about her and was at home in our circle, perhaps worked up by others who were amused at her oddities, she began to display a sort of injured antagonism and would answer any criticism very far from naively: 'Oh, I am such a poor creature, how could I change or improve? It seems I must go down to my grave just as silly and foolish.' In these words there was a note of wounded vanity, conscious or not conscious. She ceased to feel free with us and came less and less often to see us. 'Natalya Alexandrovna, God bless her,' she would say, 'no longer likes poor me.' It was not natural to Natalie to be hail-fellow-well-met with everybody or to be effusive like a schoolgirl; an element of deep serenity and great aesthetic feeling was always predominant in her. S——did not understand the value of the difference between Natalie's attitude to her and that of others, and forgot who had been the first to hold out a hand to her and warmly welcome her; with her Ketscher too drew away from us and grew more and more morose and irritable.

His suspiciousness greatly increased. In every careless word he saw an intention, a spiteful motive, a desire to wound, and not to wound him only but also S——. She for her part wept, complained of her lot, resented slights to Ketscher, and by the law of moral reverberation his own suspicions returned to him multiplied tenfold. His scolding affection began to change into a desire to find us in fault, into a supervision, a continual espionage, and the petty faults of his friends came more and more to eclipse all their other qualities in his eyes. Our pure, lofty, mature circle began to be invaded by the tittle-tattle of servant girls and the bickerings of provincial government clerks.

Ketscher's irritability became infectious; continual accusations, explanations, reconciliations, poisoned our gatherings. This corrosive dust settled in every crevice and by degrees dissolved the cement that united so firmly our relations with our friends. We all succumbed to the influence of gossip. Even Granovsky grew ill-humoured and irritable, took Ketscher's part unfairly, and lost his temper. Ketscher used to go to Granovsky with his accusations against Ogaryov and me. Granovsky did not believe them, but pitying Ketscher, 'who is ill, wounded and yet so fond of you,' took his side emphatically and was angry with me for want of tolerance. 'Why, you know what he is like; it's an illness. The influence of S——, who is good-natured but uneducated and tiresome, is driving him farther and farther in that unfortunate direction.'

To end this melancholy tale I will quote two instances. . . . They show vividly how far we had got from the theory of making coffee at Pokrovskoe.

One evening in the spring of 1846 we had five intimate friends with us, and among them Mihail Semyonovitch Shtchepkin. 'Have you taken the house at Sokolovo this year?' he asked. 'Not yet,' I answered, 'I haven't the money and one has to pay the rent in advance.' 'Surely you are not going to stay all the summer in Moscow?' 'I shall wait a little, then we shall see.' That was all. No one took any notice of this conversation, and other subjects followed peacefully a second afterwards. We were intending to go next day after dinner to Kuntsovo, which we had loved from childhood. Ketscher, Korsh, and Granovsky went with us. The excursion took place, and everything went well except that Ketscher raised his eyebrows more gloomily than ever. But in the end we all came in for a storm.

It was a spring evening, warm but not scorchingly hot; the trees had only just come out into leaf. We sat in the garden jesting and talking. All at once Ketscher, who had been silent for half an hour, got up and stood facing me. With the face of a prosecutor of the Vehme,[1] and with his lips quivering with indignation, he said: 'I must say that you were clever in the way you reminded Mihail Semyonovitch yesterday that he hadn't paid you the nine hundred roubles he borrowed from you.'

I really did not understand; especially as I certainly had not thought of Shtchepkin's debt for the last four months.

'It was delicate I must say: the old man has no money now and he is just going to the Crimea with his immense family, and here you tell him in the presence of five persons: "I haven't the money to take a summer villa." Ough, how disgusting!'

Ogaryov took my part. Ketscher flew at him and there was no end to the absurd accusations he brought against him; Granovsky tried to soothe him but could not and went away together with Korsh before the rest of us. I felt incensed and humiliated and answered very harshly. Ketscher looked at me from under his brows and without saying a word went back to Moscow on foot. We were left alone and in a state of something like pitiful irritability drove home. I wanted this time to give Ketscher a good lesson and to drop relations with him for a time, if I did not break them off altogether. He was penitent and shed tears: Granovsky insisted on our making peace, talked to Natalie, and was deeply distressed. I made it up, but not light-heartedly, and said to Granovsky: 'You see, it will last for three days.'

That was one pleasure excursion, here is another.

Two months later we were at Sokolovo. Ketscher and S—— were going back to Moscow in the evening.

[1] The *Vehme* or *Vehmgerichte* were mediaeval German tribunals which tried capital charges and were greatly dreaded for their severity.—(*Translator's Note*,)

Ogaryov rode part of the way with them on his Circassian horse, Kortik. There was no shadow of misunderstanding or ill-humour.

Ogaryov came back two or three hours later; we laughed together at the day having passed off so peacefully, and separated for the night.

Next day Granovsky, who had been in Moscow overnight, met me in our park; he was thoughtful and more melancholy than usual, and at last he told me he had something on his mind and wanted to talk to me. We went by the long avenue and sat down on the seat, the view of which is familiar to every one who has been at Sokolovo.

'Herzen,' Granovsky said to me, 'if only you knew how difficult, how painful it is to me . . . how I love you all in spite of everything, and I see with horror that everything is dropping to pieces. And now, as though in mockery, these petty mistakes, damnable carelessness, lack of delicacy. . . .'

'But tell me please what has happened,' I asked, genuinely alarmed.

'Why, Ketscher is furious with Ogaryov, and indeed, to tell the truth, it would be hard not to be; I try, I do what I can, but I haven't the strength, particularly when people don't care to do anything themselves.'

'But what is the matter?'

'Why, this: yesterday Ogaryov rode, part of the way with Ketscher and S——.'

'It was arranged in my presence, and indeed I saw Ogaryov in the evening afterwards and he did not say a word.'

'On the bridge Kortik shied and began rearing, and Ogaryov pulling him up was so vexed that he swore before S—— and she heard and Ketscher heard too. I dare say he didn't think, but Ketscher asks why he never happens to be so careless in the presence of your wife and mine. What is one to say to that?. . . And besides, for all her simplicity S——is very sentimental, which is quite natural in her position.'

I said nothing. This was beyond all bounds.

'What's to be done?'

'It's very simple,' I said.' We must break off all acquaintance with scoundrels who are capable of intentionally forgetting themselves before a woman. To be the intimate friend of such people is contemptible. . . .'

'But he doesn't say that Ogaryov did it intentionally.'

'Then what's the talk about? And you, Granovsky, Ogaryov's friend, repeat the ravings of a madman who ought to be put in an asylum. For shame!'

Granovsky was disconcerted.

'My God!' he said, 'is it possible that our little group of friends—the one place where I found hope, repose, and love, where I took refuge from our oppressive environment—will break up in hatred and anger?'

He covered his eyes with his hand. I took the other hand; my heart was very heavy.

'Granovsky,' I said to him, 'Ketscher is right: we have all come too close to each other, we are too cramped and we have stepped over each other's traces. . . . *Gemach!* my friend, *gemach!* We need airing, refreshing. Ogaryov is going to the country in the autumn. I am soon going abroad—we will part without hatred and anger; what was true in our friendship will be set right, will be purified by absence.'

Granovsky wept. With Ketscher I had no explanation on that subject. Ogaryov did, as a fact, go to the country in the autumn, and afterwards we too went away.

News of our Moscow friends reached us more and more rarely. Frightened by the terror that followed 1848, they waited for a safe opportunity to send letters.

These opportunities were rare, passports were hardly ever given. From Ketscher we had not a word for years together; he was never fond of writing, however.

The first living news was brought me in 1855 after I had moved to London. Ketscher, I heard, was in his element, conspicuous at banquets in honour of the heroes of Sebastopol, embracing Pogodin and Kokorev, embracing the sailors from the Black Sea, making an uproar, scolding, admonishing. Ogaryov, who had come straight from the graveside of Granovsky, told me little; what he did tell was gloomy.

Another year and a half passed. During that time I had finished this chapter, and to whom first of outsiders was it read?

Yes—*habeant sua fata libelli*.

In the autumn of 1857 Tchitcherin came to London; we were expecting him with impatience: once one of Granovsky's favourite pupils and a friend of Korsh and Ketscher, he seemed to us one of our intimate circle. We had heard of his rudeness, his conservative leanings, his boundless vanity, and his *doctrinaire* attitude, but he was still young . . . many angles are rubbed down by the passage of time.

'I have long hesitated whether I should come and see you or not; so many Russians visit you now that one needs more courage not to come than to come; I, as you know, though fully respecting you, do not agree with you in everything.'

That was how Tchitcherin began.

He made his approach not simply, not in the spirit of youth; he had stones hidden in his bosom, the light in his eyes was cold, there was a challenge and a dreadful, repellent conceit in the tones of his voice. From the first words I saw that this was not an opponent but an enemy; but I stifled the instinctive warning and we got into conversation.

Our talk soon passed to reminiscences and to questions from me. He described the last months of the life of Granovsky, and when he went away I felt better pleased with him than at first.

After dinner next day conversation turned on Ketscher. Tchitcherin spoke of him as a man whom he liked, laughing without malice at his sallies; from the details he told me I learned that his affection for his friends was still as denunciatory, that S——'s influence had reached such a point that many of his friends were up in arms against her, avoided their society, and so on. Carried away by the stories he told me and my own recollections, I offered to read Tchitcherin my unpublished chapter about Ketscher and read aloud the whole of it. I have many times repented doing this, not because he made a bad use of what I read, but because I was vexed and pained that at forty-five I was capable of exposing our past before a coarse man who afterwards jeered with such merciless impudence at what he called my 'temperament.'

The wide differences that separated our views and our temperaments were soon made plain.

From the first days an argument sprang up from which it was clear that we differed in everything. He was a disciple of the French democratic order and had a dislike for English freedom, not reduced to any logical order. He saw in the empire the education of the people, and advocated a powerful state and the abasement of the individual before it. It will be readily understood what these ideas became when applied to Russia. He was a governmentalist, looked upon the government as far superior to society and its movements, and took the Empress Catherine 11. for almost the ideal of what Russia needed. All this theory came from a regular edifice of dogma from which he could always and at once deduce his theosophy of bureaucracy.

'Why do you want to be a professor,' I asked him,

'and try to get a lecturer's chair? You ought to be a Minister and try to get a portfolio.'

Arguing with him, we saw him off at the railway station and parted agreeing about nothing but our mutual respect.

A fortnight later he wrote to me from France with enthusiasm about the working classes, about the institutions. 'You have found what you were looking for,' I answered,' and very quickly; that comes of going there with ready-made views.' Then I suggested that we should begin a correspondence in print and wrote the beginning of a long letter.

He did not care to do so and said that he had no time and that such an argument would do harm. . . .

A remark made in the *Bell* concerning doctrinaires in general he took as aimed at himself; his *amour-propre* was stung, and he sent me his 'denunciation,' which made a great talk at the time.

Tchitcherin got the worst of the campaign, of that I have no doubt. The outburst of indignation invoked by his letter printed in the *Bell* was universal in the younger generation and in literary circles. I received dozens of articles and letters, one of which was published. We were still mounting an uphill path in those days, and had no need of Katkov's[1] drags to hold us back. The coldly offensive, insolently smooth tone, more perhaps than was actually said, incensed the public and me alike; it was something new in those days. On the other hand, those who took Tchitcherin's side were: Elena Pavlovna, the Iphigenia of the Winter Palace; Timashov, the head of the Third Section; and N.H. Ketscher.

Ketscher remained true to the reaction, not because he 'preferred Grandison to Lovelace' but because

[1] Katkov, one of Stankevitch's circle, afterwards became a Slavophil of the most reactionary type and editor of the *Moscow Gazette*,—(*Translator's Note*.)

carried without a guiding compass *à la remorque* of a circle he remained true to it without noticing that it was sailing in the opposite direction. The man of a coterie, for him questions followed the banner of personalities and not the other way about.

Never having worked through to a single clear understanding or to a single clear conviction, he advanced with noble aspirations and bandaged eyes, and was continually beating his enemies, not noticing that the positions were changed and that in their game of blind-man's buff he beat us, beat others, is even now beating some one, even now imagining that he is accomplishing something.

I append the letter I wrote to Tchitcherin as the beginning of a friendly discussion which was prevented by his attacking me like a prosecutor:

'MY LEARNED FRIEND,—It is impossible for me to argue with you; you know so much, you know it so well, everything in your brain is fresh and new, and what matters most is that you are convinced you do know it, and so, untroubled, you resolutely await the rational development of events in accordance with the programme revealed by science. You cannot be in disharmony with the present; you know if the past was this and that, the present is bound to be this and that, and is bound to lead to this and that in the future; you are able to reconcile yourself to it through your ideas and your interpretation of it. Yours is the happy lot of a priest, comforting the sorrowful with the eternal truths of your theory and with your faith in them. All these advantages you derive from your dogmatic belief, because dogma excludes doubt. Doubt means that a question is open; dogma, that the question is closed, settled. And so every dogma is exclusive and uncompromising, while doubt can never attain so sharp a finality; it is the very essence of doubt to be ready to agree with the speaker or conscientiously to seek significance in his words, even to the extent of losing precious time needed for finding objections. Dogma sees truth from a definite angle, accepted as the sole stronghold of salvation, while doubt strives to escape from all angles, looks all round, returns on its tracks, and often paralyses all action by its humility before truth. You, my learned friend, know definitely in what direction to go, how to lead; I do not know. And so I feel that it is for us to observe and study, and for you to teach others. It is true that we can say what ought not to be done, we can unite men to act, rouse thought, set it free from chains, dispel the phantoms of church and police-station, of academy and criminal court—that is all; but you can say what ought to be done.

'The attitude of dogma to its object is the religious attitude, that is the attitude from the point of view of eternity; the temporary, the transitory, persons, events, generations scarcely enter into the *Campo Santo* of philosophy, or, if they enter, it is only when purified from real fife in the form of an herbarium of logical shadows. Dogma as a whole lives really in all times, and lives in its own period as though it were the past, not spoiling its theoretical attitude by too passionate an interest in it. Knowing the necessity of suffering, dogma keeps itself as a Simeon Stylites on a pedestal, sacrificing everything temporary to the eternal, the living particulars to general ideas. In short, the dogmatists are first of all historians, while we, together with the crowd, are your substratum; you stand for history *für sich*, we—for history *an sich*. You explain to us where our disease lies, but are we diseased? You bury us, reward us, or punish us after our death, you are our doctors and priests; but are we sick or dying?

'This antagonism is nothing new and it is of great value for progress, for development. If all mankind could believe you, it might be rational, but would die of universal boredom. The late Filiminov put as an inscription on his "fool's cap": *Si la raison dominate le monde, il ne s'y passerait rien*.

'The geometrical dryness of dogma, the algebraic impersonality of it, gives it the widest power of generalisation; it must shun sensations and, like Augustus, command Cleopatra to be veiled. But for active intervention passion is more essential than dogma, and man has no algebraic passions. The general he can understand, but it is the particular that he loves or hates. Spinoza with all the outspoken vigour of his genius maintained the necessity of reckoning as essential only the incorruptible, the eternal, the unchanging substance, and not resting one's hopes on the fortuitous, the relative, the personal. Every one understands this in theory, but man attaches himself only to the particular, the personal, to the accomplished fact; in the reconciling of these extremes, in their harmonious combination, lies the highest wisdom of life.

'If from this general definition of our opposite points of view we pass to particular examples we shall find that though our goal is the same, there is no less antagonism between us; even in those instances in which we start from agreement. An example will make this clear. We are completely agreed in our attitude to religion; but this only goes so far as the denial of supernatural religion, but as soon as we come into contact with *sublunary* religion the distance between us is immense. You have moved from the dark, incense-laden walls of a cathedral to a well-lighted government office, from Guelph you have turned Ghibelline, you have replaced the hierarchies of heaven by grades in the service, the absorption of the individual soul in God by its absorption in the State, God is replaced by centralisation, the priest by the police-inspector.

'You see in this change an advance, a triumph, we see new chains. We want to be neither Guelphs nor Ghibellines. Your secular, civic, and legal religion is the more terrible for being deprived of all that is poetical, fantastic, of all that is child-like in character; in place of which you have the red-tape of officialdom, the idol of the State with the Tsar at the top and the hangman at the bottom. You want man set free from the church to hang about for a couple of centuries in the hall of a government office, while the caste of high-priest officials and monks of dogma decide in what way and to what degree he is to be free, like our committees for the emancipation of the peasants. And all that repels us; we can accept a great deal, make concessions, sacrifice something to circumstance; but for you it is not a sacrifice. Of course in that too you are happier than we. Losing your religious faith you are not left without any support; and finding that faith in the State may take the place of Christianity for mankind, you have accepted it, and you have done very well for your moral hygiene, for your peace of mind. But this remedy sticks in our throat and we hate your government offices, your centralisation, quite as much as the Inquisition, the Consistory, the Book of Precepts.

'Do you grasp the difference? You, as a teacher, want to teach, to direct, to herd your flock. We, like a flock that is becoming conscious, do not want to be herded, but want to have our own village courts, our own representatives, our own delegates, to whom we can entrust the management of our affairs. That is why the authority of the government is an insult to us at every step, while you applaud it as your predecessors the priests applauded the temporal power. You may even differ from it as the clergy has sometimes differed from it or like people quarrelling on board ship: however great the distance between you may be, you are still in the same boat, and for us, laymen, you are still on the side of the government.

'Civic religion—the apotheosis of the State—is a purely Roman idea and in the modern world, principally French.

It is consistent with a strong state, but is incompatible with a free people; through it you may get splendid soldiers, but you cannot have independent citizens. The United States, on the contrary, have, so far as it is possible, abolished the religious character of the police and the administration.'

Epilogue

On re-reading the chapter about Ketscher I cannot help reflecting on the original, eccentric characters who live or have lived in Russia. What whimsical personalities occur again and again in the history of our culture! In what countries, under what degrees of latitude and longitude could a figure be found as angular, as rugged, as captious and erratic, as good-natured and ill-natured, as noisy and unmanageable as Ketscher's except in Moscow?

And how many of these original figures have I watched 'in all their varied kinds,' from my father to Turgenev's 'Children.' 'This is how the Russian oven turns them out,' Pogodin said to me. And indeed, what marvels it does turn out, especially when the head is made on the German pattern . . . from Russian buns and bread-rings to Orthodox loaves flavoured with Hegel, and French rolls *à la quatre-vingt-treixe*! It would be a pity if all these original products should be lost and leave no trace. We usually dwell only upon the leading figures.

But in them the effect of the Russian oven is less obvious; in them its peculiarities are corrected and redeemed; they are examples of the Russian type of intelligence rather than of the influence of their environment. These are followed by all sorts of unattached individuals who have lost their way; the eccentric figures among them are beyond all reckoning. The tiny connecting links that make up the chain of historical movements, the particles of yeast which are lost in the dough, they have raised it, not for their own benefit. Men who awoke early in the dark night and groped feeling their way to work, stumbling against everything in their road, they awakened others to quite different labours.

. . . I will try some day to save two or three more profiles from complete oblivion. They are almost lost already in the grey fog from which only the mountain tops and high crags stand out.

II

BASIL AND ARMANCE

(*An episode of the year* 1844.)

A VERY characteristic episode is connected with our second *villeggiatura*; it would really be a pity not to put it in, although Natalie and I had very little to do with it. This episode might be called: 'Armance and Basil, or the philosopher from civility, the Christian from courtesy, and George Sand's "Jacques" turned into the Jacques of Destiny.' It began at a French fancy dress ball.

In the winter of 1843 I went to a fancy dress ball. There were a mass of people there, five thousand if I remember right, and scarcely any one I knew. Basil was whirling round with a masked lady, he had no thoughts to spare for me. He was slightly shaking his head and screwing up his eyelashes, as connoisseurs do when they find the wine excellent and the grouse marvellous.

The ball took place in the hall of a reputable society. I walked about and sat down a little, looking at Russian aristocrats dressed up as pierrots of all sorts, zealously doing their best to look like Parisian shopmen and desperate dancers of the *cancan,* and went upstairs to supper; there Basil sought me out. He was in an utterly abnormal state, and in the first glow of the acute period of love; it was more acute as Basil was about that time forty and his hair was beginning to be thin on his lofty brow. He talked to me incoherently of some French 'Mignon,' with all the simplicity of a Klärchen and all the playful charm of a Parisian *grisette.*

At first I imagined that this was one of those romances in one chapter in which there is a conquest on the first page and a bill to pay on the last. But I became convinced that this was not the case. Basil saw his Parisian girl a second or third time and followed circumvolutionary tactics without making a direct attack. He introduced me to her. Armance really was a lively, charming child of Paris, who took after her parent. From her language to her manners and the special shade of independence and boldness—everything about her was characteristic of the respectable working-class of the great city, she was still a work-girl not a petty-bourgeoise. This type has never existed among us. The careless gaiety, the easy manners, freedom, mischief, were all combined with the instinct of self-preservation, the instinctive feeling of danger and honour. Flung as children sometimes from ten years old into the battle of poverty and temptation, defenceless, surrounded by the pestilential infection of Paris and snares of all sorts, they become their own providence and protection. Such girls may readily give themselves, but it is hard to take them by surprise, unawares. Those of them who might be bought never get into this class of working girls; they are bought before they reach that stage, are whirled off and engulfed in another type, sometimes for ever, sometimes to reappear six or seven years later in their carriage in Longchamps or in the box at the opera—*mit Perlen und Diamanten.*

Basil was over head and ears in love. A theorist in music and a philosopher in painting, he was one of the most complete representatives of the ultra-Hegelians. He spent his whole life soaring in an aesthetic heavens among philosophical and critical niceties. He looked upon life as he did upon Shakespeare, reducing everything in life to its philosophical significance, making everything lively boring and everything fresh stale; in fact, leaving no emotion of the heart in its directness and simplicity. This attitude, however, was characteristic in varying degrees of almost every circle of that period; some broke loose from it by talent, others from liveliness, but traces of it persisted for a long time with all—some kept the jargon, others the philosophy itself.

'Let us go' Bakunin said to T—— in Berlin at the beginning of the 'forties,' and plunge into the gulf of real life, let us fling ourselves into the waves'; and they went to ask Varnhagen von Ense to dip them like a dexterous bathing man into the gulf of practical life and to present them to a pretty actress. It will be readily understood that with such preparations there is no reaching a plunge into the passions that 'devour the secret sources of our spirit,' nor indeed to any action whatever. The Germans too do not get to action; but then Germans do not seek action, but simply tranquillity. Our temperament on the other hand cannot endure this attitude—*des theoretischen Schweigens*—gets entangled, stumbles, and trips up more funnily than seriously. And so our philosopher in love at forty began, screwing up his eyes, to collate all the speculative theories on the dæmonic power of love which drew Hercules and the frail youth alike to the feet of Omphale, began to explain to himself and others the moral idea of the family, the foundations of marriage (Hegel's *Philosophy of Law*, Chapter *Sittlichkeit*). There was no impediment on the side of Hegel. But the phenomenal world of fortuity and appearances—the world of the spirit not yet freed from tradition—was not so accommodating. Basil had a father, Pyotr Konytch, a wealthy man who had himself been married three times in succession and had had three children by each marriage. On learning that his son, and the eldest one too, wanted to marry a Catholic, a poor girl, and a French one, coming moreover from Kuznetzky Bridge, he resolutely refused his blessing. Basil, who had adopted the *chic* and manners of scepticism, might have perhaps dispensed with the parental blessing; but the old man associated with the blessing not only consequences *jenseits* (in the other world), but also *diesseits* (in this world), to wit, his inheritance.

The old man's opposition hurried things on, as is always the case, and Basil began to think of hastening the *dénouement*. The only thing left to do was to get married without wasting words, and later on to make the old man accept *un fait accompli*, or to conceal the marriage from him in the expectation that before long he would neither bless nor curse nor dispose of his fortune.

But the unenlightened world of tradition had to be reckoned with even then. To be married on the quiet in Moscow was not easy and was extremely expensive, and the wedding would have reached his father's ears at once through deacons, sacristans, church servitors, match-makers, clerks, shop boys, and gossips of all sorts. It was proposed to sound our Father Ioann in the village of Pokrovskoe, known to my readers from the scandal of his stealing when inebriated a silver watch and box from the sacristan.

Father Ioann, on learning that the disobedient son was about forty, that the bride was not Russian and that her parents were not here, that, besides me, a university professor would sign as a witness, began thanking me for this kind service, probably supposing that I was trying to marry Basil in order to secure him a two-hundred rouble note. He was so touched that he shouted to the next room: 'Wife, wife, bring out two or three eggs,' and a bottle wrapt in paper out of the cupboard, in order to regale me.

Everything went well.

The day of the wedding and other details were not fixed: Armance was to come to Pokrovskoe to stay with us. Basil who meant to accompany her was to return to Moscow and, after making the final arrangements, to come from his father's curse to receive the drunken blessing of Father Ioann.

In expectation of *i promessi sposi* we ordered supper to be got ready and sat down to wait for them. We waited and waited: it struck twelve o'clock at night. No one came. . . . One o'clock—still no one. The ladies went to bed. A——and Ketscher and I set to upon the supper. *Le ore suonan al quadriano, e una e due e tre . . .* but . . . still no sign of them.

At last the tinkle of a bell came nearer and nearer, there was the rumble of wheels over the bridge. We rushed into the porch. A coach drawn by three horses drove rapidly into the yard and stopped, Basil came out. I went up to give my hand to Armance; she seized my hand at once, but with such force that I almost cried out—and then flung herself on my neck repeating with a giggle, 'Monsieur Herstin' . . . it was no other than Vissarion Grigoryevitch Byelinsky in *propria persona*.

There was no one in the coach but Byelinsky who was laughing till he coughed and Basil who was crying till he had a cold in his nose. We looked at one another in amazement. I must observe that, to add to the effect, there had been no trace of Byelinsky in Moscow till two days before. 'Give me something to eat,' Byelinsky said at last, 'I'll tell you then what marvels have been happening among us; I must defend poor Basil, who is more afraid of you than of Armance.'

This is what had happened. Seeing that things were

moving rapidly to a climax Basil took fright; he began to reflect and was utterly overwhelmed as he pondered on the mercilessly fatal character of marriage, its indissolubility according to the code of Russian law and the code of Hegel; he locked himself up, a victim to the spirit of agonising investigation and ruthless analysis. His terror grew from hour to hour, the more so as the way of retreat was not easy either, and to decide to take it needed almost as much character as the marriage itself. This terror grew till Byelinsky, who on arriving from Petersburg went straight to see him, knocked at his door. Basil described to him all the horror with which he was going to meet his happiness, and all the aversion with which he was entering upon marriage with love—and asked his advice and help.

Byelinsky answered that he must be mad after this— consciously and knowing beforehand what it would be— to take such fetters upon himself. 'Herzen now,' he said, 'got married and eloped with his wife, and came from exile to get her; but ask him: he never once reflected whether he ought to do so or not and what the consequence would be. I am sure it seemed to him that he could do nothing else. Well! But you want to do the same, analysing and reflecting.'

This was all Basil wanted; he wrote to Armance that very night, a dissertation upon marriage, upon his luckless theorisings, upon the impossibility of simple happiness, from an analytic spirit, he laid before her all the disadvantages and dangers of their union and asked her advice— what they should do now.

He brought her answer with him.

In Byelinsky's account and in Armance's letter their two natures, hers and Basil's, came out vividly. A marriage between persons of such opposite temperaments would certainly have been strange. Armance wrote sorrowfully: she was surprised, wounded, did not understand his reflections, and saw in them a pretext and a sign of cooling love. She said that, since it was so, there must be no talk of marriage, gave him back his promise, and concluded by saying that after what had happened they had better not meet. 'I shall remember you with gratitude,' she wrote,' and do not blame you in the least. I know that you are exceedingly good, but even more exceedingly weak! Good-bye, and may you be happy.'

Such a letter could not have been altogether agreeable to receive. In every word there was strength, vigour, and haughtiness. The child of splendid plebeian stock, Armance was worthy of her origin. Had she been an Englishwoman, what a tight hold she would have kept of Basil's letter, how by the lips of her virtuous solicitor she would have described with indignation and shamefaced modesty his first pressure of her hand, his first kiss, and how her lawyer with tears in his eyes and chalk on his wig would have exhorted the jury to compensate injured innocence with a couple of thousand pounds.

The French woman, the poor sewing girl never thought of that.

The two or three days they spent at Pokrovskoe were depressing for the ex-bridegroom. He was like a schoolboy who has disgraced himself in class, and is afraid both of the teacher and his comrades. He wrote me a letter which showed confusion and dissatisfaction with himself and asked me to come and say good-bye. At the beginning of August I went from Pokrovskoe to Moscow; while I was away Natalie received at Pokrovskoe a new dissertation from him. I went to Basil's and came straight in upon a farewell banquet. They were drinking champagne, and in the toasts and good wishes there were strange hints. 'Of course you don't know,' Basil murmured into my ear: 'You see I . . . er . . .' and he added in a whisper: 'you see Armance is going with me. What a girl; only now I have learned to know her,' and he shook his head.

This was as great a surprise as Byelinsky's unexpected appearance.

In the letter to Natalie he explained to her at great length that thought and reflection upon marriage had brought him to hesitation and despair; he doubted both of his love for Armance and his suitability for family life; that in that way he had come to the agonising feeling that he ought to break off everything and flee to Paris, that in that state of mind he had come, pitiful and ridiculous, to Pokrovskoe. After he had reached this decision he had read the letter of Armance over again and made a fresh discovery, to wit, that he loved Armance very much, and he had therefore asked her to see him and had again offered her his hand. He had thought again of the priest at Pokrovskoe, but the proximity of Mamonov's factory frightened him. He was intending to be married in Petersburg and at once to set off for France. 'Armance is as happy as a child!'

In Petersburg Basil thought fit to be married in the Kazan cathedral. That philosophy and learning might not be forgotten, he asked the chief priest Sidonsky, the learned author of the *Introduction to the Study of Philosophy*, to perform the ceremony. Sidonsky had long known Basil from his learned articles as a free and worldly thinker and a disciple of the German philosophy. After all the strange things that had happened to Armance, she had the honour rarely vouchsafed to any of serving as the occasion for one of the most comic meetings of two sworn foes, learning and religion.

To show off his worldly culture Sidonsky began before the wedding talking of the latest philosophic *brochures*, and when everything was ready and the sacristan held up the epitrahil which, stooping, he began to put on, he said to Basil, dropping his eyes: 'Pardon me, it is a

THE WEDDING—AND AFTER

ceremony; I know very well that the Christian ritual has outlived its time, that . . .'

'Oh, no, no,' Basil interrupted in a voice full of sympathy and compassion: 'Christianity is eternal; its essence, its substance, cannot pass away.'

Sidonsky, with a chaste glance, thanked his 'chivalrous' antagonist, turned to the choir and chanted: 'Blessed be the name of the Lord, now and for ever and ever!' 'Amen,' boomed the choir, and the ceremony went on in due order, and Sidonsky led Basil in a crown and Armance in a crown round the lectern . . . making Isaiah rejoice.

From the cathedral Basil took Armance home and leaving her there spent a literary soirée at Krayevsky's. Ten days later Byelinsky saw the happy pair into the steamer. At this point it will be supposed that the story is certainly ended.

Not a bit of it.

Things went very well as far as the Cattegat; but at that point George Sand's accursed novel *Jacques* turned up.

'What do you think of *Jacques*?' Basil asked Armance as she was finishing the novel.

Armance told him her opinion of it. Basil informed her that it was quite mistaken, that her criticism wounded his spirit on its deepest side, and that his philosophy of life had nothing in common with hers.

The sanguine Armance was unwilling to change her philosophy of life, so they both crossed the Belt.

When they came out into the German Ocean Basil felt more at home, and made another attempt to persuade Armance to take a different view of *Jacques* and to change her philosophy of life.

Almost dying of sea-sickness, Armance with a last effort declared that she would not change her opinion of *Jacques*.

'What have we in common after that?' observed Basil, flying into a rage.

'Nothing,' answered Armance, 'and *si vous me cherchez querelle*, then let us simply part as soon as we touch land.'

'You have decided,' said Basil, very high and mighty; 'you prefer . . .'

'Anything in the world to living with you; you are an insufferable man, weak and tyrannical.'

'Madame!'

'Monsieur!'

She went to the cabin, he remained on deck. Armance kept her word. From Havre she went to her father, and a year later returned to Russia and indeed went on to Siberia.

This time I believe the story of this intermittent marriage is ended.

Though indeed Bar ère[1] has said:

'Only the dead do not return.'

Written 1857,
LAUREL HOUSE, PUTNIY.

[1] Barère de Vieuzac (1753-1841), a member of the Committee of Public Safety, nicknamed the Anacreon of the Guillotine. — (*Translator's Note.*)